ORACLE®   *Oracle Press*™

Oracle HTML DB Handbook

Lawrence Linnemeyer
Bradley Brown

McGraw-Hill/Osborne

New York   Chicago   San Francisco
Lisbon   London   Madrid   Mexico City   Milan
New Delhi   San Juan   Seoul   Singapore   Sydney   Toronto

Oracle Press™

Oracle HTML DB Handbook

The McGraw·Hill Companies

McGraw-Hill/Osborne
2100 Powell Street, 10th Floor
Emeryville, California 94608
U.S.A.

To arrange bulk purchase discounts for sales promotions, premiums, or fund-raisers, please contact
McGraw-Hill/Osborne at the above address.

Oracle HTML DB Handbook

1234567890 FGR FGR 019876

ISBN 0-07-225768-7

Acquisitions Editor		**Indexer**	
	Lisa McClain		Jack Lewis
Project Editor		**Composition**	
	Mark Karmendy		Apollo Publishing Services
Acquisitions Coordinator		**Illustration**	
	Alex McDonald		Apollo Publishing Services
Technical Editor		**Series Design**	
	Vijay Lunawat		Peter F. Hancik, Lyssa Wald
Copy Editor		**Cover Series Design**	
	Bart Reed		Damore Johann Design, Inc.
Proofreader			
	John Gildersleeve		

This book was composed with Adobe® InDesign®

This book is dedicated to those that gave.
To TUSC and Brad Brown who gave me the opportunity to write this book.
To my parents who gave me the work ethic to keep going when work gets hard.
To my teenagers, Rainer and Anneke, who gave up precious family time on evenings and weekends.
To my lovely wife MaeBe of 25 years, who gave me much needed love, support, and encouragement and who also gave up so much of our together time.
Finally and most importantly to God, who gave the greatest gift, his only son, Jesus Christ, who gave me life and everything in it.

—Larry Linnemeyer

This book is dedicated to my wonderful wife Kristen, my compassionate son Austin, and my driven daughter Paige.

—Brad Brown

About the Authors

Lawrence Linnemeyer (Larry), Frederick, CO, is a Technical Management Consultant with TUSC, winner of the 2002 and 2004 Oracle Partner of the Year Award. He has been involved with Information Technology on and off since receiving a degree in Software Engineering from Mesa State in his hometown of Grand Junction, Colorado in 1986. Larry first started with Oracle technologies as a Systems Automation Officer with the U.S. Army in 1996. He has been with TUSC's Denver office since 1998, specializing in custom application development with Oracle technologies including HTML DB, Forms, Reports, JDeveloper/JSP, Warehouse Builder, PL/SQL Server Pages, Portal, Discoverer, and Designer.

Bradley D. Brown is chairman of the board, chief architect and co-founder of TUSC. Thomas Kurian, senior vice president, Oracle Server Technologies Division, says, "Brad is among the foremost experts on Oracle's technology in the world." For Brad, web development isn't just a job, it's his passion. He is the Oracle source who technologists around the world turn to when they seek expertise and experience in that discipline. Oracle Application Server 10*g*, HTML DB, Oracle Portal, XML, wireless, and Java are only a few of the technologies he has mastered over a career that spans more than 20 years.

This book marks the fifth title he has published through Oracle Press and McGraw-Hill/Osborne. Brad's most recent contribution was *Oracle Application Server 10g*, which was co-authored with TUSC Technical Management Consultant Christopher Ostrowski in 2004. In 2001, Brad combined his many years of experience into *Oracle9i Web Development*, which was a follow-up to *Oracle8i Web Development* he released two years before that. Brad's debut in the publishing industry came with *Oracle Application Server Web Toolkit Reference* in 1997.

While Brad is easily recognized as an accomplished Oracle author and world-renowned speaker, it is his technological expertise that clearly is his identity. While he has enjoyed a countless number of major implementation successes over the years, one milestone that clearly stands out centers around the development of "Periscope" that he released through TUSC in 2002. Periscope is breakthrough software that makes data from other data sources (i.e., Microsoft Access, Sybase, SQL Server, DB2, Web Services, file systems, APIs, etc.) appear as if it's in one big Oracle database. The data also can be inserted, updated, and deleted from many source databases. The groundbreaking tool works with more than 100 databases.

Brad's vast experience and expertise have earned him roles as chief information officer of Open Access Broadband Networks and board member for Geekcruises, Lantech Inc., Colorado Uplift, and Cactus Strategies. He's currently the Breakfast of Champions chairperson for the Colorado chapter of the Young Presidents Organization after having previously served as its chapter chair, on-boarding chair, education chairperson, inventory of skills chairperson, technology officer, assistant education chairperson, and membership chairperson. Brown also was a co-founder and acting chief technology officer for Eventconnex Inc.

Along with co-founders Richard J. Niemiec and Joseph C. Trezzo, Brad is part of an award-winning company that earned the 2004 North America Oracle PartnerNetwork Partner Solution of the Year in the category of Oracle Application Server, as well as Internet Platform Partner of the Year in 2002. TUSC also has won the 2001 Ernst & Young Entrepreneur of the Year Award in the category of "E-developer," was inducted into the Chicago-Area Entrepreneurship Hall of Fame in 1998, and earned an Arthur Andersen-Chicago Best Practices Award for "Unleashing the Power of Technology."

Contents at a Glance

Contents

PART I
Introduction

PART II
Creating Applications

PART III
Building Web Pages and Components

PART IV
Website and Application Examples

PART V
Security and Administration

PART VII
Advanced Topics

PART VII
Appendixes

Introduction

 really enjoyed moving from developing with Oracle Forms and Report to developing JSPs with JDeveloper, Java, and tools such as STRUTS, but the learning curve was very steep and productivity could have been much better. So I was really excited when I learned about HTML DB and how easy it was to use to quickly produce viable real-world applications.

My introduction to HTML DB came in the form of the request, "Here's a new product, install it and figure out how it works." Needless to say the user's manual that comes with it is not meant to be a tutorial, although it is a pretty good reference if you know what you are looking for. So my learning experience consisted of a *lot* of trial and error and a whole lot of frustration until I figured out how HTML DB fully functioned. Hopefully, this book will allow you to learn HTML DB without the level of frustration that I experienced.

Once developers become familiar with the HTML DB environment and its capabilities, they will truly be able to rapidly develop real-world applications. Many IT departments will come to find that HTML DB is the answer to their backlog of custom application requests.

Components Needed

To run all of the examples in this book you will need at least an installation of an Oracle Database release 9.2.0.3 or higher, and an Oracle HTTP Server and mod_plsql. The HTTP server could be in the form of an Oracle 9*i* Database release 2 (9.2) or higher or Oracle 9*i* Application Server release 1 (1.0.2.2) or higher. That being said, by the time this book is published the final version of Oracle 10*g* Express should be released, which will include HTML DB (recently renamed *Oracle Application Express*). Your last alternative is to run all of the examples on Oracle's hosted site. You can request a workspace at http://apex.oracle.com or http://htmldb.oracle.com.

Audience

This book is intended for HTML DB application developers at the beginning and intermediate levels. Due to the limitation of the number of pages that this book contains, the depth at which some subjects could be covered had to be limited.

How This Book Is Organized

This book comprises seven parts: "Introduction" (Part I), "Creating Applications" (Part II), "Building Web Pages and Components" (Part III), "Website and Application Examples" (Part IV), "Security and Administration" (Part V), "Advanced Topics" (Part VI), and "Appendixes" (Part VII). The best approach to using this book is to work through it cover to cover following along with the examples provided.

Part I: "Introduction"

Chapter 1: "An Introduction to HTML DB"

Chapter 1 explores the evolution of Oracle Web Tools and the history of HTML DB as a product. It then provides an overview of HTML DB and how it functions. Next, this chapter compares HTML DB to Portal, JDeveloper, the PL/SQL Web Toolkit, and Designer. Finally, this chapter discusses when it is best to use HTML DB.

Chapter 2: "Installing HTML DB"

This chapter covers the installation of HTML DB, both as part of an installation of a 10g database and an HTTP server or an installation of only HTML DB as a standalone addition to an existing database and HTTP server.

Chapter 3: "Using the SQL Workshops"

Chapter 3 explores the capabilities of the SQL Workshops by looking into each of the five major areas. Object Browser allows you to browse existing database objects as well as create new ones. Query Builder provides a graphical interface for generating and running queries. SQL Commands provides a command window similar to SQL Plus, where you can execute SQL commands. SQL Scripts provides a tool for maintaining and executing SQL Scripts. Utilities provide a means for data import and export, generating DDL, viewing object reports, and monitoring the database.

Part II: "Creating Applications"

Chapter 4: "Using the Application Builder"

This chapter starts to look at the heart of the HTML DB development environment, the Application Builder. Details of the application attributes are examined along with an introduction to application shared components. Finally, the main sections of the page definition are introduced.

Chapter 5: "Creating and Running Applications"

Chapter 5 walks through the various wizards by which applications can be created. This includes creating applications from scratch, based on tables, views or queries, or based on a spreadsheet. Additionally, creation of the demonstration applications is explored as well as a methodology for converting an MS Access application into an HTML DB application.

Chapter 6: "Working with Themes and Templates"

The look and feel of HTML DB applications are controlled by themes and templates. Chapter 6 explores the different types of templates, how they work, and their use of substitution variables. Finally, the chapter takes an in-depth look into all the sections of the page template.

Chapter 7: "Using the Application Utilities"

Chapter 7 examines the different utilities available in HTML DB. These utilities allow the developer to translate applications into different languages; manage Cascading Style Sheets, image files, and static files; utilize web services; and generate and view multiple application reports.

Part III: "Building Web Pages and Components"

Chapter 8: "Building Web Pages"

The main building block of an application is web pages. This chapter looks at adding, editing, and deleting pages in an application. It also examines the primary functions of the HTML DB engine, page rendering and processing, and session state management. Regions contain everything placed on a page, so this chapter also examines the different types of regions and how they are positioned on a page.

Chapter 9: "Working with Reports"

Chapter 9 examines the creation of reports including report attributes, use of custom report templates for formatting, break formatting, and pagination. This chapter also looks at the use of tabular reports that allow editing of multiple rows at one time.

Chapter 10: "Defining and Processing Forms"

Many elements are needed to implement a form in HTML DB; thankfully, a wizard is provided to greatly ease the creation of these elements. Chapter 10 addresses the automatic and manual creation of forms and looks at all of the pieces that make up a form including items, buttons, processes, and branches.

Chapter 11: "Navigating Between Pages"

The difference between a good web application and a poor web application can sometimes be attributed to the ease of navigation around the different areas of the application. Chapter 11 examines all of the different navigational elements provided by HTML DB including navigation bars, tabs, menus, lists, trees, and embedded URLs.

Chapter 12: "Building Other Components"

One of the primary benefits of HTML DB is the ability to quickly produce robust applications. This is made possible through the myriad of wizards that assist in rapidly producing standard application components. Chapter 12 covers the creation of not-so-standard components such as lists of values, shortcuts, graphs, and calendars, which can all be created through the assistance of wizards.

Chapter 13: "Adding Computations, Processes, and Validations"

Three major areas provide the brains behind an HTML DB application. Chapter 13 explores the creation and implementation of computations, processes, and validations, without which an application would be nothing more than standard web pages.

Part IV: "Website and Application Examples"

Chapter 14: "Building an Event Scheduling Application"

Chapter 14 takes a high-level look at the thought processes involved and decisions made while creating an event scheduling application. This chapter provides an opportunity to see how the different elements previously covered are used to quickly create a real-world application that shortly produces real-world costs savings.

Chapter 15: "Building a Test Administering Application"

This chapter provides yet another look at the implementation of an actual application. During this walkthrough, different approaches are examined and the benefits of each are weighed. A close look at some of the details provides insight into the use of the features of HTML DB covered in previous chapters.

Part V: "Security and Administration"

Chapter 16: "Security"

Security for a web application can often be an area of great concern—not so for HTML DB applications. Chapter 16 examines the different security elements provided by HTML DB. It includes a close look at Authentication, which controls initial access to your application, and Authorization, which extends your security by allow programmatic control of access to pages, regions, and even individual items within your application.

Chapter 17: "Administration Functions"

This chapter covers HTML DB administrative functions. It starts by providing an understanding of users and roles. It then looks at the overall HTML DB instanced administration, which includes the creation, provisioning, and monitoring of workspaces. Finally, workspace administration is covered, which includes details on managing services, managing workspace users, and monitoring workspace activity.

Part VI: "Advanced Topics"

Chapter 18: "Tips and Techniques"

For a fairly new product there is an enormous amount of tips and techniques that can be found for HTML DB, enough to fill an entire book. This chapter provides some of the more valuable ones and perhaps more importantly, it directs you to the many resources available for HTML DB.

Chapter 19: "Best Practices"

This chapter provides a number of best practices in the areas of installation, development, security, and testing.

Part VII: "Appendixes"

Appendix A: "The HTML DB Packages, Procedures, Functions, and Views"

There are many internal packages, procedures, functions, and views included in the HTML DB installation. Many of these are available to developers for their own use. Appendix A highlights the ones most commonly used by developers.

Appendix B: "PL/SQL Web Toolkit and Packages"

The PL/SQL Web Toolkit is a set of PL/SQL packages that can be used in HTML DB dynamic regions. Appendix B provides an overview of those packages. A web version of Appendix B is also available, which provides a detailed explanation of the packages.

PART
I

Introduction

CHAPTER

1

An Introduction
to HTML DB

ver the past ten years, Oracle has been a very forward-thinking company, and their products have reflected this focus. Some would argue that Oracle has always been forward looking, but this characteristic seems to be particularly true in what has become known as the "Internet Age." With the introduction of Oracle 8 and the renaming of the database and other products such as Oracle's Application Server to include the "8*i*" label, Oracle announced their intention to focus on the Internet. This trend continues as Oracle focuses their attention on the latest advances in grid computing and Service Oriented Architectures (SOAs) with the inclusion of the label "10*g*" as part of the database name. This label has also been included in Oracle's Web Application Server 10*g* and their excellent IDE, JDeveloper 10*g*.

The introduction of the Oracle 10*g* database also formalized the introduction of a new web-based development product that had previously been available as an adjunct to the database. This product, which initially bore the name Project Marvel, was given the name HTML DB and continues Oracle's tradition of providing tools for the rapid development of web applications. In this chapter, the origins of HTML DB are explored, beginning with a brief overview of the evolution of Oracle's web tools. Next, a brief description of HTML DB is provided and the characteristics of the product are listed and discussed. Because HTML DB can be integrated into your development environment in several ways, the installation options for the product are examined next. Installing HTML DB is discussed in detail in Chapter 2. As HTML DB is only one of the products that you can use in your web development efforts, it is important to understand the choices you have and when the use of HTML DB is appropriate. A comparison between Oracle's various web products (Portal, JDeveloper, the PL/SQL Web Toolkit, and Designer) and HTML DB is provided. Keep in mind that this discussion encompasses only Oracle's web development tools; other web development options, such as Perl and PHP, are not discussed here. The chapter concludes with a look at several web applications that have been built using HTML DB.

Evolution of Oracle Web Tools

Oracle's foray into web technology began in the mid-'90s. WOW, a shareware product that utilized PL/SQL to generate web pages, was made available then. This shareware product was eventually productized and became the first version of the Oracle Webserver product line. The first version of the product, which was called Oracle Webserver, was CGI based and included a web server, licensed by Oracle from Spyglass. With Oracle Webserver, developers coded their HTML by using two PL/SQL packages, htf and htp, which were given the name "PL/SQL toolkit." A web page could be created either by using the function htp.p (for print) or by using a method such as htp.table that returned a specific HTML tag. To render a web page, a browser client would pass a request to the Spyglass web server, which would spawn a CGI process. This process connected to the Oracle database, invoked the PL/SQL procedure, and returned the generated HTML code to the browser. Although the coding process was slow and nonvisual and spawning the CGI processes was relatively slow, web applications could be developed fairly easily and relatively quickly. When integrated with packages such as DBMS_SQL, for dynamically generating the SQL in the PL/SQL packages, applications could be written quickly with this technology. These same applications would have taken much longer and required a greater amount of code with the web development tools available at that time.

Improvements were made to the Webserver product line over the next few years. Version 2 moved away from the relatively slow CGI approach by providing pre-spawned processes. The PL/SQL toolkit was also enhanced to include additional tags and several additional functions and procedures in a package called OWA. Around this time, Oracle introduced cartridge technology, and the Webserver product was overhauled to use cartridges. Webserver introduced cartridges for PL/SQL, Live HTML (a Server Side Include [SSI] implementation), and Java. Custom cartridges could also be developed. The Java cartridge was appealing and reflected Oracle's growing interest in Java technology. However, the early version of the Java language itself was somewhat limited and most Webserver developers continued to use the PL/SQL toolkit. Later versions of the Webserver product also introduced the concept of a DAD, a Database Access Descriptor, which provided the flexibility to allow the connection to the Oracle database to be made using the client's login information. Before the introduction of this concept, all Webserver users logged into the database with a single login, making it impossible to differentiate one user from another.

As the Oracle community began using the Webserver product line, which now had been renamed Oracle Application Server, several other developments within Oracle led to alternatives for web development. Oracle's growing interest in Java led to the acquisition of the code for Borland's popular Java IDE (Integrated Development Environment), JBuilder. This led to the initial development of JDeveloper 1.0, which can be loosely described as an "Oracle-ized" version of JBuilder. JDeveloper 1.0 had a nearly identical user interface as JBuilder but provided an easier mechanism for connecting Java applications to an Oracle database. JDeveloper, whose current version is 10*g,* has come along way since this point. JDeveloper is compared to HTML DB as a web development environment later in this chapter.

Around this time, the Designer community was also provided a mechanism for generating web applications using the PL/SQL toolkit. One of the issues of developing applications with the PL/SQL toolkit was that a developer had to write a fair amount of code for even a simple web application. The Designer product allowed Oracle developers to define an application in a declarative manner and then generate the application code. Several new packages were included in Designer to allow PL/SQL toolkit code to be generated. This method of web application development is still in use today and is compared to HTML DB development later in this chapter.

The large amount of PL/SQL code that had to be written, as well as other issues that were surfacing with the Webserver product line, led to another internal effort within Oracle—the development of a product called Web DB. Web DB provided publishing capabilities for managing and including documents in a web application and a wizard-based approach for developing web pages. Web DB's approach to developing web pages had many of the features of what would come to be called a "portal" application. The early versions of Web DB were welcomed by the Oracle community, and a number of Web DB projects were undertaken.

Shortly after the introduction of Web DB, the limitations and problems with the technology decisions made with the Webserver product line became evident, and the decision was made to retire the Webserver product. The main problems seemed to be with scalability and dead processes that needed to be cleaned up. One alternative that Webserver developers had at this point was to continue to use the PL/SQL toolkit for web development but to switch to an Apache web server that could make use of an Apache add-on known as "mod_plsql." This add-on allowed requests handled by the Apache web server to be passed to processes that could execute PL/SQL packages with a DAD to generate HTML and return the results to the web browser that initiated the request.

The decision to terminate the Webserver product line eventually had an impact on Web DB. As Oracle internally discussed their future plans for web development, the decision was made to concentrate more heavily on portal features using Oracle's Application Server technology. As a result, Oracle decided that version 2.1 of Web DB would be the last. Additionally, a new product would be created from the ground up that could use PL/SQL but did not rely on the PL/SQL toolkit. The resulting product was the first version of Oracle Portal as a component of Oracle's Application Server.

The History of HTML DB

The termination of the Web DB product left the internal Oracle developers with a dilemma. The Web DB group, which was led by Michael Hichwa, still felt they had a viable and superior approach to web development. Not content to let their technology approach fade away, the group began the development of a new, improved version of Web DB.

This new technology was put to use in the development of Oracle's internal web-based Calendaring system. The system, which was rolled out to 40,000 Oracle employees worldwide in 1999, provided a web front end for tracking events and scheduling meetings within Oracle. The system was quite successful, and in the following year Larry Ellison gave his blessing to continue moving ahead with this technology. One requirement he did impose, though, was the development environment for the product had to be made available as a hosted service. Work on the product continued, and the resulting technology, which at the time was known as "Project Marvel," was released as a hosted service in June, 2002. After a few initial successful projects, the decision was made to productize the technology later in the year. The technology was renamed to HTML DB and first released as a support component of Oracle 9*i* Release 2 and Oracle 10*g* databases.

What Is HTML DB?

HTML DB is the latest development tool in Oracle's arsenal for developing web-based, or "thin client," applications. The most important characteristic of these applications is that the only software required by an end user (or client) of the system is a browser and an Internet/intranet connection. This makes deployment of the application quite simple and avoids the necessity of having to "touch" each client desktop to install any required software prior to the client running the application, as was required in the client/server computing era.

The following is a brief description of HTML DB that can be used as a starting point for understanding the capabilities of the product:

> *HTML DB is a RAD (Rapid Application Development) tool for developing web applications (Internet and intranet) in a browser-based declarative manner with wizards.*

This brief description does not, however, fully convey all the characteristics of HTML DB. Some of the additional characteristics to be considered include the following:

- HTML DB applications are stored as metadata and rendered at run time.

- The HTML code for each page in an HTML DB application is rapidly and dynamically generated.

- HTML DB applications are based completely on PL/SQL and do not use Java.

- Because HTML DB makes use of Oracle SQL and PL/SQL, any task that can be accomplished with these technologies can be incorporated into an HTML DB application.

- The product provides a hosted service environment for developers.

- HTML DB allows for web-based team development.

Let's take a look at these characteristics in greater detail to gain a better understanding of the full range of capabilities of HTML DB.

Web-based RAD Development Tool with Wizards

The early web-development tools required a significant amount of coding to generate a web page. HTML DB utilizes a *declarative* approach (which began with Web DB), where developers specify what they would like to build and the code is generated for them behind the scenes. Little or no coding is involved. Although a PL/SQL API is available for more advanced users, most HTML DB development is performed using wizards. A declarative approach using wizards leads to the rapid development of components, making HTML DB a "RAD" tool.

For example, suppose that you have a web page and you want to add a form for maintaining information. The information to be maintained could be parts information, employee information, addresses, or any type of information required for your application. Further, let's also suppose you want to generate a report first of the information to be maintained. Then, to edit information, you want to be able to click on the row that you want to change and have an edit form displayed. Figure 1-1 shows a report that contains project information from the Project table in your database, and Figure 1-2 shows the edit form obtained by clicking on one of the rows in the report.

Creating these two web pages in HTML DB is quite simple. After creating an application to hold your web pages (see Chapter 5), you use a report/form wizard to generate the pages that you want, as shown in Figure 1-3. The wizard walks you through a series of steps for first defining the report and then creating an edit form associated with the report. No coding is involved, and the entire process can be done in about two minutes. The wizard automatically generates the SQL for the report query and the necessary Insert/Update/Delete SQL statements on the edit form. If required, you can modify the SQL statement or include the execution of a PL/SQL procedure before or after a web page is rendered or processed.

ORACLE

Logout   Help

WRDJOCK@EARTHLINK.NET

Home   Projects   Reports

Home > Report on Projects

Projects

Reset   Create

Search [   ] Go

Spread Sheet

	Project Title ▲	Description	Projected Cost	Requested By	Needed By	Technologies	Num Developers	Num Dbas	Start Date	Status
🖉	Company-wide Datawarehouse	Implement a company-wide data warehouse to summarize data from the transactional system	500000	Juanita Simspon	01-FEB-05	PL/SQL, Discoverer, Reports	5	2		Cancelled
🖉	Customer Data Clean-up	Examine the data in the Customer tables and clean-up duplicates and inconsistent information	32000	Paula Winowsky		PL/SQL	2	0	28-FEB-04	In Progress

FIGURE 1-1   *A Project report created with HTML DB*

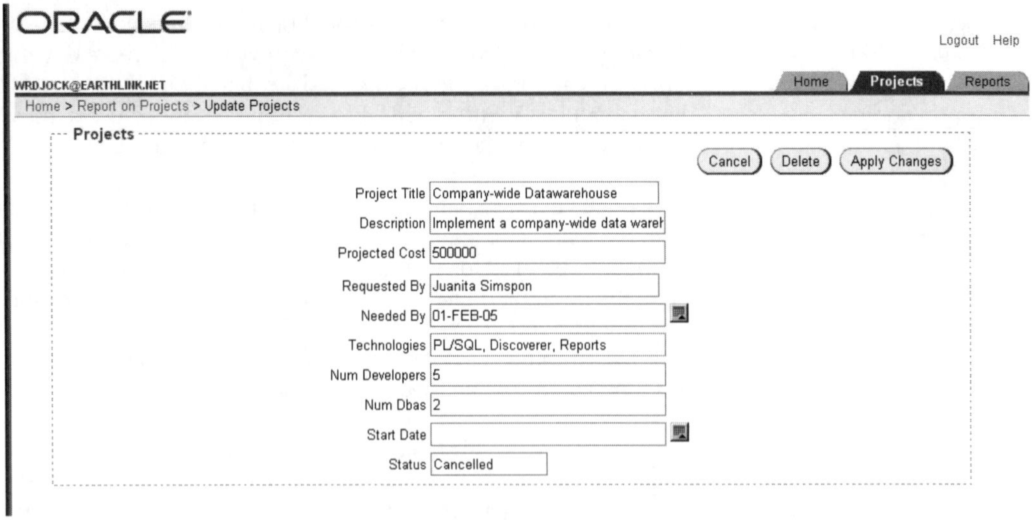

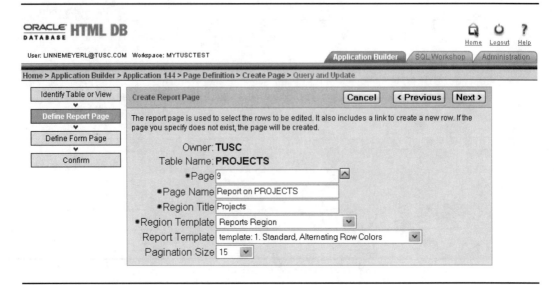

FIGURE 1-2 *The Edit form associated with the Project report*

Another important point to note is that HTML DB does not require a separate development environment. There is no separate IDE that you need to buy, and you don't need to use a product such as TOAD from Quest Software to develop your applications. The development environment for HTML DB is actually an HTML DB application that creates HTML DB applications. As a result, HTML DB development is accomplished with only a browser and an Internet or intranet connection to the HTML DB installation.

FIGURE 1-3 *The second step of the report/form wizard*

Metadata and Run-time Rendering

As an HTML DB application is being built, the information you supply in the form of the choices you make and the values you enter into the wizards are stored in a separate set of tables. These tables are associated with a separate schema, the Flows schema, which is used to store the metadata of your application. When a change is made to an application, the metadata is retrieved and displayed on the web page being used to maintain the application. As changes are made, the metadata of the application is modified or added to.

When an HTML DB application is run, the web pages of the application are generated using the metadata stored for the application. This run-time rendering is done using PI /SQL because the metadata is stored in Oracle tables.

Dynamically Generated Code

The storage of metadata and run-time rendering means that the HTML code for the web pages in your application is dynamically generated as opposed to being stored statically. HTML DB applications can be integrated with static web pages and web pages that are generated by servlets or JSPs, if required, but this is not necessary.

PL/SQL is still one of the fastest ways to execute code in an Oracle database. This translates into the rapid execution of the procedures for generating web pages, even in situations where there are a number of regions (see Chapter 8) on a web page. HTML DB provides debugging information that can be turned on and off during development and shows the processing order of the various components associated with a web page along with the time of generation of each component. Figure 1-4 shows a portion of the Projects report re-run with the Debug option turned on.

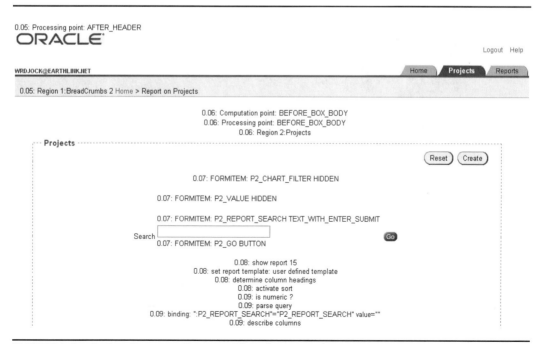

FIGURE 1-4   *Project Report web page with Debug turned on*

PL/SQL Based

Although most of your development can be accomplished in a declarative manner (using wizards) that obviates the need for coding, there are times when additional code is useful. HTML DB provides a number of points within the page-rendering cycle, including the actual generation of page components, where PL/SQL code can be added. In many cases, this code includes the use of the htp package from the PL/SQL Web Toolkit (see Appendix B). However, because the coding is being done in PL/SQL, you can take advantage of any of the available PL/SQL packages and commands, such as EXECUTE IMMEDIATE. You can also invoke any PL/SQL packages, procedures, or functions that are in common use in your organization. Figure 1-5 shows the use of an anonymous PL/SQL block on the Enter Order page of the order-processing sample application supplied with HTML DB. This procedure is invoked upon submission of an order as an After Submit process on the page.

A Hosted Service Development Environment

HTML DB was built around a hosted service model. HTML DB utilizes a concept known as an HTML DB "workspace" to control the application development process. A workspace can contain one or more applications. When a developer is ready to begin developing a new application, they can create it within an existing workspace or request a new workspace from their HTML DB administrator.

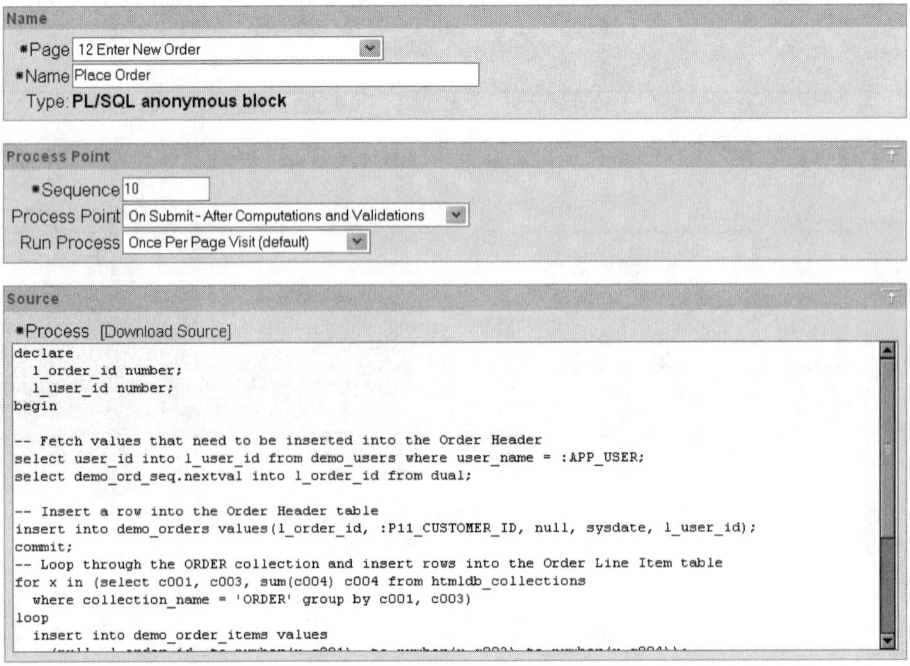

FIGURE 1-5   *Including custom PL/SQL on a web page*

The HTML DB administrator sets up new workspaces for developers and manages existing workspaces. Each workspace is given a maximum size for maintaining components and is associated with one or more database schemas. Administering workspaces is discussed further in Chapter 17.

Web-based Team Development

An application is associated with a single workspace. However, multiple developers can be granted access to the same workspace. In this way, the various components of an application can be split among multiple developers. Therefore, a team of web developers can be working on different components of the same application. Because components are stored in the database, all developers will have access to the components of an application as they are created by other developers.

The main problem with this approach occurs when two developers attempt to work on the same component at the same time. HTML DB does not currently contain any version-control capabilities to prevent this problem. In this situation, the developer who saves a component last will have their changes saved. This requires project controls to ensure that only one developer is working on a specific component at a time.

Installation Options

In the previous section, we discussed the fact that HTML DB was developed as a hosted service. This fact provides you with two options for getting started with HTML DB:

- Use HTML DB on Oracle's hosted site
- Use HTML DB internally on a server where you installed the product

Oracle's Hosted HTML DB Site

One of the quickest ways for a developer to get started with HTML DB is to utilize a hosted service provided by Oracle itself. Oracle's HTML DB hosted site is accessed on the Internet by entering the URL http://htmldb.oracle.com into your browser. This will bring you to the HTML DB's hosted site login, as shown in Figure 1-6. By clicking on the Request a Workspace link in the Task list box, you can request a workspace and a login from Oracle that will provide you access to Oracle's hosted HTML DB site. This process and using the hosted site are discussed further in Chapter 2. The Oracle hosted site should not be used for any production applications.

Installing HTML DB Internally

The other alternative for using HTML DB is to install the product locally. The HTML DB product is a series of PL/SQL packages and is loaded using a SQL*Plus script into the database. HTML DB requires that your database be at least release 9.2.0.3 or later. The majority of the product would actually work with earlier versions of Oracle, but some features require that the database be at least at this release. The installation scripts actually check that your database is at the appropriate level. Prior to the 10g release of the database, HTML DB needed to be loaded separately. With the 10g release, HTML DB is bundled with the product. Installing HTML DB within your organization is discussed further in Chapter 2.

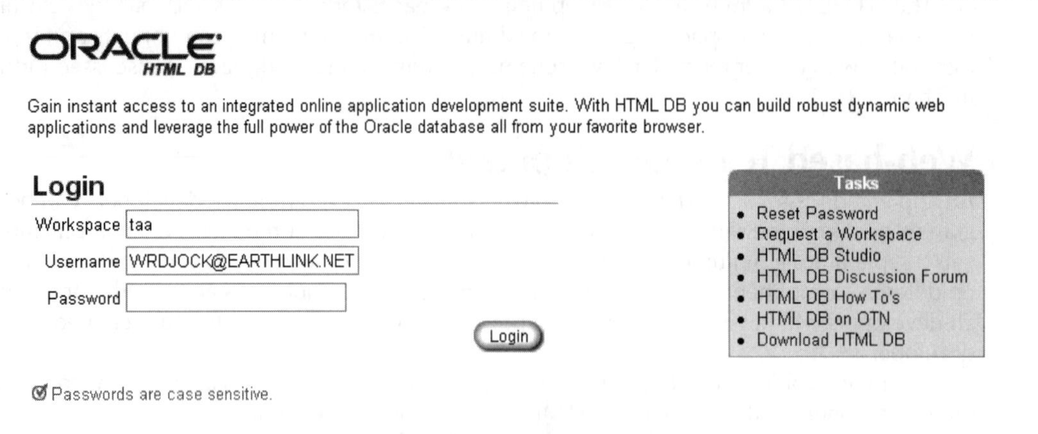

ORACLE
HTML DB

Gain instant access to an integrated online application development suite. With HTML DB you can build robust dynamic web applications and leverage the full power of the Oracle database all from your favorite browser.

Login

Workspace	taa
Username	WRDJOCK@EARTHLINK.NET
Password	

(Login)

Tasks
• Reset Password
• Request a Workspace
• HTML DB Studio
• HTML DB Discussion Forum
• HTML DB How To's
• HTML DB on OTN
• Download HTML DB

☑ Passwords are case sensitive.

FIGURE 1-6 *The Login screen of Oracle's hosted HTML DB site*

Comparison Between HTML DB and Other Oracle Products

The first step in making any product comparison involves developing a set of criteria with which to evaluate the candidate products. In most organizations, considerable time is spent evaluating which software product should be used for a particular project. Each project has its own unique requirements, including time frame, product architecture, operating system environments, whether the application is transactional or reporting, and so on. Corporate culture and available staff must also be taken into consideration. The following are some of the criteria that will be used in our comparisons between HTML DB and other Oracle web development tools, including Portal, JDeveloper, the PL/SQL Web Toolkit, and Designer:

- Productivity

- Whether the tool allows RAD development

- Declarative or coding approach

- Separate IDE required

- Whether the product requires Oracle's Application Server for deployment

- Performance of deployed application

- Types of web applications

- Robustness and scalability

- Viability of the tool

- Standards based vs. proprietary

- Organizational culture and readiness

- Security

- Integration with third-party tools

The following table describes the product characteristics of HTML DB:

Criteria	HTML DB
Productivity	High
Rapid Application Development	Yes
Declarative or coding approach	Declarative
Makes extensive use of wizards	Yes
Separate IDE required	No
Requires Oracle Application Server	No
Performance	High
Types of web applications	Individual, departmental
Robustness and scalability	High
Viability of the tool	Remains to be seen
Standards based vs. proprietary	Proprietary
Organizational culture and readiness	Oracle developers with web knowledge
Security	Adequate
Integration with third-party tools	Minimal

HTML DB vs. Portal

The product that is probably the closest in philosophy and development approach is Portal. Portal was developed in an attempt to provide a robust product for developing web applications using the concept of a portal as its paradigm. Portal provides mechanisms for developing your applications using either a declarative approach with wizards or a Java coding approach to develop your applications.

Portal makes use of a concept known as "portlets." A portlet is a region on a web page that can contain various components, including a report, a chart, and a series of URL links. In HTML DB, web pages can have regions with similar components, but in Portal the concept of a portlet is more robust.

A major difference between Portal and HTML DB is that Portal requires the installation and use of Oracle's Application Server product. This requires additional overhead and cost but allows for the development of larger-scale enterprise applications.

Table 1-1 provides a comparison between the HTML DB and Portal products.

HTML DB vs. JDeveloper

JDeveloper is Oracle's premier Java IDE for developing web-based applications using Java. JDeveloper can be used to build Java applications using a variety of approaches, including the following:

- Java applications using Swing components.

- Java applets for deployment in a browser.

- Robust J2EE applications that include JSPs (Java Server Pages), servlets, and EJBs (Enterprise Java Beans). Excellent support is also provided for Apache Struts development.

Criteria	HTML DB	Portal
Productivity	High	Medium
Rapid Application Development	Yes	Yes
Declarative or coding approach	Declarative	Declarative or coding
Makes extensive use of wizards	Yes	Yes
Separate IDE required	No	No
Requires Oracle Application Server	No	Yes
Performance	High	Medium
Types of web applications	Individual, departmental	Enterprise
Robustness and scalability	High	Medium
Viability of the tool	Remains to be seen	Currently in third release; not well promoted by Oracle
Standards based vs. proprietary	Proprietary	Proprietary
Organizational culture and readiness	Oracle developers with web knowledge	Oracle and Java developers with web knowledge
Security	Adequate	Excellent
Integration with third-party tools	Minimal	Robust

TABLE 1-1 *Comparison of Product Characteristics Between HTML DB and Portal*

The JDeveloper product has come a long way since the initial 1.0 release. The current JDeveloper release (10*g*) is a robust product that has gone well beyond its origins as a traditional Java IDE. Oracle has added a number of wizards to make the product easier to use, but development is still largely done by writing Java code. Oracle has also provided support for building robust applications using a built-in framework known as BC4J, or Business Components for Java. BC4J has largely been released with ADF, the Application Development Framework, which is a more standards-based approach to accessing server-side components in your Java applications. JDeveloper requires an application server such as Oracle's Application Server 10*g* for the deployment of J2EE applications, although other application servers such as BEA's Weblogic can be used.

When compared to HTML DB, JDeveloper's approach is intended more for the development of enterprise applications. The applications will take longer to develop and require increased manpower for both the development and maintenance.

Table 1-2 provides a comparison between the HTML DB and JDeveloper products.

HTML DB vs. PL/SQL Web Toolkit

Today, it is still possible to develop web applications using just the PL/SQL Web Toolkit. Prior to the introduction of HTML DB, this was still a viable option for developing small, robust websites that do not require an application server and rely on PL/SQL. The only requirement for the deployment of a PL/SQL Web Toolkit–based web application is a web server, such as the Apache web server, that can execute PL/SQL stored procedures. The PL/SQL Web Toolkit requires

Criteria	HTML DB	JDeveloper
Productivity	High	Low
Rapid Application Development	Yes	No
Declarative or coding approach	Declarative	Coding
Makes extensive use of wizards	Yes	Somewhat
Separate IDE required	No	Included
Requires Oracle Application Server	No	Yes, for J2EE applications
Performance	High	Medium
Types of web applications	Individual, departmental	Enterprise
Robustness and scalability	High	Medium
Viability of the tool	Remains to be seen	Strategic tool
Standards based vs. proprietary	Proprietary	Standards based
Organizational culture and readiness	Oracle developers with web knowledge	Java, J2EE developers
Security	Adequate	Robust
Integration with third-party tools	Minimal	Minimal

TABLE 1-2   *Comparison of Product Characteristics Between HTML DB and JDeveloper*

extensive coding and the use of a PL/SQL development tool such as TOAD from Quest Software or DBArtisan from Embarcadero Systems. Performance of this type of application is high because the code is all in PL/SQL.

Table 1-3 provides a comparison between HTML DB and the PL/SQL Web Toolkit.

HTML DB vs. Designer

Oracle's Designer product was once considered an excellent choice for speeding up and formalizing the development process. Designer allows a developer to specify the requirements for a system and then provides the technology for generating the application for a variety of environments. Several years ago, Designer was enhanced to provide generation capabilities using the PL/SQL Web Toolkit. Several internal packages were provided that offered wrappers for the PL/SQL Web Toolkit and generated PL/SQL code for generating web applications. Although there are still segments of the Oracle community using Designer for their web development, the product is in decline. HTML DB offers a more productive and up-to-date alternative to using Designer for developing web applications in the future.

Table 1-4 provides a comparison between the HTML DB and Designer products.

Criteria	HTML DB	PL/SQL Web Toolkit
Productivity	High	Low
Rapid Application Development	Yes	No
Declarative or coding approach	Declarative	Coding
Makes extensive use of wizards	Yes	No
Separate IDE required	No	Yes
Requires Oracle Application Server	No	No, but a web server is required
Performance	High	High
Types of web applications	Individual, departmental	Individual, departmental
Robustness and scalability	High	High
Viability of the tool	Remains to be seen	Introduced with first web products but rarely used today
Standards based vs. proprietary	Proprietary	Proprietary
Organizational culture and readiness	Oracle developers with web knowledge	Oracle developers with web knowledge
Security	Adequate	Provided by web server
Integration with third-party tools	Minimal	None

TABLE 1-3   *Comparison of the Product Characteristics Between HTML DB and the PL/SQL Web Toolkit*

Criteria	HTML DB	Designer
Productivity	High	Medium
Rapid Application Development	Yes	Yes
Declarative or coding approach	Declarative	Declarative
Makes extensive use of wizards	Yes	No
Separate IDE required	No	No
Requires Oracle Application Server	No	No, but a web server is required for web applications
Performance	High	High
Types of web applications	Individual, departmental	Departmental, enterprise
Robustness and scalability	High	Medium
Viability of the tool	Remains to be seen	Use is in decline
Standards based vs. proprietary	Proprietary	Proprietary
Organizational culture and readiness	Oracle developers with web knowledge	Oracle developers with web knowledge
Security	Adequate	Adequate
Integration with third-party tools	Minimal	None

TABLE 1-4   *Comparison of the Product Characteristics Between HTML DB and Designer*

When to Use HTML DB

After looking at the various alternatives for developing web applications, you can see that there are various considerations for when to use a particular product. It is important to understand the capabilities of the products and then compare these capabilities with the requirements for a particular project.

This leads one to ask the following question:

What are some of the considerations that I should take into account when selecting HTML DB as the product for developing my web applications?

The following considerations provide an answer to this question. HTML DB should be considered as the web development product of choice when:

■   Your organization is new to the Web and not very Java literate. This will mean that the majority of your developers are skilled in Oracle SQL and PL/SQL.

- The majority of your applications are database-centric. This is in contrast to applications that have requirements for processing flat files or need to communicate with other applications using messaging. This is the case unless the messaging will be done using Web Services, which is supported by HTML DB.

- Your application can be developed in a hosted service environment.

- Your developers are comfortable with a declarative, wizard-based approach to development.

- You want to migrate an Access database or Excel spreadsheet application to the Web. This is currently one of the major uses of HTML DB and is discussed in detail in Chapter 3.

- You have an internal web application to develop.

This last point needs some additional discussion. Some people see HTML DB as a product for developing individual or departmental web applications. As IT departments have been given more and more to do with fewer resources over the past few years, these applications have largely been ignored as IT developers concentrate on mission-critical systems. With HTML DB, these applications can now be addressed. Internally, HTML DB is the product of choice for these types of applications.

This does not mean that HTML DB cannot be used for enterprise applications within an organization. Because HTML DB applications do not require an Application Server and utilize PL/SQL, these applications perform well and are scalable.

Applications Developed Using HTML DB

As time goes by there will be more and more examples of HTML DB applications. Many of the applications that have already been and will be developed are intranet applications to be used within an organization. Typically, these applications will not be available on the Internet. The applications discussed in the next few sections are Internet applications that have been developed using HTML DB.

Before we review these applications, one other application should be mentioned. One of the early applications developed with HTML DB was an application developed by Oracle for the Chicago Police department. The application is used by the Chicago police to log and track evidence that is collected to be used in criminal proceedings. The application was developed quickly over a three-month period and currently receives over 1 million page hits per month.

SELECT Magazine Article Review

SELECT magazine serves as the technical journal for the Oracle community of the International Oracle Users Group (IOUG). Several years ago, the Executive Editor of the magazine at the time, Paul Dorsey of Dulcian Inc., instituted a review process for selecting the best articles from each issue of the magazine. The review process included a mechanism for rating each article in several categories. Reviewers with varying expertise were recruited from the Oracle community to assess the articles. Each article was assigned to a contributing editor who coordinated the reviews of the article and worked with the author to make any changes. The initial mechanisms for coordinating the reviews and sending articles to each reviewer were manual and cumbersome.

As the mantle of Executive Editor passed to Tony Jedlinski of Roman Inc., an HTML DB system was developed by Tony to coordinate the review process. Roman Inc. was an early adopter of HTML DB and still utilizes the product extensively for departmental applications. The *SELECT* Journal Article Review application is available to all *SELECT* editors as well as the article reviewers. Upon logging in to the application, an editor or reviewer is presented with a main application screen that provides a report with all the articles of interest to that person, as shown in Figure 1-7. Also, several buttons can be clicked to select areas of interest and to update personal information. A download icon can be clicked to download a copy of an article of interest for reviewing. After the download, the articles are tracked along with the reviews of those articles. In addition, the application has a mechanism for sending an e-mail to any editor or reviewer who indicated an interest in the article.

A Collaboration Application

One of the major advantages of the Web for application deployment is the ability to collaborate and work with others. Roman Inc., needed an application to review business ideas and concepts as part of their ongoing strategic analysis process. An HTML DB application, shown in Figure 1-8, was developed in two days to support this process. The application allows an employee to add and edit the Idea list, rate ideas and suggestions, and provide pros or cons or any comments for an idea.

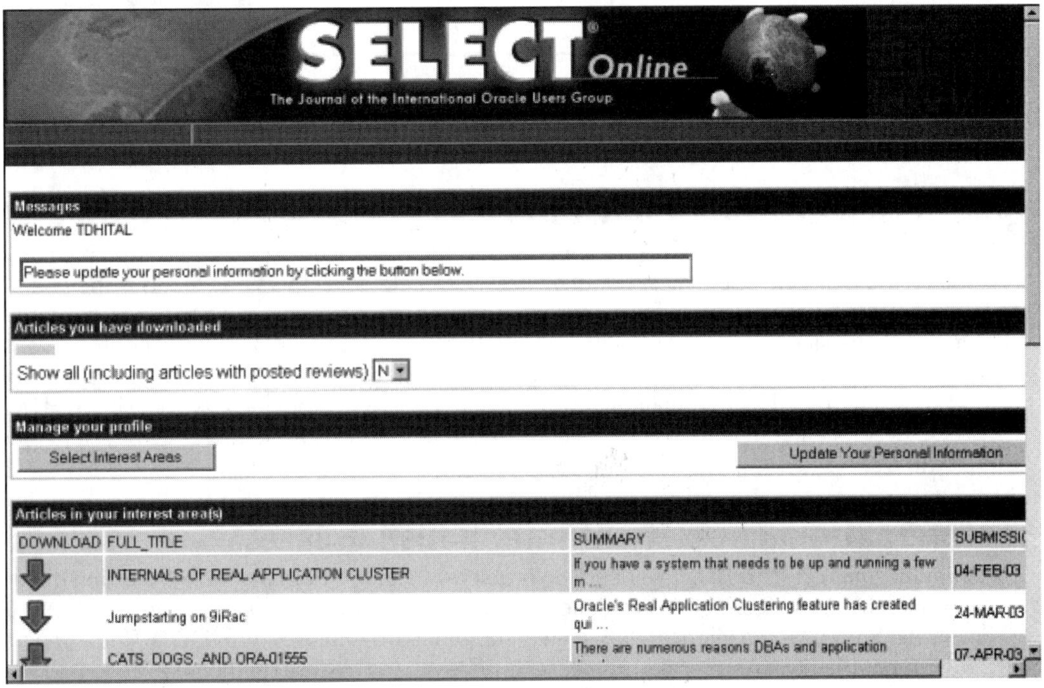

FIGURE 1-7 *The* SELECT *Journal Article Review application*

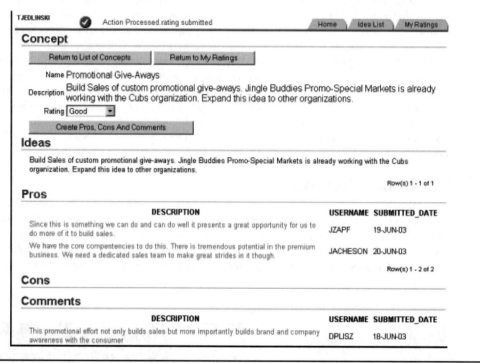

FIGURE 1-8 *Business idea review application*

External Oracle Applications

Oracle has several customer-facing applications that have been developed or rewritten to use HTML DB. One of the most popular sites for Oracle developers and DBAs is the Ask Tom site on the Web. This site is hosted by Tom Kyte, Vice President in Oracle's Government practice. The site, which is shown in Figure 1-9, allows you to ask a technical question and get a detailed answer to a particular problem you are having with Oracle. To provide a more robust solution and a more maintainable website, Oracle rewrote the Ask Tom site in HTML DB. The Developer Trends site, http://devtrends.oracle.com, is another Oracle site developed using HTML DB.

International Society of Infectious Disease

With the threat of terrorist activity and the problems that arise from naturally occurring diseases, it is important to understand and track infectious disease information. One website, the ProMED-mail website, hosted by the International Society for Infectious Diseases, provides a global reporting system for identifying outbreaks of infectious diseases and toxins. The home page for the site, which is shown in Figure 1-10, provides access to a calendar of events, information about recall and alerts, a map of outbreaks, and various announcements. The site is available in several languages, including English, Spanish, Portuguese, Chinese, and Japanese.

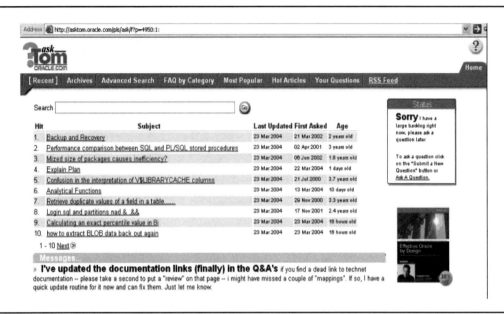

FIGURE 1-9   *AskTom.Oracle.com application*

FIGURE 1-10   *ProMED-mail HTML DB application*

It is important to point out that this home page looks like any other web page you might find on the Internet. By working with a graphics artist and defining templates (which are described further in Chapter 6), you can achieve whatever look and feel you require for your HTML DB application.

In this chapter we have looked at the evolution of the HTML DB development environment, how it compares to other development tools, and when it should be utilized. In the remainder of the book we will delve into the capabilities of HTML DB.

CHAPTER
2

Installing HTML DB

hether you're using an existing database on an existing application server or if you have created a new database along with a new application server instance, you'll find the installation and configuration of HTML DB to be a simple task.

Installation and Configuration

If you wish to try HTML DB out before you install it in your own environment, Oracle provides a hosted (non-production) HTML DB environment for your use. This chapter will discuss the following topics:

- Installation-less test drive

- HTML DB prerequisites

- Installing an Oracle 10*g* Database for HTML DB

- Downloading HTML DB

- Installing and configuring the Oracle HTTP Server

- Installing and configuring HTML DB

Installation-less Test Drive

When it comes to using HTML DB, you have the option of test driving the product from Oracle's hosted HTML DB site. This site can be found at http://htmldb.oracle.com. As shown next, you can "request a workspace" and, once it's granted, you'll be able to do everything you can from a standard workspace (outside of the administration of HTML DB discussed in this chapter).

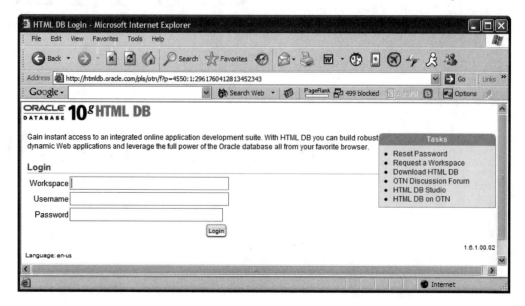

Prerequisites

HTML DB requires an Oracle Database to store its metadata repository, stored procedures, and data. HTML DB requires version 9.2.0.3 or higher of the Oracle Database. If you don't have the database installed, go to the Oracle site (http://www.oracle.com) and click on Downloads. On the downloads page, shown here, you'll notice the Database section. This section contains a link for the Oracle 10*g* Database.

Database

× Oracle Database 10*g*
  10*g* download page includes:
  - Companion CD (HTML DB, HTTP Server, more..)
  - Client CD
  - Cluster Ready Services CD
  - Oracle HTML DB standalone

Click on the link and download the database version/release for your platform and operating system. Read and acknowledge the license terms. From the next page you'll want to download both the database software and the companion CD. If you already have a 9.2.0.3 (or greater) version of the database that you can use for the HTML DB repository, you do not need to download the database. If you already have an existing 10*g* application server on which to run HTML DB, you can download the Oracle HTML DB standalone version.

If you don't already have an existing database for HTML DB, after downloading the database, perform the database installation on your platform.

Installing Oracle 10*g* Database

After downloading the necessary files, follow the "readme" instructions for pre-installation and installation of the Oracle Database. You may need to extract or unzip the files to begin the installation. Start the setup program for the installation. Here are the steps of importance for the database installation:

1. Be sure to place the database into its own Oracle home.

2. Perform a standard or enterprise installation of the database.

3. For your starter database, you can choose a general-purpose (or a transaction-processing or data warehouse) database.

4. Name your database engine using whatever global database name and SID you want. The default name of orcl is fine. You can check the "Create database with sample schemas" check box.

5. You can select e-mail notification using your outbound e-mail server and e-mail address for the management of the database.

6. Create a standard file system-based database.

7. Choose the backup and recovery method that best suits your needs.

8. You can choose individual passwords or the same password for all accounts.

9. The installation wizard will provide you with a real-time update of the status of the installation. You'll want to write down the log information for the database configuration assistant. It's important to note the URL for enterprise manager (typically port 5500).

10. You'll likely want to click on the Password Management button to unlock the sample and other schemas in the database.

11. Be sure the configuration assistants are successful. If not, click on Retry.

NOTE
*For a complete reference on installing Oracle 10*g, *refer to Oracle Database 10*g, The Complete Reference *from Oracle Press.*

Downloading HTML DB

As mentioned in the previous section, you'll need to download the companion CD for Oracle 10g. This CD (or image) contains HTML DB as well as the Oracle 10g Application Server. As mentioned, if you already have an application server on which to run HTML DB, you can simply download the standalone version of HTML DB, which is discussed next. Shown here are the two options available for download.

Oracle Database 10*g* Companion CD Release 1 (10.1.0.2) for Microsoft Windows (32-bit)

☒ 10g_win32_companion.zip (353,867,577 bytes) (cksum - 3498046895) *Includes: Examples, HTML DB, HTTP Server, JPublisher, JavaVM ncomps, Legato Single Server, Text Knowledgebase, InterMedia ncomps

☒ Oracle HTML DB v1.6 (47,913,091 bytes) - latest standalone version of HTML DB New (29-Dec-04)

Installing the Companion CD

Once you have downloaded the necessary files, follow the "readme" directions for pre-installation and installation. You may need to extract or unzip the files to begin the download. In Windows, start the Setup program for the Companion CD; for UNIX platforms, run the eunInstaller executable. Skip past the welcome message. Here are the steps of importance for the Companion CD installation:

1. As shown next, you must place the Companion components into a different Oracle home from that of the database. If the database is on another machine, you'll also want to create a new Oracle home for these components.

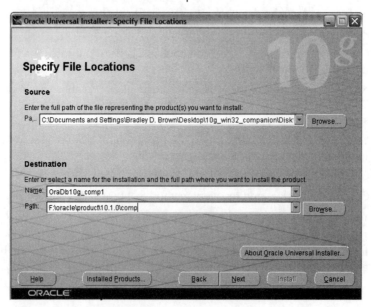

2. As shown here, choose the products to install—that is, the Oracle HTTP Server and HTML DB.

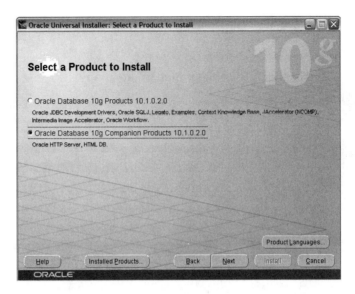

3. Next, you can see that you need to select the specific products to install. Choose both the Oracle HTTP Server and HTML DB.

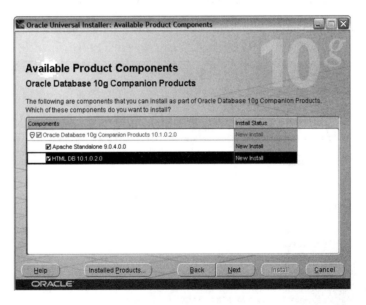

4. As demonstrated in the following illustration, you'll need to enter the specific database connection information for the HTML DB and its repository. An important parameter

to remember on this page is the HTML DB password. This will be the password of the "INTERNAL" workspace in HTML DB.

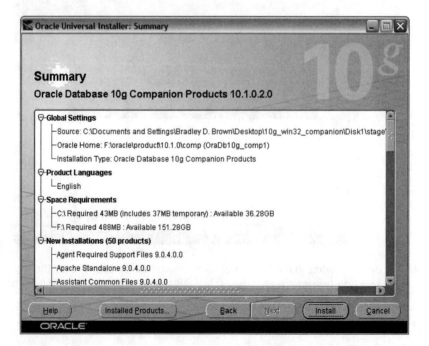

5. Confirm the installation summary information, shown here, and click on Install.

6. The installation status will be updated in real time as the HTML DB (and HTTP Server) is installed.

7. You'll want to take note of the installation summary messages displayed on the "End of Installation" page, as shown next. The port on which the HTTP Server was installed is an important parameter to note. The message also contains the path and filename to a log file where all this information is recorded for later reference.

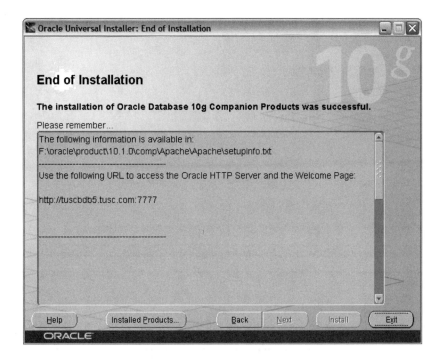

8. As demonstrated in Figure 2-1, from your browser, you'll want to test your access to the HTTP Server with the URL http://*servername:portnumber,* which is your server name followed by the port number noted in the prior step.

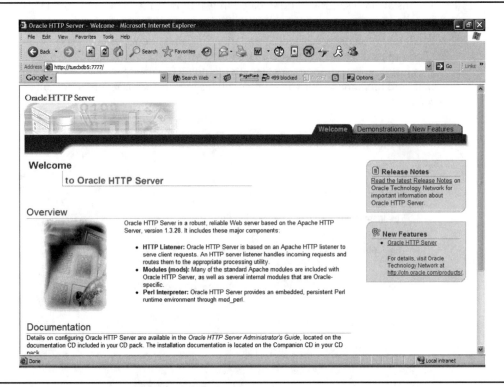

FIGURE 2-1 *Testing access to the HTTP Server*

   9. Additionally, you'll want to test your access to the HTML DB application. As shown here, simply add **/pls/htmldb/** to the end of the URL specified in the previous step.

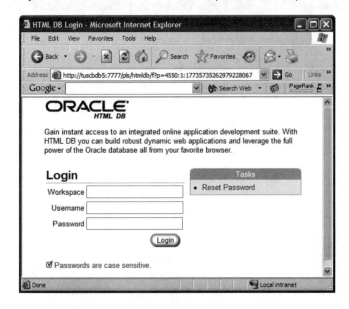

Installing the Standalone HTML DB Version

If you already have a database (greater than version 9.2.0.3) into which you can install the HTML DB repository and you already have an Oracle HTTP Server (or full-blown Oracle Application Server) from which to run HTML DB, you can download the standalone version of HTML DB from the Oracle downloads page. You can also download the standalone version if you are running a prior version of HTML DB and you wish to upgrade to version 1.6.

After downloading the 50MB compressed image, extract the files into a directory of your choice. Here's an example:

```
C:\oracle
```

(Note that the size of the file might change with different releases.) This will create an htmldb directory structure under this directory. You'll find a readme.html file in the root htmldb directory. Open this HTML document:

Read the Installation or Upgrade document before performing your installation or upgrade for more detailed information. To install (or upgrade) HTML DB in the database, simply run the ins. sql script from the same directory where you found the readme.html file. Note that the name of this file is subject to change, so pay close attention to the readme file. Running this script will prompt you for a number of answers to questions. Here's an example:

```
sqlplus sys/password@conection
Sqlplus> @ins
. HTML DB Hosted Development Service Installation.....................................>\>
Which directory should be used for the log file?   [./] >\>
Is this a (1) New install or an (2) Upgrade?     [1] >\>
What is your net8-9 connect string (Enter for none)?  [] >\>
What is your Oracle SYS password?   [CHANGE_ON_INSTALL] >\>
What is the HTML DB Admin password         [admin] >\>
What is the application tablespace?        [USERS] >\>
What is your file upload/download tablespace?    [USERS] >\>
What is your temporary tablespace?        [TEMP] **
Press return to begin the install (logfile=./install.1st)
```

The installation guide discusses the necessary pre- and post-installation steps. Be sure to read these steps in the guide. The installation document is found in an install directory under the documents directory of the location where you unzipped the file.

Configuring the HTTP Server

You may want to configure your HTTP Server for HTML DB. For example, this section will discuss changing the default port that the HTTP Server runs on, the server administrator, and virtual directories. For information about the configuration of the Oracle HTTP Server, you may wish to purchase an Apache or Oracle Application Server book, such as *Oracle 10g Application Server Web Development* by Chris Ostrowski and Bradley D. Brown.

Changing from Port 7777 to Port 80

To change the HTTP Server's port, you must edit the Apache configuration file (httpd.conf in the $oracle_home/Apache/Apache/conf directory). Open this file with a text editor. Assuming the existing port is set to 7777, search for the lines that read

```
Port 7777
Listen 7777
```

and change them so that they read as follows:

```
Port 80
Listen 80
```

Server Administrator

You may want to change the server administrator for the server. When errors occur on the server, the following e-mail will appear in the error message:

```
ServerAdmin youradmin@yourcompany.com
```

Virtual Directories

In your HTML DB application, you may wish to reference additional physical directories for HTML content or images on your server. The HTML DB installation automatically adds a virtual directory for /i/ that contains the images for HTML DB. You can find the entry for the /i/ alias and add more of your own in the marvel.conf file, which is located in the ORACLE_HOME\htmldb\ Apache\modplsql\conf directory. Note that HTML DB uses a virtual directory of /i/ for the images. You can add your own virtual directory that references an absolute directory. Here's an example:

```
Alias /photography/ "C:\PHOTOGRAPHY\BDB/"
```

Configuring HTML DB

Before you use HTML DB for development, you may wish to configure it. This section will discuss logging in to the INTERNAL workspace, turning on and managing the provisioning of new workspaces, configuring your e-mail server, and creating new workspaces manually.

Logging in to INTERNAL

To administer HTML DB, log in to the INTERNAL workspace with the username ADMIN, and the password that you specified during installation. After logging in, you'll see the HTML DB Administration page, as shown in Figure 2-2.

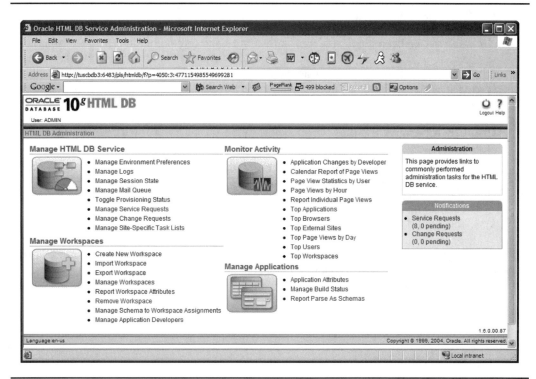

FIGURE 2-2 *HTML DB Administration page*

Provisioning

By default, the provision mode when you install HTML DB is set to MANUAL. As you can see in Figure 2-2, there is no option to allow a user to request a new workspace. Only the HTML DB administrator can provision a new workspace.

HTML DB can also run in REQUEST mode. In this mode, your user community can initiate workspace provisioning by requesting a new workspace. On the HTML DB login page, a link titled "Request Workspace" will appear. This link will pop up the Request Workspace Wizard (flow 4700). Once the request is made, the HTML DB administrator can approve, adjust, or deny the user's request.

To change the provisioning mode, click on the Toggle Provisioning Status link from the Internal Administration page and then click on the Toggle Status button.

Configure to Send E-mail

HTML DB sends mail by storing it in a queue and then periodically pushing the queue. By default, a DBMS job is created to push this queue every 15 minutes.

In order for mail to be sent correctly, two preferences need to be created. The first one, called "SMTP_HOST_ADDRESS," should be the address of an SMTP server to which the machine where HTML DB is installed has access. A second preference, called "SMTP_HOST_PORT," must be created and must be the port where the SMTP server listens for requests (this is usually 25, so the value of the preference should usually be "25").

Provisioning Workspaces

If provisioning is on, users will be able to request their own workspace. To check to see if any workspaces have been requested, look at the right-hand section of the HTML DB Administration screen (refer to Figure 2-2) in the "Pending" service requests (that is, new workspace requests) and change requests. If any workspaces are pending, you can click on the number and you'll see a list of service or change requests. Using the links on this page, you can approve, change, or deny any request.

Creating a New Workspace

From the HTML DB Administration screen (refer to Figure 2-2), click Create New Workspace. You'll be prompted, step by step, through a wizard to create a new HTML DB workspace. If you have a question about any of the prompts, you can click on the prompt for context-sensitive help about the information being requested.

As you learned in this chapter, you can create a new HTML DB environment in no time at all. Managing the HTML DB workspaces requires the wizard-based administration tool. You're now ready to begin building new HTML DB applications in your HTML DB workspaces. Note that this installation discussion was done from version 1.6. Because HTML DB is a new product and is changing quickly, it is wise to refer to the official Install doc that comes with each version.

CHAPTER
3

Using the SQL Workshops

ost of the HTML DB applications you develop will be based on one or more Oracle tables or views. In some cases, these tables or views will already exist; in other cases, they will need to be created. Existing tables may also need to be altered to include additional columns to support the HTML DB application you are developing. In addition, you will often need to make use of other Oracle database objects, including PL/SQL procedures and functions, packages, triggers, sequences, and synonyms.

To facilitate ease of use, HTML DB includes a fairly complete and easy-to-use facility, called the SQL Workshop, for working with these Oracle database objects. This workshop includes capabilities for executing SQL commands, for browsing or creating any of the Oracle objects required for your application, and for building and executing script files. The workshop also includes access to Explain Plan information for tuning your SQL queries and a facility for managing the user interface defaults associated with a table.

Another common set of functions you will need to perform relate to the data associated with an application. Often, this data is locked in a desktop application, such as an Excel spreadsheet or a Microsoft Access database, and will need to be imported and loaded into an Oracle table. The data might also be stored in a simple text file or, increasingly these days, in an XML file. HTML DB includes utilities within the SQL Workshop that allow you to work with the data your application needs. These utilities provide functions for importing data into your applications as well as the ability to export data from your applications.

Invoking the SQL Workshop

You have several ways to invoke the SQL Workshop. As you'll recall from Chapter 2, the HTML DB logon page is reached with a URL such as http://servername:7777/pls/htmldb. After you log in to HTML DB, the HTML DB Home page is displayed, as shown in Figure 3-1. The three main areas of HTML DB are accessible through the large navigation icons on the page or through the tabs across the top of the page:

- Application Builder

- SQL Workshop

- Administration

The tabs will always remain available once you are in any one of the main areas of HTML DB. In version 2.0, the navigation icons also have drop-down menus that are accessible by clicking on the down arrow on the right side of each icon. These menus allow you to navigate directly to sub-areas of each of the major areas.

Once you select the SQL Workshop, the main page of this workshop is displayed, as shown in Figure 3-2. All the different areas of the SQL Workshop are accessible through the large navigation icons on the SQL Workshop main page. Once you have navigated to one of the different areas within the SQL Workshop, you can always return to the main page by clicking on the SQL Workshop link in the breadcrumb menu just below the tabs. Here's a list of the icons on the main page:

- **Object Browser** Provides a graphical interface for browsing all types of database objects.

- ■ **Query Builder**   Provides a graphical tool for building and executing SQL queries.

- ■ **SQL Commands**   Provides an interface for directly executing SQL commands and viewing the resulting output.

- ■ **SQL Scripts**   Used to manage script files, create and execute script control files, and generate DDL for database objects.

- ■ **Utilities**   Contains icons to invoke various utilities for importing/exporting data, generating DDL, creating object reports, and monitoring the database.

Like the main navigation icons on the HTML DB Home page, these icons also offer the drop-down menus that allow direct access to the sub-areas.

Using Object Browser

Clicking on the Object Browser icon on the SQL Workshop main page will navigate you to the Object Browser page, shown in Figure 3-3. This page is implemented as frames. In the panel on the left, you can choose which type of object you wish to browse and select from the list below. You may also search for an object name by entering a value in the field with the magnifying glass. Note that the pop-up menu on the SQL Workshop main page allows you to select to browse different types of objects; each selection navigates to this same page, it just pre-selects the type of object you wish to browse. Otherwise, this page will start with Table objects.

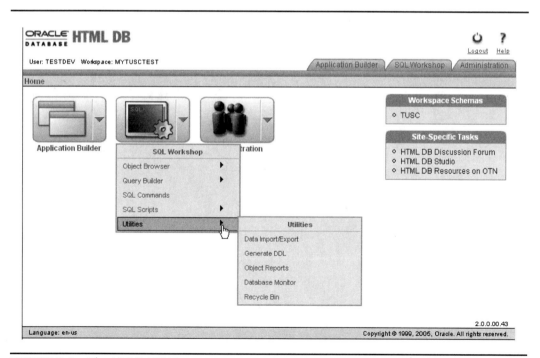

FIGURE 3-1   *The HTML DB Home page*

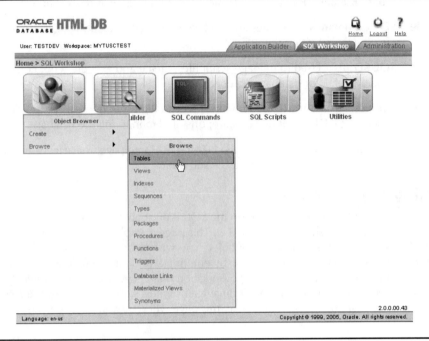

FIGURE 3-2 *The SQL Workshop Home page*

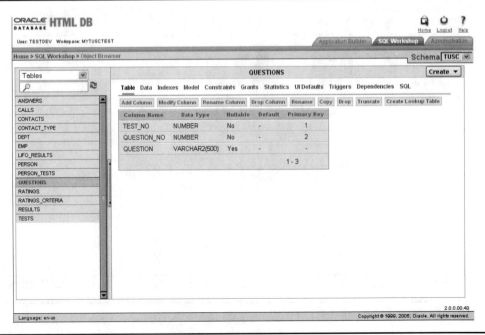

FIGURE 3-3 *Browsing the list of Table objects in the current schema*

The panel on the right shows details for the currently selected object on the left. Depending on the type of object you are browsing, different sub-tabs will be displayed along the top of the right panel. These tabs navigate to additional information about the currently selected object. Additionally, there might be buttons below the sub-tabs, as shown in Figure 3-3, that initiate different actions on the currently selected object.

You can see that there are a large number of sub-tabs that offer additional information about tables. This information includes data, indexes, triggers, constraints, grants, UI defaults, dependencies, and a model, which shows the foreign key references to and from the table. Clicking on any one of the sub-tabs displays the corresponding information in the right panel. The following illustration shows the right panel with the trigger information for the QUESTIONS table.

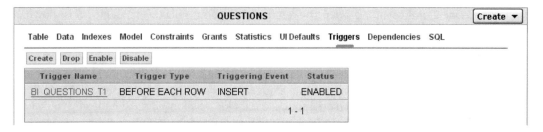

Note that the name of the trigger is a hyperlink that will navigate you to the object detail for that trigger, as shown in Figure 3-4. Notice that it changed the left panel to Trigger objects and selected the BI_QUESTIONS_T1 as the current object. Again, notice the new sub-tabs and the buttons that offer actions on the current object.

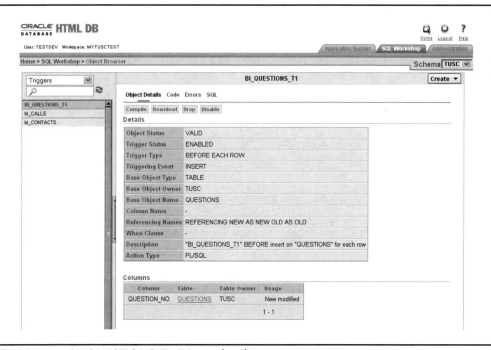

FIGURE 3-4   *BI_QUESTIONS_T1 Trigger details*

Due to space constraints, we cannot explore every option under every object type, but I will highlight a few. You should take the time to explore the entire Object Browser. When you are browsing a table and click on the Data sub-tab, a Query button appears that allows you to perform a query-by-example style query, as shown in Figure 3-5.

The query-by-example function provides a powerful and easy-to-use facility for examining data in the table. The form presented for a particular table lists all the columns of the table along with the data type of the column. A check box in front of the column needs to be checked if you want the column to appear on the report. A Column Condition box follows each column and is used to enter a value that acts as a filter on the column. For text columns, you can use special characters such as % and _ because the generated query uses the LIKE predicate for these columns. The form also provides up to three fields for sorting with corresponding radio buttons to indicate an ascending or descending order. The result of the options selected in Figure 3-5 is shown in Figure 3-6. The query results display only the columns selected and are in ascending order by test number and question number, but only for questions that contain "DOS," as requested. The query results screen has several nice features. It has an edit icon on each row for updating the data. It also provides the ability to drill up to the tests lookup because the Show option of the "Drill Up and Drill Down Links" radio button on the query-by-example form was checked. The drill up and down functionality is implemented through foreign key relationships. Additionally, you can change the number or rows displayed, start a new query, or initiate the process of creating a new row.

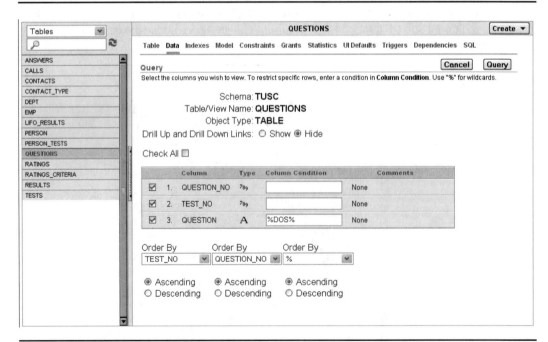

FIGURE 3-5   *The query-by-example form*

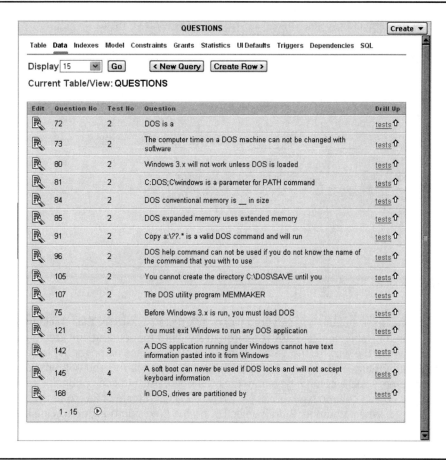

FIGURE 3-6 *Query-by-example results*

TIP
Do not use single quotes in the Column Condition box. These are supplied automatically when the SQL for the query is generated.

Creating New Objects

In addition to browsing existing objects, the Object Browser also allows you to create new objects. You can start creating a new object by selecting the object type under the Create option in the drop-down menu on the Object Browser navigation icon, shown earlier in Figure 3-2. Alternatively, you can click the Create button that is always present in the upper-right corner of the right-hand panel of the Object Browser. This gives you the screen shown next.

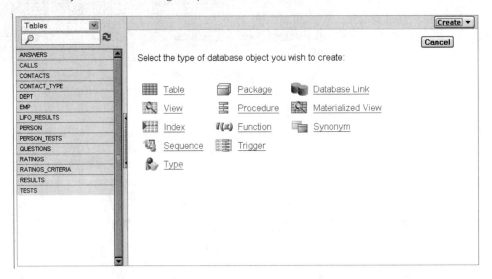

Clicking on one of the object types invokes a "Create" wizard for that object type. For example, clicking on the Table object walks you through a wizard for defining and creating a new table. In the first page of the wizard, shown in Figure 3-7, you provide a name for the table and then define each column that will be included in the table. For each column, you will provide a valid Oracle column name, select a column type from the drop-down list, and can optionally specify a comment. When you enter a column type, boxes for the precision and scale of the column appear as required. For example, when a number field is selected, both a precision box and a scale box are displayed for entry, whereas only a scale box is presented for a VARCHAR2 field. Selecting a field type of CLOB displays neither box.

The second step of the Create Table Wizard allows you to specify the field that should be used as the primary key for the table, as shown in Figure 3-8. You can select this field from a drop-down list of the fields in the table. The name of the primary key for the table will default to the table name followed by an underscore and the letters "PK" (for example, PRODUCT_PK). The radio button group determines whether or not the primary key is generated. You can select from one of three primary key population options: Not Generated, Generated from an Existing Sequence, Generated from a New Sequence. The default option is that the primary key is generated from a new sequence. If you select one of the other options, you will need to specify the name of the sequence to be used. If you select to generate the primary key from an existing sequence, you must select the sequence name from a drop-down list box of the sequences from the current schema. Selecting the option of generating the primary key from a new sequence requires that you provide a name for the sequence, although it will be defaulted for you. This option also automatically generates a trigger for maintaining the sequence.

TIP
If your table requires a primary key with multiple fields, you should select the first field of the primary key at this point because you can only select one field with the wizard. You will have to modify the primary key after the table is created.

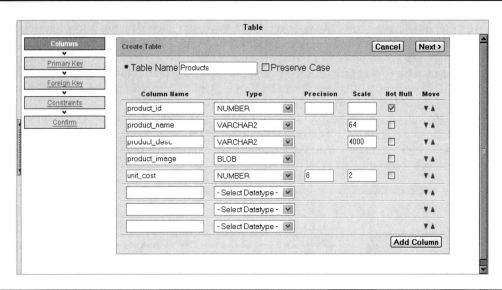

FIGURE 3-7   *The first step of the Create Table Wizard*

The next step in the wizard allows you to create foreign keys through a process of selecting a column (or columns) from the new table and then selecting a reference table and a column (or columns) from that table. The step after that allows you to add either unique or check constraints for the table. The final step is the confirmation, where you can view the SQL that will be used to create the table, constraints, and triggers. Prior versions gave you the option of saving the SQL as a script so it could be modified—for instance, to add other columns to the primary key. What you can do is to highlight the SQL, copy it, modify it as needed, and then run it through the SQL Command window.

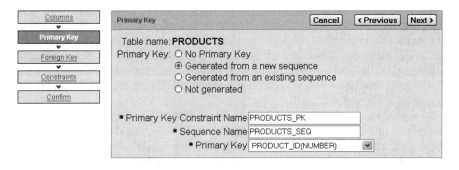

FIGURE 3-8   *The second step of the Create Table Wizard*

Managing User Interface (UI) Defaults

The user interface (UI) defaults associated with tables and their columns allow developers to control the default look and feel of fields and columns on HTML DB forms and reports. HTML DB defaults to the UI properties based on the metadata about the table stored in the Oracle Data Dictionary tables—that is, it uses the column name for a report column or a form's field label. HTML DB provides the ability to enter UI data for tables and columns; this data is maintained internally by HTML DB and used instead of the defaults it would normally use.

UI Defaults is one of the many sub-tabs in the right panel of the Object Browser for table objects (refer to Figure 3-5). If UI defaults exist for a table when you click on the UI Defaults tab, a report of current defaults is displayed, as shown in the next illustration. Clicking on the Edit button takes you to the Table Defaults edit page.

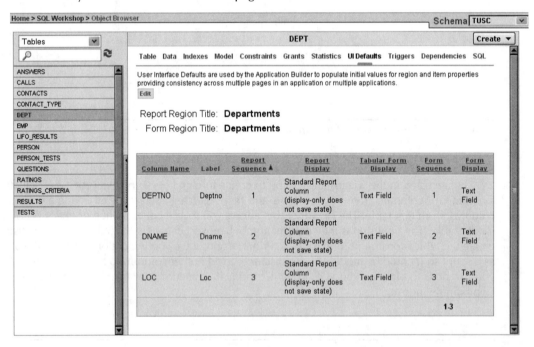

If no UI defaults are specified for a table when you click on the UI Defaults tab, a message stating that there are no defaults and a Create Defaults button appear. If you click on the Create Defaults button, HTML DB will populate the defaults and navigate to the same Table Defaults edit page (see Figure 3-9). Note that the main tab is now Application Builder and that the breadcrumb menu indicates the path of the page from the Shared Components section of the Application Builder. This is the other path you can use to manage table UI defaults. Shared Components will be covered in more detail in Chapter 4.

To modify the UI defaults for a column, click on the Column name, as shown in Figure 3-9. The Edit Column Defaults page is displayed for the column, as shown in Figure 3-10. This page has two tabs: Column Definition for defining the column's defaults and List of Values for specifying a list of values, if so desired. The Column Definition page has four sections for types of defaults you can specify: Label Default, Report Defaults, Tabular Form Default, and Form Defaults. At the

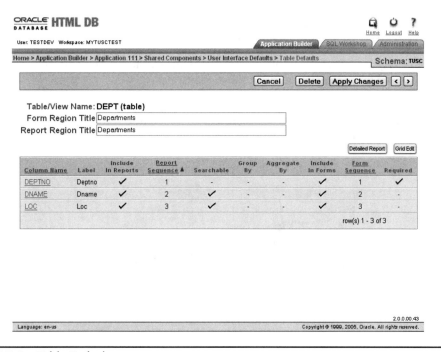

FIGURE 3-9 *Table Defaults page*

top of the page are internal page hyperlinks for quickly navigating to any of the four sections. Along with the hyperlinks you'll find information listed about the column and a link to pop up a window to display information about the column from the data dictionary. The first section allows you to specify the label that will be used for the column. This will be used for column headings on reports and for individual field labels on forms.

The Report Defaults section contains defaults for the following items:

- **Display** This is a yes/no option that determines whether the column will be displayed on the report.

- **Display Sequence** This determines the order of placement of the column on the report. A separate display sequence report for forms allows for a different sequence of columns on reports and forms.

- **Mask** This defines an edit mask that is used to display the field. You can specify an edit mask of your own using standard Oracle masking characters or select from a list of built-in masks by clicking on the arrow to the right of the field.

- **Alignment** This specifies whether the values in the field will be left-aligned, centered, or right-aligned. The default value for this field varies depending on the type of the field. For Date and VARCHAR2 fields, the default value is left-aligned, whereas for NUMBER fields, the default value is right-aligned.

■ **Searchable**   This indicates whether the field can be used in searches.

■ **Group By**   Another yes/no field that determines whether the Group By option displays for this column when a report is created.

■ **Aggregate By**   Still another yes/no field that specifies whether the column should be used for aggregation in reports and charts.

The Tabular Form Default section allows you to specify the type of field the column will be displayed as when the table is used as the source for a tabular form. You specify the value for this field by selecting the field type from a drop-down list of nearly 20 different types. Normally

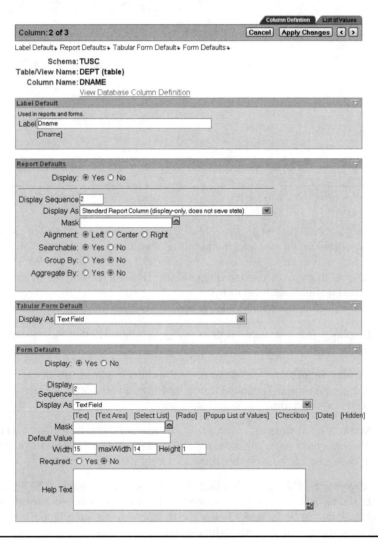

FIGURE 3-10   *The Column Definition tab*

the field type will be a text field, but if the column is a date you might specify a Date Picker type field, or if you supply a list of values for the column, the field type you choose could be a Select list or a pop-up List Of Values.

The Forms Defaults section contains default UI options for when the table is used as the source for a form. As you can see, some of the UI defaults you can specify for a form are the same as for reports:

- **Display**   This is a yes/no option that determines whether the column will be displayed on the report.

- **Display Sequence**   This determines the order of placement of the column on the form. A separate display sequence report for forms allows for a different sequence of columns on reports and forms.

- **Display As**   This specifies the type of form field on the HTML page that should be used to represent this field. You specify the value for this field by selecting the field type from a drop-down list of nearly 60 different types or by clicking one of the hyperlinks below this field. The hyperlinks represent the common field types you would specify. Field types are discussed more fully in Chapter 10.

- **Mask**   This defines an edit mask that is used to display the field. You can specify an edit mask of your own or select from a list of available edit masks.

- **Default Value**   This is a default value to be entered into the field when a new form is being filled out. For a Date field, the value could default to the current date (that is, sysdate).

- **Width**   This defines the width of the display of the field.

- **MaxWidth**   This defines the maximum width of the field. If the width is less than MaxWidth, the text entered into the field will automatically scroll.

- **Height**   This determines the field's height when displayed on the form.

- **Required**   A yes/no option that specifies whether or not the field must be entered on the form.

- **Help Text**   This is the text that will be displayed if the user clicks on the label for the field.

The other tab for Edit Column–level defaults is the List of Values tab. If the column has no list of values, you can choose to create either a dynamic or a static list of values for the column you are editing. Figure 3-11 shows a static list of values for the TEMP column of the EMP table. For a dynamic list of values, you would specify a Select statement for the values to be listed. The Select statement must select a value to be displayed and a value to be returned—for example, a query for the DEPNO field on the EMP table might look like this:

```
Select dname r, deptno d from dept order by dname
```

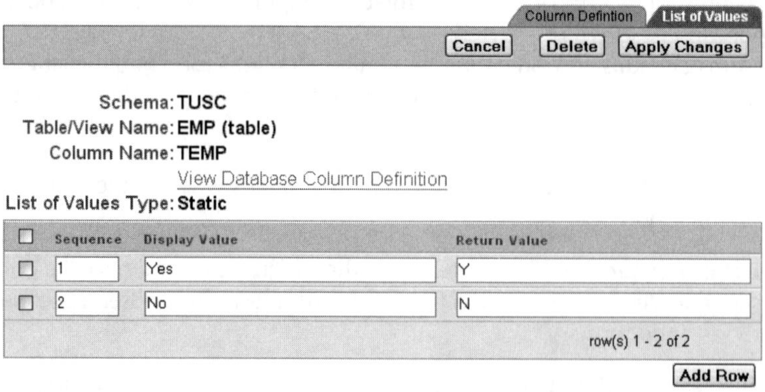

FIGURE 3-11 *The List of Values tab*

The UI information can be entered either on a column-by-column basis, as described previously, or by clicking on the Grid Edit button above the Column-level UI defaults (refer to Figure 3-9). This option redisplays the column report with the columns in an editable form, as shown in Figure 3-12. The editable form does not allow for all the UI attributes of forms and reports to be modified, but it does allow for the more important fields to be changed. This format is also useful when you want to change the order in which the columns appear on a report or on a form because you can see the values of all the columns.

Using the Query Builder

New to version 2.0 is a graphical query builder, started from the Query Builder icon on the main SQL Workshop page, which navigates you to the Query Builder page shown in Figure 3-13. You add tables to the query by clicking on the table name in the left panel. Checking the box next to a column name adds it to the query. To join two tables, click on the box to the right of the column name in one table and then click on the box to the right of the joining column in the second table.

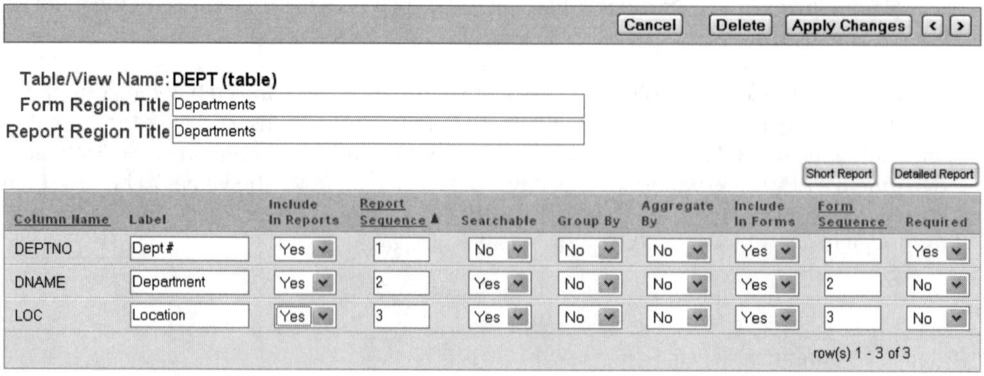

FIGURE 3-12 *User Interface Defaults Grid Edit form*

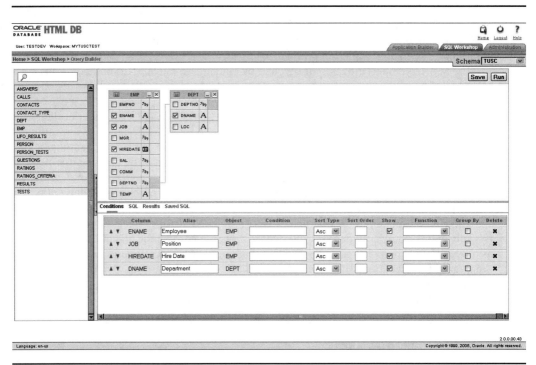

FIGURE 3-13 *Graphical query builder*

You may also specify conditions on columns that will build the WHERE clause, and you can specify the sort type and order for the ORDER clause. The Function field provides access to a number of functions that can be applied to individual columns. The Group By check box allows you to build the GROUP BY clause.

The bottom portion of the panel on the right contains sub-tabs. The SQL tab allows you to examine the SQL that is generated, whereas the Results tab allows you to view the results of the query. The Run button in the upper-right corner of the upper-right section also executes the query and navigates to the Results tab in the bottom frame to display the results. The Save button allows you to save a query for later recall. To recall saved queries, use the Saved SQL tab to see all saved queries and then click on the name of a query to load it into the current window.

Invoking the SQL Command Processor

The SQL Command Processor can be used to process either SQL commands or PL/SQL statements against any schema for which you have privileges. The SQL Command Processor is a useful facility that allows you to develop and save SQL statements that you can use to examine the data in your tables or use as the basis for a report. You can also make minor changes to the data in a table by executing Update or Delete statements. Prior to version 2.0, you needed to be careful when executing DML statements in the SQL Command Processor because any changes were automatically committed and could not be rolled back. However, you can now turn off the Autocommit option.

Similarly, you can write small PL/SQL procedures and test them before using the code elsewhere in your application. Although this facility is not as robust as other third-party SQL and PL/SQL IDEs, it does provide a convenient mechanism for executing SQL and PL/SQL statements without having to utilize another product.

The SQL Command Processor is invoked by clicking on the SQL Commands icon on the main SQL Workshop page (refer to Figure 13-2). This displays the SQL Command Processor page with an edit area for entering SQL commands or PL/SQL statements, as shown in Figure 3-14. The upper portion of the page contains an area to enter a SQL statement. The lower portion of the page displays the result and offers other features through the sub-tabs along its top. After entering your statements into the edit area directly or by cutting and pasting them from another application, you execute these statements by clicking on the Run SQL button or by pressing CTRL-ENTER. If there are any mistakes in the SQL statements entered, an error message is displayed in the results section at the bottom part of the page. If there are no errors, the results of the SQL statement will be displayed. If the SQL is a query, the results will be in the form of a report, as shown in Figure 3-14.

The History sub-tab at the bottom portion of the page provides access to the list of the most recently entered SQL commands. Within this list of SQL commands, the SQL query is displayed as a hyperlink. When clicked, this hyperlink will copy the SQL command to the SQL command area, ready for execution. The Saved SQL tab displays a list of the SQL commands you saved into the SQL Archive by clicking on the Save button in the SQL Command Processor. The Explain tab runs an Explain Plan on a piece of SQL. An example of the results is shown in Figure 3-15.

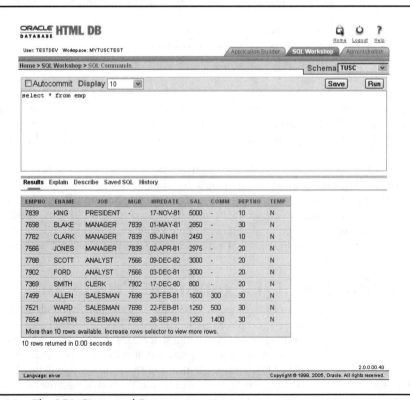

FIGURE 3-14 *The SQL Command Processor page*

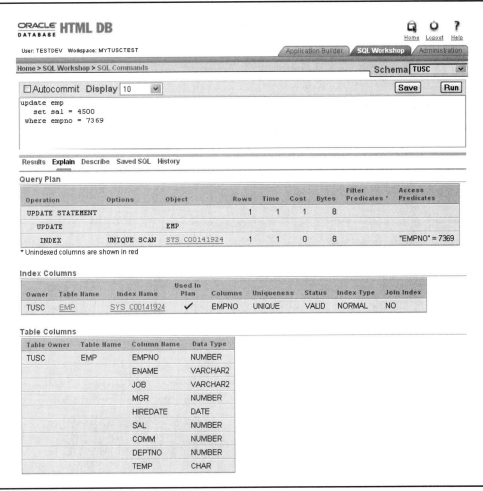

FIGURE 3-15 *Explain Plan results*

Not only does this show you the query's Explain Plan, but the results show you the indexes on the tables and a list of table columns. A Query Plan is an explanation of how the optimizer will execute the query. For more information on Explain Plan and tuning SQL queries, see Richard Niemiec's book *Oracle Performance Tuning,* by Oracle Press.

When you enter PL/SQL statements into the edit area, as shown in Figure 3-16, and click on the Run SQL button, the statements are compiled and then executed. If errors occur, as shown in the figure, the error messages are displayed along with the line (or lines) of code in error. If there are no compilation errors, the PL/SQL code is executed and a success message is displayed. There is no way to display results from executing PL/SQL statements because there is no output window, and including a statement such as

```
DBMS_OUTPUT.put_line(...)
```

or

htp.p(...)

has no effect.

Creating and Executing Scripts

In addition to the ability to execute single SQL statements, HTML DB has the ability to execute scripts that contain multiple SQL statements, which are usually designed to accomplish a specific purpose. For example, you may need a script to create a new table that has several steps, including dropping the table if it already exists, creating the new table with the required columns and keys,

FIGURE 3-16 *Entering PL/SQL statements for execution in the SQL Command Processor*

creating a new sequence for the primary key, and specifying a trigger to populate the primary key on Insert. A script to accomplish these tasks can either be entered into a script file directly or uploaded from an existing script file. Although version 2.0 offers a nice new interface, it lost some functionality previously available for scripts. Prior to version 2.0, HTML DB included a facility known as a *script control file,* which allowed you to execute more than one script file at the same time. Scripts could also use substitution variables prior to version 2.0.

To invoke the SQL Script facility, you can click on the SQL Scripts icon on the main SQL Workshop page. The Scripts Repository page, shown in Figure 3-17, displays a list of all the scripts that have been created or uploaded previously. This page allows you to manage your script files. You can create a new script file by clicking on the Create button, or you can upload a script file by clicking on the Upload button. Newly created or uploaded scripts are stored as files within HTML DB and are assigned unique names. You can delete an existing script file by clicking the Delete check box and then clicking the Delete Checked button. Existing script files can also be modified by clicking on the Edit icon or run by clicking on the Run icon. You can manage script files from other users by selecting a different user from the drop-down list box.

If you upload a script file from an existing file, the script file is simply added to the list of script files you can execute. When you create a new script file, a simple editor opens where you can either paste in your script contents or type in your script contents, as shown in Figure 3-18. Note that this same editor page is what you will get when you click on the edit icon on the Scripts Repository page. When creating a script, you should provide a meaningful name for it. If you change the name of the script when editing it, a new copy will be saved with the new name.

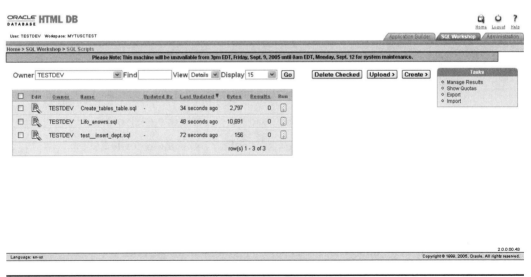

FIGURE 3-17 *The Scripts Repository page*

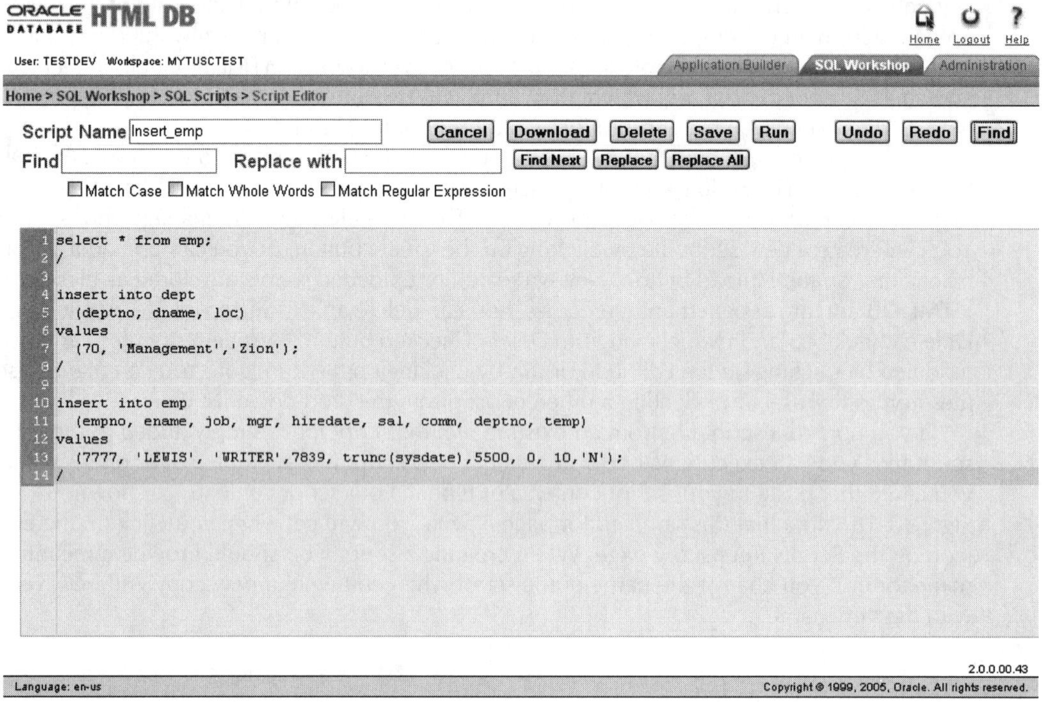

FIGURE 3-18   *The Script Editor*

Here's a list of the buttons available in the editor:

■ **Cancel**   Discards any changes since you last saved.

■ **Download**   Allows you to download the contents of the editor to your machine.

■ **Delete**   Deletes the script after you confirm you want to delete it.

■ **Save**   Saves the new script or saves changes to the script you are editing. Remember that if you change the name of the script when editing, it will become a new script.

■ **Run**   Brings up the same Run Script page (see Figure 3-19) as the Run icon on the Scripts Repository page (refer to Figure 3-17).

■ **Undo**   Will undo your last edits. This is the same as the CTRL-Z keystroke.

■ **Redo**   Will redo your last undo operations. This is the same as the CTRL-Y keystroke.

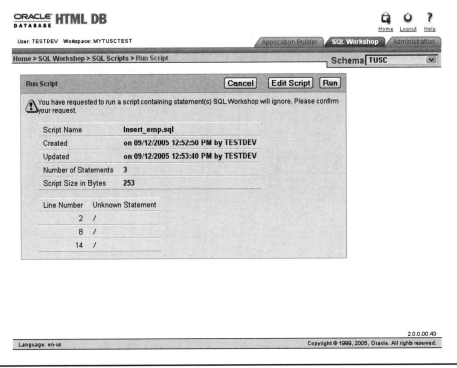

FIGURE 3-19   *The Run Script page*

■   **Find**   Brings up the fields and buttons associated with the Find and Replace
functionality. This functionality is just as it is in most editors, and even allows you to
search by regular expressions.

As you can see in Figure 3-19, the Run Script page evaluates your script prior to running it.
Previous script files required slashes (/) to be present to run statements. Here, however, you can
see that the page identified the slashes as statements that will be ignored. If your script has a
problem, the Edit Script button on the page will return you to the script editor. Just because it
shows no problems with your script does not mean there won't be any errors. If you are satisfied
with your script, click on the Run button to execute it. The script will be executed in the
background and you will navigate to the Manage Script Results page, shown in Figure 3-20,
where you can see the status of your script—Complete, Canceled, Executing, or Submitted. For
a very long running script, you can view its status in the Long Operations report, available in the
Database Monitor under the Utilities section of the SQL Workshop.

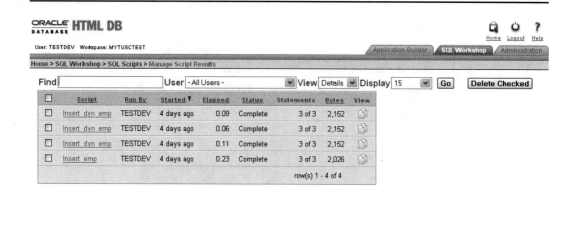

FIGURE 3-20 *The Manage Script Results page*

Once your script completes, you can view the results by clicking on the view icon that corresponds to your script run. This will take you to the Results page, where you can view either summary or detail results of your script. The summary results comprise a simple report, as shown in the following illustration. In the report, you can see the result of each statement and the time that it took to execute.

Script: **Insert_dyn_emp** Status: **Complete**

View: ○ Detail ◉ Summary Display [15 ▾] [Go] [Edit Script]

Number ▲	Elapsed	Statement	Feedback	Rows
1	0.03	select * from emp	15 rows selected.	15
2	0.00	insert into dept (deptno, dname, loc) values (70, 'Manag	ORA-00001: unique constraint (TUSC.SYS_C00141921) violated	-
3	0.00	insert into emp (empno, ename, job, mgr, hiredate, sal, co	ORA-00001: unique constraint (TUSC.SYS_C00141924) violated	-
			row(s) 1 - 3 of 3	

Statements Processed	3
Successful	1
With Errors	2

You can also select to view detailed results of your script, as shown in Figure 3-21. In the Detail view, you can select which detail you want to view by checking the boxes at the top of the page. The Statements check box determines whether the actual statements are displayed. The Results check box is for the results from Select statements in your scripts that are displayed in

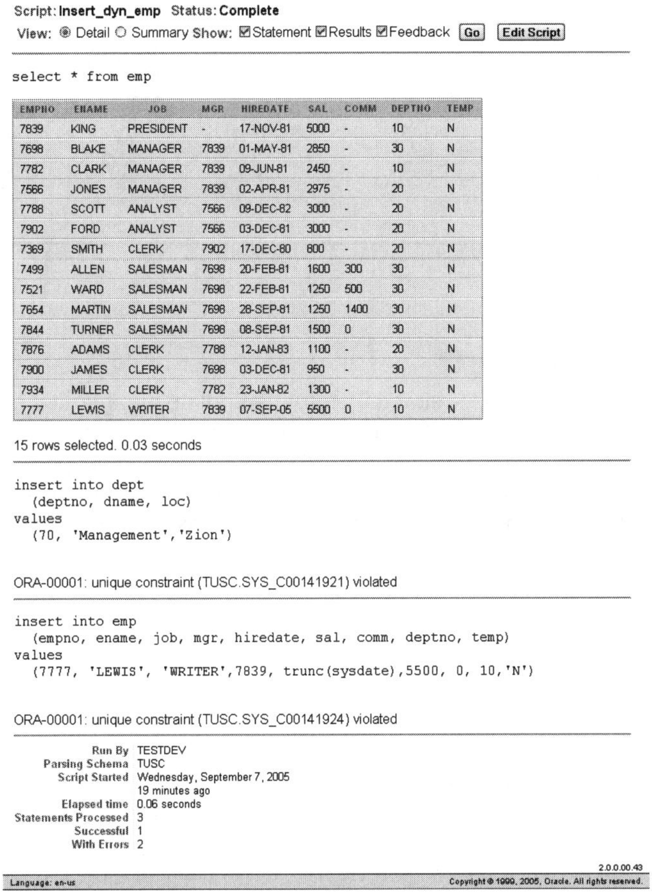

Script: **Insert_dyn_emp** Status: **Complete**

View: ◉ Detail ○ Summary Show: ☑Statement ☑Results ☑Feedback [Go] [Edit Script]

```
select * from emp
```

EMPNO	ENAME	JOB	MGR	HIREDATE	SAL	COMM	DEPTNO	TEMP
7839	KING	PRESIDENT	-	17-NOV-81	5000	-	10	N
7698	BLAKE	MANAGER	7839	01-MAY-81	2850	-	30	N
7782	CLARK	MANAGER	7839	09-JUN-81	2450	-	10	N
7566	JONES	MANAGER	7839	02-APR-81	2975	-	20	N
7788	SCOTT	ANALYST	7566	09-DEC-82	3000	-	20	N
7902	FORD	ANALYST	7566	03-DEC-81	3000	-	20	N
7369	SMITH	CLERK	7902	17-DEC-80	800	-	20	N
7499	ALLEN	SALESMAN	7698	20-FEB-81	1600	300	30	N
7521	WARD	SALESMAN	7698	22-FEB-81	1250	500	30	N
7654	MARTIN	SALESMAN	7698	28-SEP-81	1250	1400	30	N
7844	TURNER	SALESMAN	7698	08-SEP-81	1500	0	30	N
7876	ADAMS	CLERK	7788	12-JAN-83	1100	-	20	N
7900	JAMES	CLERK	7698	03-DEC-81	950	-	30	N
7934	MILLER	CLERK	7782	23-JAN-82	1300	-	10	N
7777	LEWIS	WRITER	7839	07-SEP-05	5500	0	10	N

15 rows selected. 0.03 seconds

```
insert into dept
  (deptno, dname, loc)
values
  (70, 'Management','Zion')
```

ORA-00001: unique constraint (TUSC.SYS_C00141921) violated

```
insert into emp
  (empno, ename, job, mgr, hiredate, sal, comm, deptno, temp)
values
  (7777, 'LEWIS', 'WRITER',7839, trunc(sysdate),5500, 0, 10,'N')
```

ORA-00001: unique constraint (TUSC.SYS_C00141924) violated

Run By TESTDEV
Parsing Schema TUSC
Script Started Wednesday, September 7, 2005
19 minutes ago
Elapsed time 0.06 seconds
Statements Processed 3
Successful 1
With Errors 2

2.0.0.00.43

Language: en-us Copyright © 1999, 2005, Oracle. All rights reserved.

FIGURE 3-21 *Script Results page*

table form output. Finally, the Feedback check box is for the error messages or normal feedback resulting from executing your statement. If you want to edit and then rerun the script, press the Edit Script button at the top of the page.

SQL Workshop Utilities

The SQL Workshop Utilities are accessed via the Utilities icon and menu on the SQL Workshop main page (refer to Figure 3-1). The icon takes you to the Utilities page, shown in Figure 3-22, which provides five navigational icons with pop-up menus for each major area. Data Import/Export provides the functionality that used to be in the Data Workshop. Generate DDL allows you to produce script files for creating all objects in your schema. Object reports provide access to a myriad of reports about objects. Database Monitor (which requires a DBA username/password) provides access to a variety of reports that describe the activity, storage, and configuration of the current database instance. Recycle Bin allow you access to database objects that have been dropped but are still available to be recovered.

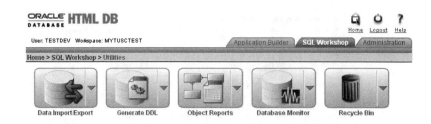

FIGURE 3-22   *Utilities page*

Data Import/Export

The Data Import/Export utilities enable you to manipulate another key element in your application—the data itself. The Data Import/Export page, shown next, has three navigational icons that correspond to the three major areas of data import and export—one for importing data into Oracle tables, another for exporting data from your database schemas into files on your computer, and the final one for keeping track of what has been imported. The Data Import/Export utilities are invoked from the Utilities icon and pop-up menu on the SQL Workshop's main page (refer to Figure 3-1).

Import

HTML DB allows data to be imported in one of two formats. The first format is for simplex text data or spreadsheet files and makes use of the comma-delimited (.csv files) or tab-delimited format. The second is an XML format. This format makes use of a series of XML elements that represent the columns in a table and <row> elements that represent the individual rows.

Importing Text and Spreadsheet Data   Although there appears to be two separate functions—one for importing text and another for importing spreadsheet data—the links to these functions take you to the same place. You can, therefore, click on either the Import Text Data or Import Spreadsheet Data image or hyperlink to start the import process. You can also click on the Data Import tab to be taken to the first step of the Data Import Wizard, as shown in Figure 3-23, where you select the target and method of the import.

On this page, you specify whether your method of import will be to copy and paste your data into the wizard or whether you will upload your data from a file in comma- or tab-delimited format. You will also specify whether the target of your import is an existing table or whether you will create a new table.

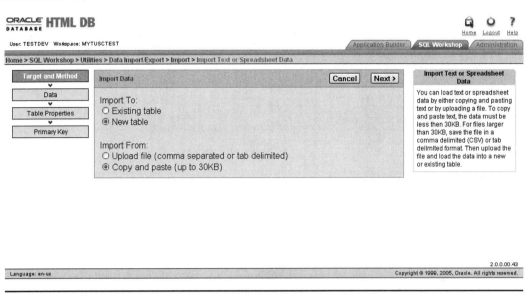

FIGURE 3-23 *The first step of the Data Import Wizard*

When you're using the copy-and-paste method, the total size of your data must be less than 30KB. If you use this method, you highlight the portion of the spreadsheet of interest and then copy the data to the clipboard. The import process is much smoother if your spreadsheet contains column names in the first row. If your spreadsheet is set up in this fashion, it is advisable to include the column names in your copy-and-paste operation. If your spreadsheet is too large, you will need to save the data as a tab-delimited or comma-delimited file. If your Excel spreadsheet is a workbook with multiple worksheets, you will need to import each worksheet, one at a time. With the first worksheet, you can create a new table and load the subsequent worksheets into the same table by selecting the Existing Table option.

If your data is not stored in an Excel spreadsheet, you have several options. One option is to create an Excel spreadsheet from your data. You can then either copy and paste the data if the size of the data is less than 30KB or create a tab- or comma-delimited file from the Excel spreadsheet. If the data is contained in a Microsoft Word document, you may be able to directly copy and paste the data from the document. You can directly import data through a copy-and-paste operation if the data is in a Word table within the document. If the data is stored as text in the Word document, you can use the Convert Text to Table option and then copy the data from the table. You can also use data from any application that can create a file that is in comma- or tab-delimited format.

Let's examine how the import process works by uploading a spreadsheet using the copy-and-paste method and creating a new table during the process. The spreadsheet that we will use to demonstrate the process is one that an IT manager might use to keep track of and manage the list of projects their department is or will be working on, as shown in Figure 3-24. For each project, the manager provides a title, a description, an estimated cost, who requested the project, the require completion date, the technologies that will be used, the number of developers and DBAs required to complete the project, the project status, and the start date of the project.

	A	B	C	D	E	F	G	H	I	J
1	Project Title	Description	Projected Cost	Requested By	Needed By	Technologies	# of Developers	# of DBAs	Status	Start Date
2	Single Sign On	Upgrade to security to allow applications to use a single signon procedure	$153,000.00	Security Manager	12/1/2005	iAS PL/SQL, Java	3	1	Approved	11/15/2004
3	Standard Addresses	Standardize the use of addresses across applications	$92,000.00	James Johnson	2/15/2006	C++, Java, PL/SQL	2	1	Pending	6/1/2005
4	Public Web Site Update	Make a number of requested changes to the website	$36,000.00	Sally Woo	9/1/2005	HTML DB, Javascript	1	0	Complete	6/1/2005
5	On-line Entry	Improvements in the ability of internal reps to enter data	$75,000.00	Warren Olsen	2/1/2006	Forms	2	1	In Progress	1/1/2003
6	Personnel System Updates	Various updates required to the Peoplesoft HR system	$186,000.00	HR Manager	12/15/2005	Peoplesoft, PL/SQL	3	1	Cancelled	
7										

FIGURE 3-24   *A portion of the Projects spreadsheet*

To begin the import process, click on the Import Spreadsheet Data icon. On the Target and Method page that is displayed, select the Import to a New Table option and the Copy and Paste method option. Clicking on the Next button takes you to the second step where you will import the data. An edit area is provided where you can paste the spreadsheet data after you have saved the data to the clipboard from within Excel, as shown in Figure 3-25. At the bottom of the page is a check box, which is checked by default, where you can indicate that the first row of data contains column names. Because our data contains column names, we will leave this check box checked and click the Next button.

The next page of the Data Import Wizard displays the proposed properties for the new table based on the data imported from the Excel spreadsheet, as shown in Figure 3-26. This page displays the properties of each column by analyzing the data contained in each column and determining a name for the column, the data type of the column, and the length of the column. The column name and column length are text fields that you can and, in many cases, will need to modify. For example, if a column is determined to be a NUMBER field, the length automatically defaults to 30, which you will want to change to a more appropriate value. The Data Type field is a drop-down list that currently has six values: NUMBER, VARCHAR2, DATE, CLOB, BINARY_ FLOAT, and BINARY_DOUBLE. The Data Import Wizard initially identified the date fields in the spreadsheet data as VARCHAR2 fields, and they need to be changed to DATE fields. There is also a text field for specifying a format mask to be used on the Insert statement. The dates in our spreadsheet data are not in standard Oracle format and need to be converted. Specifying a format mask of "mm/dd/yyyy" will cause the data to be loaded correctly; otherwise, the Insert will fail with an ORA-01843 error message. The page also contains an Upload drop-down list that has a value of Yes or No. This determines whether the column should be uploaded or ignored. The page also contains the rows of data for each column that will be imported.

The final page of the Data Import Wizard allows you to specify the primary key for the table, as shown in Figure 3-27. The Data Import Wizard does not allow a table to be created without a primary key, and you will need to specify a new column to be added as the primary key or select one of the columns in the data be imported as the primary key. The default is to create a new column, but you can click on the Primary Key From radio button to select one of the columns from the drop-down list that is then displayed. In either case, you will need to specify a constraint name for the primary key. When a new column is being created for the primary key, you will also

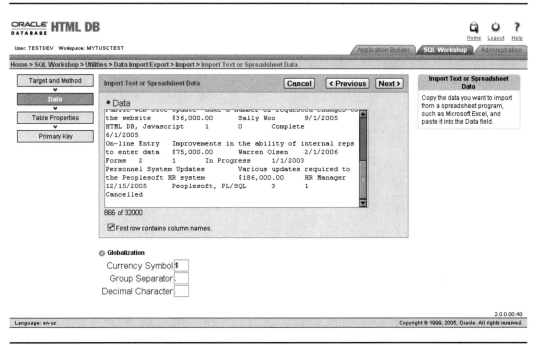

FIGURE 3-25   *The second page of the Data Import Wizard*

need to specify the method of populating the primary key. You can choose to not generate the key, to generate the key from an existing sequence, or to generate the key from a new sequence. The last option, which is the one you will most likely select, also requires you to specify a sequence name. If the last option is selected, the Data Import Wizard will also create a trigger to populate the primary key.

	Column Names				
Column Names	Project_Title	Description	Projected_Cost	Requested_By	Needed_By
Data Type	VARCHAR2	VARCHAR2	NUMBER	VARCHAR2	DATE
Format					MM/DD/YYYY
Column Length	30	255	30	30	30
Upload	Yes	Yes	Yes	Yes	Yes
Row 1	Single Sign On	Upgrade to security to a	$153,000.00	Security Manager	12/1/2005
Row 2	Standard Addresses	Standardize the use of a	$92,000.00	James Johnson	2/15/2006
Row 3	Public Web Site Update	Make a number of request	$36,000.00	Sally Woo	9/1/2005
Row 4	On-line Entry	Improvements in the abil	$75,000.00	Warren Olsen	2/1/2006
Row 5	Personnel System Updates	Various updates required	$186,000.00	HR Manager	12/15/2005

FIGURE 3-26   *The third page of the Data Import Wizard*

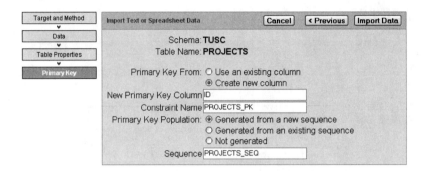

FIGURE 3-27 *The fourth and final page of the Data Import Wizard*

The Import process begins when you click on the Import Data button. At that point, the various Oracle objects are created first, including the table, the primary key constraint, the primary key sequence, and the trigger for the primary key. This is followed by the actual import of the data. When the import is successfully completed, the Data Import Repository page is displayed, which provides a list of the previous imports that have taken place. The list contains a hyperlink with the table name, which displays the Object Details page for the table from the SQL Workshop. This page allows you to make additional enhancements to the table you have just created, including creating lookup tables from columns in your new table and managing the UI defaults for the table. Some of these enhancements will be examined in Chapter 5, where we will discuss how to create a complete application using the imported Projects spreadsheet data.

Importing XML Files   The other input format supported by the Data Workshop is XML. The XML Data Import Wizard allows you to import data that represents the rows and columns of a table in an XML format. Unlike the text and spreadsheet data import process, XML data can only be uploaded from a file into an existing table.

The XML data to be imported must be in a specific format, which could be called "ROWSET/ ROW" format, as shown next. This format, which is used extensively in Oracle's XML Development Kit (XDK), makes use of a <ROWSET> tag for the root element and uses the <ROW>…</ROW> tag to encapsulate the data for each row. Within each <ROW> tag, the data for each column is represented as a separate XML tag where the element name is the same as the column name.

```
<ROWSET>
    <ROW>
        <PROJECT_TITLE>Unpaid Invoices</PROJECT_TITLE>
        <DESCRIPTION>Move unpaid invoices &gt; $10,000 into a
            separate application for processing</DESCRIPTION>
        <PROJECTED_COST>45000</PROJECTED_COST>
        <REQUESTED_BY>President</REQUESTED_BY>
        <NEEDED_BY>2004-12-15T00:00:00.000</NEEDED_BY>
        <TECHNOLOGIES>PL/SQL,JSP,XML</TECHNOLOGIES>
        <NUM_DEVELOPERS>2</NUM_DEVELOPERS>
        <NUM_DBAS>1</NUM_DBAS>
        <STATUS>Approved</STATUS>
        <START_DATE>2003-12-01T00:00:00.000</START_DATE>
    </ROW>
</ROWSET>
```

TIP
If your XML data is not already in this format, you can use an XSLT stylesheet and transformation to format your data in this fashion.

When creating the XML elements, you will need to take several precautions to ensure that the data is loaded properly. For example, when an XML element represents a NUMBER field, you should make sure that the XML data does not include formatting characters such as periods, dollar signs, and commas. For example, if you attempt to import a file that contains a <PROJECTED_COST> tag with formatting such as

```
<PROJECTED_COST>$45,000 </<PROJECTED_COST>
```

you would receive the following error message:

```
ORA-29532: Java call terminated by uncaught Java exception: oracle.xml.sql.
OracleXMLSQLException: 'java.lang.NumberFormatException $45,000' encountered
during processing ROW element 0. All prior XML row changes were rolled back in
the XML document.
```

Any errors that occur during the XML data import process will produce a similar error message. Another precaution you will need to take involves text fields. Any text fields that contain special characters, such as a greater-than sign (>), will need to be escaped. Date fields can also be a problem because the XML format for dates is quite different from the standard Oracle format. For a date to be processed properly, it must be in the following date/time format: yyyy-mm-ddThh:mi:ss.ms. For example, to represent the date and time of 6:30 A.M. on November 15, 2003, you would specify 2003-11-15T06:30:00.00.

There are several ways to specify null values in your XML files. The easiest way is to simply omit the tag from the XML file for a specific column. In this case, the XML data import process inserts a null for the column. Another mechanism is to use an empty XML tag, which can be represented in XML either as <NUM_DBAS></NUM_DBAS> or as <NUM_DBAS />.

TIP
Misspelling the name of a column or specifying the column name in lowercase letters will cause the XML Data Import Wizard not to recognize the column and inadvertently insert a null value.

To start an XML import, click on the XML Import icon on the Data Workshop home page. This invokes the XML Data Import Wizard, which walks you through three steps for importing XML data, where you specify a schema, a table for the import, and a filename that contains the XML data, as shown in Figure 3-28.

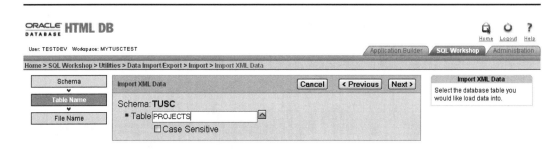

FIGURE 3-28 *The XML Data Import Wizard*

Exporting Text and XML Data

The Data Workshop allows data to be exported in either a text format or an XML format. Both export processes are quite similar.

To initiate a text export, click on the Export Text Data icon on the Data Workshop home page. This invokes the Text Export Wizard, which offers a four-step process for exporting data in text format. First, you specify the schema name and then the table name. The table name can either be entered directly in the text field or selected from the pick list field. Once the table is selected, the third step of the Text Export Wizard allows you to specify which columns you want to include in a multiselect box, as shown in Figure 3-29. The final step of this wizard allows you to specify certain options for the output text file, including the field separator, an optional character to enclose the text fields with, a file format of either DOS or Unix, and which character set to use. The default character set is Unicode UTF-8, which is the equivalent of ASCII. Clicking on the Export Data button initiates the export.

Performing an XML export is almost identical. You initiate an XML export by clicking on the XML Export icon on the Data Workshop home page. This invokes a three-step wizard whose steps are basically the same as the Text Export Wizard, except the fourth step is not required. Another difference is that on the third step of the wizard, where you select the columns to include, there is an extra check box. This text box determines whether the XML extract will be loaded into a file or whether the extract will be performed and then displayed in a browser.

Generate DDL

The Generate DDL section of the SQL Workshop Utilities allows you to create and export the DDL for schema objects. Once you select the Generate DDL icon on the Utilities page (refer to Figure 3-22), you will see a report that summarizes how many objects are in the current schema. From there you click on the Create Script button, which takes you to the start page of the Generate

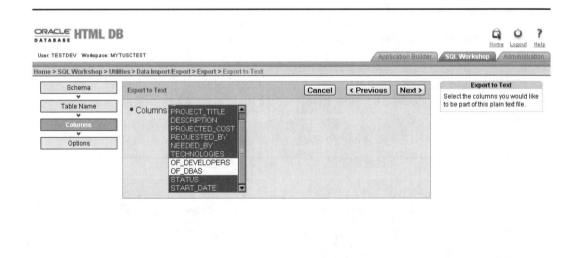

FIGURE 3-29   *The steps of the Text Export Wizard*

DDL Wizard. In this four-step wizard, you select the schema and then select the object types for which you want to create a script, as shown next. You also specify whether you want to generate the DDL as a script file or display it inline. If you select to generate the DDL from this step, you will get DDL for every object of the types you specified. If you proceed to the next step, you will be presented with a list of the objects of the types you selected. There you can select each object you want to include in the script. Finally, you can specify the name of the script file if you selected to save it as the DDL in this format.

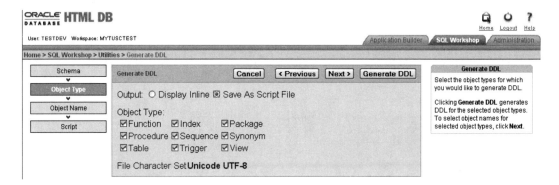

Object Reports

The Object Reports section of the SQL Workshop Utilities is accessed via the Object Reports icon and menu on the SQL Workshop Utilities main page (refer to Figure 3-22). From here you can access over 20 different reports about objects in the workspace schemas. Access to the individual reports is controlled through the navigational icons and pop-up menus on the Objects Report page, shown next. Due to space constraints, we cannot explore all the reports, but you should take the time to familiarize yourself with the ones available. They are broken into the following major categories: Tables, PL/SQL, Security, All Objects, and Data Dictionary.

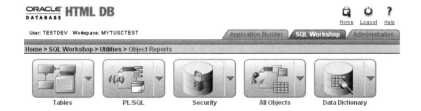

Database Monitor

The Database Monitor section of the SQL Workshop Utilities, which is accessed through the Database Monitor navigation icon and menu on the SQL Workshop Utilities main page (refer to Figure 3-22), allows you to monitor the activity of the current database instance. In order to access this section, you will have to provide the username and password of a database user who has been granted the DBA role. This section allows you to monitor database activity, database storage, and database configuration. Due to space limitations, we are unable to explore this area in detail. For more information, refer to the online user manual.

Recycle Bin

The Recycle Bin section of the SQL Workshop Utilities allows you to view and recover database objects that have been dropped and are still available. When an object is dropped, Oracle does not immediately remove the space associated with that object but rather renames and places the object in the Recycle Bin, where it can be recovered. The Recycle Bin section is accessed through the Recycle Bin navigation icon and menu on the SQL Workshop Utilities main page (refer to Figure 3-22). From the icon, you can navigate to a page to purge the Recycle Bin or to the Dropped Objects report page, shown here.

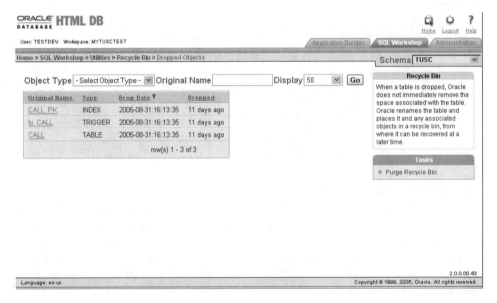

Each item under Original Name is an active link that navigates to a page where you can view information about the dropped object and choose either to restore or to purge the object.

In this chapter, we just scratched the surface of the functionality available in the SQL Workshop area of the HTML DB development environment. Version 2.0 brought a lot of major improvements in the user interface and the functionality of this section of the HTML DB development environment. Although a web interface is never the optimal method for interacting with a database and its objects, this interface offers a viable one.

PART
II

Creating Applications

CHAPTER
4

Using the Application Builder

n this chapter we will explore the Application Builder interface of the HTML DB application.

Invoking the Application Builder

The Application Builder interface is the heart and soul of the HTML DB development process. It allows the developer an easy method for creating, reviewing, editing, running, and deleting application elements. Once you have a workspace and a developer's username and password, you are ready to log on and get started. Refer to Chapter 17 for details on the administration functions for creating workspaces and users. Whether you are using a local installation of HTML DB or using Oracle's hosted site, the initial login screen will look very similar to the one shown in Figure 4-1. You must enter a workspace name along with the customary username and password.

Once logged on, you will see the HTML DB home page. From the home page, you can quickly navigate to any part of the HTML DB application, such as an application edit page like the one shown in Figure 4-2. Keep in mind that the HTML DB development environment is itself an HTML DB application; anything you see done in the development application can be done in an application you create. The Application page shown in Figure 4-2 uses many of HTML DB's available items, such as a logo image, navigation bar, breadcrumb menu, navigational lists, buttons, text fields, pick lists, and report areas.

The Home, Logout, and Help items in the upper-right corner are an implementation of a navigation bar. It is highly recommended that you frequently use the Help link to open the well-written HTML DB help document. The three tabs in the upper-right are used to navigate to the three main areas of the HTML DB development environment: Application Builder, SQL Workshop, and Administration. Each of these takes you to its corresponding start page. Home | Application Builder | Application 154 is a breadcrumb-style menu, which will be present on every page of the

---

ORACLE **HTML DB**
DATABASE

Gain instant access to an integrated online application development suite. With HTML DB you can build robust dynamic Web applications and leverage the full power of the Oracle database all from your favorite browser.

Login

Workspace	mytusctest
Username	linnemeyerl@tusc.com
Password	******

[Login]

2.0.0.00.36

FIGURE 4-1 *HTML DB Login screen*

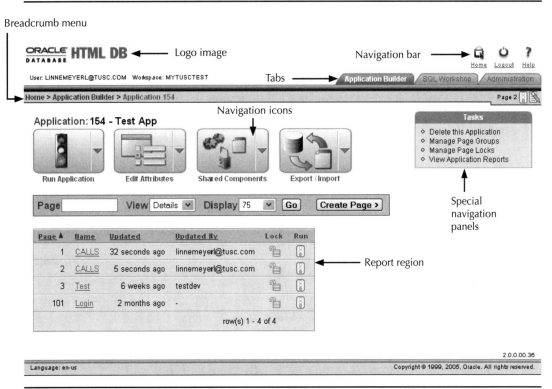

FIGURE 4-2   *HTML DB Application page*

development environment. Clicking on any of the items in the list will bring you back to that page. Breadcrumb menus indicate your current location (last item on the menu) relative to other pages in the current application. The four large images across the page are for navigation. They are implemented with a hierarchical navigation list. Clicking on the down arrow on the right side of each image will bring up a multilevel pop-up menu. The Create Page button takes you to the start page of the Page Creation Wizard.

The list panel on the right side is an implementation of a single-level navigational list. The Tasks panel provides links to infrequently used tasks for the current page. A lot of pages in the development environment have these side panels, which contain links to special tasks.

The table is an example of a report region. This table displays all the pages in the current application. The report utilizes many easily available features. Notice that each of the report's column headers appears as a link. Clicking on any one of the linked labels reorders the report by the contents of that column. Clicking on the header the first time orders in ascending order, and clicking on the header the second time places the contents in descending order. Notice the little up arrow next to the Page column header; this indicates the report is currently ordered by page in ascending order. From this report, you can run any of the application's pages by clicking on the Run Application icon. Likewise, you can jump to the edit page for any of the pages by clicking on the page name. The Go button and the Page text box, View pick list, and Display pick list allow you to search for a specific page, control the way the pages are displayed (details or icons), and control the number of rows displayed in the report, respectively.

You have a couple of ways to navigate an application's Application page (see Figure 4-3). From HTML DB's home page, you can click on the down arrow on the side of the Application Builder icon and then click on the name of your application in the list of recently edited applications at the bottom of the menu. Alternatively, you can click on the Application Builder icon or Application Builder tab, either of which will take you to the Application Builder main page, which is a list of all applications. From there, you click on the name of the application you wish to edit.

Once you are in the process of editing an application, you have two methods of returning to the Application page. The first is to click on the application name in the breadcrumb menu that appears at the top of every page. The second is to use the Developer's toolbar (shown next) that

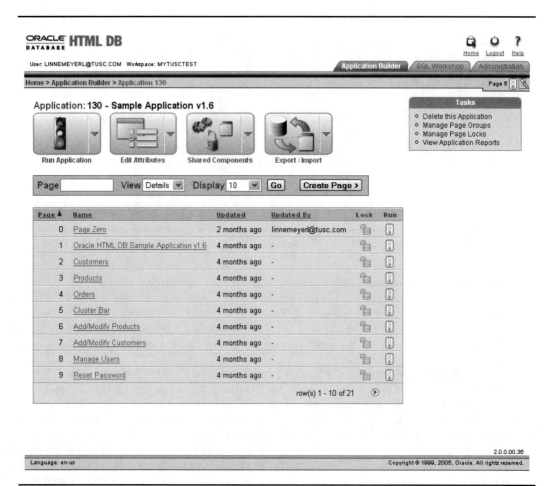

FIGURE 4-3 *Application Builder main page*

appears at the bottom of the page when you run a page while developing. The Edit Application link returns you to the Application page.

| Edit Application | Edit Page 1 | Create | Session | Debug | Show Edit Links |

Navigating the Application Builder

Because the HTML DB development environment is a web application, it can sometimes take several clicks to get to where you want to go. Oracle has done a nice job with version 2.0 of adding more navigational items throughout the application, thus making it easier for you to get to where you want to go with the fewest possible clicks. It is to your advantage to become familiar with all the navigational items, because this will make you more efficient. A good example of this is the quick navigation icons on the right, just under the tabs (refer to Figure 4-3). Here, you will see the Run Application (traffic light) and Edit Attributes (paper and pencil) icons for the most recently visited page, which is indicated by page number next to the icons.

The Application Builder main page contains four main navigational icons, shown at the top of Figure 4-3. The first icon, Run Application, simply runs the current application. Edit Attributes allows you to edit application-level attributes such as Authorization, Globalization, and Availability. Shared Components takes you to a page where you can access items that are shared between the pages of this application, such as lists, tabs, menus, build options, and computations. The last icon is for the Import/Export section. This section allows you to export and import workspaces, applications, Cascading Style Sheets, script files, themes, and user interface defaults. Importing and exporting is covered in more detail in Chapter 7. New in version 2.0, drop-down menus appear off the side of the large navigational icons. Click on the down arrow next to an icon to activate that menu. The menus allow you to navigate directly to subordinate sections of the main navigation area.

Edit Application Attributes

As of version 2.0, the editing of application attributes has been broken up into three main areas, each with its own edit page: Standard Attributes, Security Attributes, and Globalization Attributes. The Edit Attributes icon (refer to Figure 4-3) takes you to the Application Attributes page, which contains three more large navigation icons, one for each of the attribute areas, leading you to their respective edit pages. You can skip this page and navigate directly to each of the edit pages from the drop-down menu using the down arrow on the right side of the Edit Attributes icon.

Edit Standard Attributes

The Edit Application Attributes page, shown in Figures 4-4, has five sections where you can edit application attributes and four sections that display details about other application attributes that are actually edited through the application's Shared Components section, which is covered next in this chapter.

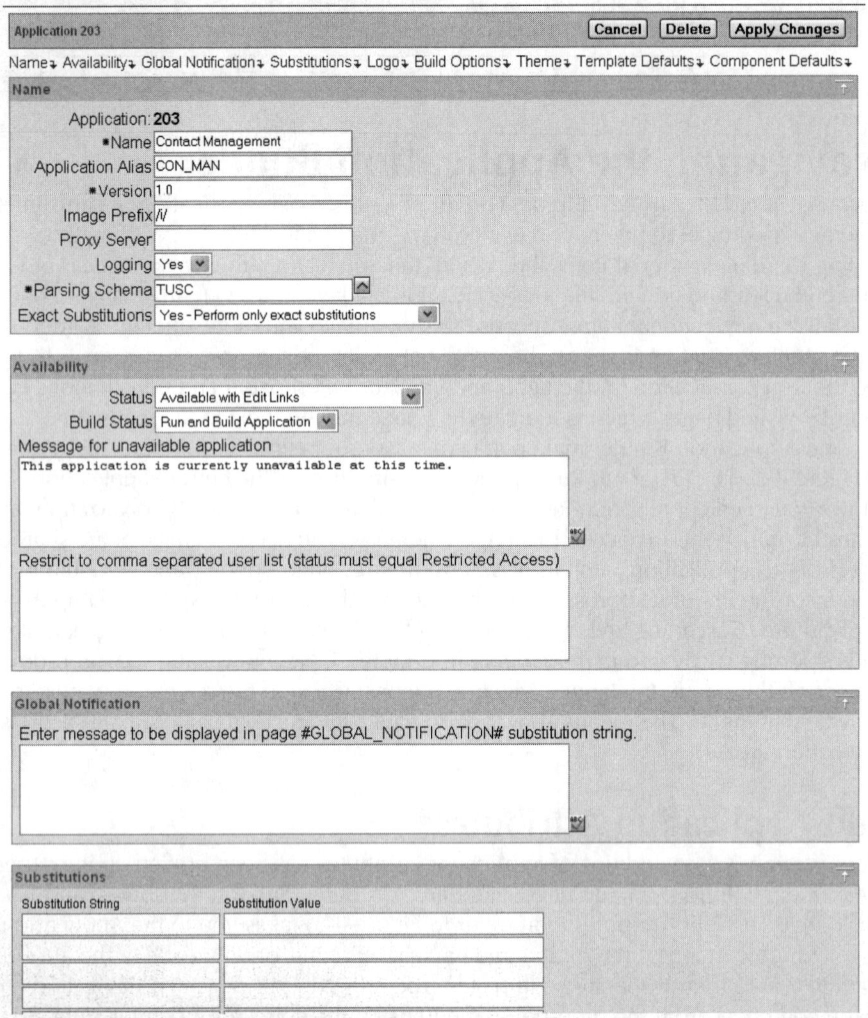

FIGURE 4-4 *Edit Application Attributes page*

Name Section

- **Application** As each application is created, HTML DB automatically assigns a unique identifier for the application. This value cannot be changed. It is used in the URL for the application. For example, the application's number is 100 in the following URL: http://servername:7779/pls/htmldb/f?p=100.

- **Name** A short descriptive name used to identify the application in the application report list on the Application Builder main page.

- **Application Alias** An alternate identifier that can be used in place of the application ID in the URL (for example, http://servername:7779/pls/htmldb/f?p=CON_MAN).

■ **Version**   Allows you to track the version number of an application. You can display the version in your application by using the substitution variable #APP_VERSION# in either the header or footer section of a page template (see Chapter 6). You can also specify just a format mask of YYYY.MM.DD or MM.DD.YYYY or DD.MM.YYYY, and HTML DB will replace the mask with the date of the last modification of any application attribute.

■ **Image Prefix**   Specifies the virtual directory set up during installation that points to the actual path of the file system directory where images are stored. This value will be used for the substitution variable #IMAGE_PREFIX# when referring to images (see Chapter 6 for more details). You could change this prefix if you define another alias in C:\Oracle\ htmldb\Apache\modplsql\conf\marvel.conf, but most likely you will not modify this attribute.

■ **Proxy Server**   Used to specify a proxy server when you are referencing a region source– type of URL and the target of the URL is on the other side of a firewall.

■ **Logging**   When Logging is set to Yes, an entry will be generated in a log for each page visited by a user. This allows a workspace administrator to view reports on an application's user activity.

■ **Parsing Schema**   Specifies the schema that all SQL and PL/SQL in the application will be parsed against. This value can be referenced with the substitution variable #OWNER# in any SQL or PL/SQL.

■ **Exact Substitutions**   The item should be set to "Yes – Perform only exact substitution." Only change it for backward compatibility. The normal substitution format is "&ITEM." and non-exact substitution is "&ITEM" (notice the missing period). This is a deprecated feature. See Chapter 6 for more information on different substitution syntax.

Availability Section

■ **Status**   Allows you to change the status of the application. With Status, you can make the application temporarily unavailable so you can do maintenance. You can restrict access to users with developer roles only, or you can restrict access to a specified list of users. You can also redirect to a different URL.

■ **Build Status**   Specifies whether developers can both run and build the application or only run the application.

■ **Message for unavailable application**   Allows you to specify the message to be displayed when a user tries to access an unavailable application.

■ **Restricted user list**   Allows you to specify a comma-separated list of users who are allowed access to the application. This lists only works when the status is set to Restricted Access.

Global Notification Section

■ **Message**   Text that you enter here will be displayed on any page that has the #GLOBAL_ NOTIFICATION# substitution variable used in its template. See Chapter 6 for more detailed information.

Substitutions Section

- **Substitution String and Substitution Value**   These fields allows you to enter a substitution string and a value that will be available globally for substitution. For example, if you develop an application that will be used by many different organizations, you can create a substitution string such as ORG_NAME and, when the application is deployed to a new organization, change the corresponding substitution value to the new name of the organization. This way, you only have to make a change in one place. It is used throughout the application with the syntax &ORG_NAME.

Logo Section (Not Shown)

- **Image**   If you specify an image here, any place in the application's page templates that you place the substitution variable #LOGO#, an image tag will be generated.

- **Logo Image Attributes**   Allows you to enter the HTML attributes that will be included in the generated image tag for the substitution variable #LOGO#. You would want to include items such as width and height.

Display Only Sections (Not Shown)

- **Build Options**   This section shows you the current status of any application build options. These are defined and controlled in the Shared Components section, discussed later in the chapter. Build options allow you to include or exclude certain elements. One common use is for debug items that you might include while developing an application. When you are ready to deploy the application, simply change the status of the build option to exclude. Then, when the application is built, it will be as if the items with this build option do not exist.

- **Theme**   Specifies the currently selected theme. Themes are made up of templates, which control the look and feel of the application. Themes and templates are covered in detail in Chapter 6.

- **Template Defaults**   This section shows you the current default page templates. These are defined when you create or alter a theme and will be used in the creation of new pages. See Chapter 6 for more details.

- **Component Defaults**   This section displays the templates that will be used by default when creating components through wizards. Component defaults are also defined with each theme. See Chapter 6 for more details.

Edit Security Attributes

The Edit Security Attributes page, shown in Figure 4-5, contains five sections for editing application attributes that control different security aspects for the current application. Authentication is the logic that controls a user's access to the application; the user generally sees this in terms of a login screen. Authorization can be used to control access to particular pages or parts of your application once a user is authenticated. Database Schema controls the schema used to parse your application. Session State Protection is new to version 2.0 and can be used to help prevent hackers from tampering with your application's URLs. Virtual Private Database (VPD) can be used to enhance data security based on row- and column-level security.

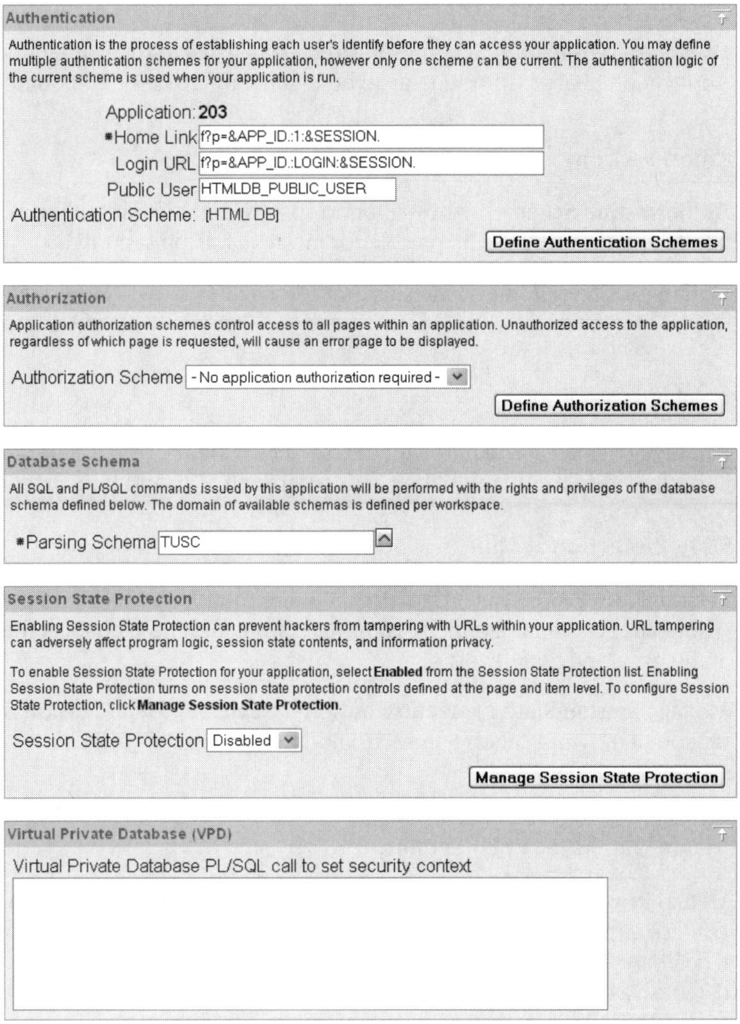

FIGURE 4-5   *Edit Security Attributes page*

Authentication Section

- ■ **Home Link**   This can be either a relative URL, as displayed in Figure 4-5, or a procedure that calls an HTML page. The result is the location for the home page of your application. Whatever value you enter here will be used for the substitution variable #HOME_LINK# within application templates.

- ■ **Login URL**   Specifies the location of the login page.

- **Public User**   Identifies the Oracle database schema that will be used to connect to when generating unprotected pages.

- **Define Authentication Schemes button**   Navigates to the Authentication section of the Application Shared Components, where you can create or edit authentication schemes.

Authorization Section

- **Authorization Scheme**   Allows you to specify a particular authorization scheme for the whole application (see Chapter 16 for more details on security).

- **Define Authorization Schemes button**   Navigates to the Authorization section of the Application Shared Components, where you can create or edit authorization schemes.

Database Schema Section

- **Parsing Schema**   From here you can select a schema, from those associated with the current workspace, that will be used to parse all SQL and PL/SQL commands.

Session State Protection Section

- **Session State Protection**   Used to enable or disable session state protection for the whole application. Enabling session state protection here enables the controls defined at the page and item levels.

- **Manage Session State Protection button**   Navigates to the Session State Protection section of the Application Shared Components, where you can view the status of session state protection controls.

Virtual Private Database (VPD) Section

- **Virtual Private Database PL/SQL call to set security context**   Place the PL/SQL that you use to normally set the VPD context in this field. This code is normally placed in a database login trigger. However, because all users of this application connect to the database as the same user, you can place the call here and change the VPD based on the HTML DB login user.

Edit Globalization Attributes

The Edit Globalization Attributes page, shown in Figure 4-6, allows you to set several application attributes that control the globalization of the application. This page also displays information about existing translations and provides links to areas of the Applications Shared Components, where you can manage translation elements.

Globalization Section

- **Application Primary Language**   Specifies the primary language for the application. This will be the language in which the application is developed. An application can be translated into multiple languages.

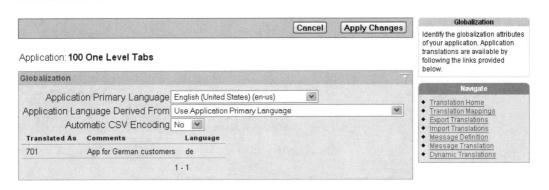

FIGURE 4-6 *Edit Globalization Attributes page*

■ **Application Language Derived From** Allows you to select what will determine the language of the application. The choices are Application Not Translated, Use Application Primary Language, Use Browser Language Preference, Application Preference, and Use Item Containing Preference.

■ **Automatic CSV Encoding** Determines if the output of all CSV reports will be automatically converted to a character set compatible with localized desktop applications. The character set used for CSV encoding is determined by each translated application's language setting.

■ **Translated As report** Shows the application number, language, and comments of any existing translations for the current application.

■ **Navigate side panel** Provides the same navigation that is found in the Translate Application section of the Application Shared Components.

Shared Components

The Shared Components icon at the top of the Application Builder main page will take you to another navigational page, shown in Figure 4-7. Shared components are elements available to all pages throughout your application and are grouped into six major categories:

■ Logic

■ Navigation

■ Security

■ User Interface

■ Globalization

■ Files

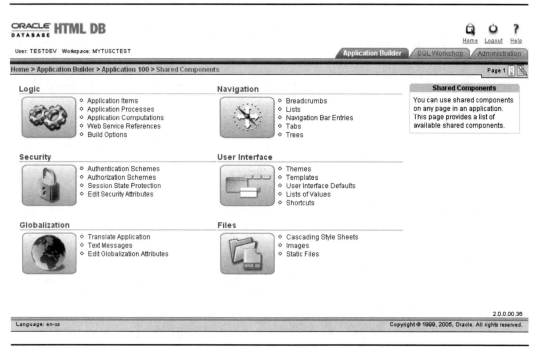

FIGURE 4-7 *Shared components*

Logic | Application Items

The Application Items link takes you to a page that lists the current application-level items and allows you to create new ones for the current application. In short, application-level items are global variables. They do not display, but they are available throughout the application. Application-level items may be set using application or page computations. Use the ON_NEW_ INSTANCE frequency of an application-level computation to set an initial value for an application-level item.

Logic | Application Processes

Like the Application Items link, the Application Processes link takes you to a page that lists the current application-level processes and allows you to create new ones; additionally, you can run a report on the utilization of your application-level processes. Application-level processes are used to run PL/SQL logic at specific points for each page in the application. Alternatively, you can set conditions to control when a process will execute. Additionally, a special type called On Demand will only be run when specifically called from a page.

Logic | Application Computations

The Application Computations link takes you to a page that lists current computations and allows you to create new ones for the current application. Application-level computations are most commonly used to assign values to application- and page-level items for each page displayed or for a new page instance. You are allowed to specify conditions for the execution of the application-level computations, so they can be conditionally executed for multiple pages, but not for all.

Logic | Web Services References

The Web Services References link takes you to a page that displays any current web service references and allows you to create more through a wizard. HTML DB is able to access web services across the network and then incorporate them into your application to process data submitted by a form or to render output in a form. A web service performs an action and then sends back a response—for example, one of HTML DB's sample applications uses an entered ZIP Code to look up the city and state and populate the corresponding fields. In order to utilize a web service in HTML DB, you must create a web service reference. The Web Services References Creation Wizard helps you create a reference to a web service so you can submit parameters and parse out responses from the web service for use in your application. Refer to Chapter 13 for more details on web services.

Logic | Build Options

Build options are a way of controlling the inclusion and exclusion of certain elements of your application. You can create any number of build options to suit your needs. One common use of build options is to include or exclude items used for debugging. Deploying applications with different levels of features is another way build options could be used. Most items would be included in the standard release of your application and therefore would have no build option associated with them. However, certain features may be part of a deluxe version of your application and could easily be include or excluded with an export by changing the build option status.

The Build Options page allows you to create, edit, and delete build options as well as report on the use of build options (see Figure 4-8). To create a build option, click on the Create button. You will be asked to name the build option, set its current status (Exclude or Include), set its option for exports, and provide comments describing the use of the build option. Click on the name of a build option to edit any of its attributes. Click the Utilization sub-tab to go to a report page to view a report about build options utilization.

A build option can have one of two statuses: Include or Exclude. Build options can be associated with almost any item—from a single button to an entire page—and they usually appear in a section labeled Configuration, as shown next. When an item is set to a build option and that build option is set to Exclude, it will be like the item does not exist. However, if the option is set to Include, the item will be included. When an item is set to the {not} build option and that build option is set to Include, it will be like the item does not exist; if the option is set to Exclude, the item will be included.

Navigation | Breadcrumbs

A breadcrumb menu item provides a hierarchical navigation method. Menu items can be used to display different types of menus, such as breadcrumbs or single-level menus. For instance, the breadcrumb menu shown in Figure 4-7 is an example of a menu created from a menu item. For a more detailed discussion of menus, see Chapter 11.

Navigation | Lists

A list is a template-driven, shared collection of links used for navigation. For instance, the task panels shown in Figures 4-6 and 4-7 are examples of list-driven navigation. Version 2.0 has

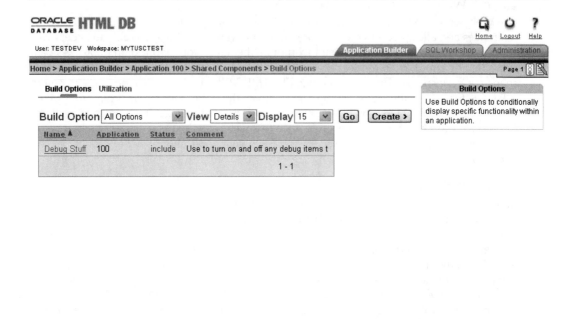

FIGURE 4-8   *Build options*

added the ability to use multilevel pop-up list navigation menus. For more detailed discussion of lists, see Chapter 11.

Navigation | Navigation Bar Entries

Navigation bars offer yet another method of providing easy navigation to your users. Navigation bars are typically used to provide standard navigation to every page. Although you can have multiple menus or lists defined for an application, you can only have one navigation bar. Items in a navigation bar can be text or icons. Although you can have only one navigation bar, you can conditionally display elements of a navigation bar for different pages. The Home, Logout, and Help text and icons seen on the top of every page comprise an example of a navigation bar (see Figure 4-8). For a more detailed discussion of navigation bars, see Chapter 11.

Navigation | Tabs

Tabs have become one of the most commonly used forms of navigation in applications for moving from major section to major section. HTML DB allows you to implement single-level and dual-level sets of tabs within your application. For instance, the tabs shown in Figure 4-7 allow you to move between the major areas of the HTML DB development environment. For a more detailed discussion of tabs, see Chapter 11.

Navigation | Trees

Trees are the final method of presenting navigation. Trees are ideal for hierarchically structured menus, such as a site map. Figure 4-9 shows an example of a tree. This particular example is actually one of HTML DB's application reports that displays the attributes for a page in a tree structure. Some of the branches are active links that take you directly to the edit page for their respective objects. For a more detailed discussion of trees, see Chapter 11.

Security | Authentication Schemes

Authentication is the method used to identify individual users who access your application. You can use a number of preconfigured authentication schemes or create a custom authentication scheme to control and track users of your application. If you do not need to distinguish between individual users in your application, you can use one of the standard authentication schemes. However, if you need to identify your users individually, you will need to implement a custom authentication scheme. For a more detailed discussion of security and authentication schemes, see Chapter 16.

Security | Authorization Schemes

Whereas authentication schemes control access to your application, authorization schemes allow you to secure individual items, such as pages, tabs, regions, menus, and buttons, by associating an authorization scheme with a component. An authorization scheme either succeeds or fails; if it fails, the component is not available. For a more detailed discussion of security and authorization schemes, see Chapter 16.

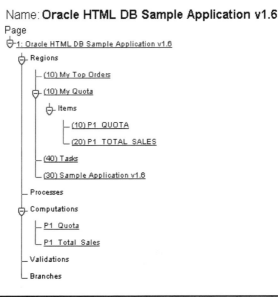

FIGURE 4-9   *Tree Navigation menu*

Session State Protection

Use this link to navigate to a page where you can report on current session state controls implemented at the page, item, and application item levels. From there, you can also set and configure session state protection. For a more detailed discussion of session state protection, see Chapter 16.

Edit Security Attributes

This link navigates you to the Edit Security Attributes page discussed earlier in the section "Edit Application Attributes."

User Interface | Themes

Themes and templates control the look and feel of every part of an application—from page layouts, to report regions, to individual items and buttons. Themes are used to group together sets of templates. Use the Theme link to navigate to the Themes page, where you can manage themes for the current application. For a more detailed discussion of themes and templates, see Chapter 6.

User Interface | Templates

Templates provide a method of segregating the look and feel of an application from the applications logic and database access. Use the Templates link to navigate to the Templates page, where you can manage templates for the current application. Refer to Chapter 6 for more details on templates.

User Interface | User Interface Defaults

User interface defaults can be created for each table in the schema(s) associated with an application. User interface defaults are not actually application specific but rather apply to the entire workspace. The defaults allow you to specify details about tables and their columns for when the tables are used in creating regions and items. You can control items such as table and column labels, whether or not to include columns in reports or forms, and the order of columns when used in reports or forms. User interface defaults enable you to provide consistency when a table is used across multiple pages or even applications.

User Interface | Lists of Values

Lists of values are either dynamically created lists or static lists used to display a specific type of page item. They can be used for a variety of types of items, such as a pop-up list of values, a select list, or even a group of radio buttons. For a more detailed discussion of user interfaces and lists of values, see Chapter 12.

User Interface | Shortcuts

Shortcuts are another way that HTML DB helps reduce the amount of work that a developer has to do. Shortcuts allow a developer to write and maintain frequently used code in a single place and reference it in as many places as desired throughout the application. In addition to minimizing copies of codes, shortcuts allow you to place dynamically generated code in places that normally only support static text. For a more detailed discussion of the use of shortcuts, see Chapter 12.

Globalization | Translate Application

Translate Application enables you to deploy an application in multiple languages from a single HTML DB and database instance. Stated simply, to translate an application, you map the primary and target application, create an XML export file for the translation, manually translate the target text in the XML file, import the resulting file, and then publish the application. For a more detailed discussion of Translation Services, see Chapter 7.

Globalization | Text Messages
Another tool for deploying your application in multiple languages is the Text Messages utility. When a translated application includes PL/SQL regions, processes, or calls to PL/SQL program units, you may need to translate the dynamic results. For example, you may select a name and city from a table based on some parameters and wish to display them as part of a sentence. Text Messages allows you to create a translation of the sentence for each language in which you are deploying your application. For a more detailed discussion of translatable messages, see Chapter 7.

Globalization | Edit Globalization Attributes
This section allows you to set variables that control an application's globalization. Items include the application's primary language, the source from which that language is to be derived, and the action that will be taken when encoding CSV reports.

Files | Cascading Style Sheets
Through the Cascading Style Sheets (CSS) link, you navigate to a page where you can see a report on CSS files that have already been imported into the current workspace. These files are available to all applications in the current workspace. From this page, you can edit or download existing files or create/import a new one. For more details about importing and exporting CSS files, see Chapter 7.

Files | Images
The Images link navigates to a page where you manage images for the workspace and the current application. Images may be associated with a particular application or the entire workspace and therefore are available to all applications within the workspace. A report shows you existing images and allows you to create/import new images for the current application or for use by all applications within the workspace. For more details about importing and exporting files, see Chapter 7.

Files | Static Files
The Static Files link navigates to a page where you manage static files for the workspace and the current application. Files may be associated with a particular application or the entire workspace and therefore are available to all applications within the workspace. Files containing JavaScript code are a typical use for static files. A report shows you existing files and allows you to edit or download existing files. You can also create/import new files for the current application or for use by all applications within the workspace. For more details about importing and exporting files see Chapter 7.

Working with the Page Definitions
The report section on each application's main page displays a list of the current pages for the application, as shown in Figure 4-10. The run icon allows you to immediately run a specific page, whereas the lock icon displays whether a page is locked or unlocked. The locking feature allows you to have multiple developers working on the same application without stepping on each others' toes. Click on the lock/unlock icon to change the status of a page. The history of page locks with comments is maintained for each page and can be viewed from the Locked Pages page, which is accessed through the Manage Page Locks link in the Tasks panel.

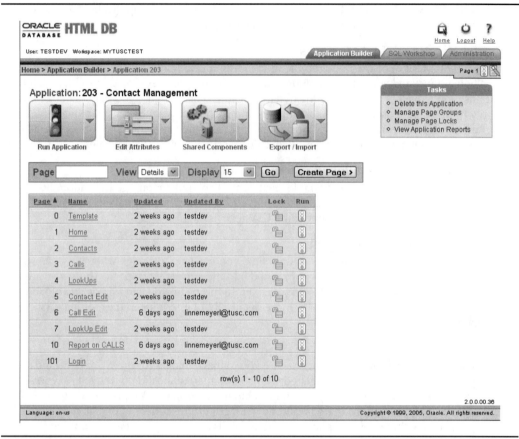

FIGURE 4-10 *Application main page*

When applications become very large and the number of pages becomes unmanageable, HTML DB offers a method of grouping similar pages together. Following the Manage Page Groups link in the Tasks panel takes you to a page that allows you to create page groups and associate pages with those groups. From the Page Group page, you can run a group report for a particular group. From the resulting report, you can easily navigate to the Page Definition page by clicking on the page name.

Likewise, on the page report, clicking on the name of a particular page will take you to the Page Definition page for that page. The Page Definition page contains links to edit definitions of every portion of a page. The definition page is divided into three major categories: Page Rendering, Page Processing, and Shared Components. Keep in mind that HTML DB renders a page of an application based on metadata defined for that page. Then it processes that page according to other metadata you have defined. The Page Rendering section contains the metadata unique to the page. This combined with the Shared Components is used render the page. The Page Processing metadata is used to validate, process, and move on to the next page.

Page Rendering Section

Pages are made up of regions. Regions are containers for content on a page. The layout of regions on a page is controlled by a page template. Regions can contain different elements, depending on the type of region they are. Some of the more frequently used types of regions are HTML, Report, PL/SQL Dynamic Content, Menu, and List. Regions contain elements; the layout of elements within a region is controlled by a region template. In addition to elements specific to a particular type of region, buttons and items can be added to the region as well. The look and feel of the items and buttons are also controlled by templates. The types of items that can be added to a region include text fields, text areas, radio groups, select lists, date pickers, password fields, file browsers, and display text. Figure 4-11 shows the Page Definition page for a page from the HTML DB sample application that creates and modifies a record in the products table, shown in Figure 4-12.

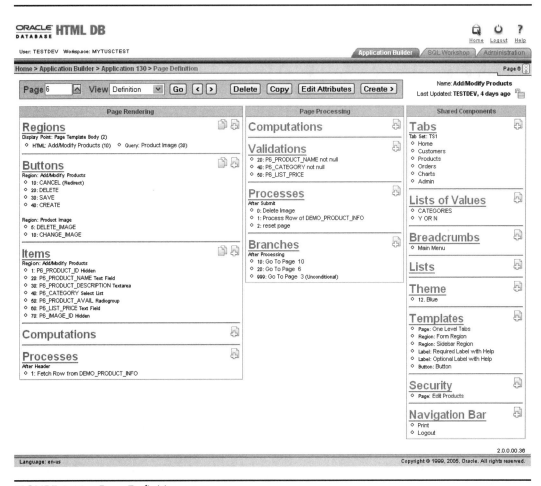

FIGURE 4-11 *Page Definition page*

FIGURE 4-12 *Add/Modify Products page*

The page shown contains two regions: the Add/Modify Products region and the Product Image region, both of which are listed in the Regions area under the Page Rendering section. Both of the regions contain buttons. You can see they are listed by region in the Buttons section in Figure 4-11. Notice the Add/Modify Products section has four buttons; only the Cancel and Create buttons are displayed when the page is in the add mode, as shown in Figure 4-12, whereas the Cancel, Delete, and Save buttons are displayed when the page is in the edit mode, as shown in Figure 4-13. Note, the Save button's text label is defined as Apply Changes. For most items you define for a page, you will specify a sequence. This sequence is the order in which the items will be processed within their group. Look at the Items section in Figure 4-11. Notice the numbers before each item listed. Notice the items appear in Figures 4-12 and 4-13 in the same order as they are listed here, and they are listed in numeric sequence order.

Shared Components Section

You can see most of the shared components on both pages. The tabs are displayed across the top. The lists of values are implemented in two different types of items. The CATEGORIES list of values is implemented in P6_CATEGORY select lists, whereas the Y_OR_N list of values is implemented in the P6_PRODUCT_AVAIL radio group. The MAIN_MENU menu is the breadcrumb menu that is found on every page; it is implemented through a menu-type region that is defined on page 0 of the application. Page 0 is a special page definition that allows you to define elements that are common to every page. The Blue theme is the theme for this application; all the templates from the Blue theme that are utilized on this page are listed in the Shared Components Templates section. The Print and Logout links seen in the upper-left corner of each page are the Navigation Bar shared components. Their placement is controlled by the One Level Tabs page template.

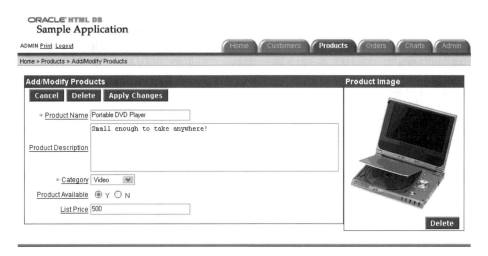

FIGURE 4-13 *Add/Modify Products page in edit mode*

Page Processing Section

The center section in the Page Definition page, titled "Page Processing," contains metadata for the processing of the page. Page processes execute some logic or interact with the rendering engine, typically to perform some action when a specific event occurs, such as validating the contents of a field when the page is submitted. The Page Processing section has three groups: Validation, Processes, and Branches. Generally, the HTML DB engine runs the processes in the order as they appear on the page definition, and always in their numeric sequence order.

The validation items validate fields before they are submitted; in this case, they check to see that the product name and category are not null and the list price is a number. When you define validation for an item, you specify the conditions the item must meet and the message that will be displayed if the conditions are not met. Validation is covered in more depth in Chapter 10.

Process definitions handle the processing of the data on a page at predefined points in the life of a page, including on new instance, on load before header, on load after header, on submit before computations and validations, on submit after computations and validations, and more. Processes are also covered in more detail in Chapter 10.

Branching items take care of the navigation between pages. Because they are almost always conditional, you may have many different branching options defined. As you can see in Figure 4-11, which is the definition page for page 6, one of the branching options returns to itself. Branching will be discussed further in Chapters 10 and 11.

Other Navigational Items

Aside from the three main regions on the Page Definition page, there are quite a few more buttons and navigational aids. In the Page field, you can directly enter the number of another page and press ENTER or click on the Go button to navigate directly to the Page Definition page for the selected page. You can also select another page from a list of page numbers and names that is displayed in a pop-up window when you click on the up arrow next to the Page field. Additionally, the left and right arrows allow you to navigate to the numerically previous and next pages, respectively. The Delete and Copy buttons allow you to delete and copy the current page, whereas the Create button starts a page creation wizard for creating a new page in your application. The Edit Attributes button takes you to a page to edit attributes specific to the page, which is discussed more in Chapter 8. The View pick list, along with the Go button, offers a number of different views for the current page:

- **Definition**   The current page.

- **Event**   Takes you to a page that displays a report that details all the page controls and processes in chronological view of how they will be rendered by the HTML DB engine. Figure 4-14 shows an example of the Page Application view report for the page we have been looking at.

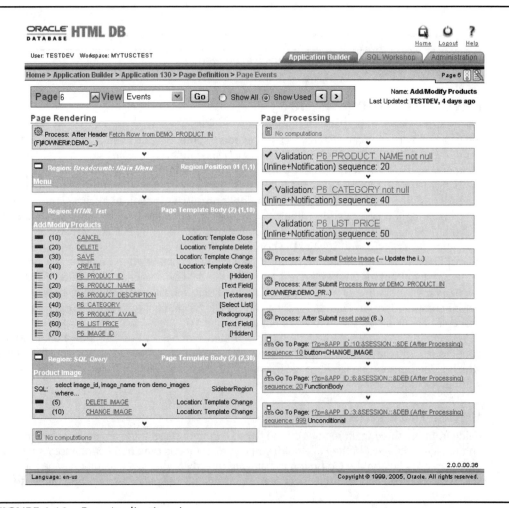

FIGURE 4-14   *Page Application view*

- **Objects**   Takes you to a page with a report that displays database objects that are referenced by components in the current page.

- **History**   Takes you to a report page that lists the change history of the page and a history of the locks and unlocks.

- **Export**   Allows you to export the current page (for more information on importing and exporting, see Chapter 7).

- **Groups**   Takes you to a list of pages in the same page group. This allows you to move quickly between related pages.

- **Referenced**   Navigates to a report that lists page components and shared components that link to the current page. From the report, you can easily navigate to each item.

In this chapter, we explored the major components of the HTML DB Application Builder, including the application's attributes, the application's shared components, and the Page Definition page. In coming chapters, we will go into much more detail on the individual pieces used to build robust applications through the HTML DB development environment.

CHAPTER
5

Creating and Running
Applications

he Application Builder is HTML DB's main facility for working with applications. In the last chapter, we examined how the Application Builder is used to switch between the different applications you have access to and to view and edit the pages of the application currently selected. In this chapter, we examine the other major functionality of the Application Builder: the ability to create and run applications.

HTML DB walks you through the process of creating a new application with the Create Application Wizard. The Create Application Wizard is started from the Create button on the Application Builder main page. In the first step of the Create Application Wizard, you select the method you will use to create the new application. Version 2.0 revamped the entire Create Application Wizard, making many improvements. The following table shows the options that used to be available in the first step of the wizard, along with the options now available.

Pre-V2.0 Options	V2.0 Options	Comments
From Scratch Based on Existing Tables Based on Existing Application	Create Application	All of these options are incorporated in the new Create Application path of the Create Application Wizard. In addition to creating from tables, the new wizard allows you to base pages on SQL queries.
Based on Spreadsheet	Create from Spreadsheet	Creates an application from a single table loaded from a single spreadsheet. More tables can be imported through Data Import utility in SQL Workshop.
Demonstration Application	Demonstration Application	Installs demonstration applications that come with HTML DB.
From an Application Export File		This option is available from the Import button on the Application Builder main page.

Most of the applications you create will be through the Create Application option. Within this option, you choose to create an application from "scratch" or based on an existing application.

Previously, when creating an application from scratch, the Create Application Wizard provided only a basic shell with tabs to which you could add pages with forms and reports to develop your complete application. Now when you create an application from scratch, you can create just the shell or also create many pages based on existing tables or views.

Using existing Oracle tables as the basis for an application allows for a rapid method of developing a complete web application with almost no work on your part, assuming you can accept the default application that is generated. Prior to v2.0, when creating an application based on an existing table, you could only choose a single table. Now you have the ability to add reports and forms for any number of tables or views.

Basing a new application on an existing application gives you a head start in defining your new application and can be used to standardize HTML DB applications within your organization. When you create new applications through the wizard, you have the option, on the final confirmation page, of saving the application as an application design model. These models provide a method by which you can base new applications on existing applications. Each of these methods is described further in this chapter.

The creation methods can be used in conjunction with the objective of creating an HTML DB application from one of two data sources: an Excel spreadsheet or a Microsoft Access database. In Chapter 1, we discussed the types of applications HTML DB is best suited for, along with the difficulties and limitations of using Excel and Access as technologies for developing and maintaining applications. One of the main limitations of these technologies is their inability to provide web-based access to the data they maintain. In this chapter, we will also discuss how to convert applications using Excel and Access into HTML DB applications.

Creating New Applications

To initiate the creation of a new application, click the Create Application button on the Application Builder main page. The first step of the Create Application Wizard is displayed, as shown in Figure 5-1. On this page, you are presented with the three paths for creating a new application: Create Application, Create from Spreadsheet, and Demonstration Application. The choices are presented as radio buttons because they are mutually exclusive. Click on the radio button next to the option you want and then click on the Next button, or you can simply click the icon.

NOTE
Most of the large icons in version 2.0 have two features. Clicking on the icon will select the option that it represents and move you on to the next page. Many have a down arrow on their right side; clicking on this down arrow brings up a hierarchical submenu.

The remainder of the steps of the Create Application Wizard will vary depending on the option you select. Before we begin our examination of these methods, let's look at a sample application that will be used throughout the remainder of the chapter.

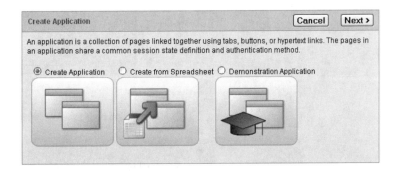

FIGURE 5-1   *Selecting the creation method for a new application*

The Contact Management Application

In order to compare the various options for creating an HTML DB application, a simple contact management system will be used. This system will be re-created throughout this chapter using the various creation methods. In addition, we will also take a look at how to create an HTML DB application assuming that the data is stored in an Excel spreadsheet as well as in a Microsoft Access database.

The sample Contact Management system that is examined in this chapter is, in fact, based on one of the sample applications delivered with Microsoft Access. The application contains several components, including the following:

- Three tables

- A form for displaying, entering, and editing information in each table

- Two reports

- Navigation between the forms and reports

The three tables in the application maintain basic contact and call information. The three tables and their relationships are shown in Figure 5-2. The diagram in this figure was generated by the Relationship Editor in Microsoft Access. The main table is the Contacts table, which maintains the name, address, and contact information for a contact. The field ContactTypeID is a foreign key reference to the Contact Types table, which identifies the type of the contact. The remaining table is the Calls table, which tracks calls made to a contact over time.

The application includes several forms that are required for maintaining information in the three tables. The Contacts form is where the name, address, and contact information is added for a new contact or edited or deleted for an existing contact. The form also requires the ability to navigate between contacts and a button to link to the Calls form, where call information for the contact can be added, edited, or deleted. A separate form is required for maintaining contact types.

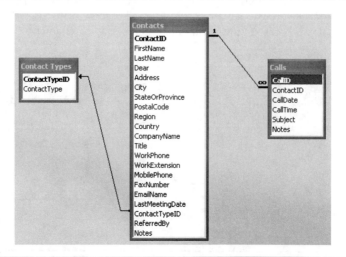

FIGURE 5-2 *The Contact Management system's tables and their relationships*

The contact type for a contact is specified on the Contact form using a drop-down list box. The system also requires a parameter form that is used to specify the range of dates for the Call report.

The application produces two reports. The first is the Contact Listing report, which lists contacts in alphabetical order. The other report is the Call Summary report, which displays call information for a specified date range. The date range is specified on the parameter form mentioned previously.

Navigation between the various components of the application is also required. The application requires the ability to select a form or a report as well as the ability to move from one form to another.

In this chapter, we examine several different ways to create applications. First, a shell for our sample Contact Management system is created using the Create Application method. This shell will be enhanced by adding forms, reports, and navigation in subsequent chapters. Next, we will explore the ability to create an application directly from tables/views and SQL queries, followed by an examination of creating the application from an existing application. Then, the application will be developed from a spreadsheet containing the Contact Management system data. Finally, we will take a look at a process for migrating a Microsoft Access version of the Contact Management system to HTML DB.

Creating a New Application from Scratch

Before proceeding with application creation, you should have an idea of the basic functionality and layout of the application. I see this application having a main home page and then a series of reports based on each table and a corresponding edit form based on each table. These could be organized with three main tabs—Home, Reports, and Edits—with a page for each table under the Reports and Edits tabs.

Upon selecting the Create Application option in the first step of the Create Application Wizard, you will be given two choices: create the application from scratch or create the application based on an existing application design model. To create an application from scratch, you specify an application name and an application number. The application number must be unique within the current workspace. Select an application schema and click on the Next button. You will be taken through a series of additional steps that define a shell for the application you are creating. Here are the subsequent steps you will go through:

1. Add pages.

2. Specify the tab style.

3. Select to copy shared components from another application.

4. Specify application attributes, including authentication and language.

5. Select a UI theme. You select a standard page theme from the themes provided by HTML DB.

6. Confirm your choices and initiate creating the new application.

Adding Pages

The next step of creating a new application from scratch is to add the pages. Notice that the list of steps for creating an application from scratch is displayed in the Navigation pane at the left of the page, as shown in Figure 5-3. The upper portion of the center of the page contains a list of pages that have already been added, whereas the bottom portion provides the ability to add pages. This is the area of the Create Application Wizard to which the most changes have been made in v2.0. With this new design, you can add as many pages as you like. They can be blank, or you can create forms and reports based on tables or queries (this is covered in the next section).

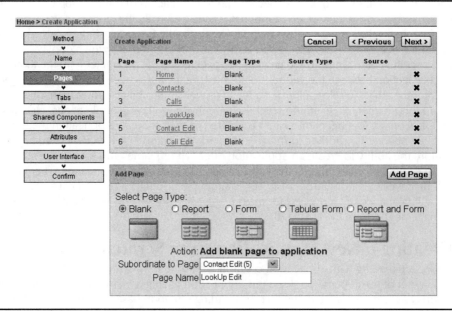

FIGURE 5-3 *Adding pages to the application*

To add a blank page, select the Blank Page type, specify the page name and whether the page is subordinate to other pages, and then click on the Add Page button. I added the pages shown based on the three-tab functional layout discussed at the beginning of this section. The current wizard does not allow you as much control as previous wizards when it comes to naming and associating pages with tabs. However, it is much faster, and any modifications can be made once the application is created. There will be a home tab, a tab for reports, and a tab for edit forms. Contacts was the first page specified for reports and edits, so I specified the others as subordinate to Contacts. We will look at how this works with tabs next. After adding all the blank pages, click on the Next button to proceed.

Understanding the Available Tab Options

The next step of the Create Application Wizard is to select a tab style for the application you are creating, as shown in Figure 5-4.

HTML DB offers three styles of tabs. You select a tab style by clicking on the radio button next to the style you want:

- No Tabs

- One Level of Tabs

- Two Levels of Tabs

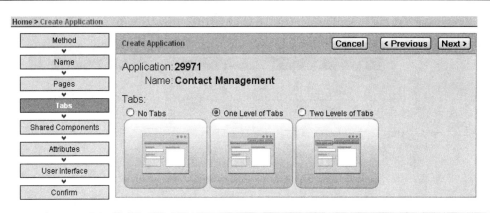

FIGURE 5-4 *Specifying the tab style*

Based on the style of tabs you select, HTML DB will do different thing for the navigation between the pages you created. If you select No Tabs, the only navigation created will be between pages defined as subordinate. List-type navigation will be created on the master page with links to each of the subordinate pages, as shown next. Note that there is no way to navigate between the top-level pages.

For the One Level of Tabs style, HTML DB creates one tab on each page for the number of pages you specify, unless subordinate pages are defined. In the case of subordinate pages, there is a tab for each non-subordinate page, and then list-style navigation is created on the master page with links to each of the subordinate pages, as shown here.

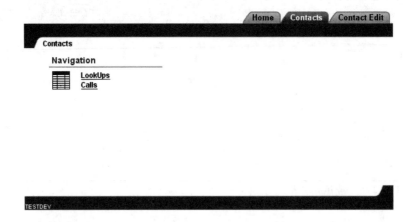

For the Two Level of Tabs style, HTML DB creates one parent tab for each top-level page and a second-level tab for each subordinate page and the page that is the master page of the subordinate page, as shown next. If any of the subordinate pages also has subordinate pages, list-style navigation will be created for the subordinate pages.

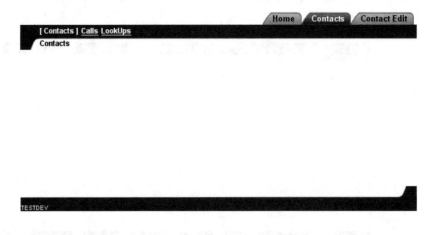

TIP
Even though you might have selected the No Tabs option during this step, you have the ability to add one-level or two-level tabs to a page after the application has been created by editing the page and creating a new tab set for your page. Adding tabs after an application is created is described in Chapter 8.

Shared Components

The next step of the wizard allows you to copy certain shared components from another application in the current workspace. If you select the Yes radio button, further options will be displayed, as shown in Figure 5-5. You may select as many options as you like; some of the options, if selected, will bring up additional pages when you click on the Next button. If you want to create an application that serves as your "master template" application, where you have your standard custom theme, navigation bars, lists of values, authentication schemes, and authorization schemes, this is where you would "copy" all the information from your master template application. The option of copying components from existing applications prior to version 2.0 was only available when you created an application from an existing application. After specifying whether or not to copy shared components, click Next to move to the next step.

Application Attributes

In the next step, you specify the type of authentication, as shown in Figure 5-6. You can specify whether to use HTML DB authentication or no authentication. HTML DB authentication, which is selected by default, can be used to associate authentication and authorization schemes to your application. When HTML DB authentication is used, anyone attempting to access your application will be presented with an HTML DB login screen and will have their credentials checked on each page to determine which items they are allowed access to, based on their level of authorization. Selecting the No Authentication option does not necessarily indicate that there will be no security within your application. You may choose to leave off any security constraints while the application is being developed and tested. You can later go back and add HTML DB authentication if you wish. Later, you can also choose to use the authentication offered by the Database Access Descriptor (DAD) provided by the mod_plsql plug-in to Apache or use the Single Sign-On (SSO) functionality offered by either the Oracle 9*i* or Oracle 10*g* Application Server. Securing HTML DB applications is discussed further in Chapters 16 and 17.

The other fields on the page are two options for globalization. If your application will be done completely in English and does not have an international component, you can ignore these options. For those situations where another language is required, you will need to specify these options. The Globalization region of the page is initially displayed in a collapsed format. When you click the plus sign next to Globalization, two drop-down lists appear. The first drop-down list allows you to select the language for your application, with over 50 language choices being provided. The second drop-down list provides several choices for determining where the user's language

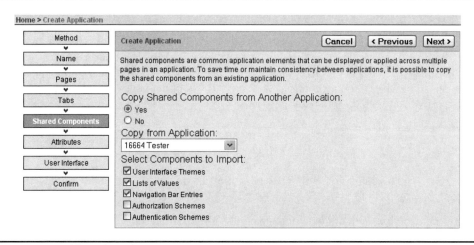

FIGURE 5-5 *Adding shared components*

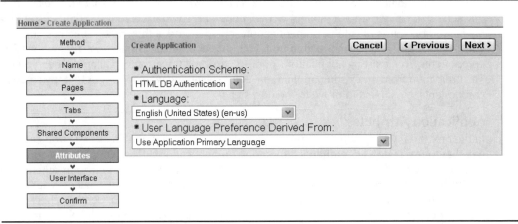

FIGURE 5-6 *Application Attributes page*

preference should be derived from. The default is Use the Application's Primary Language. Here's a list of the other options:

- No NLS (application not translated)

- Browser (use browser language preference)

- Application Preference (user FSP_LANGUAGE_PREFERENCE)

- Item Preference (use item containing preference)

For more information about globalizing your HTML DB applications, see the "Managing Globalization" section of the Oracle HTML DB user's guide.

Selecting a User Interface Theme

After clicking on the Next button on the Attributes page, the User Interface (UI) Theme page is displayed. The UI Theme page, which is shown in Figure 5-7, presents the 12 application themes available for selection in the current version of HTML DB. Make your selection by clicking on the radio button next to the theme you want and then click the Next button.

The UI theme provides templates for the pages and the regions within the pages of your application. The UI theme controls the look and feel of the pages in an application by specifying the HTML required for the following items:

- The color scheme of the pages and the regions on a page

- Images, such as the Oracle logo, placed in page headings

- The layout, color, and behavior of the tabs on a page (if you have selected tabs for your application)

- The location and type of page navigation for the reports of your application

- The layout and style of buttons on your forms

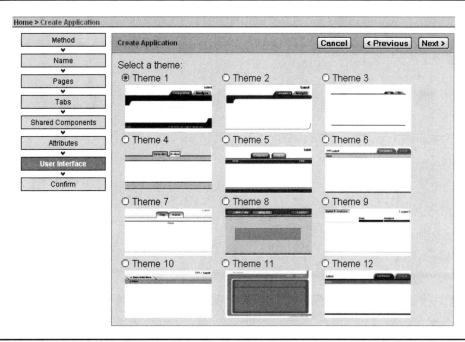

FIGURE 5-7 *User interface selection page*

TIP
There is currently no way to add any templates that you might create to the list of available templates on the UI Theme page. You could edit the HTML DB–supplied templates and change them for any future applications you create, but that practice is not recommended. The best way for you to create and use your own templates is to create a template, as described in Chapter 6, and then create your new application with the Based on an Existing Application creation method, discussed later in this chapter.

To demonstrate the differences between selecting different UI themes, let's look at the Contact Management system created with two different UI themes. In the first example, the application is created using Theme 1, whereas the second example shows the use of Theme 11. In both examples, Two Levels of Tabs was selected as the tab style. The Contacts Report page shown in Figure 5-8 is from an application created using the red UI theme. With this UI theme, there are actual tabs in the upper-right corner of the page that represent the parent tabs. The selected tab is in red, along with the attached bar that has the tabs associated with the parent tab displayed in the bar, in white, at the left side of the screen. The non-selected parent tabs are displayed underlined. The selected second-level tab, which is Contacts on this page, is enclosed in brackets ([]), whereas the non-selected tabs are not. The report title is shown in red above the report with a line drawn across the page under the title.

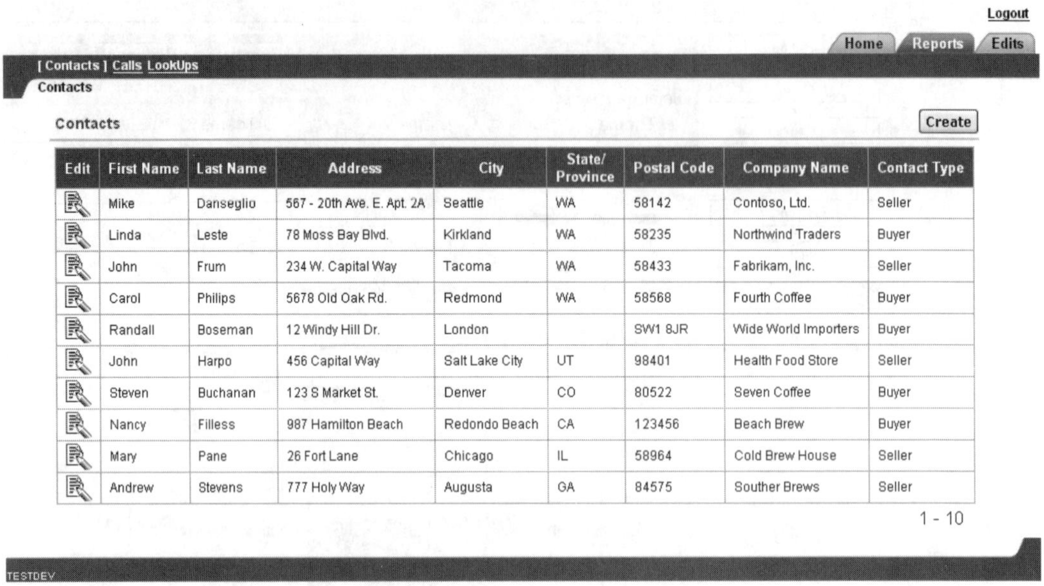

Edit	First Name	Last Name	Address	City	State/ Province	Postal Code	Company Name	Contact Type
	Mike	Danseglio	567 - 20th Ave. E. Apt. 2A	Seattle	WA	58142	Contoso, Ltd.	Seller
	Linda	Leste	78 Moss Bay Blvd.	Kirkland	WA	58235	Northwind Traders	Buyer
	John	Frum	234 W. Capital Way	Tacoma	WA	58433	Fabrikam, Inc.	Seller
	Carol	Philips	5678 Old Oak Rd.	Redmond	WA	58568	Fourth Coffee	Buyer
	Randall	Boseman	12 Windy Hill Dr.	London		SW1 8JR	Wide World Importers	Buyer
	John	Harpo	456 Capital Way	Salt Lake City	UT	98401	Health Food Store	Seller
	Steven	Buchanan	123 S Market St.	Denver	CO	80522	Seven Coffee	Buyer
	Nancy	Filless	987 Hamilton Beach	Redondo Beach	CA	123456	Beach Brew	Buyer
	Mary	Pane	26 Fort Lane	Chicago	IL	58964	Cold Brew House	Seller
	Andrew	Stevens	777 Holy Way	Augusta	GA	84575	Souther Brews	Seller

FIGURE 5-8 *Contacts report page using Theme 1*

Compare this page with the page created using the green UI theme, shown in Figure 5-9. With this theme, both the parent tabs and the second-level tabs are part of the top region of the page, with white letters displayed on a solid green background. The currently selected parent tab is indicated with the small white arrow pointing down to its name, whereas the currently selected second-level tab has a small green arrow pointing up at its name. The report is displayed in an area with a white background below the report title that is shown in a light green bar above the report.

Once you select the UI theme and click on the Next button, a confirmation page is displayed, as shown in Figure 5-10. The confirmation page displays the options you have selected in the various steps of the Create Application Wizard. Look over your choices carefully. If you are satisfied that everything is correct, click the Create Application button. Note the check box at the bottom of the page. If this box is checked, a design model will be created based on this applications definition. That design model will then be available to create other applications based on it. At any point up to and including this step, you can click the previous buttons and make any changes that need to be made. You can click on the Cancel button at any point if you need to start over. After you click on the Create Application button, HTML DB creates a new application based on your selections, storing the information in its metadata tables, and returns you to the Application Builder main page with an "Application Created" success message and the new application selected as the current application.

At this point, you can click Run to examine the application shell that was created. The functionality of the application in the form of reports, forms, and charts can then be added. In the next section, we examine the Create Application Wizard for generating a complete application from tables as views. When this type of application is created, it already has the functionality included.

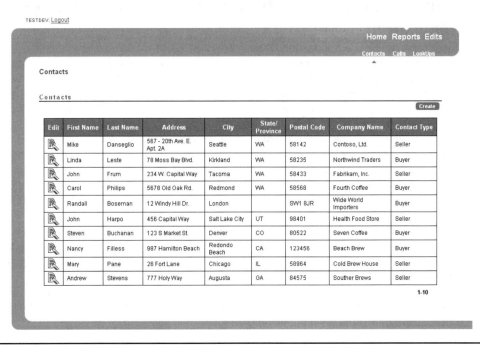

FIGURE 5-9 *Contacts report page using Theme 11*

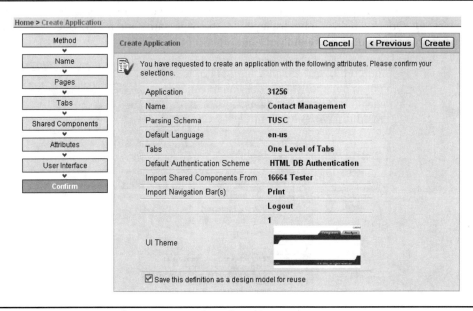

FIGURE 5-10 *Create Application Wizard confirmation page*

Using SQL Queries, Tables, or Views to Create a New Application

When using the Create Application Wizard, version 1.6 only allowed you to select a single table or view, whereas previous versions had allowed you to select multiple tables. With version 2.0, not only can you use multiple tables or views, but you can also use SQL queries for reports. Previous versions also offered no choice when it came to the type of pages that were created. These versions would create a report page, similar to those shown in Figures 5-8 and 5-9, and an edit page for a single row of the table that was linked through an edit icon on the individual rows of the report.

The same process we used to create a new application from scratch can be used to create an application based on SQL queries and existing tables or views. You start with the Create button on the Application Builder main page and then select the Create Application option, shown earlier in Figure 5-1. As before, you specify an application name, number, and schema and select the radio button to create the application from scratch. Clicking the Next button will take you to the page where you add pages, shown previously in Figure 5-3.

For our shell application, we only used the Blank Page option when adding pages. All the other options will utilize an existing table/view or a SQL query. When adding pages, you may choose to add a report and a form, a report only, a form only, or a tabular form, which is a multirow edit form similar to a spreadsheet.

For the purpose of illustration, we are going to create a small application using the Oracle EMP and DEPT sample tables. This way, we can look at some of the analytical options available when creating an application based on tables. Our Contact Management system does not really have any data suitable to analyze.

When you select the Report option on the Add Pages step in the wizard, you may specify the page source to be either a table or a SQL query, as shown in the next illustration. If it is not the first page to be created, you will have a select list field that allows you to specify the page to which the new page will be subordinate if it is not a top-level page. If you select Table, a field will be displayed with a pop-up list that allows you to select an existing table or view. If you select SQL Query, a field will be displayed for the page name and for the query. There will also be a button to pop up a query builder.

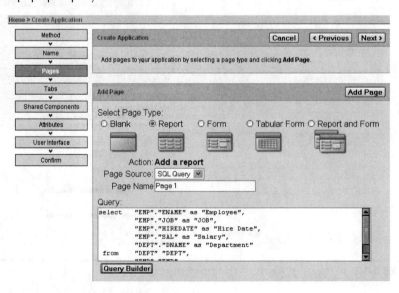

The query shown was created using the query builder shown next. The Report option is the only option that will give you the ability to specify a SQL query.

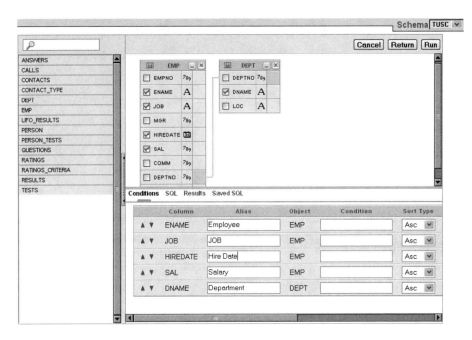

If you select one of the remaining options—Form, Tabular Form, or Report and Form—you will have the field for the subordinate page and a field with a pop list for selecting a table or view. If you select Report and Form or the Report option for a table, there will also be a check box that specifies to include analysis pages, as shown next. For the example, I selected the EMP table with the analysis pages.

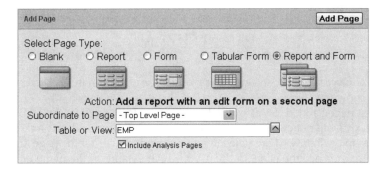

When you click on the Add Page button and you have selected the Include Analysis Pages option, a window will pop up to collect additional information for the analysis. The first step allows you to select summary columns, as shown next. Detail reports and charts will be created for each summary column; the summarized information will be grouped by the columns specified.

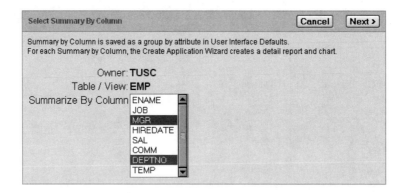

The next step in the pop-up allows you to specify the columns for which values will be aggregated. You may select the columns and select whether to sum or average their values, as shown in the next illustration. The final step of the pop-up allows you to specify whether the pages will be Read Only or Read and Write. For the Report and Form option, the default is Read and Write; for the Report Only option, the default is Read Only. You may also specify whether you want pie charts or vertical bar charts used in the analytical pages.

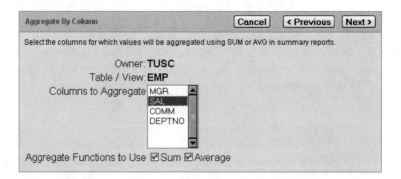

Once you confirm your selections, pages will be added. In this case, seven new pages are added, as shown in Figure 5-11.

The last page I added to this example is a tabular form page on the DEPT table. Once pages are added, you will notice that their name in the page listing is a hyperlink. Clicking on a page name pops up a window where you can edit certain attributes for the page and columns, as shown next. You may change the name of the page, which defaults to the name of the table. You can also change whether the table is subordinate to another page. For each of the columns, you can change user interface defaults such as the column heading or label, the alignment, and format mask. The UI attributes are used in creating the reports or forms. Although this is a convenient method of setting these items prior to the application being created, the best place to define UI

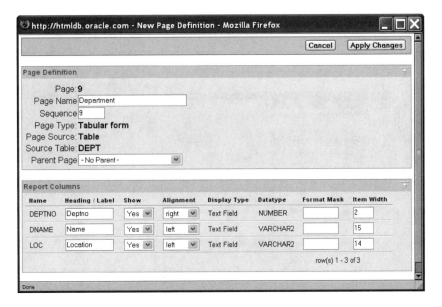

FIGURE 5-11   *Create Application page listing*

defaults is on each table. If the UI defaults have previously been specified on the table, as explained in Chapter 3, they will be used here.

After adding all pages, the remaining steps in the Create Application Wizard are identical to those covered in the preceding section. Once those steps are completed and the application is created, you can run the application, which should look similar to what's shown in Figure 5-12. Although the "application" that is created through the wizard is far from a real-world application, it can provide you a good start or at least a nice application to analyze methodologies that you can apply in your own applications. As you can see, the names of the tabs are based on the names of the page you provided, which is not always desirable. The report in Figure 5-12, which was created from the query of the EMP and DEPT tables, has many helpful features. Notice that the labels for each column are hyperlinks; each one can be clicked on to order the report. The small up arrow next to the Employee column label indicates the table is currently ordered in ascending order. The search box and Go button allow you to search all columns for any given value. Once the resulting rows are displayed, the Reset button will return the user to the full set of data. Also note the Spread Sheet link just below the report. Clicking on this link will bring up a dialog box to either save or open a comma-separated value (CSV) file of the report's results.

The form under the Department tab is an example of a tabular form, shown next. Tabular forms allow you to edit multiple rows at the same time. You may also delete multiple rows by selecting the check box for those you wish to delete and clicking on the Delete button, or you may add new rows to the table by clicking on the Add Row button, which will add a new blank row at the bottom of the report.

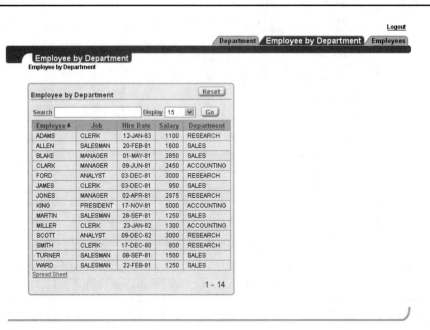

FIGURE 5-12 *Employee by Department page from a query*

The report under the Employee tab is the one that was made as part of the Report and Form on the EMP table, shown in Figure 5-13. Notice the sub-tabs under Employee: Employees, EMP, and EMP Analysis. These correspond to the hierarchical listing in Figure 5-11. I used the page link in Figure 5-11 for page 2, EMP, to change the name of the page from EMP to Employees. From this page the main tab, Employees, and the first sub-tab, Employees, was created. The other two sub-tabs, EMP and EMP Analysis, were created from the two pages that are directly subordinate to page 2 in Figure 5-11. Note that there are four pages subordinate to EMP Analysis; when you go to that sub-tab, you'll find list-style navigation for moving to those pages.

The report, shown in Figure 5-13, is basically the same as the first report we looked at in Figure 5-12, with the addition of the pencil and paper edit icon and the Create button. Each of these will navigate you to the same data entry form (the form part of Report and Form, page 3, shown in Figure 5-11) that handles both the inserting and updating of rows to the EMP table, as shown next. The only difference between the edit and creation screens is which buttons are displayed. Notice that the

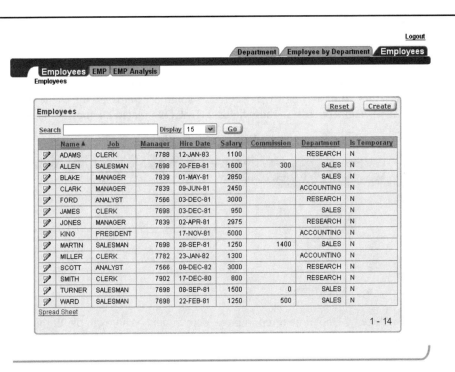

FIGURE 5-13 *Application based on existing table*

Department field is defined as a select list field; this is because an LOV was associated with the field in the table's default user interface attributes.

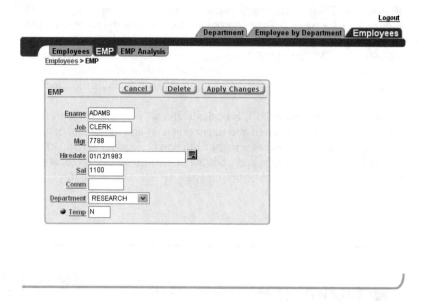

The contents of the EMP Analysis tab, displayed next, provide links to the Analysis Reports and Charts pages. The two fields we selected as summary fields are the MGR field and the DEPARTMENT field. For each of these fields, HTML DB created an analysis page and a chart page.

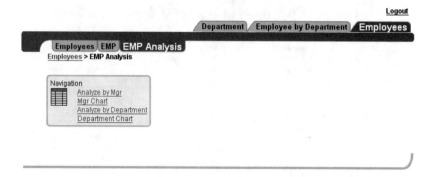

The Analyze by Department report page, shown next, is an example of the analysis reports that HTML DB will create for you. The analysis report is aggregated for the Salary column, which was specified as the aggregation column in the wizard. You may or may not be able to utilize these types of reports; if nothing else you can examine and learn from how they were created. Even though the manager column on the EMP table has an LOV defined, it only shows the department number. You would most likely want to modify the query for this report so as to display the department name rather than the number. In order to navigate to the other analysis report and chart page, you return to the Emp Analyze main page by clicking on the EMP Analysis link in the breadcrumb menu.

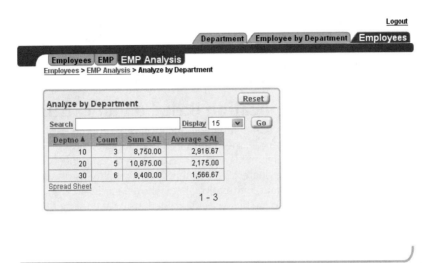

The chart for the distribution of employees by manager, shown next, is an example of the analysis chart pages that HTML DB creates for you. The pie chart that is presented is a Scalable Vector Graphics (SVG) chart that can only be displayed after the plug-in is installed. If the plug-in is not present, you will be provided with a link to Adobe's website so you can download and install the plug-in. We will discuss charts and graphs in more detail in Chapter 12. The pie charts are based on the counts of record for each Summary column group. Again, it would be helpful to have the manager names displayed rather than the manager numbers.

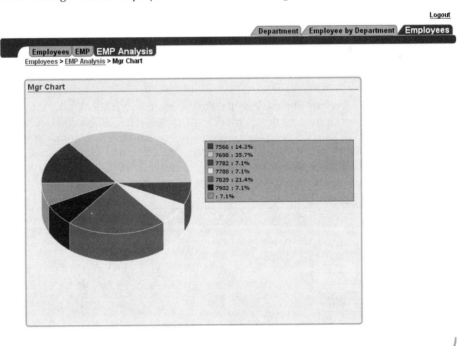

Although the application created with the wizard and existing tables and queries is probably not ready for deployment to production, it is a good start. There may be instances where you can use this ability to quickly generate an application. More likely than not, your users will have different or addition requirements, but you can use this as a good place to start, or at least as a great example to look at for the types of things you can accomplish with HTML DB.

Creating a New Application Based on an Existing Model

Prior to version 2.0, when you created a new application based on an existing application, you only picked up the common shared components and none of the pages of that application. In the Create Application Wizard in version 2.0, you can copy shared components from other applications with any new application in the Shared Components section that was discussed earlier and was shown in Figure 5-5. On the final confirmation page, shown earlier in Figure 5-10, you'll see a check box at the bottom of the page that specifies whether to save the definition as a design model. If you select that check box, the definition will be available as a design model.

To create an application based on an existing design model, you start with the Create button on the Application Builder main page and then select the Create Application option, shown earlier in Figure 5-1. The next step, shown here, where you specify the application's name, number, and schema, has a radio button option titled "Based on existing application design model."

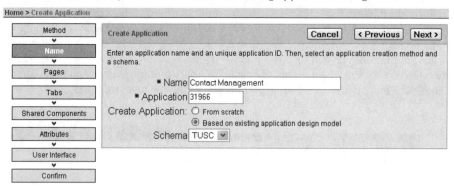

When you select this option and click on the Next button, you will navigate to a page that presents a report of your existing design models, as shown next. When you select an existing design model and click on the Next button, you will navigate to the Pages page. All the pages that were present during the original creation of the application will be shown, whether those pages were simply blank pages or were forms and reports based on tables/views or SQL queries. You may choose to keep all the pages, delete some, or add more.

All the steps that follow in the Create Application Wizard are the same as before. On the Shared Components page, shown earlier in Figure 5-5, you may select to copy shared components from the application whose design model you are using or from another application. The Shared Components section is where the real power of using existing work happens. Creating an application from an existing design model is really only useful if you need the same number and organization of pages as an existing application.

Creating a New Application from a Spreadsheet

Many applications that become important to an organization begin as data stored in an Excel spreadsheet or a Microsoft Access database. In this section, we take a look at Excel spreadsheets and how they can be converted into web-based applications using HTML DB; Microsoft Access applications are considered in the final section of this chapter.

Over the years, the functionality available in Excel has increased tremendously, such as improved formatting and the ability to designate a portion of the spreadsheet as a database. Also, improved charts and pivot tables allow users to easily enter data, perform calculations, and display their data. All too often, however, the data stored in these spreadsheets becomes important to an organization, and critical business decisions are made using the data that they contain. A number of issues are associated with this approach:

- There is no way to share the information contained in the spreadsheet because only one person can have the spreadsheet open at a time.

- Spreadsheets are not directly available via the Web. They can be converted to HTML, but this is not always a straightforward process. Components such as charts and pivot tables are also not available on the Web.

- Large volumes of data present a problem.

- Spreadsheets do not provide transactional capabilities. Therefore, data being entered can be lost if the computer housing the spreadsheet crashes.

- Data stored in a spreadsheet cannot be easily shared with other applications.

- Excel does not contain functions for developing a front end for entering and manipulating spreadsheet data.

These issues can be eliminated by migrating the data from the worksheets of an Excel workbook into Oracle tables and creating an HTML DB application that uses these tables.

A Step-by-step Approach to Migrating Spreadsheet Data

The latest versions of HTML DB have included an option to create an application based on a spreadsheet. This is seen as one of the options on the Create Application main screen, shown earlier in Figure 5-1. Although this is a new application creation option with version 1.6, the functionality was previously available. The Data Workshop allows you to import spreadsheet data into an existing table or a new table, and the Create Application Wizard allows you to create an application based on an existing table. Version 1.6 has combined these two processes into a single wizard. With a couple of simple steps you can transform your existing spreadsheet data into an application.

Identify the Data to Be Uploaded

Before uploading the spreadsheet data into Oracle tables, you need to examine the data. Many Excel workbooks contain multiple worksheets with data. A determination must be made of which worksheets are required and what columns of data from each worksheet will be needed. If the worksheet contains column names in the first row, it is recommended that you include the column names. This saves you from having to enter a column name for each column of data that is uploaded. You can modify the proposed name that the Data Import Wizard creates during the import process.

NOTE
You do not need to eliminate any columns that you don't want to be included in your Oracle tables. During the upload process, the Data Import Wizard provides you an opportunity to include or exclude a column.

Prepare the Data for Import   Because the Data Import Wizard and the Create Application Wizard do not import directly from the Excel file, you will either need to cut and paste the data you need separately for each worksheet in the workbook or export each sheet as a separate CSV file. You can use the cut-and-paste method for sheets up to 30KB in size; otherwise, you will have to use the CSV import file method. This is accomplished by making a copy of the workbook and then performing a Save As operation, where you select "CSV (comma-delimited)" in the Save As Type drop-down list. This operation must be performed separately for each worksheet in the workbook. The Create Application from Spreadsheet Wizard, like the Create Application from Existing Table Wizard, only allows you to create from one table. You can use the wizard to create the initial application and then add more to the application manually.

Figure 5-14 shows a portion of an Excel workbook that contains three worksheets for the Contact Management data discussed earlier in the chapter: Contacts, Calls, and Contact Types. The initial application will be created based on the data from the Calls worksheet.

Use the Create Application from Spreadsheet Wizard   After you select the Based on Spreadsheet option from the Create Application main page, the first step of the wizard is presented, as shown next. This step allows you to select the method for importing the spreadsheet data—CSV file upload or copy and paste.

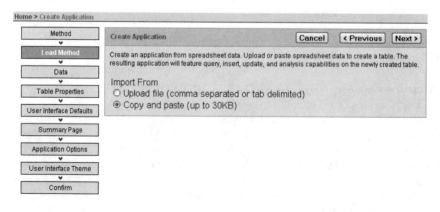

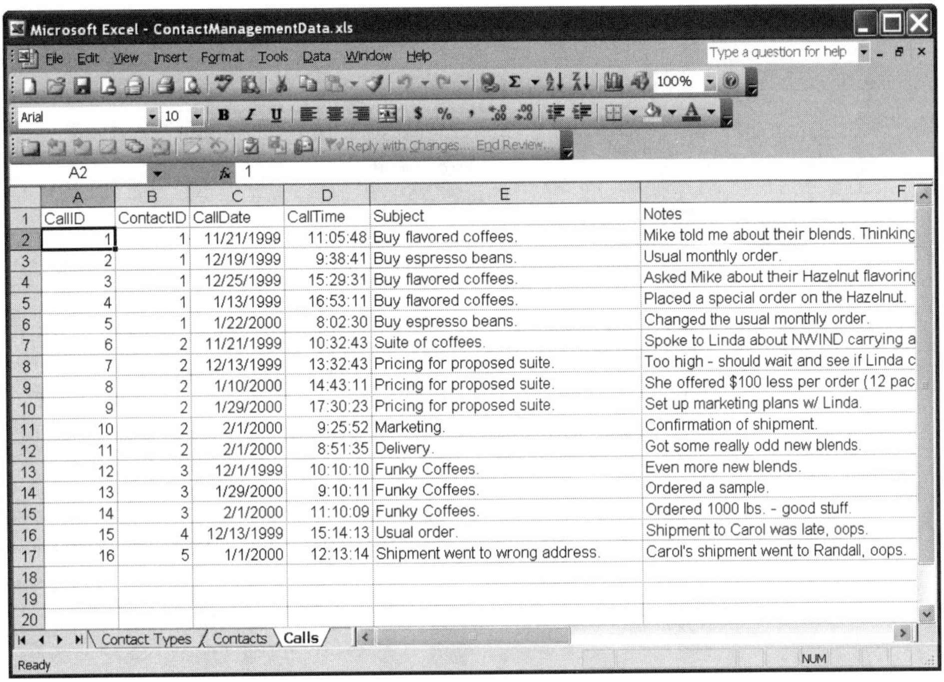

	A	B	C	D	E	F
1	CallID	ContactID	CallDate	CallTime	Subject	Notes
2	1	1	11/21/1999	11:05:48	Buy flavored coffees.	Mike told me about their blends. Thinking
3	2	1	12/19/1999	9:38:41	Buy espresso beans.	Usual monthly order.
4	3	1	12/25/1999	15:29:31	Buy flavored coffees.	Asked Mike about their Hazelnut flavoring
5	4	1	1/13/1999	16:53:11	Buy flavored coffees.	Placed a special order on the Hazelnut.
6	5	1	1/22/2000	8:02:30	Buy espresso beans.	Changed the usual monthly order.
7	6	2	11/21/1999	10:32:43	Suite of coffees.	Spoke to Linda about NWIND carrying a
8	7	2	12/13/1999	13:32:43	Pricing for proposed suite.	Too high - should wait and see if Linda c
9	8	2	1/10/2000	14:43:11	Pricing for proposed suite.	She offered $100 less per order (12 pac
10	9	2	1/29/2000	17:30:23	Pricing for proposed suite.	Set up marketing plans w/ Linda.
11	10	2	2/1/2000	9:25:52	Marketing.	Confirmation of shipment.
12	11	2	2/1/2000	8:51:35	Delivery.	Got some really odd new blends.
13	12	3	12/1/1999	10:10:10	Funky Coffees.	Even more new blends.
14	13	3	1/29/2000	9:10:11	Funky Coffees.	Ordered a sample.
15	14	3	2/1/2000	11:10:09	Funky Coffees.	Ordered 1000 lbs. - good stuff.
16	15	4	12/13/1999	15:14:13	Usual order.	Shipment to Carol was late, oops.
17	16	5	1/1/2000	12:13:14	Shipment went to wrong address.	Carol's shipment went to Randall, oops.
18						
19						
20						

FIGURE 5-14 *An Excel workbook containing the Contact Management data*

After you select the copy-and-paste method, the next step provides a place to paste up to 30KB of data. A check box is available to indicate whether the first column of data contains the column names. If the Globalization options (at the bottom of the page) are expanded, you can enter a currency symbol, group separator, or a decimal character. If you selected the option to upload a CSV file, this screen allows you to select the file to upload, specify a field separator and character set, and indicate if the first column contains the column names.

Once the data has been imported, you are allowed to specify properties for the table, as shown in Figure 5-15. The wizard initially identified the date fields in the spreadsheet data as VARCHAR2 fields, and they need to be changed to DATE or NUMBER fields as necessary. There is also a text field for specifying a format mask to be used on the INSERT statement. The dates in our spreadsheet data are not in standard Oracle format and need to be converted. Specifying a format mask of "MM/DD/YYYY" will cause the data to be loaded correctly; otherwise, the INSERT will fail with an ORA-01843 error message. You can also see that a format mask of "HH24:MI:SS" has been specified for the times. The page also contains an Upload drop-down list (with values of Yes and No) that determines whether that column should be uploaded or ignored. The display also contains the rows of data for each column that will be imported.

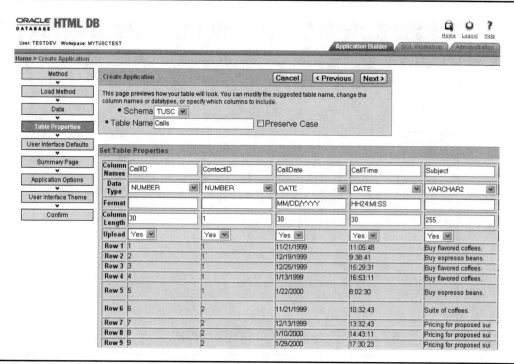

FIGURE 5-15 *Table properties*

The next page allows you to specify user interface defaults for the table, including singular and plural names for the table and labels for the columns. By default, when you're creating an application from a spreadsheet, the wizard runs as if you were creating a report and form with analytical pages based on the table you just created by uploading the data. Therefore, the remaining steps in the Create Application Wizard are the same steps discussed earlier using the other paths through the wizard:

1. Summary Page (specifies summary columns and aggregation columns for analysis reports)
2. Application Options (specifies the application name as well as Read and Write mode)
3. User Interface Theme
4. Confirm

Once the initial piece of the application is created, you can add more tables and pages to the application.

Creating Demonstration Applications

One of the Create Application options first introduced in version 1.6 is to create demonstration applications. After selecting this option from the Create Application main page, you will navigate to the Demonstration Applications page, shown in Figure 5-16. To create any of the available applications, click on the corresponding Install link. This will take you to a page to select the schema in which to install the application. The final step will be to confirm your choices. After that, the selected demonstration application will be installed.

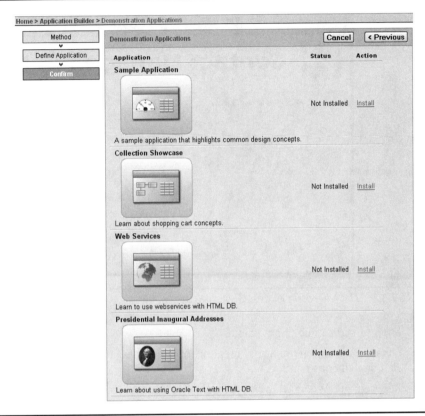

FIGURE 5-16 *Demonstration Applications page*

Converting a Microsoft Access Application to HTML DB

Whereas a spreadsheet contains data that you can use to build a web-based application, Microsoft Access applications are more complicated. An Access application typically contains data tables with relationships, forms for maintaining data, and highly formatted reports. Access also has a facility known as the Switchboard that allows you to navigate between these components, as shown in Figure 5-17.

A Step-by-step Approach to Migrating an Access Application

Due to the additional complexity of Access applications, a step-by-step approach is required for converting them to HTML DB. The following steps define one approach you can use:

1. Read any available documentation, especially the user's guide.
2. Run the application and become familiar with its functionality.
3. Examine the data tables and their relationships.
4. Export the Microsoft Access data tables.

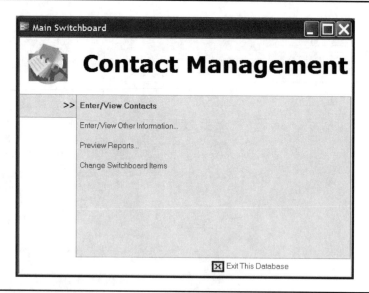

FIGURE 5-17 *The Microsoft Access Switchboard*

5. Import the data into Oracle tables.

6. Enhance the imported data by creating lookup tables, adding data relationships, and defining UI constraints.

7. Redesign the Access UI to be representative of a web-based application.

8. Determine which application template to use.

9. Create an HTML DB application to contain the converted application.

10. Add the functionality of the existing application to the HTML DB application shell.

These steps are described in greater detail in the following sections.

Read Any Available Documentation

Most existing applications have some documentation available. Often, a user's guide has been developed that describes the application from the user's point of view. The user's guide is one of the most important document to locate. If a user's guide was not written, examine the application and determine whether any online help screens are available that you can examine to understand the application.

Also, determine whether any technical documentation was prepared. The most important technical document is the data dictionary, which documents the definition and purpose of the columns of every table in the application. Any documents describing the user interface and the reports would also be useful.

Run the Application and Become Familiar with Its Functionality

It is important to understand the functionality of the existing system. Microsoft Access applications are Windows-based and take advantage of many of the capabilities of running on a single desktop computer. You will need to understand how the application works so that you can translate the functions from the single-computer client/server model to a web-based application.

The Contact Management application discussed in this chapter is one of the sample applications available with Microsoft Access. To access this application on your machine, perform the following steps:

1. Start Microsoft Access.

2. Select the New Database link from the File menu or press CTRL-N.

3. In the New dialog box that appears, click the Databases tab.

4. You will see a list of about 20 different sample databases that demonstrate different features of the Access product. Click on the Contact Management sample database and then click on OK.

5. The File New Database dialog box is presented for you to select a location for the Microsoft Access database, which is saved with a file type of .MDB. Select a location on the file system and click on the Create button.

6. This invokes the Access Database Wizard, which walks you through the options for creating the sample database. If you wish to select the Access defaults for the database, you can click Finish.

When the Finish button is clicked, the database .MDB file is created and the data for the application is loaded. After the data is loaded, you are presented with a tabbed interface for examining the tables, queries, reports, macros, and modules that are part of the application.

If the application is being supplied by one of your clients or users, all that is required is a copy of the .MDB file.

The best way to run the application is by using the Switchboard. From the Switchboard, you can invoke the Enter/View Contacts link to display the form shown in Figure 5-18. This form allows you to enter, edit, and delete the contacts within the system. Navigational control and a paging mechanism are also provided. You'll also see a button on the page to invoke the Calls form, which is shown in Figure 5-19.

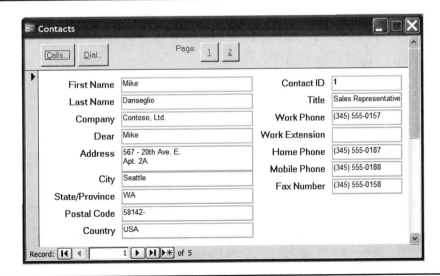

FIGURE 5-18   *The Enter/View Contacts form*

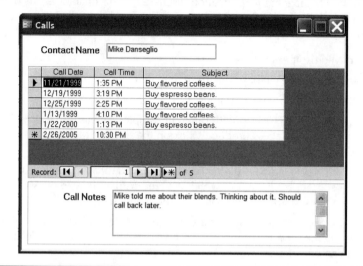

FIGURE 5-19 *The Enter/View Calls form*

You should also run the reports for that system that will be re-created in HTML DB. The Contact Management system has two built-in reports: an alphabetical list of contacts, as shown in Figure 5-20, and a calls report. The calls report is invoked from a parameter form for providing a date range.

Examine the Data Tables and Their Relationships

You can examine the individual tables of the application by clicking on the Tables tab and selecting each table separately. Access also has a tool, available on the Tools menu, for displaying the relationships between the tables of the application. Figure 5-2, which shows the relationships

Alphabetical Contact Listing

	Contact Name	Company Name	Title	Work Phone	Ext.	Fax Number
B						
	Boseman, Randall	Wide World Importers	Purchase Manager	(71) 555-0122		
D						
	Danseglio, Mike	Contoso, Ltd.	Sales Representative	(345) 555-0157		(345) 555-0158
F						
	Frum, John	Fabrikam, Inc.	Sales Representative	(345) 555-0182		(345) 555-0183
L						
	Leste, Linda	Northwind Traders	Vice President, New Products	(345) 555-0112		(345) 555-0113
P						
	Philips, Carol	Fourth Coffee	Purchase Manager	(345) 555-0122		(345) 555-0123

FIGURE 5-20 *The alphabetical contacts report*

between the three tables of the Contact Management application, was generated using the Relationships tool. The Relationships tool shows each table in the application and the primary/ foreign key relationships. The names of the columns on each table are also included.

To view the data types of the columns in one of the Access tables, double-click the table and then select Design View from the View menu. A list of the columns in the table is presented, as shown in Figure 5-21 for the Calls table. The key field is usually an AutoNumber field, which is Access's equivalent of tying a sequence to a field without having a separate sequence object. These AutoNumber fields are mapped to Oracle as follows:

1. Create a new Oracle sequence.

2. Define the field as a NUMBER field.

3. Define a BEFORE INSERT trigger that increments the sequence and then use the next value of the sequence as the primary key of the row to be inserted.

You will need to map the other Access data types to Oracle data types. TEXT fields are the equivalent of VARCHAR2 fields. NUMBER and CURRENCY fields are mapped to NUMBER fields with a specific precision. DATE/TIME fields in Access are mapped to Oracle DATE fields. Access also has a MEMO data type for columns that require a larger amount of text data. These can either map to larger VARCHAR2 fields, which can be up to 4,000 characters in length, or CLOB or BLOB columns, which can be very large.

The list of fields also has valuable information that you can capture in HTML DB. Several of the fields, such as Caption, Input Mask, and Required, can be mapped as UI defaults. The validation rules can be translated into validation rules in the application or as CHECK constraints.

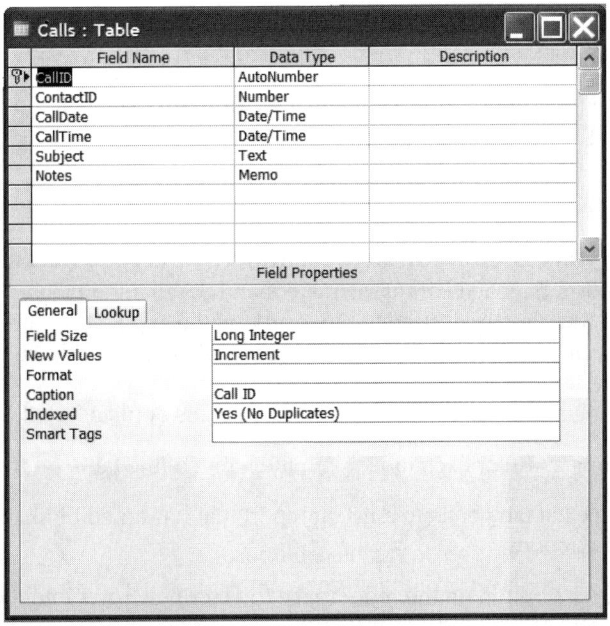

FIGURE 5-21   *Access properties sheet for the Calls table*

Export the Microsoft Access Data Tables

The data from each of the tables can be exported from Access into a text file using the Save/Export function. This function is invoked from the File menu or by right-clicking on the table and selecting the function. Here are the steps to follow to perform the export:

1. From the Save As dialog box, leave the To an External File or Database option selected and click on OK.

2. From the Save Table dialog box, browse through the file system and select a location for the export file. Change the Save As type to text files and click on Export.

3. The Export Text Wizard is invoked. Leave the default of Delimited selected and click on Next. The other option is Fixed Width.

4. Leave the default value of a comma for the delimiter and a double quote as the text delimiter. Click on the Include Field Names on First Row check box, which is unchecked by default, and then click on Finish to begin the export.

Import the Data into Oracle Tables

The process of importing the Contact Management data into Oracle tables was discussed earlier in this chapter, as well as in Chapter 3.

Oracle does provide another mechanism for creating Oracle tables from Microsoft Access tables—the Data Migration Workbench. The Data Migration Workbench is useful for larger Access application with many tables. A discussion of this facility is beyond the scope of this book.

Enhance the Imported Data

In the previous section on migrating spreadsheet data, several enhancements to the Contact Management data were examined. These include:

■ Creating lookup tables from the imported data

■ Defining new indexes and foreign key constraints to identify data relationships

■ Specifying UI defaults

These operations are also required when migrating Access data.

Redesign the Access UI to Be Representative of a Web-based Application

Access applications have a different interface than is available in web applications. In an Access application, the Switchboard is used to move around the application and invoke different functions. Although this approach could be emulated, web applications tend to use tabs, menus, and navigation panes for moving between pages.

Several changes are required to translate the Access application to a web-based application:

■ Providing a tab for each table, with the name of the table on the tab.

■ Having each tab generate a listing report that has an edit link to change the values in the row of a report.

■ Including a button on the report page to enter new rows into the table.

■ Including a Delete button on the edit screen for removing rows.

■ On the Contacts page, including a link to the Calls report for the specific contact.

Determine Which Application Template to Use

Access applications are developed using templates. The Contact Management system uses a background image of clouds and specific font settings. In HTML DB, you can create templates that emulate the Access templates. Templates are discussed further in Chapter 6.

Create an HTML DB Application to Contain the Converted Application

After creating a template to emulate an Access template, you can build an HTML DB application template to house it. You can then create other applications based on this template.

You can also choose to migrate away from the Access template and use one of the templates available within HTML DB. This is accomplished by creating an application from scratch and choosing one of the HTML DB templates in the Create Application Wizard.

Add the Functionality of the Existing Application to the HTML DB Application Shell

Once the shell of the application has been created, you can begin the process of creating an HTML DB application that provides the same functionality as the Access application. Adding the needed additional functionality to this sample application will be done in following chapters.

CHAPTER
6

Working with Themes and Templates

TML DB utilizes various templates to implement the look and feel of an application. A *theme* is a collection of these templates. This arrangement allows for a single implementation point of an application's look and feel and the segregation of visual elements from the application logic and database access. Development tasks can be divided up by skill sets; one developer can work on the look and feel of the user interface while another simultaneously works on the business logic and flow of the application. A centralized implementation of the visual elements also allows changes to the entire application to be made in a single location.

Templates are made up of HTML and substitution variables that allow the page to be dynamically generated at run time. An application is associated with a theme, which has a default set of templates that will be utilized throughout the application unless a different template is selected during development. Here are the different types of templates available:

- Button templates

- Calendar templates

- Label templates

- List templates

- Menu templates

- Page templates

- Popup LOV templates

- Region templates

- Report templates

In this chapter, we will examine the use of themes, the different types of templates available, and the use of substitution strings in template definitions. Also, we will dig into great detail on page templates.

Themes

The look and feel of an application is controlled by the theme that is associated with the application. Themes are managed on the Themes page, which is accessible from the Themes link in the User Interface section of the Shared Components drop-down menu, as shown here.

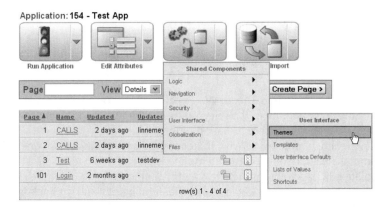

The drop-down menu is activated by clicking the down arrow on the right side of the Shared Components navigation icon. If you click on the icon, it will navigate you to the Shared Components page, where you can click on the Themes link in the User Interface section.

From this page, you can create a new theme, edit existing themes, delete a theme, or switch the current theme for the application. The current theme for an application is indicated by a check mark in the Current column on the Themes page, as shown in Figure 6-1. You can easily switch the current theme for an application. Starting in version 1.6, you are allowed to copy templates from other applications within your workspace; previously, this had not been possible. From this page, you can also access the individual templates that belong to a theme by clicking on the magnifying glass icon in the View column for the theme. Note that the Themes page has two different displays: a summary display and a detail display. You switch between displays by selecting from the display LOV and clicking on the Go button. You can also display themes by icons, although this view is the least informative.

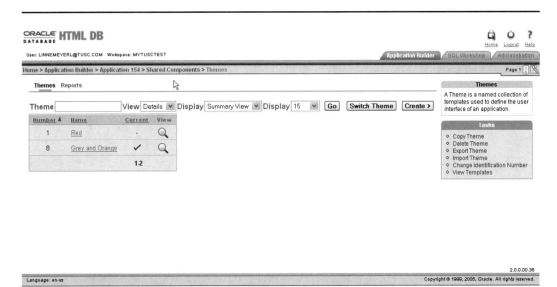

FIGURE 6-1   *Themes page*

Switching an Application's Theme

Clicking the Switch Theme button on the Themes page shown in Figure 6-1 takes you into a wizard that walks you through the steps necessary to change an application's current theme. The Switch Theme button is not available if there is only one theme; you must create another before this button will appear.

The first page of the Switch Theme Wizard allows you to select a new theme. The second page verifies the compatibility of the selected theme with the application's existing pages and objects. The last page asks for confirmation of the switch.

When switching templates, HTML DB accomplishes mappings from one theme to another through template class identifiers. Each template is assigned to a template class in the first section of the template edit page. For instance, a specific button template might be associate with the "Button" or "Button – Alternate 1" class identifier, among others. By checking the compatibility of themes, HTML DB ensures the new theme contains a template of the same class for every class of template being used. For example, if the application has a button that uses a button template with a "Button – Alternate 1" class identifier, HTML DB ensures that the new theme contains a Button template also associated with the "Button – Alternate 1" class.

If the new theme has two or more templates of the same class, you will see "Warning" in the Status column and a pick list in the To Template column on the Verify Theme Compatibility pages, as shown in Figure 6-2. The pick list allows you to select which template you want to map to in the new theme. Note that the columns are actually mislabeled; they are in fact To and From Template, not To and From Template Class. The To and From templates are matched by their corresponding template classes.

If one of the mappings fails, you will see "Error" in the Status column and you will not be allowed to proceed to the next page of the wizard. An error occurs if either a From template is not associated with a template class or a To theme does not have a template of the same class.

To resolve these errors, note the template name, listed under the From Template column, for each one that has an "Error" status. Cancel out of the switch process. This returns you back to the main Themes page. Click on the small Theme Reports tab, just below the breadcrumb menu, and view the Application Templates report for the existing theme. The report lists each template in the theme by theme type along with its name and associated template class. Observe the template classes for the template name noted earlier. If there is no template class listed, that is part of the

Template Type ▲	From Template Class	To Template Class	Status
Breadcrumb	Breadcrumb Menu	Breadcrumb Menu	✓
Button	Button	Button	✓
Label	Optional with help	Optional with help	✓
Page	Login	Login	✓
Region	Breadcrumb Region	No Template	Error
	Reports Region	Reports Region	✓
	Report List	Chart List ▼	Warning
Report	Standard	Standard	✓
		row(s) 1 - 8 of 8	

FIGURE 6-2   *Theme compatibility*

problem. You must edit your existing template and assign a template class to each template and then try the switch again. If a template class is listed for the template, you must have a template with a corresponding template class in your To theme. In the theme you wish to switch to, create a new (or edit an existing) template of the proper type and associate it with the same template class.

NOTE
When an application is converted from version 1.5 to 1.6 or 2.0, an initial theme will be created from the application's templates. The templates will not be assigned a template class. If you want to switch templates, you will have to edit each template and assign it a template class.

Creating New Themes

Like the theme-switching process, the process to create a new theme is also accomplished through a wizard. Start the wizard by clicking on the Create Theme button on the Themes page, as shown earlier in Figure 6-1. The first screen of the wizard presents the three options for creating themes: From the HTML DB Repository, From Scratch, and From Export.

HTML DB comes with a repository of a dozen different themes. If you decide to create a theme based on one from the repository, you will be taken to a screen to select from one of the canned themes. After you have created the new theme, you can alter it in any way you would like. If you select the option to create a theme from an export, the wizard will take you through the process of importing an export file from another application. Exporting and importing of applications and their components is covered in Chapter 7. This is the method you would use to copy a theme from one application to another.

If you select to create a theme from scratch, you will be taken to a screen to name your new theme and then an empty theme will be created. This is the method you use if you want to create all your own templates or copy templates from other different themes. When you create new templates, you can copy them from templates in themes in other applications within your workspace. Before version 1.6, it was not possible to copy templates between applications. When you copy a template, you can subscribe to the original template. If changes are made to the original template, you can update the subscribed template. However, if you do update the subscribed template, any modifications you made will be lost. For more information, refer to the upcoming section, "Creating and Copying Templates."

NOTE
Versions 1.6 and above allow you to share templates between applications in the same workspace.

Specifying a Theme's Default Template

Within a theme you can specify a default template for each type of template. When an application uses a theme and a specific template is not specified for an object, that object will use the theme's corresponding default template. Clicking the name of a theme listed on the Themes page, as shown earlier in Figure 6-1, will navigate you to the Create/Edit Theme page, shown in Figure 6-3. Here, you can select a default template for each type of template. For page- and region-type templates, you may specify several defaults based on the type of page or type of region. Notice there is no place to set a default template for Popup LOVs; this is because only one Popup LOV template is allowed per theme.

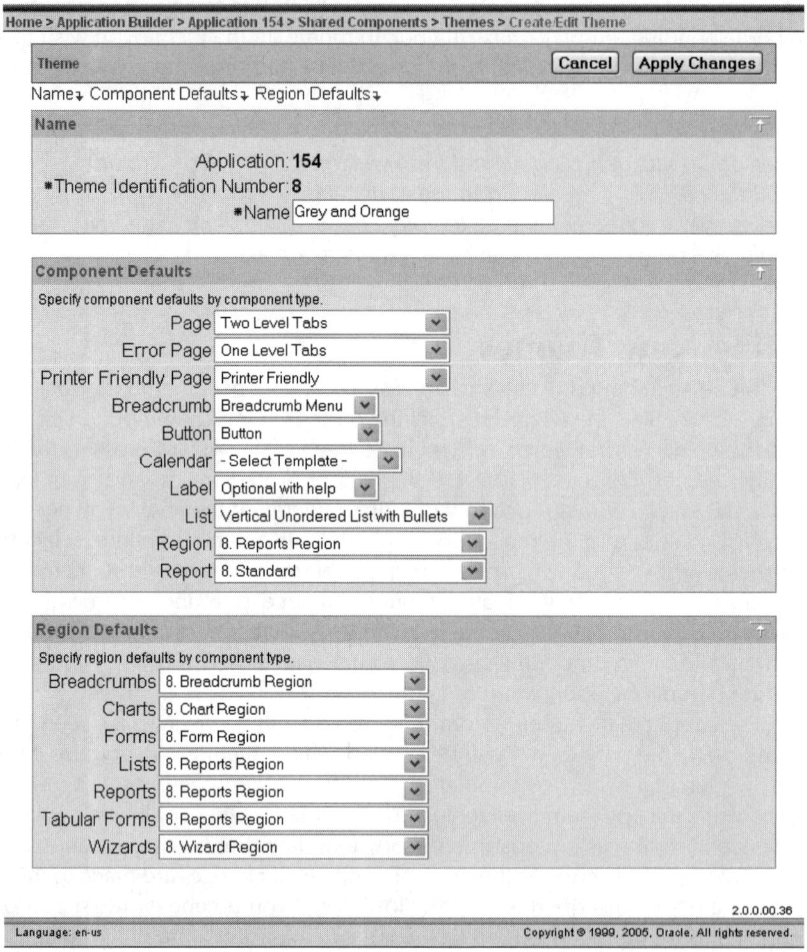

FIGURE 6-3   *Create/Edit Theme page*

Templates

HTML DB uses templates to control the look and feel of an application. Templates are made up of HTML code and substitution variables. At run time, the HTML DB engine uses information from your object definitions to dynamically fill in information for the substitution variables and create the final HTML pages. The large number of template types available allows you to precisely control the way your application looks while centralizing the administration of the look and feel.

Template Types

HTML DB has nine different types of templates, as listed in the introduction of this chapter. The templates apply to all different types of objects. Objects that use templates go from more general type objects, like pages and regions, to more specific type objects, like lists and buttons.

Page Templates

Page templates control the look and feel of common items on a page, such as headers, footers, parent tabs, standard tabs, and navigation bars. As shown in Figure 6-3, a typical application needs three different page templates: Page, Error Page, and Printer Friendly Page. Although it is possible to use only one page template for an entire application, a more professional look and feel can be accomplished with a variety of templates.

Region Templates

Region templates control the look and feel of regions within a page. They control items such as region borders, titles, and the placement of buttons.

Report Templates

Report templates format the results of a database query. They control the look of headers and rows. Conditional row formatting can be used to dynamically change the look of a row based on the row's content and whether it is an odd or even row.

List Templates

List templates control the look and feel of a shared group of links. You can control before and after list formatting as well as current and noncurrent link formatting.

Label Templates

Label templates control the look and feel of item labels. Typically label templates are used to distinguish between required and nonrequired fields.

Calendar Templates

Calendar templates control the look and feel as well as the placement of a calendar. They are typically made from an HTML table to control the placement of dates.

Menu Templates

Menu templates control the look and feel of menus. Menu templates are selected for creating a menu-type region.

Button Templates

Button templates are used to control the appearance of buttons. Buttons can be created using multiple images or with HTML. The use of templates is optional for buttons.

Popup LOV Templates

Popup LOV templates are used to control the look and feel of items of type POPUP. Only one Popup LOV template can be specified for an application; therefore, it is the only template type for which a developer does not specify a default.

Managing Templates

Templates are managed from the Templates page. To get to the Templates page, click on the magnifying glass icon in the View column on the Themes page. The Templates page allows you to see all templates for all themes within your application. The selection boxes at the top of the page, as shown in Figure 6-4, allow you to limit the templates displayed by selecting a theme, a template type, and whether the template is referenced in your application. This page tells you a lot about your templates, such as which ones are the defaults, how many references there are to a template, and whether the template is subscribed to a master template. From this page, you can also create a new template, edit any existing template, and even do a mass replacement of templates from another application.

Editing an Existing Template

To edit any existing template, simply click on the template name from the Templates page. This will take you to a type-specific template edit page. In order to edit templates, you need at least a good working knowledge of HTML. See the following sections for specifics on Page and Report templates. Due to space limitation, we are not able go into complete detail on all nine different types of templates. However, you will come to find that they are very similar when it comes to editing them. With a good working knowledge of HTML, an understanding of the substitution variables, and some hands-on experimentation, you should be able to fully understand each type of template.

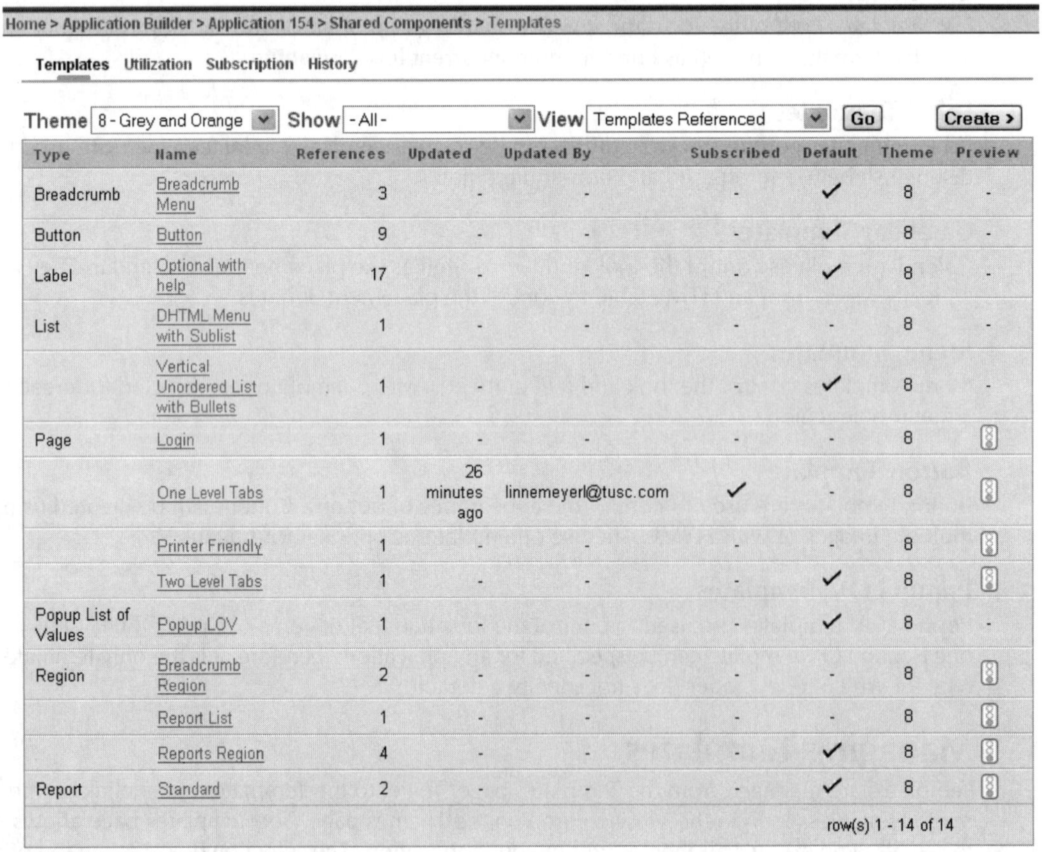

Home > Application Builder > Application 154 > Shared Components > Templates

Templates   Utilization   Subscription   History

Theme [8 - Grey and Orange ▾]   Show [- All - ▾]   View [Templates Referenced ▾]   [Go]   [Create >]

Type	Name	References	Updated	Updated By	Subscribed	Default	Theme	Preview
Breadcrumb	Breadcrumb Menu	3	-	-	-	✓	8	-
Button	Button	9	-	-	-	✓	8	-
Label	Optional with help	17	-	-	-	✓	8	-
List	DHTML Menu with Sublist	1	-	-	-	-	8	-
	Vertical Unordered List with Bullets	1	-	-	-	✓	8	-
Page	Login	1	-	-	-	-	8	▣
	One Level Tabs	1	26 minutes ago	linnemeyerl@tusc.com	✓	-	8	▣
	Printer Friendly	1	-	-	-	-	8	▣
	Two Level Tabs	1	-	-	-	✓	8	▣
Popup List of Values	Popup LOV	1	-	-	-	✓	8	-
Region	Breadcrumb Region	2	-	-	-	-	8	▣
	Report List	1	-	-	-	-	8	▣
	Reports Region	4	-	-	-	✓	8	▣
Report	Standard	2	-	-	-	✓	8	▣

row(s) 1 - 14 of 14

FIGURE 6-4   *Templates page*

Creating and Copying Templates

Like themes, templates can either be created from scratch or copied from another location. With templates, you don't copy from the HTML DB repository, but rather from other templates in other themes, including themes from other applications. Like with themes, template creation is accomplished through a multiscreen wizard. The first screen allows you to select the type of template you are going to create. On the next screen you choose to create the template either from scratch or as a copy of an existing template.

If you choose to create the template from scratch, you will be asked to name the template, select the theme it will belong to, and specify the template class. Upon confirmation, a nearly blank template will be created; it will include some very basic HTML along with the minimal substitution variables.

If you go the route of creating a template as a copy of an existing template, you select the application to copy from and then select the theme to copy from and the theme to copy to. At this point, the wizard will present to you a list of templates from the selected theme that are of the type you chose to copy, as shown in Figure 6-5. For each of the templates listed, you can choose to copy and subscribe, just copy, or not copy. If you subscribe to a template and changes are later made to the master template, you can update the subscribed template by entering the edit template page and clicking on the Refresh Template button found in the Template Subscription section of the edit template page. Be aware that any changes you make to the subscribing template will be lost when you refresh the template.

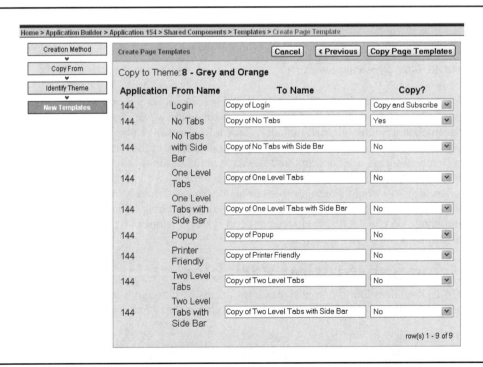

FIGURE 6-5   *Creating templates by copying*

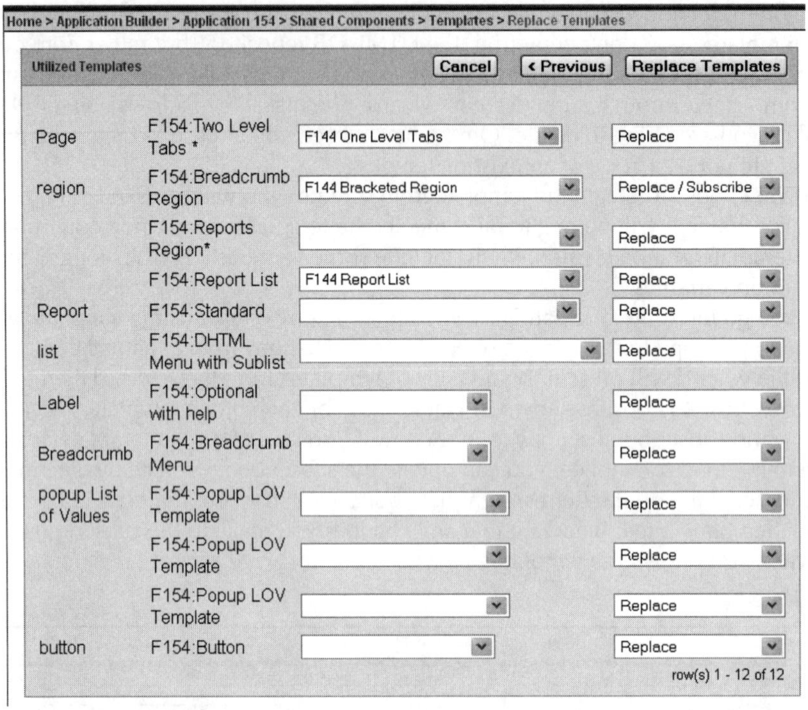

FIGURE 6-6 *Replacing templates*

There is one other powerful feature available for copying templates. If you have copied templates from another application but did not subscribe when you copied, you can still refresh the template from the original. Actually, you can replace *any* utilized template in your current application with another template in another application. In the Tasks box on the right side of the Templates page is an option titled "Replace templates in this application with templates from another application." If you follow this link, you will be asked to select the source application from which you would like to replace templates. You will then be presented with a list of the templates for your current application that are currently being utilized. For each of these templates, you can choose a replacement and select whether to replace or to replace and subscribe, as shown in Figure 6-6.

Using Substitution Variables

HTML DB utilizes four different syntaxes for accessing different types of variables throughout the HTML DB application. The following table shows the different syntaxes.

Syntax	Usage
#VARIABLENAME#	For system-defined substitution variables such as those used in templates
&VARIABLENAME. (note the trailing period)	For global application variables, session variables, and page items

Syntax	Usage
v('VARIABLENAME')	For use in PL/SQL for character-type variables, including session variables and page items
nv('VARIABLENAME')	For use in PL/SQL for number-type variables, including session variables and page items
:VariableName	Bind variable syntax also used in PL/SQL to refer to global application variables, session variables, and page items

Substitution variables are used in template definitions as placeholders for values that will be filled when the page is generated. HTML DB has a large number of predefined substitution variables that are used in template definitions. Those used in template definitions always start and end with the pound symbol (#). For example, #TITLE# is the substitution variable that will be replaced with the page title that is defined when a page is created. Each type of template has a number of substitution variables predefined for use with the template. The best way to know what variables are available for a particular section of a template and which ones are required for that section is to click on the section title to access the help text for that section.

TIP
Utilize HTML DB's extensive built-in context-sensitive help, available by clicking on most item's labels.

A complete list and description of each of the substitution variables available for each type of template can be found in HTML DB's online help, accessible from the Help icon located in the upper-right corner of each page. Once you open Help to the contents page, select the Customizing Templates link under the Controlling Page Layout and User Interface section. Near the top of the page is a list of links that will take you to a section for each of the different types of templates. Each section lists the substitution variables and a brief description of the template's major sections.

Page Template

In this section, we will look at the details in a Page template to see how the template works with substitution variables and where those substitution variables tie back to what was specified when the pages were created.

The Edit Page Template screen contains 12 sections. Several of these sections are common to all or most of the other template-editing pages. We will address those sections before moving on to the page-specific ones. Navigate to an edit template screen by clicking on the name of the template from the list on the Templates page, as shown earlier in Figure 6-4.

Common Template Sections

All templates have a corresponding edit page. Many of the items on these pages are specific to only one type of template; however, there are a number of sections in the edit pages that are common to most types of templates.

Page Template Identification

The first common section is the Template Identification section. Here, you provide a unique descriptive name for the template as well as select the theme to which the template belongs. Additionally, in this section you specify the template class for the template and select whether the template is translatable (which has to do with deploying a template in multiple languages). See Chapter 7 for more details on deploying applications in multiple languages.

Template Subscription

The next section is the Template Subscription section. This section lists details about subscriptions. Was this template copied from another template? Is this template subscribed to another template? Does this template have any subscribers?

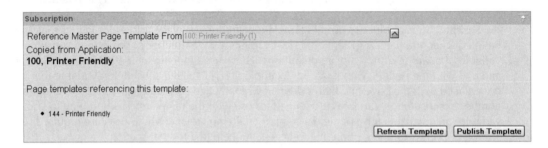

The first line contains a pick list for a master template. If the template was copied from another template, it will have a meaningless reference number listed in the pick list field, as previously shown. Otherwise, it will be empty, as shown next. In either case, you can select another template from the pick list and then refresh this template from the selected template. In instances where there already is a master (as in the previous example), you would click on the Refresh Template button. If this template never had a master template, like in the following example, a Refresh check box will appear next to the pick list. If this is checked and you apply changes to the page, it will refresh from the master.

The section then displays where the template was copied from and a list of templates that are subscribed to it. If the template is subscribed to another template, you'll see a Refresh Template button. Clicking that button recopies from the subscribing template, overwriting everything. If this template has other templates that subscribe to it, you'll see a Publish Template button. Clicking the Publish Template button will copy the current template out to all templates that are subscribed to it, overwriting any changes that may have been made to them.

Configuration Management

This section contains a single field to select the build option for this template. Build options are used to include or exclude certain components of an application. There can be any number of build options. You will have a pick list that includes a selection for each build option and a {Not} selection for each build option. Refer to Chapter 4 for more details on build options.

Comments

The last common section is the Comments section. This section allows the developer to enter any pertinent comments about a template. Comments should be used to document anything that is done out of the ordinary.

Header/Body/Footer Definitions

The next section contains the definitions for the header, the body, and the footer of the page. Remember, the HTML DB engine generates each page at run time by combining the static HTML defined in your template with the dynamic pieces derived from the metadata you used when building the pages. This connection is made through the use of substitution variables. There is an area for entering the HTML for the Header section, the Body section, and the Footer section. Let's take a closer look at an example of each of these definitions.

Header

The Header section contains the HTML for the HEAD section of an HTML document. Everything you would normally include before the BODY tag in an HTML document belongs here. Someone familiar with web page layout and HTML should make the modifications to templates. However, if you must do it and are not familiar with HTML, then try *HTML & XHTML: The Complete Reference* by Thomas Powell (McGraw-Hill/Osborne, 2003).

The following is a listing of code from the header definition:

```
<!DOCTYPE html PUBLIC "-//W3C//DTD HTML 4.01 Transitional//EN">
<html>
<head>
    <title>#TITLE#</title>
    #HEAD#
    <link rel="stylesheet" href="#IMAGE_PREFIX#css/einstein.css"
      type="text/css" />
    <script src="#IMAGE_PREFIX#javascript/functions.js"
            type="text/javascript"></script>
</head>
```

Notice the example contains normal HTML items such as the title tag and includes statements for a Cascading Style Sheet and a file containing JavaScript. It also contains several substitution variables.

The substitution variable #TITLE# will be replaced at run time with the value from the Title field in the Primary Page Attributes section of the Edit page, or "Form on CONTACTS," as shown in Figure 6-7. The substitution variable #HEAD# will be replaced with the value entered in the HTML Header section of the Edit page, as shown in Figure 6-7. You might have HTML to reference additional JavaScript libraries or Cascading Style Sheets.

The other substitution variable seen in this code block is #IMAGE_PREFIX#. This is a predefined variable that contains the directory on the server for the images that come with HTML DB. If you look at the source of a generated page, you will see that it resolves to /i/, which is mapped to ORACLE_HOME\marvel\images. The Cascading Style Sheet (CSS) file is located in ORACLE_HOME\ marvel\images\css, and the JavaScript file is located in ORACLE_HOME\ marvel\images\javascript. At a minimum, the Header section should contain the #TITLE# and the

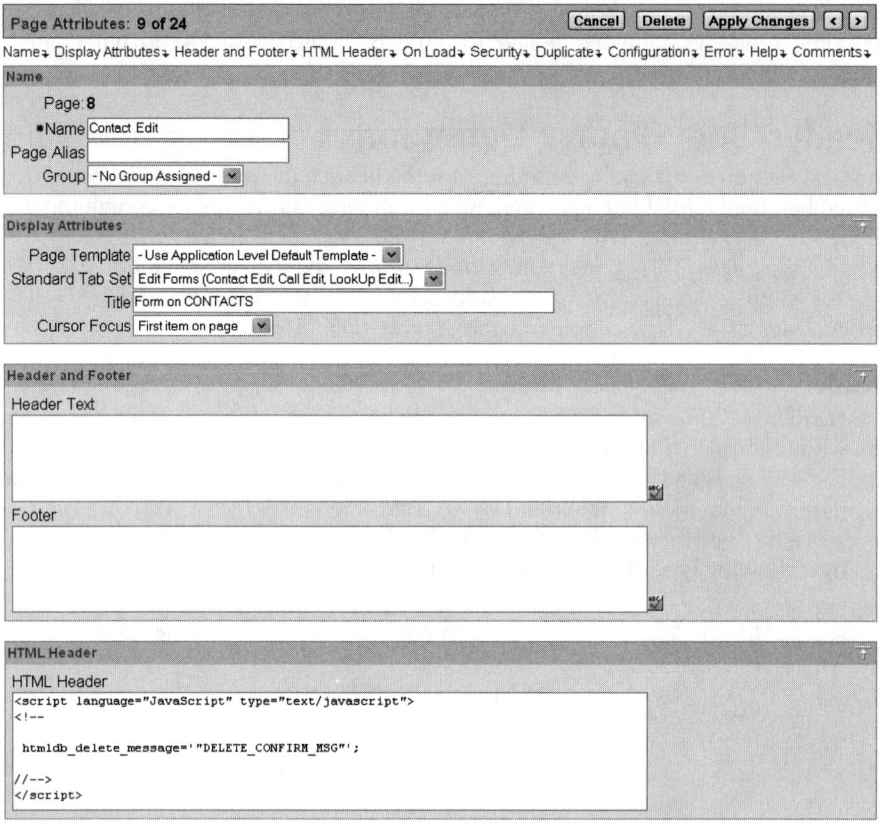

FIGURE 6-7   *Edit page—source for substitution variables*

#HEAD# substitution variables. Here's a list of the other substitution variables allowed in the Header section:

    #ONLOAD#
    #NAVIGATION_BAR#
    #FORM_OPEN#
    #NOTIFICATION_MESSAGE#
    #SUCCESS_MESSAGE#
    #GLOBAL_NOTIFICATION#

Body Section

The Body section contains the HTML tags and substitution variables for the BODY section of the HTML document. This is the section through which the majority of your page will be created. You can define the location of your main body content and position up to eight different regions for your page. If you are using tabs and sub-tabs, their location will also be defined here. The following is a listing of code from a BODY section definition:

```html
<body #ONLOAD#>
#FORM_OPEN#
<table width="100%" cellpadding="0" cellspacing="0" border="0" summary="">
  <tr>
    <td valign="top" class="t1Logo">#LOGO#</td>
    <td valign="top" class="t1Logo">
      <img src=#WORKSPACE_IMAGES#change_user2.gif />
    </td>
    <td align="right" valign="top">#NAVIGATION_BAR#</td>
  </tr>
  <tr>
    <td>&APP_USER.</td>
  </tr>
</table>
<table width="100%" cellpadding="0" cellspacing="0" border="0" summary="">
  <tr>
    <td colspan="5" class="t1ParentTabHolder">
      <table border="0" cellpadding="0" cellspacing="0" summary="" align="right">
        <tr><td><br/></td>
          #TAB_CELLS#
        </tr>
      </table>
    </td>
  </tr>
  <tr>
    <td class="t1topbarLeft" valign="top">
      <img src="#IMAGE_PREFIX#themes/theme_1/top_bar_far_left.png" alt="" />
    </td>
    <td align="right" class="t1topbarLeft" colspan="2"  valign="top">
      <img src="#IMAGE_PREFIX#themes/theme_1/top_barleft2_1.png" alt="" /></td>
    <td align="right" class="t1topbarLeft" valign="top">
      <img src="#IMAGE_PREFIX#themes/theme_1/top_barleft2_2.png" alt="" /></td>
    <td class="t1topbarMiddle" valign="top">
      <table height="100%" cellpadding="0" cellspacing="0" border="0" summary="">
        <tr>
          <td height="20"><br/></td>
        </tr>
        <tr>
          <td valign="bottom" height="20">#REGION_POSITION_01#</td>
        </tr>
      </table></td>
    <td valign="top">
      <img src="#IMAGE_PREFIX#themes/theme_1/top_bar_right.png" alt="" /></td>
  </tr>
  <tr>
    <td class="t1PageLeft" colspan="3" align="left" valign="top">
      #REGION_POSITION_02#
    </td>
    <td><br/></td>
    <td class="t1PageRight" colspan="2">
      <table summary="" cellpadding="0" width="100%" cellspacing="0" border="0">
        <tr>
          <td width="100%" valign="top" class="t1PageBody">
            <div class="t1messages">
              #GLOBAL_NOTIFICATION##SUCCESS_MESSAGE##NOTIFICATION_MESSAGE#
            </div>
            #BOX_BODY##REGION_POSITION_04##REGION_POSITION_05##REGION_POSITION_06#
            #REGION_POSITION_07##REGION_POSITION_08#
          </td>
          <td valign="top">#REGION_POSITION_03#<br /></td>
        </tr>
```

```
      </table>
    </td>
  </tr>
</table>
```

This example contains a lot of HTML tags that you would expect to see in the body of a regular HTML page, but it also has a large number of substitution variables. This particular example defines a page that has a logo image, a navigation menu, one set of tabs, a side navigation bar, a breadcrumb-type menu, and a region for a report. Figure 6-8 shows a page based on this template.

The #ONLOAD# substitution variable in the <body> tag is used for JavaScript that will be executed when the page is first loaded. The value that will be substituted at run time is entered in the On Load JavaScript section of the Edit Page section, as shown here.

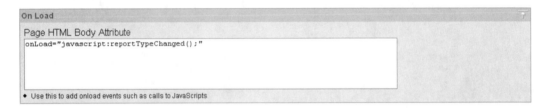

The #FORM_OPEN# substitution variable is placed where you would normally place the HTML <form> tag. If a page using this template is to be submitted, you must include this substitution variable in your template. There is no source for this substitution variable; HTML DB will generate the necessary code.

The next section of HTML code defines a table that contains the two logo images and the navigation bar. The first logo image is placed using the #LOGO# substitution variable, which

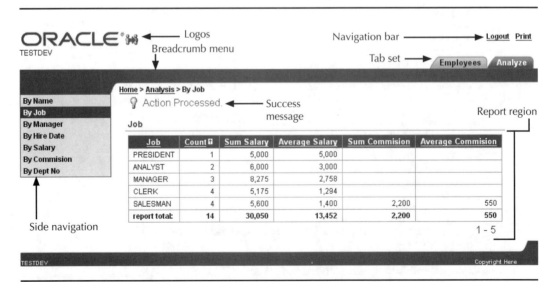

FIGURE 6-8 *Template base page*

derives its source from the Image and Logo Image Attributes fields in the Logo section of Application Attributes. We have already seen the use of the #IMAGE_PREFIX# for an image that came with HTML DB, but here we see another substitution variable, #WORKSPACE_IMAGES#, which allows you to use an image that is imported into your workspace. Simply include this substitution variable before the name of the image. For further details on managing image files, see Chapter 7. The #NAVIGATION_BAR# substitution variable specifies the location of the navigation bar. For more information about navigation bars, see Chapter 11. The source for the substitution variable comes from the navigation bar sub template definition (see the "Sub-template Definitions" section, later in this chapter).

Notice the use of both regular HTML style elements, such as <td height="20">, and Cascading Style Sheet classes, such as <table class="t1Logo">. Remember, the CSS was specified in the Header section of the template. Also note the use of the substitution variable &APP_USER. in <td> &APP_USER.</td>, which retrieves the current username.

The next section of HTML code defines a table and a table row that displays the standard tabs. The substitution variable #TAB_CELLS# is used to position the display of the tabs. The value for this variable comes from the Standard Tab Attribute section of the page template (for further explanation, see the "Standard Tab and Parent Tab Attributes" section, later in this chapter). It is possible to position your tabs anywhere on the page you would like. The #TAB_CELLS# substitution variable can be placed in the Header, Body, or Footer section. If your page also contains parent tabs, you would place the #PARENT_TAB_CELLS# substitution variable in its own table row. This could be in the same table or a different table definition.

The next group of HTML, which includes three image definitions that use the #IMAGE_PREFIX# substitution variable and the #REGION_POSITION_01# substitution variable, make up the bar below the tab and the region used for the breadcrumb menu. The following group uses one image, and the #REGION_POSITION-02# substitution variable is used to define the region where the side navigation bar is located.

The next three substitution variables used are #GLOBAL_NOTIFICATION#, #NOTIFICATION_MESSAGE#, and #SUCCESS_MESSAGE#. The #GLOBAL_NOTIFICATOIN# substitution variable gets its source from the Global Notification field in the Application Attributes. The substitution variable #NOTIFICATION_MESSAGES# will be replaced with a summary of inline error messages from item validation. When creating a validation, you may choose to display the error messages next to the associated items, all together in the #NOTIFICATION_MESSAGE# location, or in both places. The #SUCCESS_MESSAGE# substitution variable defines the location for the display of the page-level success and error messages.

In the remainder of the HTML code, a number of substitution variables are used, #BOX_BODY# and #REGION_POSITION_O3# through #REGION_POSITION_08#. The region position variables specify the locations for different regions within the page. You may create a template with up to eight different regions, #REGION_POSITION_01# through #REGION_POSITION_08#. When designing your template, you might use one region on the side of your page for a navigation section, another for a breadcrumb menu across the top, one in the center for the main content, and another at the bottom of the page. It does not matter in what order you place the region positions within your HTML code. Notice that #REGION_POSITION_03# is actually placed after all the other region positions.

The region positions are used in your page definition. As you define a page and create its regions, you specify, through a pick list, the template region position in which you would like your regions displayed. It is not necessary to use every template region position when creating a page that uses that template.

Footer

The Footer section contains the HTML tags and substitution variables for the Footer section of the HTML document. Generally little is placed in this section. If you want to consistently conclude your page with something, this is where it will go. The following is a listing of code from the Footer section of the template for the page displayed in Figure 6-8.

```
<table width="100%" cellpadding="0" cellspacing="0" border="0" summary="">
  <tr>
    <td>
      <img src="#IMAGE_PREFIX#themes/theme_1/bot_bar_left.png" alt="" />
    </td>
    <td class="t1BotbarMiddle">
      <div id="t1user">&APP_USER.</div>
    </td>
    <td class="t1BotbarMiddle">
      <div id="t1copy">Copyright Here</div>
    </td>
    <td>
      <img src="#IMAGE_PREFIX#themes/theme_1/bot_bar_right.png" alt="" />
    </td>
  </tr>
</table>
<br/>
#FORM_CLOSE#
</body>
</html>
```

This example contains several substitution variables. The #IMAGE_PREFIX# variable is used again in specifying the images that make up the solid bar seen across the bottom of the screen in Figure 6-8. Notice that the user and the copyright notice appear to be in the solid bar. The bar is actually made up of the left image and the right image and two <td class="t1BotbarMiddle"> tags. The class definition gives the table cells the proper background and size to blend seamlessly with the two images.

The last substitution variable is the #FORM_CLOSE# variable. Although Oracle recommends this variable be placed in the Body section, it is acceptable to place it in the Footer section. In fact, this code was clipped from one of the templates that came in the HTML DB repository. If you have a #FORM_OPEN# substitution variable in your template, you must have a #FORM_CLOSE# substitution variable. It simply specifies the position for the HTML form close tag. The only requirement is that it must be placed after the #BODY_BOX# substitution variable.

Default Display Points

The Default Display Points section contains two sections: Breadcrumb Display Point and Sidebar Display Point. Each of these fields allows you to select a position for each element's default display position. This information is only used by the Create Application Wizard. If the template is used while creating an application that has a breadcrumb menu or a side navigation bar, those elements will be placed in the selected positions.

Sub-template Definitions

Some templates contain sub-templates. A sub-template is a portion of a template that is defined in the later part of the template definition page and referred to in an earlier section of the template with a substitution variable.

Success Message

This sub template will be the value for the #SUCCESS_MESSAGE# substitution variable used in the Body section. This sub-template is where you specify the HTML for formatting the content of the success message. This sub-template also uses the #SUCCESS_MESSAGE# substitution variable. This could be a little confusing because the same substitution variable is used for two different things. When it is used here, it is substituted with the actual text of a success message after a page is processed successfully; when it is used in the Body section, it is substituted with the value of this sub-template. The light bulb and "Action Processed" text seen in Figure 6-8 are the results of the following code:

```
<table class="std">
  <tr>
    <td align="right" width="24">
      <img src="#WORKSPACE_IMAGES#wwv_light.gif>" width="24" height="23"
       alt="success" >
    </td>
    <td>
      <span style="color:#336699;font-size:10pt;text-align:left;
                 vertical-align:bottom;">
        #SUCCESS_MESSAGE#
      </span>
    </td>
  </tr>
</table>
```

Navigation Bar

This sub-template is the source for the value of the substitution variable #NAVIGATION_BAR# used in the Body section. This is where you format the navigation bar specified in the Shared Components section of an application. Two items—Help and Logout—were defined for the navigation bar shown in Figure 6-8. The following listing of code is used to display the example's navigation bar. The substitution variable #BAR_BODY# is used to place the actual contents of the navigation bar. The contents of this substitution variable can be controlled even further if desired. See the upcoming "Navigation Bar Entry" section for more details.

```
<table>
  <tr>
    <td>
      <br/>
    </td>
    #BAR_BODY#
  </tr>
</table>
```

Navigation Bar Entry

If you want extreme control of the way the items in the navigation bar are displayed, this is the section where that is accomplished. Note that it is not necessary to define this sub-template; the items in a navigation bar will display fine without any entry here. The code entered here controls the presentation of each individual navigation item placed in the navigation bar's #BAR_BODY#. You can use eight different substitution variables in creating this sub-template. They can all be found in the help for the section by clicking on the title of the section. The following code listing uses two of the substitution variables. The first, #LINK#, will receive the actual URL link of the navigation item. The second, #TEXT#, will receive the text of the navigation item.

```
<a href=#LINK# style="color:#336699;font-size:10pt;text-align:left;
                      vertical-align:bottom;">
   #TEXT#
</a>
```

Notification

This sub-template defines the value for the #NOTIFICATION_MESSAGE# substitution variable used in the header. The only substitution variable available for this section is the #MESSAGE# variable. Include this variable in any HTML code you would like to use to format the notification message. This section is very similar to the "Success Message" section, earlier in this chapter.

Standard Tab and Parent Tab Attributes

The two sections for controlling the look and feel of the page tabs are the Standard Tab Attributes section and the Parent Tab Attribute section. The fields in these sections are identical. If your template contains only one set of tabs, they will be defined in the Standard Tab Attribute section. If your template contains parent tabs and sub-tabs, the parent tabs are defined in the Parent Tab Attribute section and the sub-tabs are defined in the Standard Tab Attribute section.

Each of these sections contains two fields: Current Tab and Non Current Tab. If the template was defined in an earlier version of HTML DB, the fields Current Tab Font Attribute and Non Current Tab Font Attribute will appear after each corresponding tab field. These fields were removed in version 1.6. The formatting that was contained in these fields can simply be included in the tab definition fields.

NOTE
The Tab Font Attribute fields were deprecated in version 1.6.

The HTML specified in the Standard Tab Attributes will be substituted within the header, body, or footer—wherever you placed the #TAB_CELLS# substitution variable. The code for the parent tabs will go wherever the #PARENT_TAB_CELLS# substitution variable is placed within the header, body, or footer definition. Remember, these substitution variables can be placed anywhere on the page. Therefore, your tabs could be at the top part of the page like most HTML DB standard themes, or they could be placed at the bottom of the page like a spreadsheet application.

We will look at two methods for tabs. These methods have a similar structure—a three-cell, single-row table within a table cell. The three table cells format the look of the tab. The first is the start of the tab, the second is the center and is where the name will appear, and the third is the close of the tab, as demonstrated by the following code outline:

```
<td>
  <table>
    <tr>
      <td> table cell for front part of tab </td>
      <td> table cell for middle part of tab, with tab name and link</td>
      <td> table cell for end part of tab </td>
    </tr>
  </table>
</td>
```

The first method is the easiest method, in that it uses only one substitution variable. This code listing produces a tab set similar to the one shown here.

The first table cell uses an image that makes up the slanting part of the left side of the tab. The second table cell uses a CSS class that simply has a background color that matches that of the image in the first cell. The #TAB_TEXT# substitution variable takes care of displaying the label and creating the link for the target page. The #TAB_INLINE_EDIT# substitution variable is used internally by HTML DB to display edit links when a developer runs the page and clicks on the Show Edit Links in the Developer's Toolbar. The last table cell uses an image that makes up the right side of the tab. The following listing of code was for the Current Tab Attributes section. The only difference in the code between the current and noncurrent version is the CSS class and the images referenced in each cell.

```
<td>
  <img src="#IMAGE_PREFIX#themes/theme_1/tab_on_left.png" border="0"/>
</td>
<td class="t1ParentTabCenterOn">
  #TAB_LABEL##TAB_INLINE_EDIT#
</td>
<td>
  <img src="#IMAGE_PREFIX#themes/theme_1/tab_on_right.png" border="0"/>
</td>
```

The second method also follows the same basic outline. However, it uses individual substitution variables for the tab's link and label, #TAB_LINK# and #TAB_LABEL#, respectively. Like in the first method, the first cell is the left part of the tab, the second is the middle of the tab, and the last cell is the right side of the tab. This code produces the tabs shown here.

In this code, you will notice that each of the three table cells has an <a> tag defined with an href element that utilizes #TAB_LINK#. This allows the user to click on any part of the tab to activate the link. In the previous example, only the center part of the tab would activate the link. Although this seems like a minor detail, it makes the user's experience that much easier. In this example, no CSS classes are used; rather, the images are referenced directly. This set of tabs uses six different images—three for the active tab and three for the inactive tab. The code example is for the active tab. Again, there is an image for the left part of the tab, one for the center of the tab, and one for the right side of the tab. These images were created using a good image editor. The left and right images are the size of the curved parts of the tab; however, the center image is only a few pixels wide. The left and right images are used as the actual source for the <a> tag, whereas the center cell uses the image as a background for the entire table cell. This allows the tabs to be a variable width depending on the label of each tab.

```
<td>
  <table cellpadding="0" cellspacing="0" border="0" style="margin-left:6px;">
    <tr>
      <td style="width:20px;">
        <a href="#TAB_LINK#">
         <img src="#WORKSPACE_IMAGES#tab_active_left.png"
              alt="#TAB_LABEL#" border="0" />
        </a>
      </td>
      <td background="#WORKSPACE_IMAGES#tab_active_center.png"nowrap="nowrap">
        <a href="#TAB_LINK#">
          #TAB_LABEL#
        </a>
      </td>
      <td style="width:15px;">
        <a href="#TAB_LINK#">
          <img src="#WORKSPACE_IMAGES#tab_active_right.png"
               alt="#TAB_LABEL#" border="0" />
        </a>
      </td>
    </tr>
  </table>
</td>
```

Image-based Tab Attributes

This section allows you to use an image for a specific tab. If you are going to use images for your tabs, you need to place <td>#TAB_IMAGE#</td> in each of these fields, although the help for each of these fields tells you to put in <td>#TAB_TEXT#</td>. The images that will be displayed are actually defined in the definition of the individual tabs. The Edit Standard Tab page contains an Images section. In this section, you specify two images for the tab—one for when the tab is the current tab and one for when the tab is not the current tab. There is also a field for entering HTML attributes for the images, such as border, width, and height.

Multicolumn Region Table Attributes

When the HTML DB engine displays regions in columns in the same region position, it renders them in an HTML table. This section contains a single field, Region Table Attributes. This field allows you to control the attributes of the table that the HTML DB engine creates for displaying multiple columns of regions in the same region position. The values entered in this field will be incorporated into the <table> tag.

Error Page Template Control

This section is where you format the display of the error message and the link to return to the page that produced the error. A default error page can be specified for a theme, as described in the earlier section "Specifying a Theme's Default Template" and shown in Figure 6-3. In the template specified as the default error page, you would want to add code to this section for formatting the error message. If you do not specify a default template for the error page, and an error is specified to display on a separate error page, the template for the current page will be used as the template for the error page. Therefore, this section can be utilized in any page template, whether it is the default error page template or not.

Two substitution variables are used in the Error Page Template field: #MESSAGE# and #BACK_LINK#. These two variables take care of displaying the text of the error message and providing a link back to the originating page. The following code listing is a simple example of HTML code that you might use to format this section:

```
<img src="#IMAGE_PREFIX#error.gif">#MESSAGE#
<br>
<br>
<a href="#BACK_LINK#">Return to previous page to correct the error</a>
```

CHAPTER
7

Using the Application
Utilities

n the previous chapters, we have explored the Application Builder and used many of its primary features to construct various elements of an application. In this chapter, we will delve into some less frequently used components of the Application Builder. All the features covered in this chapter are accessible from either the Shared Components icon or the Export/Import icon on the Application Builder main page.

Shared Components   Export / Import

Translating an Application into Another Language

HTML DB provides several nice utilities to make publishing your application in multiple languages relatively simple. The methodology used allows you to develop and maintain a single application while simultaneously deploying several different language versions of the same application. When you want to have multiple translations of an application, you first develop the application in a primary language and then translate that application to other languages. Because translation is a large task, the translation process can be an iterative one that occurs throughout your application development. You do not have to have the primary application totally completed before starting the translation process. The translation work that you do throughout development will not be lost.

The translation utilities are available on the Shared Components page through the Shared Components icon on the Application Builder main page. You'll find two links under the Translation section of this page: Translation Services and Manage Messages. Translation Services allows you to translate all the static text used throughout your application—column headings, button labels, link text, menu items, section headers, and much more. The Manage Messages utilities allow you to manage dynamically created portions of your application. We will look at both of these utilities.

Translation Services

Translating an application of any size is no small task. Translation Services will make it easier, but the process is tedious nonetheless. The Translation Services link from the Shared Components page takes you to the Translate Application page shown in Figure 7-1. This page lists the steps necessary to translate an application. Some of these steps are automated, and some are manual. Step 5 on this list takes you to the same location that the Manage Messages link from the Shared Components page takes you. This makes this page the home page for all translation activities. Note the breadcrumb menu at the top of Figure 7-1. The current location, Translate Application, is the last item. Every other page in the translation process will be a child of this page, and you can return to this page by clicking its link in the breadcrumb menu.

The first four steps listed in Figure 7-1 walk you through the process of translating all the static text in your application. Simply stated, the tasks are:

- Identify a new target language.

- Extract all the static text into an XML file that contains entries for your primary language and entries for your new language.

■ Manually translate the target entries.

■ Import the file back into HTML DB.

■ Publish the new application.

Clicking on the first step will take you to the Application Language Mappings page shown in Figure 7-2. This page lists any existing mappings you have and provides a Create button for creating new mappings. The table shows the unique identifier for the primary language application, the unique identifier for the translation language application, the language code for the translation, an image path if you wish to use different images, and finally any translation comments. Clicking on the Create button takes you to a page where you can enter all these fields for a new translation mapping. Even though you enter a new unique numeric application identifier, the translated application will still be accessed through the URL for the application's primary language. In this case, the URL to access all language versions of the application is http://server.here.com:7779/pls/htmldb/f?p=100. If the browser's default language setting is German (de), the 701 application will be run.

NOTE
Application identifiers must be unique across all workspaces for your entire HTML DB application.

The second link—Seed and export the translation text of your application into a translation file—takes you to a wizard. The wizard copies all the translatable text into a translation text repository. After that, you can export the repository into an XLIFF file, which is a type of XML file.

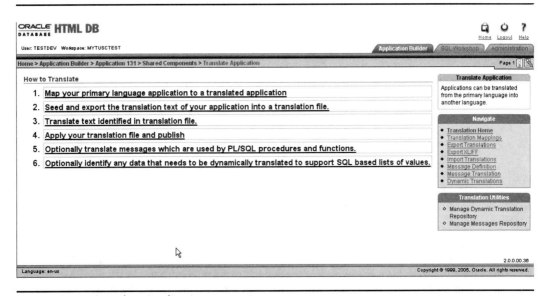

FIGURE 7-1 *Translate Application page*

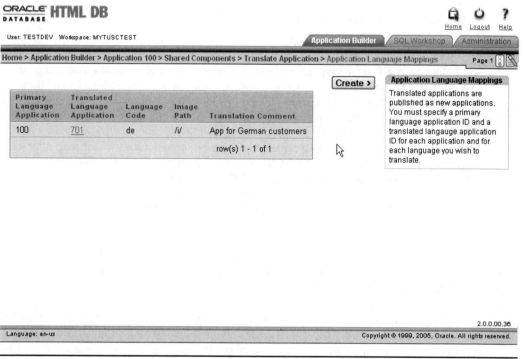

FIGURE 7-2 *Application Language Mappings*

The first step of the wizard allows you to select the mapping you want to seed and export. The mappings are listed using the unique identifiers, as shown here.

Once you select the language mapping and click on the Seed Translatable Text button, you will be taken to the next screen of the wizard, shown in Figure 7-3. This step of the wizard allows you to make some selections that will determine what is exported into the XLIFF file; XML Localization Interchange File Format (XLIFF) is an industry standard for translation. From this page, you can

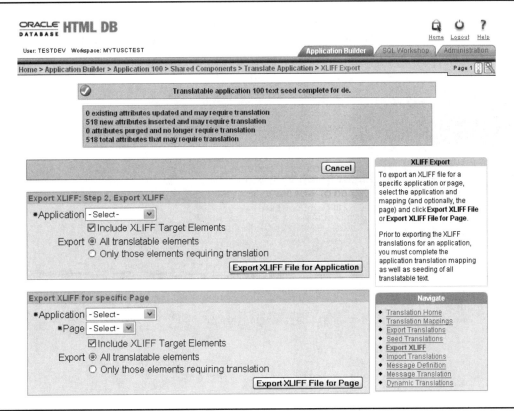

FIGURE 7-3   *Step 2 of the wizard: XLIFF Export*

select to export for the entire application or for a single page. If you have already been through this process before and are only after the new items to be translated, you can select the radio button for only those elements requiring translation. We will look at the content of an XLIFF file later, but basically it creates a source and a target element for each item that needs translating. If you only want the source items, you can exclude the target element tags from the file by deselecting the check box.

Clicking on either of the export buttons will open a dialog box to save the file to your local machine. Once you have saved the file, you can edit it with any text editor or XML file editor. Even XLIFF-specific editors are available that you can use. The code shown below is a small portion of an exported XLIFF file. When it was first exported, the text between the <source> and <target> tags was the same text. The tedious part of translating an application comes in changing all the source tags to the target language. At the top of Figure 7-3, you can see an analysis of the attributes in the application that might need translating. You'll notice that over 500 items in this sample application might need translating. For this example, I selected the display text off a couple pages and then used a free online translation page to translate the items. I then used a text editor to perform a search-and-replace operation on the target tags. Notice that there are two entries for PRINT. Each of these is for a different translation unit. This is why the search-and-replace approach makes sense. Various products and services are available to help you translate an XLIFF file.

```xml
<?xml version="1.0" encoding="UTF-8"?>
<!--
 ******************
 ** Source    : 100
 ** Source Lang: en-us
 ** Target    : 701
 ** Target Lang: de
 ** Filename:    f100_701_en-us_de.xlf
 ** Generated By: TESTDEV
 ** Date:       12-MAR-2005 11:38:48
 ******************
 -->
<xliff version="1.0">
<file original="f100_701_en-us_de.xlf" source-language="en-us"
                target-language="de" datatype="html">
<header></header>
<body>
  <trans-unit id="S-2-300454818975306150-100">
   <source>Logout</source>
   <target>Abmeldung</target>
  </trans-unit>
  <trans-unit id="S-2-300454920439306151-100">
   <source>Print</source>
   <target>Druck</target>
  </trans-unit>
  <trans-unit id="S-2.1-300454818975306150-100">
   <source>Logout</source>
   <target>Abmeldung</target>
  </trans-unit>
  <trans-unit id="S-2.1-300454920439306151-100">
   <source>Print</source>
   <target>Druck</target>
  </trans-unit>
  <trans-unit id="S-4-300454335007306144-100">
   <source>Home</source>
   <target>Heim</target>
  </trans-unit>
  <trans-unit id="S-4-300454415843306148-100">
   <source>Customers</source>
   <target>Kunden</target>
  </trans-unit>
  <trans-unit id="S-4-300454535018306149-100">
   <source>Products</source>
   <target>Produkten</target>
  </trans-unit>
```

The third step listed in Figure 7-1 is this manual process of translating the target tags in the XLIFF file. Although the step is an actual link, it takes you nowhere. The forth step on the Translate Application page allows you to apply the XLIFF file changes to your application and publish the translated application. Clicking on that link takes you to the XLIFF Translation Files page, shown in Figure 7-4. This page lists any XLIFF files that have been uploaded and allows you to upload more or delete any existing ones. Clicking on the Upload XLIFF File button takes you to a page where you can enter the title, add a description, and select a file from your local computer to upload. Once you upload the file, you return to this page and the new file will be listed. You might want to keep one or two of your previous versions just in case you want to undo any changes.

To apply the XLIFF translation file and publish your new application, click on the magnifying glass icon next to the translation file you want to apply. This takes you to the XLIFF File Details page shown in Figure 7-5. This page allows you to confirm you have selected the correct file and to specify the mapping to which you want to apply the file. If you selected the wrong version of the file, you can select another from the pick list at the top. Once you have made your selections, click the Apply XLIFF Translation File button to apply the changes. This will update the translation repository created earlier.

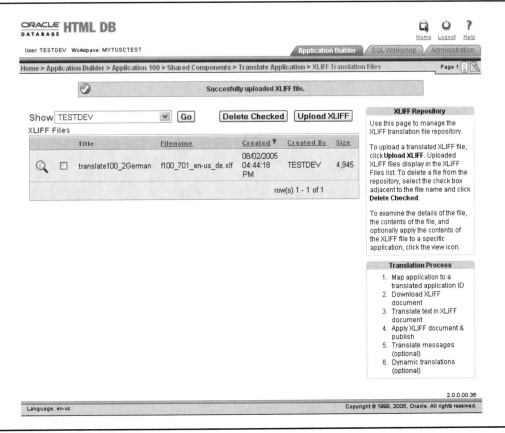

FIGURE 7-4 *XLIFF Translation Files page*

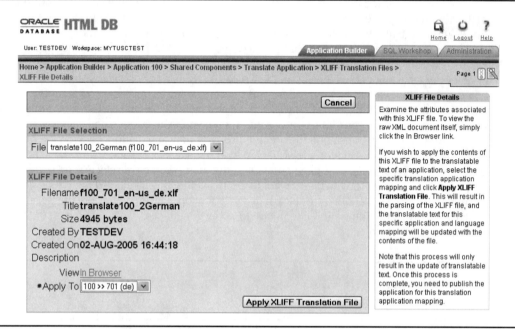

FIGURE 7-5 *XLIFF File Details page*

The following page confirms the update of the translation repository and allows you to publish the application. To create or re-create the translated application, all you must do is select the mapping from the pick list and click on the Publish Application button.

Once you have published the application, it is available for use. Figure 7-6 shows the main page of the primary language application, and Figure 7-7 shows the German version. Both examples were generated from the same URL. One of the browsers has its default language set to German (de). This works if the Application Language Derived From option in the Globalization section of the Edit Application Attributes page has been set to Browser. See Chapter 4 for more details on editing application attributes.

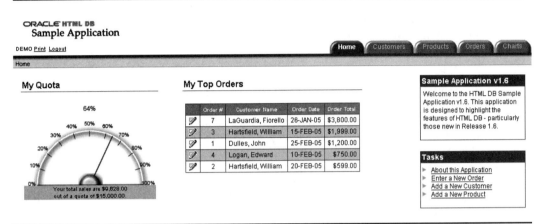

FIGURE 7-6 *Sample application primary language*

Manage Messages

If you compare Figures 7-6 and 7-7, you will see that almost all the text has been converted. The text in the logo is part of the image and therefore not translated. If you had other images, you could have specified an alternate image directory and changed the image. The other text that was not translated is the text below the speedometer graph. If you had searched the XLIFF file for this text, you would not have found it. The reason is this text is dynamically created in a region source. Although HTML DB provides a method for dealing with the translation of dynamic text, Manage Messages, it won't work in this situation because the source for the text is not a PL/SQL source. The only way around this one would be to define the region twice—once with the text in English, and the other with the text in German. On both regions you would put a conditional display for the current language.

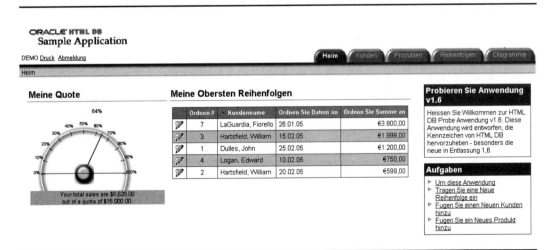

FIGURE 7-7 *Sample application translated to German*

Let's take a look at how Manage Messages works within PL/SQL for dynamic translation. First, you start with a text message, which is predefined text that contains substitution variables that can be filled dynamically at run time. We will use the text

```
Your total sales are $9,628.00 out of a quota of $15,000.00
```

as an example for translation via messages. Most of the string is constant, whereas the dollar amounts need to be supplied at run time.

Text messages need only be used when you are planning on translating an application. You get to the Text Messages page, shown in Figure 7-8, using the Manage Messages link in the Translations section of the Shared Components page. This page provides a means of maintaining existing messages as well as creating new ones.

In order to translate a message, we need to create a text message to use as the source. First, we create a text message by clicking on the Create button on the Text Messages page. This takes us to a page where we can name the text message, select the base language, and enter the message. As you can see in next, we specify location of substitutions with the percent sign (%) and a number between 0 and 9. In this example, we use two of the ten possible.

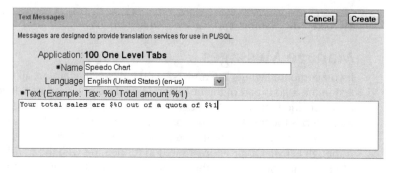

FIGURE 7-8   *Text Messages page*

After creating the new message, you will be returned to the Text Message page. Click on Shared Components in the breadcrumb menu to return to the Shared Components page. From there, you can click on the Translate Application link to return to the Translate Application page, shown earlier in Figure 7-1. Then select the fifth step, labeled "Optionally translate messages which are used by PL/SQL procedures and functions." This takes you to the Translatable Messages page, shown next, which lists all existing messages, each with an Edit and Translate icon. Click on the Translate icon of the message just created. This returns you to an entry page just like the one shown previously, with the same name of the message already filled in. Select a new language and supply the translated text. Then click on the Create button. You will be returned to the Translate Message page, where you will see both of the messages you created with the same name but with different languages, as shown here.

From	English (United States) (en-us)	To	German (Germany) (de)	Display	15	Go

Translatable Messages   Create >

Edit	Translate	Application	Name	Language	Text
📝	📝	100	GREETING_MSG	en-us	Good Morning %0 how's it going?
📝	📝	100	SPEEDO CHART	de	Ihr Gesamtverkauf ist $%0 Aus einer Q
📝	📝	100	SPEEDO CHART	en-us	Your total sales are $%0 out of a quo

row(s) 1 - 3 of 3

To utilize the message in any source of type PL/SQL, you will use the built-in function HTMLDB_ LANG.MESSAGE_P or the built-in procedure HTMLDB_LANG.MESSAGE (see Appendix I for more details). For example, the following would work as the source for a PL/SQL region:

```
HTMLDB_LANG.MESSAGE_p(p_name=>'SPEEDO CHART', p0=>:P1_TOTAL_SALES, p1=>:P1_QUOTA)
```

The function takes in the name of the message and the two values for substitution. Because a language is not specified, it will pick up the default language.

Managing CSS, Image Files, and Static Files

In Chapter 6, we talked about the use of images and Cascading Style Sheets (CSS) in template definitions. Often developers will rely on the graphic arts department to define the standard look and feel for web-based applications. Developers will be given standard classes to use in defining web elements, and the graphic arts department will create a CSS to implement the desired look and feel. Images for logos, buttons, and tabs might also come from the art department. Before images or Cascading Style Sheets can be used, they must be available to the HTML DB application.

HTML DB provides an interface for uploading and saving image files, CSS files, and even static files. The Shared Components page contains a Files section, with links for each of these types.

Cascading Style Sheet Files

Following the Cascading Style Sheet link from the Files section of the Shared Components page takes you to the CSS Repository Page, shown in Figure 7-9. From here, you can see the existing CSS files, edit existing files, and load new ones. Like with many HTML DB pages, if you have a large number of items displayed in the report area, the page provides you with a method to search for the one you are looking for. Clicking the Go button will cause the report to display

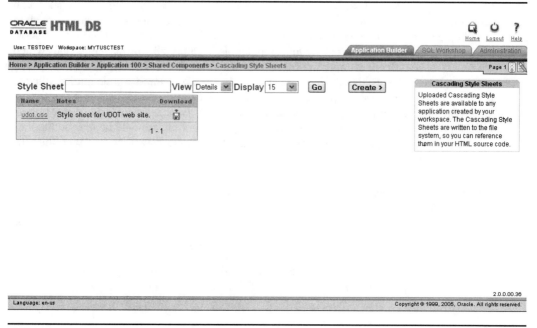

FIGURE 7-9 *CSS Repository page*

only files whose name or notes contain the text you entered into the find box. Clicking the Create button takes you to a page where you can select a file from your local machine to upload and add comments about the file before uploading. Clicking the filename for a specific CSS will take you to a page where you can actually edit the contents of the file as well as update the notes. The Download icon allows you to download the file to your local drive.

Image Files

Like the CSS link, the Images link on the Shared Components page takes you to a repository page. Figure 7-10 shows the Image Repository page. Images can be workspace images available to any application in the workspace, or they can be application images available only to the associated application. To refer to a workspace image in a template, you prefix it with the substitution variable #WORKSPACE_IMAGES#. For application images, use #APP_IMAGES#. The Image Repository includes a pick list to limit the images displayed to application images, workspace images, or both. The search function also finds images with the text of the find field anywhere in an image name. For more details on the use of images, see Chapter 6.

Static Files

The Static Files link from the Shared Components page also takes you to a repository page for managing static files. Like the other file repository pages, the Static Repository page displays a report of existing static files with a search option, links to edit each existing file, and a Create

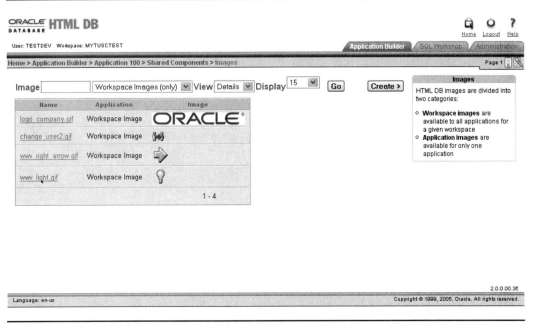

FIGURE 7-10 *Image Repository page*

button that allows you to upload a new static file. Static files can be used for static HTML pages developed outside of HTML DB, uploaded and then referred to from within any HTML region using the #WORKSPACE_IMAGES# substitution variable. For example, here's a link to a static instruction page:

```
<a href=#WORKSPACE_IMAGES#IntructionsPart1.htm>More Instructions</a>
```

Web Services

Web services are applications or segments of business logic that are accessible over the Internet using SOAP (Simple Object Access Protocol) for communicating input parameters and results. Web services can be thought of as little black-box applications that take a defined input and return an expected output. Those inputs and outputs are defined in a specification known as *WSDL (Web Service Description Language)* and can be found in UDDI (Universal Description, Discovery, and Integration) registries.

Following the Web Services link from the Shared Components page takes you to the Web Service References page, shown in Figure 7-11, which lists any existing web service references. From there, you can edit or test any existing web service or create a new web service reference through a multistep wizard started by clicking on the Create button. The paper and pencil icon allows you to edit the name and SOAP URL endpoint, while the Name link allows you view a Web Service Reference detail page.

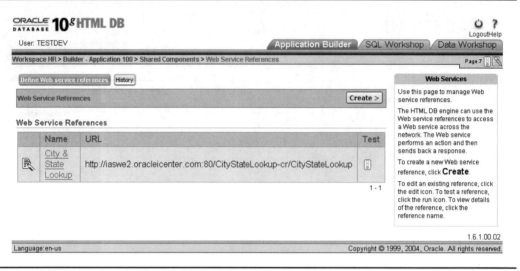

FIGURE 7-11   *Web Service References page*

As stated, the definition of a web service is contained in a WSDL. You can either directly specify the location of a WSDL or search for one in a UDDI registry. The first step of the wizard, shown in Figure 7-12, allows you to choose one of these options. Selecting the Yes option to search a UDDI registry will take you through multiple steps to find and specify a WSDL location, whereas selecting No will take you directly to specifying the WSDL location.

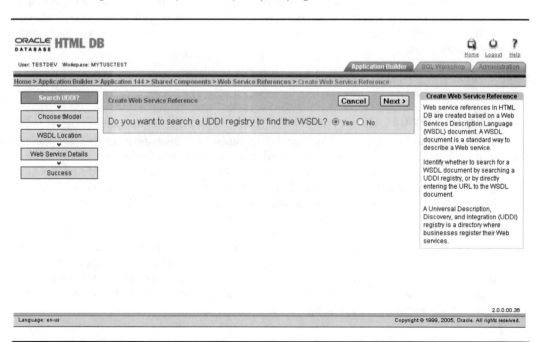

FIGURE 7-12   *Web Service References Wizard*

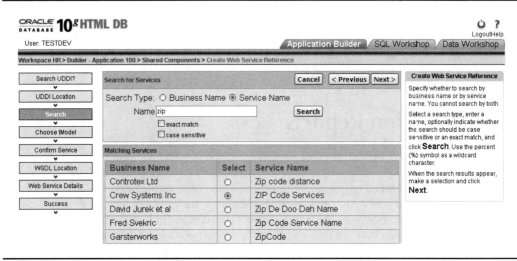

FIGURE 7-13 *Web Service References Wizard's Search page*

The first step in searching for a WSDL is to select from a list of available UDDI registries. Currently, HTML DB supplies four registries, including Oracle OTN. Once you have selected a registry, you can enter parameters to search for a particular web service, as shown in Figure 7-13. Once you click on the Search button, you can select a service from the matching results and click on Next.

If the service has multiple models, you need to select a specific model. Otherwise, you go to the confirmation page, which summarizes the service you have selected. After clicking on the Next button again, you will navigate to the WSDL location page, which will have the URL for the WSDL filled in for you. If you did not search a UDDI, you would manually enter a URL for a WSDL on this page. The next page, shown in Figure 7-14, lists the details about the service, and the final page is a success message.

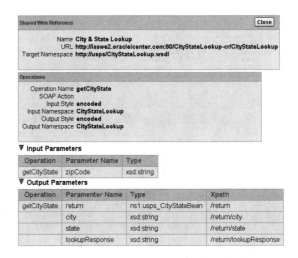

FIGURE 7-14 *Web Service References Details page*

Once a web service reference is created, it can be used in a process. The process will supply values for the input parameters and store the resulting values. For more information on processes, see Chapter 13. However, you can still test the functionality of a web service before creating a process by clicking on the stop light test icon, shown earlier in Figure 7-11. Testing a web service reference allows you to verify the functionality of the web service as well as see the XML from both the request and the response, as shown in Figure 7-15.

Application Reports

HTML DB has provided a large number of canned reports to help you manage your applications. These reports can help you view and edit attributes of your application, review a summary and details of developer changes, and view database object dependencies. With these reports, you can ensure consistency of elements throughout your entire application. The Application Reports page, shown in Figure 7-16, can be accessed through the View Application Reports link in the Tasks panel on the right side of an application's main page. Each of the navigation icons takes you to another page that lists the reports for the corresponding area: Shared Components, Page Components, Activity Reports, and Cross Application Reports. You can use the sub-pages or you can use the drop-down menus, which are activated by clicking on the down arrow on the right side of the icons.

FIGURE 7-15 *Web Service References Test page*

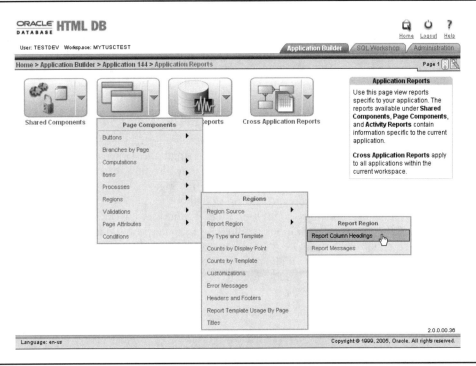

FIGURE 7-16   *Application Reports page*

The application reports are grouped into three main areas: Page Components, Shared Components, and Activity Reports. Many of the reports allow you to view attributes across your application as well as to edit certain attributes across your application. The following reports allow mass-editing of certain attributes:

List of Values

Button Labels

Computation Error Messages

Item Help Text

Error Messages

Report Messages

Validation Error Messages

Item Buttons

Menu Entries

Buttons Displayed in Item Positions

Item Labels

Process Messages

Report Column Headings

Titles

Breadcrumb Entries

Exporting and Importing Applications

HTML DB provides a set of utilities for importing and exporting almost every part of your development environment. These utilities allow you to move an application from one environment to another as well as provide an easy backup and recovery method. If your target environment is in a different instance, you will need to migrate the referenced database objects as well as the application. This can be done using the Oracle database export and import utilities. The complete process of moving an application involves three basic processes: export the application and related files from the source HTML DB instance, import the files into the target HTML DB instance, and install the imported files from the repository. The Export/Import icon on the main Application Builder page takes you to the Export/Import page, whose only option is to select to import or export.

Exporting Application Components

Exporting an application exports all of an application's attributes—from individual items and buttons to regions, pages, and templates—all into a single file. However, to completely move an application from one environment to another, you may also have to export Cascading Style Sheets and images separately. The Export interface, shown in Figure 7-17, is the starting point for all export operations. There are individual export operations for workspaces, applications, Cascading Style Sheets, images, static files, script files, themes, and user interface defaults.

All the different export operations require you to specify the file format for the export. You must choose either UNIX or DOS. A UNIX export file will contain rows delimited by line feeds, whereas DOS export file rows will be delimited by carriage returns and line feeds. For most of the exports, you simply select the specific item to export, click on the export button, and select the location to save the resulting export file.

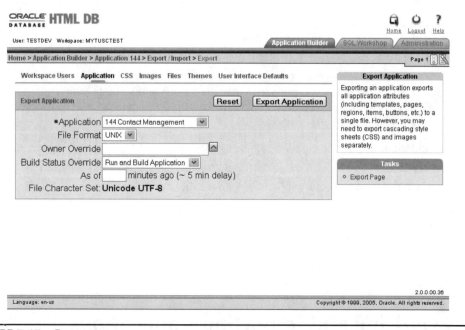

FIGURE 7-17 *Export page*

The option to export a workspace is only available to workspace administrators. This export creates a script containing users and user groups, along with their developer privileges. Selecting the file format is the only option before exporting the workspace.

To export an application, you must select the application, the file format, and the build status. The options for the build status are Run Only and Build and Run the Application. Run Only would be used to export an application to an instance where it cannot be modified. You can also override the application owner and specify a past save point.

Importing Application Components

From the Application Builder main page, follow the Export/Import icon to the Export/Import page and select the Import option. This takes you to the Import page, shown in Figure 7-18. This is the starting point for every type of file import. Click on the Browse button to select the file you wish to import. Select the appropriate file type and specify the same character set as the character set from the source database. Click on the Next button to import the selected file into the file repository.

Once a file is imported, you will receive a success message and an option to install the imported file. You can either proceed with the install at this point or choose to install later from the file repository. To navigate to the repository, use the View Repository link at the bottom of the Import page. Either way, once you select to install an imported file, you will be presented with a screen that contains some final necessary selections prior to installing the file. Figure 7-19 shows the final screen for an application import.

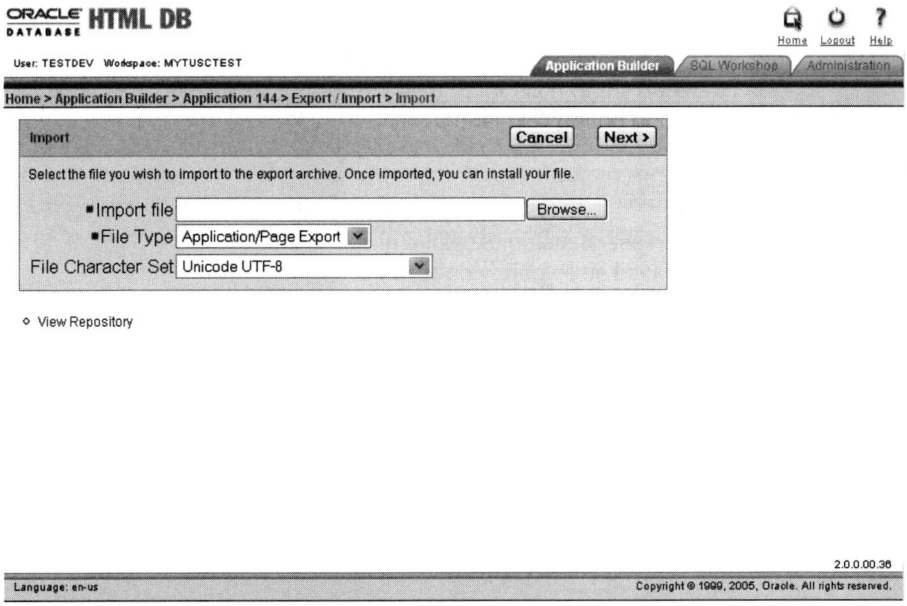

FIGURE 7-18   *Import page*

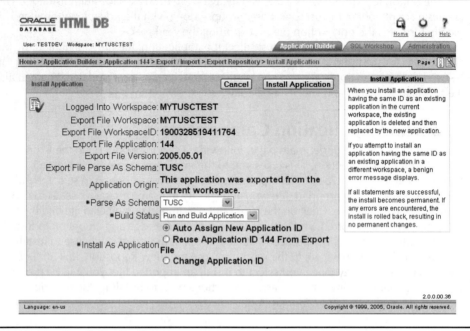

FIGURE 7-19 *Install Application page*

For an application import, you must select the schema that will be used to parse the application. This should be the schema that was exported from the source database and imported into the target database. If all the referenced database objects are not present, you will be unable to build the application. You also have an option to keep or change the application identifier.

Most of the other types of imports only require you to select the application into which you want to install the selected file. Note that at the time of writing this book, importing static files or script files was not yet supported, even though the options were available. You can go through the steps, but you will receive an error stating the operation is not yet supported.

PART
III

Building Web Pages and Components

CHAPTER
8

Building Web Pages

ages are the building blocks for applications. They are the containers for all functionality. In Chapter 5, we looked at building applications through the Create Application Wizards. Utilizing the wizards, we built applications containing functional pages based on existing applications, existing tables, or an imported spreadsheet. We also used a wizard to construct, from scratch, the shell of a new application that contained pages with no functionality. Because of the limited functionality that can be gained by building applications through the wizards based on tables and spreadsheets, the majority of the time you will start building an application using the wizard based on an existing application or from scratch.

In this chapter, we will cover many of the areas needed to construct pages manually. In subsequent chapters, we will go into great detail on the specific components of a web page, but first you need to understand the basics of HTML DB pages and how all the components come together to create a page. You will learn how to create, edit, and delete pages. We will address how a page is rendered, how regions are used, and the ways their display can be controlled. Additionally, we will cover the concepts of how the HTML DB engine produces pages, handles the submission of data, and deals with session and state management.

After you understand the concepts of an HTML DB page and how its parts all work together, you can look in the following chapters for a more detailed discussion of specific page components:

- **Chapter 9**   Reports

- **Chapter 10**   Forms

- **Chapter 11**   Navigation between pages

- **Chapter 12**   Other components, such as charts, LOVs, calendars, and wizards

- **Chapter 13**   Computations, processes, and validations

Adding, Deleting, and Editing Pages

In the section "Creating a New Application from Scratch" in Chapter 5, we created the shell of the Contact Management application. The resulting application's Pages report is shown in Figure 8-1. To navigate to this page, click on the name of the application listed in the Applications report on the Application Builder main page.

Prior to the actual construction of an application, you should have a good idea of the pages needed, based on your application's requirements and design documentation. For the Contact Management application, we determined we needed a home page, report pages for each of the tables, and an edit page for each of the tables. We also decided to use two levels of tabs—the parent tabs being Home, Report, and Edit, with the latter two having child tabs for each table (Contacts, Calls, and LookUps). The wizard helped us create the shell pages, nicely organized into the tab structure. All the pages created contained nothing more than the shared components—see the Page Definition page for the Calls report page in Figure 8-2.

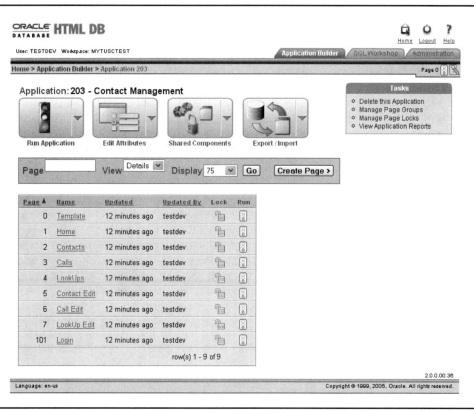

FIGURE 8-1 *Contact Management page listing*

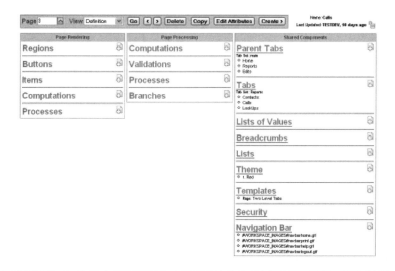

FIGURE 8-2 *Calls page definition created from scratch using a wizard*

The developer must now add all the other components to the pages, such as the reports and the forms for editing. Reports will be cover in depth in Chapter 9, and forms will be covered in Chapter 10. The idea behind having a corresponding form page for every report page is that the report page will display all the existing records with an Edit link for each row that navigates to the corresponding form page so that the user can edit the selected record. The form page can also function as an entry form for creating new records. With this idea, it is easy to see that there must be a relationship between the report pages and the form pages. Although it is possible to create a report for the Calls table on one page and an edit form for the Calls table on another page and then manually create the relationship between them, it is a whole lot easier to let an HTML DB wizard do it for you. In the following section, we walk through the steps for creating a report and the corresponding form page.

Creating Pages

HTML DB provides many wizards for creating new pages. Access to the wizards can be started by clicking on the Create Page button on the application's main page, shown in Figure 8-1, or by clicking on the Create button on a Page Definition page, shown in Figure 8-2. Before you actually start one of the wizards, you have a series of choices. If you start from the application's main page, you will want to select the Form option. If you start from the Page Definition page, you will want to select the Region on This Page option and click on the Next button. You will be presented with all the different region type options, as shown in Figure 8-3.

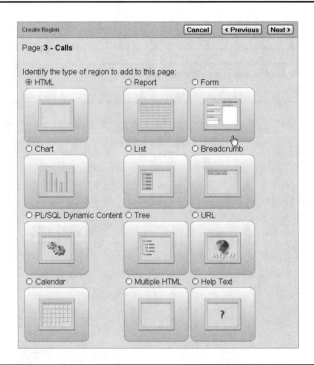

FIGURE 8-3 *Selecting a component type*

The specifics of each of these types will be discussed in more detail in the following chapters. For now, let's select the Form option and move on. The next step allows you to select a particular type of form, as shown next. Detail on each of the different form options will be covered in detail in Chapter 10. Select Form with Report and click on the Next button to start the Query and Update Page Creation Wizard.

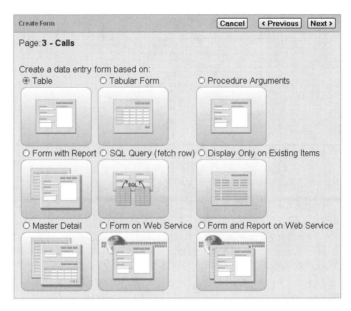

The Query and Update Page Creation Wizard has a number of steps. In the first step, you select the schema that owns the table or view. The second step provides an LOV to select the table or view on which you wish to base the pages. Select the Calls table and click on Next. The Calls table is one of the tables we imported from the spreadsheet in Chapter 5.

The next step of the wizard allows you to enter information about the page on which the report will be created (see Figure 8-4). As usual, the fields marked with a red asterisk are mandatory fields. All fields will be pre-populated with values based on the table you selected. The page number will default to a page that does not exist. We could select, from the LOV, the empty Calls page that was created with the Create Application from Scratch Wizard. If you use an existing page, the next step, Report Tabs, will be skipped. The values for the templates are the defaults specified in the application's theme definition (see Chapter 6 for more information). You may accept the defaults or select other templates from the LOV. The Region Title will be displayed above the report. The Pagination Size specifies the number of rows that will be displayed on a single page (15 is the default, but you may select another value from the LOV).

The next step in the wizard allows you to specify the tab options. You may select not to use tabs, to create a new tab in an existing tab set, or use a tab that is already defined. If you select to create a new tab, you must select the tab set to which it will belong and enter a label for the new tab. If you want to use an existing tab, you will select the tab set from one LOV and the specific tab from another LOV that is dynamically populated based on your first selection. We want to choose to use an existing tab set and reuse an existing tab within that tab set. Once you select that option, a pick list will be displayed for the tab set. Select the Reports tab set, click on Next, select the Calls tab, and then click on Next again.

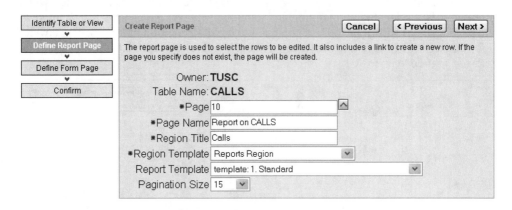

FIGURE 8-4   *Step 2 of the Query and Update Page Creation Wizard*

Selecting the columns to display on the report is the next step in the wizard. The page displays all columns from the table or view that you selected in the second step of the wizard, as shown next. Let's select all the columns except CALLID. As you can see, you can enter an optional WHERE clause (it is not necessary to include WHERE). The clause can be any WHERE clause you can use in a normal SQL statement; it can even reference values of items on other pages within the application. You can expand the Example SQL WHERE Clause entry at the bottom for an example of a WHERE clause. For now, don't include the WHERE clause; we will cover it later. Click on the Next button to continue.

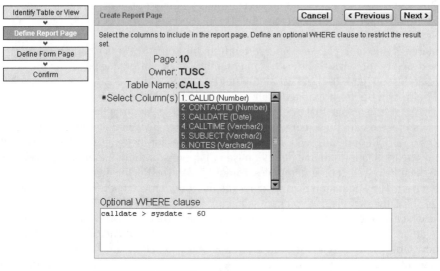

The advantage of using the wizard to create the report and form pages together is that HTML DB will do the work required to tie the two pages together. The next step of the wizard allows you to select the icon that will be used as the means to navigate between the report page and the form page. You may select one of the standard icons included with HTML DB, shown next, or you may select one of your own imported workspace images. For more information on importing images, see Chapter 7. Select an icon and click on the Next button.

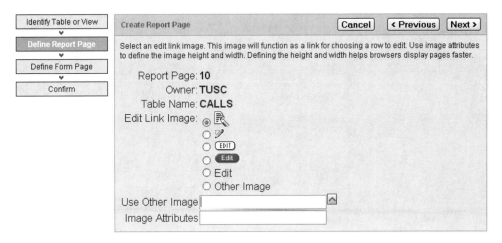

The next two steps in the wizard are for specifying information about the form page and tabs. They are almost identical to the ones used for the report page. This time, let's select an existing page from the LOV. Select the Call Edit page and click on Next. Because an existing page was selected, the step to select the tabs is skipped.

In order for HTML DB to implement the relationship between the report page and the edit page, it must know the primary key of the report table. It must also know the source of the primary key. The next step allows you to select the columns that make up the primary key, as shown next. Unfortunately, the wizard only allows you to specify two columns for the primary key. If the actual primary key is made up of more than two columns, select the first two and then add the others manually.

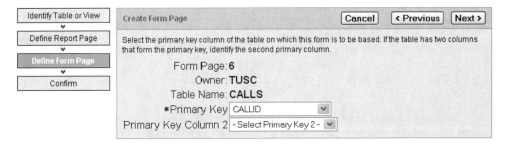

In the next step of the wizard, you specify the source of the primary key. As you can see next, you must select one of three options. If the source is an existing trigger, you only need to select the corresponding radio button. If you select the source to be a custom PL/SQL function, the page will refresh and a text box will be added so you may enter the body of a function to return a value for the primary key (naturally, this will only work if your primary key is a single column). Likewise, if you select the radio button for the primary key source to be an existing sequence, the page will refresh and add an LOV from which you can select the existing sequence. Again, this will only work if your primary key is a single column. In our case, the primary key is based on an existing trigger, so select the corresponding radio button and click on the Next button.

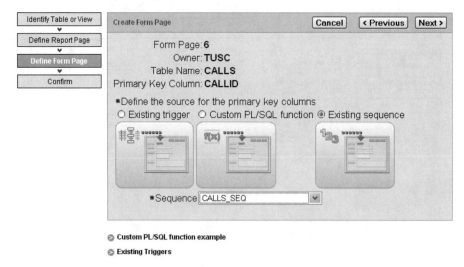

In the following step, you select the columns to be included on the form page. This page is just like the page for selecting the columns for the report page, with the exception that the primary key column is not included in the list of columns from which to select. Select all columns and click on the Next button. In the final step before the confirmation, you specify the actions that will be available on the form page, as shown next. Select Yes from the LOVs for Insert, Update, and Delete and then click on the Next button.

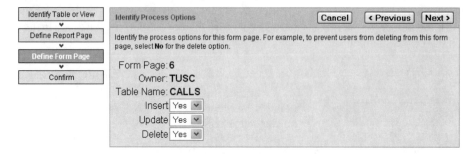

The confirmation page summarizes the choices you have made throughout the wizard. As with any of the previous pages, you may use the Previous button to return to any of the pages of the wizard and make changes. When you are satisfied with your choices, click on the Finish button. Once the pages have been created, a success page will be displayed with two icons—one to run the page and another to edit the page. If you run the page, you should get something similar to what's shown in Figure 8-5.

Notice that the active parent tab is the Reports tab and that the active child tab is the Calls tab. There are 15 records displayed, just as selected in the pagination option. The remaining records are available using the arrow, the Next link, or the row selection LOV. Clicking on either the Create button or any one of the edit icons will navigate to the edit page, shown in Figure 8-6.

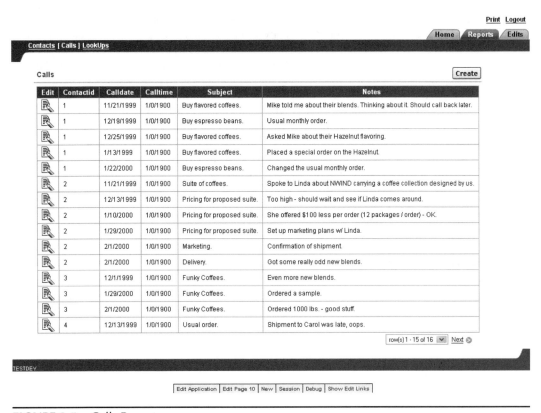

FIGURE 8-5 *Calls Report page*

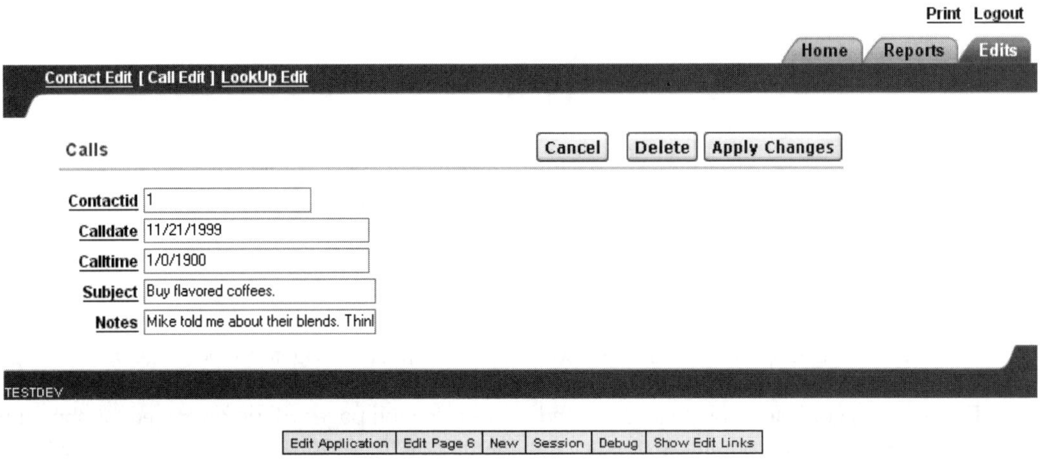

FIGURE 8-6 *Calls Edit page*

When you navigate to the edit page via one of the Edit links on the report page, the corresponding record's data is preloaded into the form and the Cancel, Delete, and Apply Changes buttons are displayed. The Cancel button will discard any changes and return to the report page. The Delete button will display a confirmation dialog box prior to deleting the record and returning to the report page. The Apply Changes button will post and commit any changes to the database and return to the report page.

If you navigate to the edit page from the Create button, shown in Figure 8-5, all the fields will be blank and the only buttons displayed will be the Cancel and Create buttons. The Cancel button has the same function of discarding any changes and returning to the report page. The Create button will insert and commit a new record into the database and return to the report page.

The navigation bar located below both the report page and the form page is commonly called the Developer's Toolbar. This navigation bar is only displayed when the application is run from the development environment. We will cover its functionality more in depth later in this chapter, but for now know that it provides an easy method to navigate to the main Application Builder page (Edit Application) or the edit page of the currently running page (Edit Page #). Use the Developer's Toolbar to navigate to the Main Application builder page.

Deleting Pages

After creating the new pages and returning to the main Application Builder page, you should see a report of pages similar to the following illustration. Because we created a new page for the Calls report page instead of using the existing one, we now have an unneeded page. In the following illustration, page 10 is the page we just created for the Calls report page, whereas page 3 is the unneeded page.

Page ▲	Name	Updated	Updated By	Lock	Run
0	Template	10 days ago	testdev		
1	Home	10 days ago	testdev		
2	Contacts	10 days ago	testdev		
3	Calls	10 days ago	testdev		
4	LookUps	10 days ago	testdev		
5	Contact Edit	10 days ago	testdev		
6	Call Edit	58 seconds ago	linnemeyerl@tusc.com		
7	LookUp Edit	10 days ago	testdev		
10	Report on CALLS	57 seconds ago	linnemeyerl@tusc.com		
101	Login	10 days ago	testdev		

row(s) 1 - 10 of 10

To delete page 3, click on its corresponding name link to navigate to the Page Definition page, shown earlier Figure 8-2. To delete the page, simply click on the Delete button on the Page Definition page. Before the page is deleted, a confirmation page will be displayed, as shown next. This page gives you a summary of what is contained on the page you have selected to delete. The pick list allows you to choose whether to delete the corresponding tabs when you delete the page. When you are sure you want to delete the page, click on the Permanently Delete Page button.

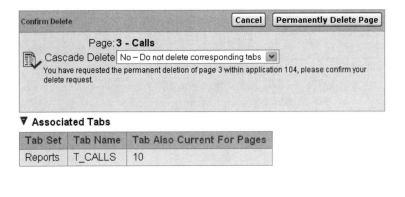

Editing Pages

Regardless of how you create a page, you will most likely want to make changes to it before you will be completely satisfied with its functionality. The application's main page, shown earlier in Figure 8-1, contains a page listing for the current application. The process of editing pages starts from there. To access the Page Definition page for any page of the current application, simply click on its name in the page listing report. After clicking on the name for the report on the Calls page we just created, you will see a Page Definition page like the one shown in Figure 8-7. You can compare this figure with Figure 8-2, which was the original page shell created for the report on the Calls table by the Create Application from Scratch Wizard. The only additional items on our functional pages are the region Calls, the button Create, and the three new templates: Reports Region, Button, and Standard. The new template items on the page are used by the other two new components. Creating and working with reports will be covered in depth in Chapter 9. Buttons are used for navigation, which is covered in Chapter 10.

HTML DB version 1.6 added some extra features that make navigating around your development environment easier. Just below the Data Workshop tab is a small traffic light icon that runs the current page. As you navigate off of the Page Definition page to edit components of this page, a paper and pencil icon is added next to the traffic light. This icon returns you to the Page Definition page. As seen next, the page number, Go button, and arrows provide easy navigation from page to page. The right and left arrows take you to the numerically previous and next pages, respectively. The up arrow pops up a selection window that lists all the application's pages by number and name. Click on the one you wish to navigate to, and the page number will appear in the text field. Then you can click on the Go button. If you are familiar with your pages, you can type a page number directly into the field and click on the ENTER key to navigate to that page. The View pick list allows you to change the view of the Page Definition page to several other useful views, including Event, Objects, History, Groups, Referenced, and Export. Explore each of these to see what it has to offer.

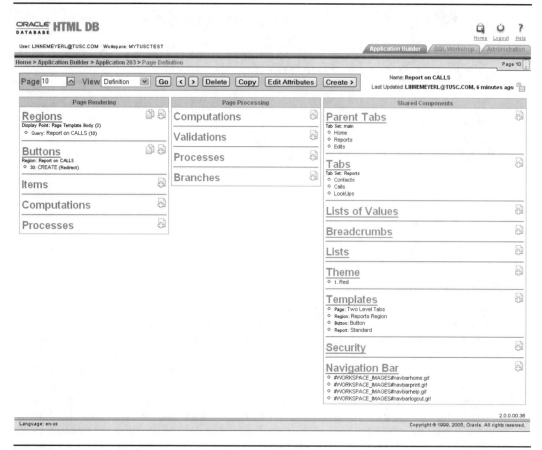

FIGURE 8-7 *Page Definition page for Report on Calls*

The series of buttons on the right side of the page provide more functionality. The Create button starts the process of creating a new page. The details of the Delete button were covered in the previous section. The Copy button starts a short wizard that allows you to copy the page. The paddle lock icon to the right allows you to lock or unlock a page to protect it from being changed by more than one developer. Finally, the Edit Attributes button navigates to the Edit page, where you can modify page-level attributes such as the page name, page group membership, page template, page-specific JavaScript, meta tags, and style attributes. Figures 8-8 and 8-9 illustrate the Edit page.

The Edit page has eight major sections that can be quickly navigated to using the links at the top of the page. The Name section, shown in Figure 8-8, contains the name of the page, the page alias, and the group to which the page is assigned. The Name field should be a descriptive name that you can easily associate with the page. It is used on multiple HTML DB screens and many reports. The value you enter into the Page Alias field can be used in specifying the navigational link within the application, rather than using the page number. This is used in something referred to as the "f?p" syntax, which is covered in more detail in Chapter 11. Using the alias makes the navigational link more understandable—rather than being f?p=100:10, for example, it would be f?p=100:CallsReport. The Group LOV allows you to assign the current page to a page group. Groups can be set up off of the main Application Builder page. They are used to group together related or similar pages in very large applications. The groups are managed from a link on the main Application Builder page, where you can list all pages belonging to a group.

In the Display Attributes section, shown in Figure 8-8, you may choose to override the application-level page template by selecting another one in the Page Template field. The Standard Tab Set field allows you to select a tab for this page. This does not necessarily mean clicking on the tab will navigate to this page, because multiple pages can be associated with a single tab. The only thing it ensures is that when this page is rendered, the set of tabs will be displayed and the tab selected will be shown as the current tab. For more information on tabs, see Chapter 11. The text entered in the Title field will be used for the #TITLE# substitution variable in the page template. This is normally used to place the title in the browser window's title bar. Finally, you can select whether or not to focus the cursor in the first item of the page when you navigate to the page.

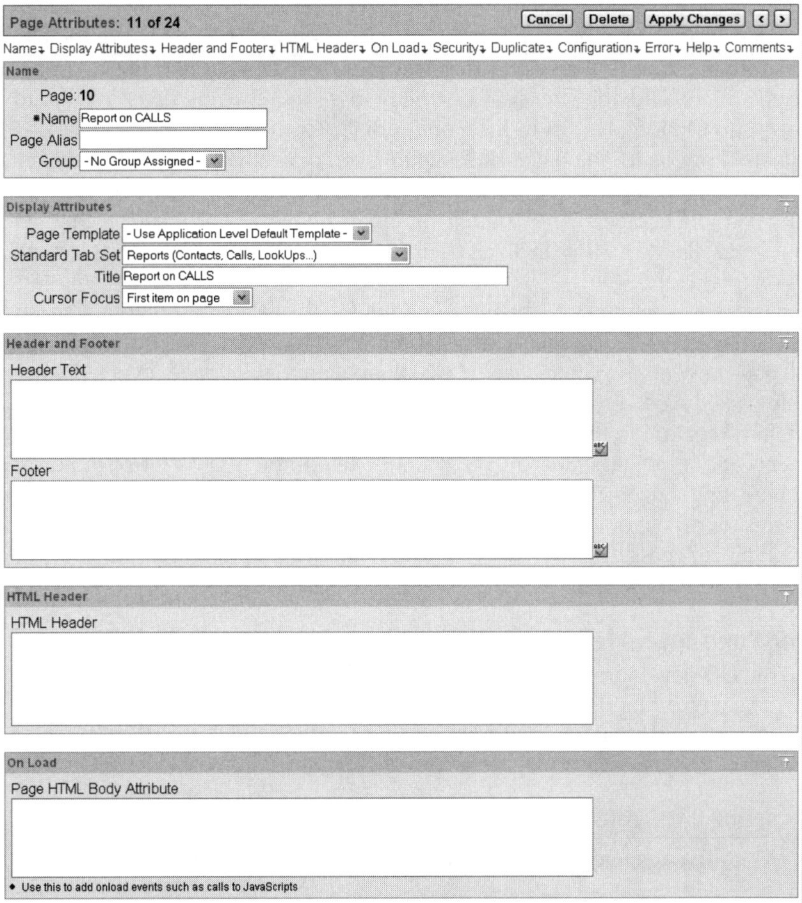

FIGURE 8-8 *Edit Page, part 1*

The value placed in the HTML Header field, shown in Figure 8-8, will be used in the page template for the #HEAD# substitution variable. Anything that you would normally place in the HTML <HEAD> tag can be placed in this text area. This might include page-specific JavaScript, a page-specific Cascading Style Sheet or inline CSS class, or page-specific HTML meta tags. Any HTML code or text you enter in the Header Text field will be placed immediately after the page header and before the HTML body content. Likewise, what is entered in the Footer field will be placed immediately after the page template body and before the page template footer.

The content of the Page HTML Body Attribute field, shown in Figure 8-8, is used for your page template's #ONLOAD# substitution variable. This can be used for onload events. Almost all the standard HTML DB templates place the substitution variable within the body tag (that is, <body #ONLOAD#>).

The Security section, shown in Figure 8-9, allows you to specify the authorization schema for the page and whether the page requires an authentication method. For further details on security, see Chapter 16. One problem with web-based transactional applications is that users might click on the Submit button more than once or use their browser's Back button rather than use the application-provided navigation. This can cause a page to be submitted multiple times. The fields in the Duplicate Page Submission Checks section provide the developer a method of preventing unwanted submissions. The pick list allows you to select whether or not the page can have duplicate submissions. If duplicate submissions are not allowed and occur, an error message will be displayed and the URL that you provide will be used to allow the user to return to the application.

The Build Option pick list in the Configuration section, shown in Figure 8-9, allows you to select a build option for the page. Build options are typically used to include/exclude debug items or to separate normal functionality from premium functionality. Build options are discussed in further detail in Chapter 4. The contents of the In-line Error Notification Text field will be used for your #NOTIFICATION_MESSAGE# substitution variable in the page template when an error occurs on this page.

The text that is entered into the Help Text field in the Page Help Text section, shown in Figure 8-9, can be displayed in a help page that you develop. Unlike item-level help text, which is displayed in a small pop-up window when a user clicks on an item's label, page-level help text must be displayed in a help page the developer creates (see the next section for how to add page-level help).

The final section in the Edit page is the Comments section. Use this section to add developer comments about the page. It is a good practice to comment any out-of-the-ordinary logic you used in creating a page. The Comments section can also be used to track changes to a page. Comments for all pages can be viewed from the Page Comments link on the Application Reports page, which is accessible from the View Application Reports link in the Tasks panel on the main Application Builder page.

Adding Page-level Help

The HTML DB development team made creating a page for page-level help very simple. If you follow the steps outlined here, you can add a Help link in your application's navigation bar that takes the user from any page in the application to a help page that displays the page's help text along with all the items and their help text.

1. Using the Create Page link, create a new blank page following the steps in the wizard.

2. Edit the page and click on the add icon next to Regions.

3. Select Help Text as the Region type and follow the remaining wizard steps.

4. From any Page Definition page, click the add icon next to Navigation Bar in the Shared Components section. Navigation bars are covered further in Chapter 11.

5. Type **Help** in the Text field. Click on Next.

6. Specify the target as Page in This Application. Enter the number of your newly created help page (or select from the pick list) and then enter **&APP_PAGE_ID.** (note the trailing period) in the Request field. Click on Next and then click Create. Chapter 11 covers navigation and URLs in more depth.

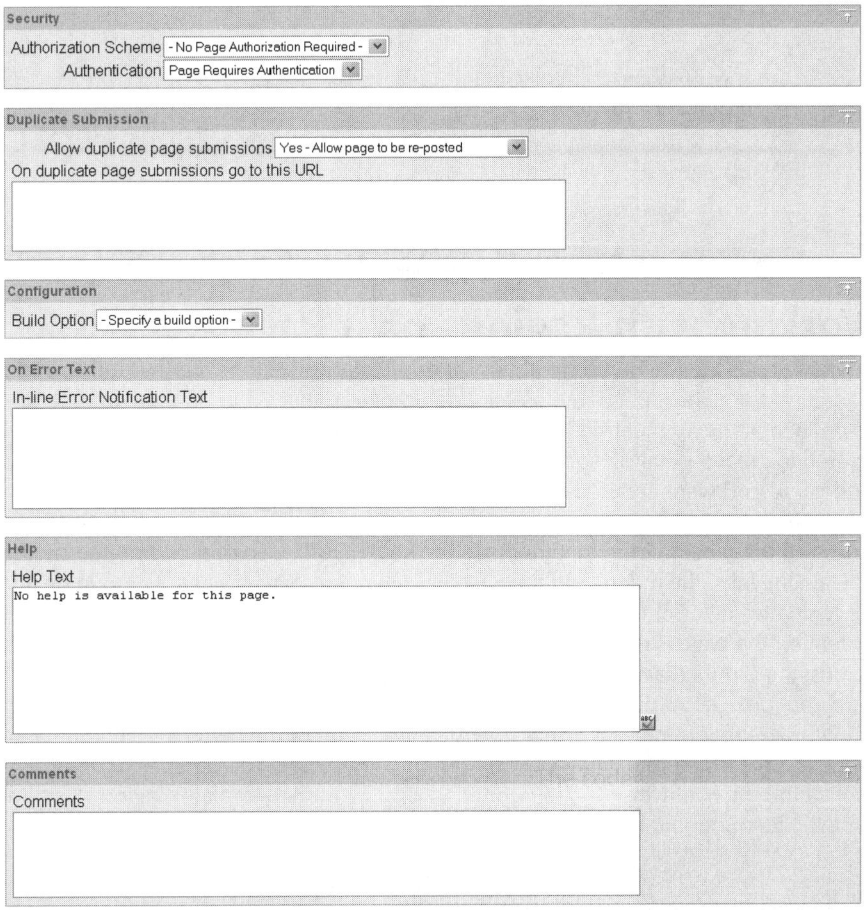

FIGURE 8-9 *Edit Page, part 2*

Now when you click on the Help link in your navigation bar, a help page will be displayed, as shown next, with any page-level help text you defined along with any item help you have defined. Note in the following illustration the Help link in the navigation bar in the upper-right corner.

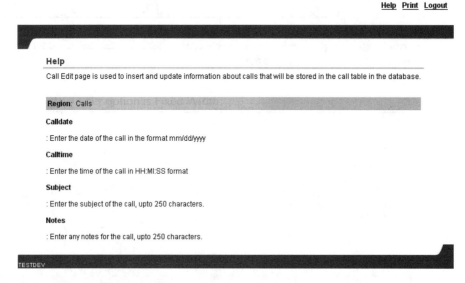

Working with Regions on a Page

Whereas pages are the building blocks for applications, regions are the building blocks for pages. In addition to regions, pages are also made up of templates and other shared components, which are defined at the application level. Shared components were introduced in Chapter 4 and are covered in greater detail in subsequent chapters. Templates are contained in a theme for the application and were covered in Chapter 6.

The home page from the sample application that comes with v1.6 and v2.0 is a good example of how all the pieces come together (see Figure 8-10). The shared components shown on this page are the tabs, the menu, and the navigation bar; all of these are covered in detail in Chapter 11. The templates determine layout and control the colors and fonts of the page. However, the real content on the page is contained in regions. As you could probably guess, this page contains four regions: the Quota dial chart, the Top Orders report, the Welcome text box, and the list of tasks.

If you look below at the Regions portion of the Page Definition page (for the home page), you will see the four regions defined. You can see two of the regions—My Quota and My Top Orders—are defined to display in Page Template Body (2). The other two regions—Sample Application v.1.6 and Tasks—are defined to display in the template Region Position 03. You can tell a lot about the regions just from the information in the Regions section.

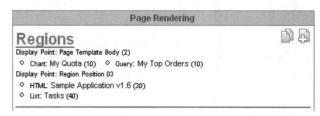

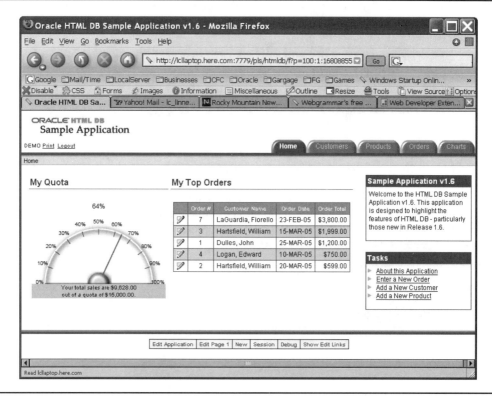

FIGURE 8-10 *HTML DB sample application's home page*

The listing of each region tells you what type of region it is, the name of the region, and its display sequence. The types of the four regions defined for this page are Chart, SQL Query, HTML, and List. See the "Region Types" section later in this chapter for a complete list of region types. You can also tell that the first two regions are defined for display in different columns because they are listed side by side. These items and much more are set on the Edit Page Region page, which is accessible by clicking on the name of the region in the Regions section. Something else to note in the Regions section is the two icons in the upper-right corner. The icon with the plus sign starts the Region Creation Wizard; the other icon starts a wizard that allows you to copy an existing region.

Edit Page Region

The majority of the Edit Page Region page is the same, no matter what type of region you are editing. In this section, we will look at the common pieces of the Edit Page Region page.

The first section is the Name section, shown next, where you specify the title of the region and the type of region. The value in the Title field will be displayed only if the selected region template uses the #TITLE# substitution variable. The type of region is set when you create a region through the wizard. You can only change the type of a region if you are changing it to a similar type—for instance, if you change it from an HTML region to an HTML region with shortcuts.

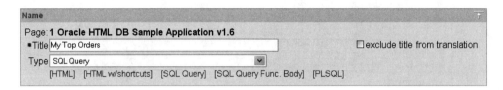

The next section is the User Interface section, shown here. Items specified here control where and how the region will be displayed on the page. The Template field provides an LOV of all the region templates for the application's current theme. If you look at Figure 8-10, you can tell by the look of each of the regions that the two on the left use one region template and the two on the right each use a different template. Templates control the background color, the font, the display of the region title, and whether or not they have borders. The Display Point field specifies where within a page template the region will be displayed.

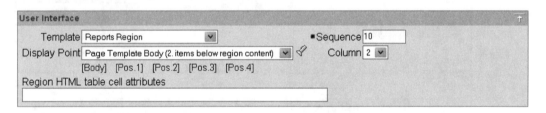

Clicking the flashlight icon will display a pop-up that shows the location of the different options within the current page template, as shown in Figure 8-11. See Chapter 6 for more details on templates. The sequence number controls the order in which regions will be displayed within the same display regions. The column pick list allows you to place regions side by side within a display region. When you use more than one column, HTML DB places the multiple regions in cells in an HTML table. The Region HTML Table Cell Attributes field can be used to specify additional attributes for those table cells. The regions in the home page, shown earlier in Figure 8-10, were defined to display in two display points: Page Template Body(2) and Region Pos 03. You can see their relationship in Figure 8-11.

The next common section in the Edit Page Region page is the Conditional Display section. Not only is this section common to all region definitions, but you will also find a Conditional Display section for items, buttons, tabs, navigation bar items, processes, computations, and validations. See the "Conditional Rendering and Processing" section later in this chapter for more information.

The following section is the Header and Footer Text section, which contains a text area field for entering region header text and one for region footer text. Use these fields to enter HTML text that will be displayed in the header or footer section of a region. The on-page navigational links, which allow you to jump to a particular region on that page, are implemented using the Header Text field. Figure 8-8 shows some of these links at the top. These links are implemented with an HTML region at the top of the page that has a source such as

```
<a href='#auth'>Jump to Authorization<a>
```

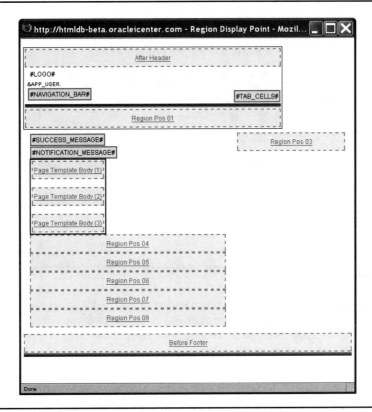

FIGURE 8-11 *Region Display Point Selection page*

which references an HTML anchor tag entered in the region Header Text area (that is, <a name="auth">). Report regions have a number of special substitution variables that can be used in the region's Footer Text area. These will be covered in Chapter 9.

The Authorization section and the Configuration Management section are not only common to all regions but are also common to many other HTML DB components, including pages, items, buttons, tabs, navigation bar items, processes, computations, and validations. Authorization is covered in Chapter 16, whereas configuration management was covered in Chapter 4.

The last section common to all regions is the End User Customization section, shown next. End-user customization is the ability for users to select whether or not a region of a page is displayed when they visit that page. If you choose to allow a region to be customizable, you can set to either be shown or not shown by default. This selection is made with one of the radio buttons shown here.

If the region is customizable, you must supply a name for the option that will be displayed in the customization options pop-up, shown next. In order for users to access the customization options pop-up, the page template must include the #CUSTOMIZE# substitution variable, which will display a Customize link if any regions are customizable.

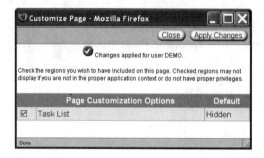

Region Types

The home page for the HTML DB sample application, shown earlier in Figure 8-10, has four of the 12 different types of page regions: Chart, Report, HTML, and List. The best way to see the different types of regions is to start the Create Region Wizard. The Create icon in the Region section of the Page Definition page, shown earlier in Figure 8-7, starts the Create Region Wizard, from which you can create any type of region. The first page of the wizard contains a list of the different types of regions that can be created, as shown in the following table. This table also provides a description of each region type.

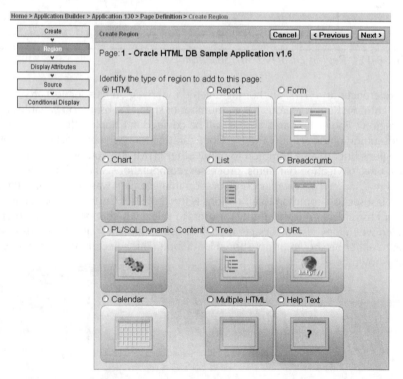

Region Type	Description
HTML	Creates a region to display HTML entered by the developer and/or acts as a container for items and buttons. HTML code can include substitution variables. The next step allows you to select from three different variations of the HTML region. These types can also be specified in the Type field on the Edit Page Region page.

HTML	Normal HTML Region
HTML Text (escape special characters)	Special characters are escaped before they are rendered. For example, you could type in a block of HTML code and the entire block would be displayed, not the results.
HTML Text (with shortcuts)	Allows the use of shortcuts. Shortcuts are discussed in detail in Chapter 12.

Region Type	Description
Report	Displays data based on a SQL query.
Form	Form regions are used to provide users with the ability to edit data. They are made up of HTML items such as Text, Text Areas, Hidden, Select List, and more. The following screen allows you to select from nine different types of forms. All of these types are covered in detail in Chapter 10.
Chart	Can contain various types of charts based on a SQL query, such as line, bar, pie, and dial.
List	Lists are made up of links or images and are used for navigation. Each list item can be conditionally displayed.
Breadcrumb	Menu regions are also for navigation. Menu items are defined in a hierarchical manner with parent and child elements.
PL/SQL Dynamic Content	The PL/SQL Web Toolkit enables you to dynamically render HTML content from PL/SQL. See Appendix B for further detail on the PL/SQL Web Toolkit.
Tree	A tree region is another navigational control region. It is based on a SQL query executed at run time. The tree structure allows the user to expand and collapse nodes.
URL	Based on a URL, this region retrieves its content by calling a web server.
Calendar	Calendar regions display a monthly calendar with details displayed on certain dates based on a SQL query.
Multiple HTML	This option allows you to create multiple HTML regions.
Help Text	Help Text regions are a variation of HTML regions, but they automatically create the content necessary to display developer-defined help content for pages and items.

Page Concepts

So far we have demonstrated how to create pages within an application and we have looked at some of the components that make up pages. We have done this, though, from a high-level wizard-driven perspective, without really getting into the low-level details of how things work. However, before we can explore the fine details of page components, it is imperative that you have an understanding of how the HTML DB engine creates and processes pages and how the information in those pages is maintained and used from page to page.

At the very basic level, when a user requests a web page using a URL, the web server does not know that request from any other request. It simply provides the requested page, which for most web pages is just static HTML. The user views the page and requests another. Again, the web server doesn't know that request from any other and there is no connection between the first request and the second request. Some web pages have fields where data can be entered and then submitted along with the request for another page. In this case, the web server will "process" the data sent back before returning the next page. You need to understand how HTML DB takes these unrelated requests and ties them together to appear as a coordinated application.

Everything we have worked with to this point—templates, tabs, menus, pages, regions, items, buttons, and more—have all been created or defined through wizards or edit pages. What we have really done is to define all the pieces that are used to make the pages in an HTML DB application. All this information is referred to as *metadata* about the application. The HTML DB engine must use this metadata to create the actual HTML pages and to process those pages.

When a page of an HTML DB application is requested, the HTML DB engine uses a process known as *Show Page* to transform the metadata defined about the page into the plain HTML code that will be returned to the requesting browser. This process is referred to as *page rendering,* which corresponds to the first section of the Page Definition page, shown in Figure 8-12. Aside from the shared components, the Page Rendering section contains all the metadata that the Show Page process uses to create the HTML page.

When a page of an HTML DB application contains data and is submitted, the HTML DB engine uses a process know as *Accept Page* to process that data, including doing any validations, performing any calculations or processes, and then branching to yet another page of the HTML DB application. This process is referred to as *page processing,* which corresponds to the second section of the Page Definition page shown in Figure 8-12. In this section, you define the metadata that the Accept Page process uses to perform these tasks.

This still leaves the question as to how HTML DB ties the page requests together and makes data available from one page to another. The HTML DB engine accomplishes this task through a logical construct called a *session*. Each session is given an identifier that uniquely identifies that session across the entire HTML DB instance. The HTML DB engine uses that session identifier to store and retrieve the current state of application data from the Oracle database as it is rendering and processing pages. This whole process is referred to as *session state management.*

In the rest of this section, we will look in detail at page rendering, page processing, and session state management.

Page Rendering and Processing

Page rendering refers to the HTML DB engine process Show Page, which builds an HTML page based on that page's metadata that is stored in the HTML DB repository. The metadata used will be the application's applicable shared components and those items defined in the Page Rendering section of that page's Page Definition page.

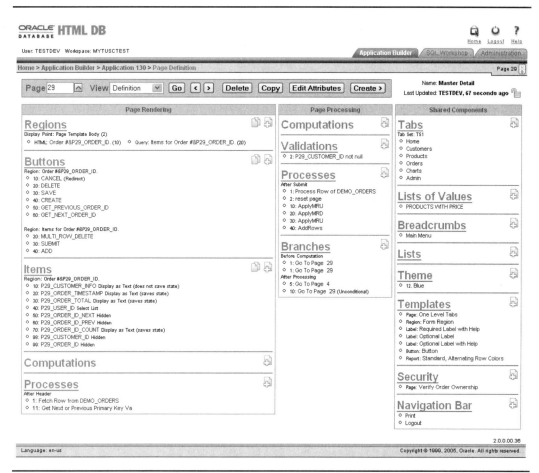

FIGURE 8-12   *Master Detail Page Definition page for the sample application*

As shown in Figure 8-12, the Page Rendering section contains regions, buttons, items, computations, and processes. As shown earlier in this chapter, regions are containers for the different types of content that can be displayed on an HTML DB page. Chapter 10 will cover in detail the use of items and buttons.

Computations are units of logic executed when the page is rendered, and they are used to assign values to items within the application. The item can be on the current page, another page, or it could be an application-level item. Processes are logical controls executed when the page is rendered and are used to perform tasks such as managing session state, changing pagination, and invoking an API, Web Service, or PL/SQL program unit. Computations and processes are covered in depth in Chapter 13.

Page processing refers to the HTML DB engine process Accept Page, which accepts the page's submitted data and processes it according to that page's metadata stored in the HTML DB repository. The metadata used comes from those items defined in the Page Processing section of that page's Page Definition page.

As shown in Figure 8-12, the Page Processing section contains computations, validations, processes, and branches. As with page-rendering computations, page-processing computations are used to assign values to items within the application. In fact, the only difference between a processing computation and a rendering computation is that its computation point is defined as "after submit." Likewise, page-processing processes are like page-rendering processes, except their process point is defined as "after submit." Typically, rendering processes are used to execute data-manipulation language statements (insert, update, or delete database records), execute PL/SQL program units, or manage session state.

Validations are units of logic that allow you to ensure the data entered by the user is valid. The checks can be as simple as ensuring a mandatory field is not null or as complex as your PL/SQL skills will allow you to make them. Branches are logical units used by the developer to control navigation throughout the application.

HTML DB versions 1.6 and above provide links to pages that offer access to some additional useful information about each page. In version 1.6, these links were buttons across the top; in version 2.0, you access the pages by selecting a different view from the View field's pick list at the top of the Page Definition page and clicking on the Go button (this can be seen in Figure 8-12). By far the most useful of these is the Events view. This page, shown in Figure 8-13, will help you fully understand the order in which the page is rendered and the order in which the page is processed. The page allows you to select whether you want to see all the items or just those being used.

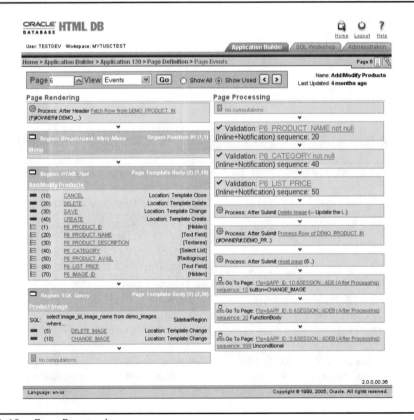

FIGURE 8-13 *Page Events view*

Conditional Rendering and Processing

All the components listed for page rendering and page processing can be controlled so that they display or process depending on the outcome of a given condition. If a component has a condition, the HTML DB engine will evaluate that condition before processing the component.

Each type of component has a corresponding edit page that contains a Conditional section, like the one shown next. Only page-rendering components will have the option to specify a "when button clicked" condition, which checks the name of the button that was clicked to submit the page. If the submitting button matches the one selected, the condition evaluates to true. The pick list for the Condition Type field provides more than 50 different types of conditions that can be used. The arrow next to the field will bring up a searchable page containing all the applicable condition types for the current object. The fields Expression 1 and Expression 2 are used to provide values for the condition. For example, the condition displayed here is for a PL/SQL function body that returns a Boolean value. Expression 1 contains the function body that checks the request to see if it equals the name of two different buttons.

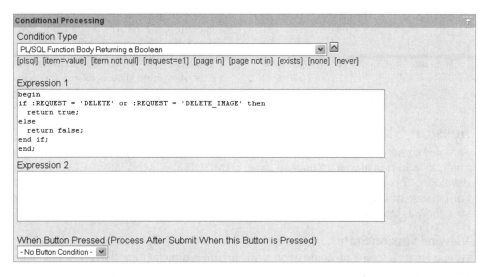

Some of the more common condition types can be selected quickly utilizing one of the shortcuts below the Condition Type field. The following table lists some of the common condition types. Note that when the condition type reads "Value of Item in Expression," it is looking for the name of an application item, such as P6_PRODUCT_NAME. Also, SQL or PL/SQL used in the expressions can reference application items using the bind variable syntax (for example, :P6_PRODUCT_NAME). See the following section on session state and referencing page items.

Condition Type	Description
Value of Item in Expression 1 is NOT NULL	Verifies that the value of the item specified in Expression 1 has a value.
Value of Item in Expression 1 is NULL	Verifies that the value of the item specified in Expression 1 has no value.
Value of Item in Expression 1 = Expression 2	Verifies that the value of the item in Expression 1 equals the value of the item in Expression 2.

Condition Type	Description
Value of Item in Expression 1 is Numeric	Verifies that the value in the item in Expression 1 contains only numbers.
Value of Item in Expression 1 is Alphanumeric	Verifies that the value of the item in Expression 1 contains only alphanumeric characters.
When any item in comma-delimited list of items has changed	Evaluates to true when the value of any non-NULL session state item in the list of items in Expression 1 has changed.
When any item in current page has changed	Evaluates to true when the value of any non-NULL session state item in the current page has changed.
PL/SQL Expression	Evaluates any valid PL/SQL statement that evaluates to true or false.
Exists (SQL query returns at least one row)	The SQL query entered in Expression 1 is executed. If it returns at least one row, the condition evaluates to true.
NOT Exists (SQL query returns no rows)	The SQL query entered in Expression 1 is executed. If no data is found, the condition evaluates to true.

Session State Management

As stated earlier, the HTML DB engine uses a logical construct called a *session* to maintain application information from page to page. HTML DB makes this information available to the developer. This information is commonly referred to as *session state* because it maintains the current state of items for a given session. In this section, we will look at how to view session state, how to reference session state, and how session state is set and cleared.

Viewing Session State

As you are developing an application, you can run it directly from the development environment by clicking on any of the many traffic light icons available on most pages of the Application Builder. As you run an application from the development environment, a navigation bar will be displayed below your application's page, as shown earlier in Figure 8-5 and 8-6. This navigation bar is referred to as the Developer's Toolbar, and it contains a link to view the current session state.

The Developer's Toolbar is displayed under each page of an application as you run the application from within the development environment. If the bar is not present as you run the application from the development environment, make sure the application status in the Application Availability section of the Edit Application Attributes page is set to Available with Edit Links. The Developer's Toolbar provides the developer with several very useful quick links.

The first links on the Developer's Toolbar, shown next, are the Edit Application and Edit Page # links, which navigate to the Application Builder main page and the Page Definition page, respectively. The Create link takes you to a page from which you can start the wizards for creating almost any component, including a blank page, a new component (report, chart, form, and so on) on either a new page or the existing page, page controls (including regions, items, and buttons), and shared components.

| Edit Application | Edit Page 6 | Create | Session | Debug | Show Edit Links |

The links Debug and Show Edit Links redisplay the currently running page. Debug runs the page in debug mode, which displays HTML DB engine actions, with timing stamps, as the page is processed. Show Edit Links runs the page and displays edit links (four dots) next to most of the page's control items. These links allow you to jump directly to each item's corresponding edit page. As you are running the page in either of these modes, the links change to No Debug and Hide Edit Links, respectively, as shown in Figure 8-14.

You can view session state from the Session link on the Developer's Toolbar. Let's take a look at the session state for the Calls Edit page we created at the beginning of the chapter. I ran the Calls report page directly from the Application Builder main page and then clicked on the edit icon for one of the calls. Figure 8-15 shows the results in the Calls Edit page.

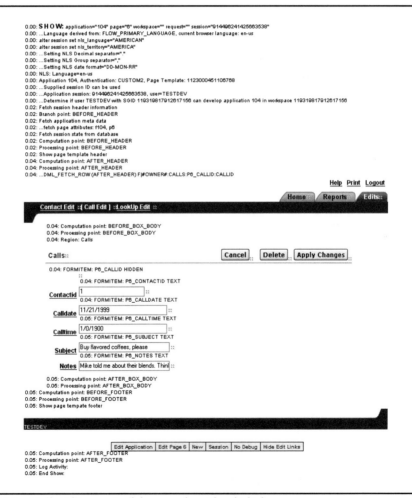

FIGURE 8-14 *Calls Edit page in debug mode with edit links*

Help Print Logout

Home | Reports | Edits

Contact Edit [Call Edit] LookUp Edit

Calls   Cancel | Delete | Apply Changes

Contactid | 4
Calldate | 12/13/1999
Calltime | 1/0/1900
Subject | Pricing for proposed suite.
Notes | Too high - should wait and see if Lind

TESTDEV

Edit Application | Edit Page 6 | New | Session | Debug | Show Edit Links

FIGURE 8-15 *Calls Edit page*

If we were to edit the page and look at the page items, we would see those shown next. Each of these items can contain a value. The P6_CALLID item is a hidden field, and the rest are defined as text fields. Working with fields will be covered more in depth in Chapter 10, but for now you only need to understand that these items correspond to the HTML items on the rendered HTML page, shown in Figure 8-15.

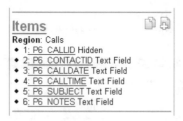

If we click on the Session link in the Developer's Toolbar, we will get a pop-up window that displays the current session state, as shown in Figure 8-16. You may change the page number to see the session state for another page within your current application, but typically you are interested in the page you are currently running.

The application environment section at the top, shown in Figure 8-16, provides the session ID, current user, workspace ID, and browser language. The Page Items section provides the current session state for the items on the current page. The elements displayed are self-explanatory except for Status, which can be any of the following:

- **I** Inserted
- **U** Updated
- **R** Reset

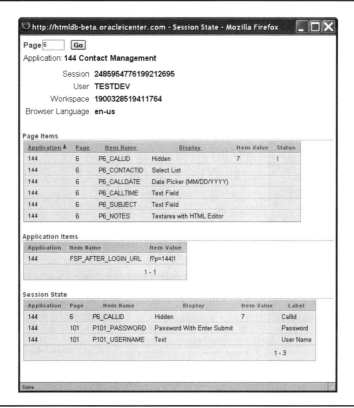

FIGURE 8-16   *Session state for the Call Edit page*

The Session State section provides the entire session state for the user. Items listed in the Application Items section are session state variables that do not reside on a page. These items are defined from the application's Shared Components page (see Chapter 4 for more details).

You might be asking yourself, Why is P6_CALLID the only item with a value? When you look at the page, all the items are populated. This is because the state of these items has not been specifically set or the values have not been submitted. P6_CALLID is populated because the edit icon on the Calls Report page we clicked on to get to this page is defined as a link to the Call Edit page, and it sets the value of P6_CALLID to the call ID of the current row. The Call Edit page executes a query using the session state of P6_CALLID as the primary key to populate the other fields on the Call Edit page. If we update the value of the Subject item and click on the Apply Changes button, we will be returned to the Calls Report page and see that the change we entered has been made to the record.

It is not important at this point that you understand every detail of what happens behind the scenes, but you should start to get an idea of how session state is being used. Here is a high-level view of what happens:

1. When the Apply Changes button is clicked, the browser submits the Call Edit page back to itself, including the value of all the text fields.

2. The HTML DB engine runs the Accept Page process and utilizes the Page Processing metadata to process the values passed.

   a. The values are saved to the session.

   b. The values are used to update the row in the database.

   c. The page branches back to the Calls Report page.

3. The HTML DB engine runs the Show Page process using the Page Rendering metadata for the Calls Report page and returns the resulting HTML page to the browser.

4. If there had been some validation in the page processing that failed, the Call Edit page would be regenerated using the values from the session state so you would not lose your changes.

If we now look at the session state from the Calls Report page, we would see something like what's shown in Figure 8-17. Note that there are no page items listed, because the Calls Report page does not contain any items. Also note that all the values from the previous page are now in the Session State section.

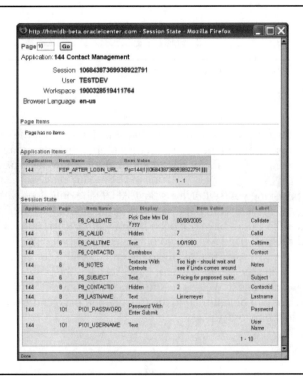

FIGURE 8-17 *Session state for the Calls Report page*

At this point, you should understand how to look at the current session state. It is also possible to examine session state for applications that other users are running outside of the development environment. See Chapter 17 for administrative functions that allow you to monitor session states.

Referencing Session State

We have seen session state ID maintained for page items and for application items. These session states are available to the developer to use throughout the HTML DB application. The following table shows how they can be referenced in SQL, PL/SQL, or in static text such as an HTML region.

Syntax	Where Used	Description
:P6_SUBJECT	SQL or PL/SQL	Reference the values of items using standard bind variable syntax. Good for items 30 characters or less.
V('P6_NOTES')	PL/SQL	V is an HTML DB database function that returns the value of items. Returns a character value.
NV('P6_CALLID')	PL/SQL	NV is an HTML DB database function that returns the value of numeric items. Returns a number.
&P6_NOTES.	Static Text	Note the trailing period. The item name must be in capital letters. Acts as a substitution variable.

Setting Session State

We have already seen that values submitted from a page are automatically stored in session state. We also saw in the walkthrough as we navigated from the report page to the edit page via the edit icon that P6_CALLID was set so that the edit page could query the proper record. The following illustration shows a small portion of the report definition that defines the link for the edit icon on the Calls Report page, shown earlier in Figure 8-5. You can see that item P6_CALLID is assigned the value #CALLID#, which is the value of the callid column for the current row. HTML DB actually accomplishes this by constructing a relative URL—something like f?p=104:6:585955298 3631133758::::P6_CALLID:14. At this point, it is not necessary to understand the workings of reports or the use of f?p syntax URL, only that the session state was set in one page for the use in another. Reports will be covered in depth in the next chapter, and the use of the f?p syntax for navigation will be covered in Chapter 11.

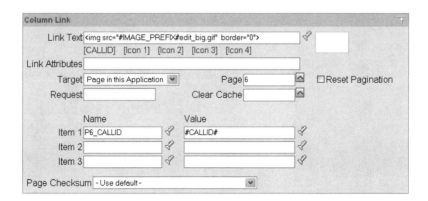

You can also set session state directly in a PL/SQL anonymous block. Here's an example:

```
:P6_SUBJECT := 'A new subject';
```

Clearing Session State

After posting the new values from the Call Edit page and returning to the Calls Report page, we saw that the session state for the items from the Call Edit page were still present, as shown in Figure 8-17. Once set, these values will remain in the session. Therefore, you will probably find it necessary at times to clear the session state of certain items. Clearing session state is also accomplished when navigating using the f?p syntax URL. Through the f?p syntax, you can clear a single item, all the items on a single page, all the items on several pages, or even all the items in the entire application.

Many times the f?p syntax will be created for you through the metadata you provide, as shown earlier. Part of the Clear Cache option allows you to specify a page number whose cache you would like cleared through the navigation. Again, it is not necessary that you fully understand everything at this point, just that clearing the session state is something you will want to do and that it is accomplished through the f?p syntax. You will see in upcoming chapters many places in edit pages that allow you to specify the clearing of cache. The f?p syntax and all its options for clearing cache will be covered in Chapter 11.

CHAPTER
9

Working with Reports

TML DB reports are columnar displays of the data returned from a SQL query. In Chapter 8, while walking through the Page Wizard, we used the Report Wizard to create a report page for Calls with a corresponding form page. The report page produced, shown in Figure 9-1, is a typical example of a basic HTML DB report.

In this chapter, we will explore some of the more advanced features of reports, including user-selectable sort order, column links, column breaks, multilined records, and pagination controls.

Help Print Logout

Home   Reports   Edits

Contacts [Calls] LookUps

Calls   Create

Edit	Contactid	Calldate	Calltime	Subject	Notes
📝	1	21-NOV-99	1/0/1900	Buy flavored coffees, please	Mike told me about their blends. Thinking about it. Should call back later.
📝	1	19-DEC-99	1/0/1900	Buy espresso beans.	Usual monthly order, not usually
📝	1	25-DEC-99	1/0/1900	Buy flavored coffees.	Asked Mike about their Hazelnut flavoring.
📝	1	13-JAN-99	1/0/1900	Buy flavored coffees.	Placed a special order on the Hazelnut.
📝	1	22-JAN-00	1/0/1900	Buy espresso beans.	Changed the usual monthly order.
📝	2	21-NOV-99	1/0/1900	Suite of coffees.	Spoke to Linda about NWIND carrying a coffee collection designed by us.
📝	2	13-DEC-99	1/0/1900	Pricing for proposed Vacation.	Too high - should wait and see if Linda comes around.
📝	2	10-JAN-00	1/0/1900	Pricing for proposed suite.	She offered $100 less per order (12 packages / order) - OK.
📝	2	29-JAN-00	1/0/1900	Pricing for proposed suite.	Set up marketing plans w/ Linda.
📝	2	01-FEB-00	1/0/1900	Marketing.	Confirmation of shipment.
📝	2	01-FEB-00	1/0/1900	Delivery.	Got some really odd new blends.
📝	3	01-DEC-99	1/0/1900	Funky Coffees.	Even more new blends.
📝	3	29-JAN-00	1/0/1900	Funky Coffees.	Ordered a sample.
📝	3	01-FEB-00	1/0/1900	Funky Coffees.	Ordered 1000 lbs. - good stuff.
📝	4	13-DEC-99	1/0/1900	Usual order.	Shipment to Carol was late, oops.

row(s) 1 - 15 of 16 ▾   Next ◉

TESTDEV

FIGURE 9-1   *Calls report*

Creating Reports

Reports are one of the many types of regions that can be defined on an HTML DB application page (see Chapter 8 for a complete listing of region types). You have three different ways to start the process of adding a report region, but once you get into the report-building section of each of these wizards, you'll find that they are very similar:

- **Create Page Wizard (Page with Component option, Report option)**   You start the Create Page Wizard by clicking on the Create Page button on the Application Builder main page or the Create button on any Page Definition page.

- **Create Region Wizard (Report option)**   You start the Create Region Wizard by clicking on the Create icon in the Regions section of any Page Definition page.

- **New Component Wizard (Component option, Report option)**   You start the New Component Wizard by clicking on the New link on the Developer's Toolbar.

Recall that the Contact Management application we have been building is based on three tables we defined in Chapter 5. In Chapter 5, we created a shell for the application consisting of seven blank pages organized under two levels of tabs. In Chapter 8, we walked through the steps to create a page with a report region for the Calls table, along with another form page for editing the Calls table. This was accomplished through the Create Page Wizard. We will now build a report for the Contacts table so that we can explore further capabilities of HTML DB report regions.

Navigate to the Page Definition page for the Contacts report. Aside from the shared components, this page definition is empty. Click on the Create icon in the Regions section under Page Rendering. This starts the Create Region Wizard. Select the Report option and click on Next. The page presented, shown in Figure 9-2, provides three paths for creating a report. You will run through

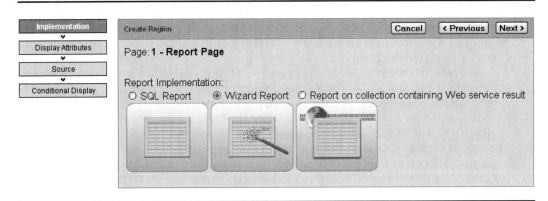

FIGURE 9-2   *Select Report Implementation*

this same page whenever you start any of the three wizards. However, each one has slightly different options, as shown in the following table.

Option	Description	Create Region Wizard	New Component Wizard	Create Page Wizard
SQL Report	Creates a report based on a SQL query you write from one or more tables.	X	X	X
Wizard Report	The wizard helps you build a SQL query from one or more tables.	X	X	X
Report with Form	Creates a Report and Edit form for a single table. (This option was used in Chapter 8.)		X	
Report on Collection Containing Web Service Results	Creates a report based on a Web Service Reference created in Shared Components	X		

The Contacts table, as defined in Chapter 5, was joined to the Calls table and the Contact_Type table. Also in Chapter 5, we created a lookup table, Title_Lookup. The Contacts table provides details about the Calls table, whereas the Contact_Types and Title_Lookup tables provide details about the contact. To get all pertinent information about contacts, we will need to join the Contacts, Contact_Types, and the Title_Lookup tables. We could write our own query and use the SQL Report option, shown in Figure 9-2, but let's choose the Wizard Report option and let HTML DB build the query for us. Another advantage of using the Wizard Report option is that, unlike a SQL report, this report will take advantage of any column-level user interface defaults that have been defined on the tables. User interface defaults provide column labels, column widths, and more. They are discussed in Chapter 3.

After selecting the Wizard Report option and clicking on the Next button, you will navigate to a screen where you specify the region's display attributes (see Figure 9-3). The Title field is the title of the report region. This is displayed or not depending on whether the selected region template uses the #TITLE# substitution variable. The Region Template field allows you to select a region template from a list of region templates included in the current theme for the application. The Display Point field specifies where within the page template the region will be displayed. You may either select from the LOV or click on the flashlight icon, which will display a pop-up window. This window shows a page mockup with each display point on the current page template. Simply click on one of the display points to close the window and populate the Display Point field with your selection. The sequence determines the order in which regions will be shown within the display point. If you want regions displayed in columns, select different columns for each.

Once all the region display attributes are set, click on the Next button, shown in Figure 9-3, to proceed to the Source section of the wizard. The first page in the Source section allows you to select tables and then select columns from those tables. Figure 9-4 shows the screen after selecting the CONTACTS table and then selecting all columns except those that are foreign keys

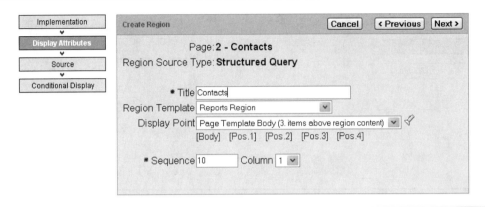

FIGURE 9-3 *Region display properties*

to the CONTACT_TYPES and TITLE_LOOKUP tables. Once a table is selected, radio buttons are displayed that limit the LOV of tables to only those that are related to the selected table. Select the CONTACT_TYPES table and then select the CONTACTTYPE column. Next, select the TITLE_ LOOKUP table and select the TITLE column. If you select columns from tables that are not related, you will have to provide the join conditions in the next step.

The next page of the source selection section allows you to specify all the join conditions for the tables selected. Join conditions will be pre-populated based on the foreign key relations of the tables selected. Figure 9-5 shows those pre-populated for the tables we selected. If you need to add more conditions, you may type them directly into the fields or you may use the LOV to select a column. If you type them in, they need to be fully qualified with the table name and column name, but they don't need to be enclosed in quotes as the pre-populated ones are. If you need more lines to add additional conditions, click on the Add More Join Conditions button. If you need to do an outer join, you can add (+) after all the join conditions for the table that might not have matching columns.

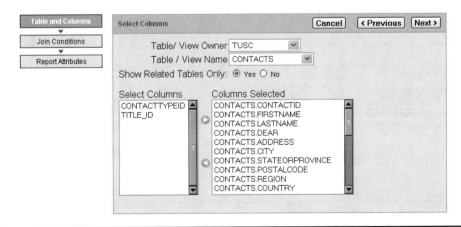

FIGURE 9-4 *Source table and columns selection*

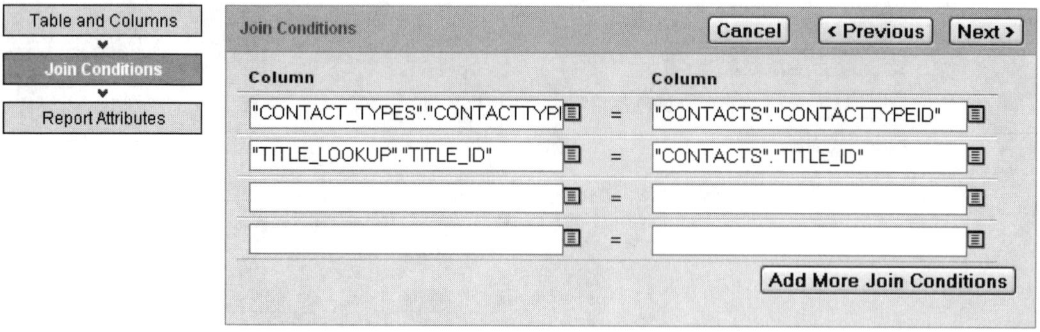

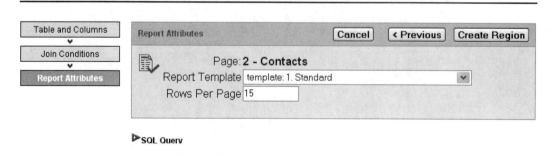

FIGURE 9-5 *Source table join conditions*

The final step in creating the report region is to specify the report attributes, as shown in Figure 9-6. The Report Template field allows you to select any report template from the current theme. We will use the standard, but we'll change it later. The Rows Per Page field sets up the pagination for the report. If there are more rows in the result set than specified in the Rows Per Page field, the report will only display that number of rows and will provide navigation to display the remaining rows in groups of the same size. If you want to see the SQL query, you can expand the field located just below the box.

Once you have created the region, run the page by clicking on the stop light icon in the upper-right corner just below the tabs. Your report should look similar to the report shown in Figure 9-7. The standard template used defines a simple columnar report. However, with a table like the CONTACTS table, which has 29 columns, a simple columnar layout does not present an easily viewed report. The user must scroll to the side for several screens to see all the columns, and when any field contains a large amount of data, the entire row becomes very wide. Another option would be to select a default template that is laid out vertically. This is typically a two-column report—the first column displays the field name, and the second column displays the field's value. Again, for a large table, the user would probably not be able to see an entire record on a single screen and would be required to scroll.

FIGURE 9-6 *Report attributes*

Help Print Logout

[Contacts] Calls LookUps

Contacts

Contactid	Title	First Name	Last Name	Contacttype	Dear	Address	City	State	Zip	Region	Country	Company Name	Work Phone
5	Purchase Manager	Randall	Boseman	Buyer	Randy	12 Windy Hill Dr.	London		SW1 8JR		UK	Wide World Importers	715550122
4	Purchase Manager	Carol	Philips	Buyer	Carol	5678 Old Oak Rd.	Redmond	WA	58568		USA	Fourth Coffee	3455550122
3	Sales Representative	John	Frum	Seller	John	234 W. Capital Way	Tacoma	WA	58433		USA	Fabrikam, Inc.	3455550182
1	Sales Representative	Mike	Danseglio	Seller	Mike	567 - 20th Ave. E. Apt. 2A	Seattle	WA	58142		USA	Contoso, Ltd.	3455550157
2	Vice President, New Products	Linda	Leste	Buyer	Linda	78 Moss Bay Blvd.	Kirkland	WA	58235		USA	Northwind Traders	3455550112

FIGURE 9-7 *Contacts report*

A better solution to using one of the standard templates would be to create a custom template that utilizes the space on the page more efficiently. Figure 9-8 shows the same report run with a custom template. Chapter 6 addresses working with themes and templates, but does not specifically cover details on report templates, so we will look at the template for this example.

From the Contacts Page Definition page, click on the add icon next in the Templates section in the Shared Components column on the right side of the screen. This will start the Create Template Wizard. On the first page, select the Report option and click on Next. On the following page, select the option to build the template from scratch. As shown next, on the final page, give the template a meaningful name, select the Red theme, select a custom template class, and choose the Named Column template type. Generic Columns templates use the same template for every column, whereas Named Column templates allow you to position and format each column individually. After you click on the Create button, you will be returned to the Page Definition page.

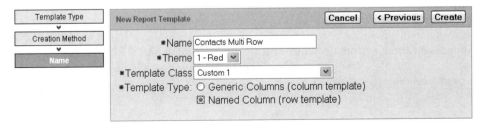

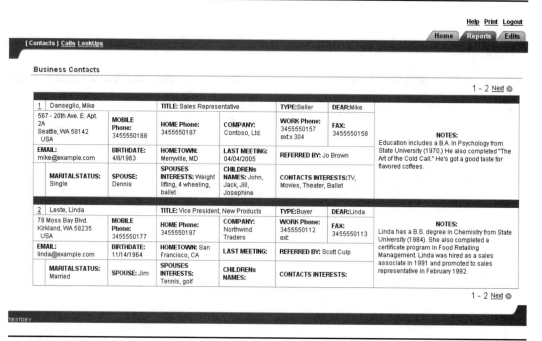

FIGURE 9-8 *Contacts report with custom template*

To navigate to the edit page for the new template, follow these steps:

1. Click the application name in the breadcrumb menu at the top of the Page Definition page. This will return you to the Application Builder main page for the current application.

2. Click the Shared Components icon.

3. Click the Templates link under the User Interface section.

4. Find the name of the template you just created under the Reports section in the list of templates. The Reports section is at the bottom of the page. You could limit the templates displayed by selecting Report in the Show field and then clicking on the Go button.

Remember that templates are a combination of HTML code and substitution variables that are replaced with values when the page is rendered. In order to customize templates, you need to have a basic understanding of HTML. Before we enter the code for the Named Column template, let's look at a portion of a Generic Column report template. The following listing of HTML code comes from the Standard Report template of the Red theme. The report in Figure 9-7 was formatted with this template, which is a Generic Column template. You can see that the code contains one table within another. The inner table contains the columnar report made up of the column headings and the data rows.

```
1.  <table cellpadding="0" border="0" cellspacing="0" summary="">
2.     #TOP_PAGINATION#
3.     <tr>
4.        <td>
5.           <table cellpadding="0" border="0"
                       cellspacing="0" summary=""
                       class="t1standard">
6.              <th#ALIGNMENT# id="#COLUMN_HEADER_NAME#"
                          class="t1header">
7.                 #COLUMN_HEADER#
8.              </th>
9.              <tr #HIGHLIGHT_ROW#>
10.                <td#ALIGNMENT# headers="#COLUMN_HEADER_NAME#"
                             class="t1data">
11.                   #COLUMN_VALUE#
12.                </td>
13.             </tr>
14.          </table>
15.          <div class="t1CVS">#CSV_LINK#</div>
16.       </td>
17.    </tr>
18.    #PAGINATION#
19. </table>
```

Lines 1–5 come from the Before Rows section of the template. This section establishes the outer table and the inner table and will also display the pagination options if specified. Line 6 comes from the Column Heading Template section and is repeated for each column's heading. Notice the lack of the <tr> and </tr> tags; these will be automatically supplied. Line 9 comes from the Before Each Row section. It allows formatting of the data rows. #HIGHLIGHT_ROW# works in conjunction with a "[row selector]" column to highlight a row when it is selected. A row selector column is a special type of column, created by some report wizards, that displays a check box to select the column for deletion. Once the check box is checked, JavaScript is used to highlight the column as selected.

Lines 10–12 come from the Column Template section and are repeated for each cell of data displayed. Line 13 comes from the After Each Row section, and it closes out each row. Lines 14–19 come from the After Rows section, and they close out the tables opened in the first lines. They also display the pagination options and the link to export to a CSV file. This option is covered later in this chapter.

The main point to see in this code, from a Generic Column template, is that only one table cell is defined, and it is reused for every column. The only thing that can be different from column to column is the alignment. On the other hand, in a Named Column template, you can format each data element differently.

The edit page for a Named Column report template contains seven main sections, several of which are common to most types of templates. See Chapter 6 for more details on these common sections. The three sections we will be concerned with here are the Row Templates section, the Before First and After Last Row Text section, and the Pagination section. The following HTML code is a combination of the code from those three sections. As with the code from the Generic Column template, you can see that this code contains one table within another.

```
1.<table cellpadding="0" border="0" cellspacing="0" summary="">
                                                #TOP_PAGINATION#
2.   <tr>
3.     <td>
4.       <table cellpadding="0" border="0"
5.               cellspacing="0" summary="" class="t1standard">
6.         <tr> <td colspan=8 BGCOLOR="#FF0000"> </td></tr>
7.         <tr>
8.           <td class="t1data">#CONTACTID#</td>
9.           <td class="t1data" colspan=2>#LASTNAME#, #FIRSTNAME#</td>
10.          <td class="t1data" colspan=2><cTypeface:Bold>TITLE:</b> #TITLE#</td>
11. <script language="javascript">
12.   if ("#CONTACTTYPE#" == "Seller")
13.   {
14.    document.writeln('<td class="t1data"><cTypeface:Bold>TYPE:</b>
                         <font color=#FF0000> #CONTACTTYPE#</font></td>')
15.   }
16.  else {
17.    document.writeln('<td class="t1data"><cTypeface:Bold>TYPE:</b> #CONTACTTYPE#</td>')
18.   }
19.  </script>
20.          <td class="t1data"><cTypeface:Bold>DEAR:</b> #DEAR#</td>
21.          <td class="t1data" rowspan=4>
22.            <cTypeface:Bold><center>NOTES:</center></b>#NOTES#</td>
23.        </tr>
24.        <tr><td class="t1data" colspan=2>#ADDRESS# <br>
25.                             #CITY#, #STATE# #POSTALCODE#<br>
26.                             #REGION#  #COUNTRY#</td>
27.          <td class="t1data"><cTypeface:Bold>MOBILE Phone:</b><br>#MOBILEPHONE#</td>
28.          <td class="t1data"><cTypeface:Bold>HOME Phone:</b><br>#HOMEPHONE#</td>
29.          <td class="t1data"><cTypeface:Bold>COMPANY:</b><br>#COMPANYNAME#</td>
30.          <td class="t1data">
31.            <cTypeface:Bold>WORK Phone:</b><br>#WORKPHONE# ext:#WORKEXTENSION#</td>
32.          <td class="t1data"><cTypeface:Bold>FAX:</b><br>#FAXNUMBER#</td>
33.        </tr>
34.        <tr><td class="t1data" colspan=2><cTypeface:Bold>EMAIL:</b> #EMAILNAME#</td>
35.          <td class="t1data"><cTypeface:Bold>BIRTHDATE:</b> #BIRTHDATE#</td>
36.          <td class="t1data"><cTypeface:Bold>HOMETOWN:</b> #HOMETOWN#</td>
37.          <td class="t1data"><cTypeface:Bold>LAST MEETING:</b> #LASTMEETINGDATE#</td>
38.          <td class="t1data" colspan=2 >
                             <cTypeface:Bold>REFERRED BY:</b> #REFERREDBY#</td>
39.        </tr>
40.        <tr><td class="t1data"> </td>
41.          <td class="t1data"><cTypeface:Bold>MARITALSTATUS:</b> #MARITALSTATUS#</td>
42.          <td class="t1data"><cTypeface:Bold>SPOUSE:</b> #SPOUSENAME#</td>
43.          <td class="t1data"><cTypeface:Bold>SPOUSES INTERESTS:
                                    </b> #SPOUSESINTERESTS#</td>
44.          <td class="t1data"><cTypeface:Bold>CHILDRENs NAMES:</b> #CHILDRENNAMES#</td>
45.          <td class="t1data" colspan=2>
46.            <cTypeface:Bold>CONTACTS INTERESTS:</b>#CONTACTSINTERESTS#</td>
47.        </tr>
48.      </table>
49.      <div class="t1CVS">#CSV_LINK#</div>
50.    </td>
51.  </tr>
52.  #PAGINATION#
53. </table>
```

Lines 1–5 come from the Before Rows field, and lines 48–53 come from the After Rows field of the Before First and After Last Row Text section. These open and close the tables for the report. Like their counterparts in the Generic Column template, they allow for pagination and placement of the CSV file link. Lines 6–47 come from the Row Template 1 field in the Row Templates section and make up the custom formatting that results in the Row Template sections outlined in Figure 9-9. This section is repeated for each row of the report, whereas in the Generic Column template the formatting was repeated for each table cell. The resulting report is by no means a work of art, but you can see that with a little knowledge of HTML you can produce a custom template that greatly improves the readability of a table with a large number of columns. You are limited only by your knowledge of HTML. Note the use of JavaScript in lines 11–19, which will highlight the contact type if it is equal to Seller.

Editing Report Attributes

Once you have created a report, you can make further refinements to the report by editing the report's attributes. You can navigate to the edit page from the Regions section of the Page Definition page, which was discussed in Chapter 8. The Regions section shown next has two reports. The first report was created using the wizard; this is indicated by its region type, which is RPT. The second report was created as a plain SQL report; this is shown by its region type of Q. Clicking on the report type will take you directly to the Report Attributes edit page. If you click on the name of the region, you will navigate to the Edit Page Region page.

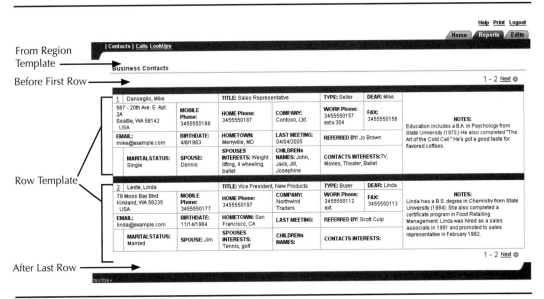

FIGURE 9-9   *Contact report template sections*

Edit Page Region Page

The Edit Page Region page is where you control elements such as the region template, conditional display, region header and footer text, authorization, configuration management, and end-user customization. Refer back to Chapter 8 for more details on these items. You need to know a few things specific to report regions. If the region is a wizard-created report, the Region Source section will only display the query generated by the query builder, whereas if the region is a manually written SQL query, the query is entered and modified in the Region Source section. Additionally, two more items appear below the Region Source area, as shown next. The Region Error Message field allows you to enter a message that's displayed in case of an error. You can display the SQL error message with the #SQLERRM# substitution variable. The radio buttons allow you to specify that the column names will be generic and come from the query when it is parsed at run time. Normally, you will use the Use Query-Specific Column Names and Validate Query option.

```
Region Source

Region Source
declare
   avar varchar2(10) := 'ename';
begin
   if   :p6_showall = 'N' then
      return 'select empno,'||avar||', job from emp';
   else
      return 'select * from emp';
   end if;
end;
```

◉ Use Query-Specific Column Names and Validate Query
○ Use Generic Column Names (parse query at runtime only)

Region Error Message
```
#SQLERRM#
```

The Use Generic Column Names option should be used if the query you are writing cannot be validated when you are creating the report region—for instance, when you are writing a query against a table that will be created and populated during the execution of the application. Another time you would use the Generic Column option would be in the case of a dynamically created query, like the one just shown. This is just a simple example, but you can make it as complex as you need to. You can dynamically choose the columns you want to select and you can even change the table you will select against.

To create a report with a dynamic query, first create a report region with a straight SQL query, then edit the region and change the region type in the Region section of the Edit Page Region page from SQL Query to SQL Query(PL/SQL Function Body Returning SQL Query). At the same time, change the region source from the straight query to a function body.

Report Attributes Page

You navigate to the Report Attributes page from the Page Definition page by clicking on the region type for the report, which will either be RPT or Q, as discussed previously. This will take you directly to the Report Attributes page. Once at the Report Attributes page, you can switch back and forth to the Edit Page Region page by using the tabs at the top of the page. The Report Attributes page allows you to further control the look and behavior of your report by arranging the order of columns, changing column headings, enabling sorting, changing pagination, enabling report breaks and totals, and allowing a CSV export of your report. The Report Attributes page is divided into six main sections. You can navigate quickly to any section via the quick links at the top of the page.

NOTE
Using the tabs to navigate back and forth between the Region Definition page and the Report Attributes page also applies any changes that you have made.

The first section, Report Column Attributes, shown in Figure 9-10, allows you to control certain aspects of the report's columns. This section contains a radio button group to specify the column heading type and a table of attributes for each column in the report. If you select to use generic column names in the Region Source section of the Edit Page Region page, the table of column attributes in the first section will contain 60 generic columns with aliases COL01 through COL60. You may still change the attributes in the table, and they will apply to whatever column happens to be in that position.

Report Column Attributes

The paper and pencil edit icon will navigate you to the Column Attributes page, which is covered later in this chapter. The alias is the name of the column from the query that is used when you refer to the value of the column with the #ALIAS# syntax. We did this in the Named Column template example earlier, and we will look at another example of this in the "Column Attributes Page" section later in this chapter.

The Link and Edit columns will contain a check mark if a particular column is either a link or has been set to an editable column. These are both done in the Column Attributes page and will be covered later. The up and down arrows allow you to rearrange the order in which your columns are displayed. The Heading column allows you to edit the text for the heading if the Custom radio button is selected as the heading type, located above the table of columns.

The Headings Type radio button group allows you to specify the source for your column headings. The default is Column Name, which uses the column name from the query in all capital letters; you can also select for the column name with initial letters capitalized. The Custom option allows you to supply your own heading in the heading column. The PL/SQL option can be used if you are doing a dynamic query. You must supply a function that returns a colon-delimited list of the column headings. The same logic that you use in determining which columns and what table you are going to query could be used to create the list of column headings. You may also select the None option to use no headings at all.

The Column and Heading Alignment LOVs allow you to specify the horizontal justification of the header and data. The Show check box allows you to hide or show a column. If you select the Sum check box for a numeric column, a summed total will be displayed at the bottom of the report. The labeling of this summation can be controlled and is discussed later in the section "Break Formatting."

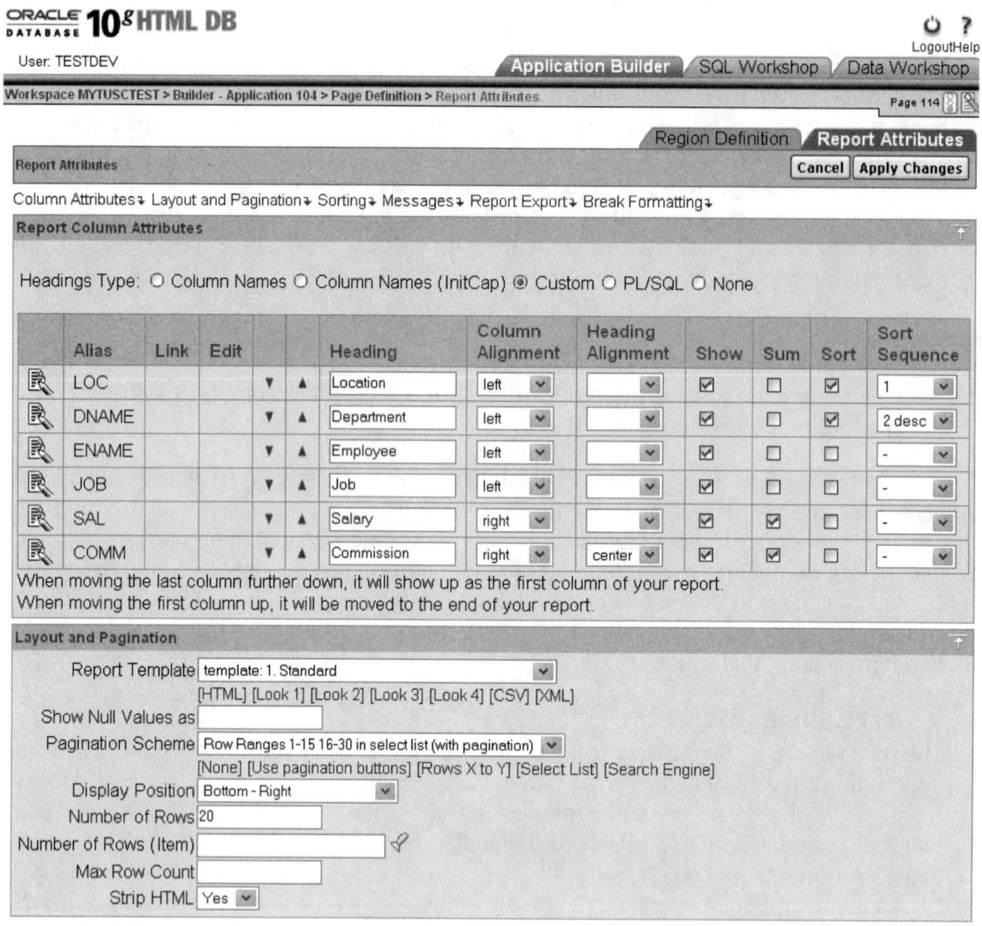

FIGURE 9-10 *Report Attributes page, part 1*

The Sort check box enables user-initiated sorting on the selected column. The column heading will be made into an active link. The first time it is clicked on, the report will rerun and be sorted in ascending order of the column selected. The next time it will be sorted in descending order. An icon, as defined in the Sorting section, will be displayed next to the column heading to indicate that the data is sorted on that column in either ascending or descending order. Sort Sequence specifies how you initially want the report ordered. You may specify multiple columns to sort on and whether you want each one to sort in ascending or descending order. If you specify a sort sequence, the columns you include in the sort sequence will automatically have their Sort check box checked and the user-initiated sorting will be enabled for each column specified in the sort sequence.

NOTE
Once a user reorders a report from its initial ordering through the use of the column-ordering feature, each time they return to the report it will be ordered the same way in which they last left it. This is stored as a user preference. These preferences can be removed through workspace administration, covered in Chapter 17, or programmatically with the HTMLDB_UTIL package, which is introduced in Appendix I.

Layout and Pagination

The Layout and Pagination section allows you to change items that influence the display of the report and the way pagination is implemented for the report. The item that most influences the layout of the report is, of course, the report template used to render the report. The report template is specified during the creation of the report but may be changed at any time. The Report Template LOV allows you to select from a list of standard report templates or from all the report templates in the theme associated with the application. Some of the default templates may quickly be selected via the links directly below the LOV.

The Show Null Values As field allows you to specify a value that will be displayed for any null column throughout the entire report. If you need to have different values for nulls in different columns, use the NVL function in the query for each of your columns. If the Strip HTML field is set to YES, this tells the rendering engine that you might be selecting values from the database that contain HTML tags that could interfere with the rendering of the report and that the tags should be stripped out of the data before being displayed.

Pagination refers to how all the rows of a report will be broken into logical "pages." In other words, if your report returns 57 rows, pagination could display the report on three pages, with 20 rows on the first two pages and 17 rows on the last page. The Pagination Scheme selected, as detailed in the following table, determines if all rows of a report will be available, determines how the information about the number of rows in the result set and the current position in the result set will be displayed, determines the type of navigation options that will be provided for moving from page to page of the report, and can influence the performance of the report. The list may still include the Use Externally Created Pagination Buttons option, but this option has been deprecated and is only present for version 1.5 backward compatibility.

Pagination Schema	Example Display	Complete Result Set Available	Counts All Rows (Decreases Performance)
No Pagination Selected	Nothing displayed	No. Limited to value specified in Number of Rows	No
Row Ranges 1–15 16–30 (with set pagination)	**1-10** 11-20 21-30 31-40 41-50 Next Set ⊚	Yes	Yes
Row Ranges 1–15 16–30 in select list (with pagination)	row(s) 1 - 10 of more than 200 ⊻ Next ⊚	Yes	Yes

Pagination Schema	Example Display	Complete Result Set Available	Counts All Rows (Decreases Performance)
Row Ranges X to Y (no pagination)	row(s) 1 - 10 of 11	No. Limited to value specified in Number of Rows	No
Row Ranges X to Y of Z (no pagination)	row(s) 1 - 10 of more than 200	No. Limited to value specified in Number of Rows	Yes
Row Ranges X to Y of Z (with pagination)	row(s) 1 - 10 of more than 200 Next ◉	Yes	Yes
Search Engine 1, 2, 3, 4 (set-based pagination)	**1** 2 3 4 5 6 7 8 9 10 Next Set ◉	Yes	Yes
Row Ranges X to Y (with next and previous links)	◉ Previous 11 - 20 Next ◉	Yes	No

The Number of Rows field determines how many rows will be displayed per page. The Number of Rows (Item) field allows you to specify a page item that contains the number of rows to be displayed per page. This way, the number can be set dynamically. The Max Row Count field specifies a maximum number of rows that will be returned by the report. If left blank, this value is set internally and will not allow a report to display more than 500 rows unless you manually enter a larger value. The following table shows the basic steps for implementing a user-defined Number of Row item. Some of the items in the steps are concepts that have not yet been covered. Refer to later chapters for more details.

Steps for Implementing User-controlled Report Lengths

1. Create a page item of type Text Field (always submits a page when ENTER is pressed) named P4_ROWS_PER_PAGE, positioned at the top of your report region, and give it a default value of 15.

2. Create a Go To Page branch that unconditionally branches back to the same page number on which you are implementing the report.

3. Set the Number of Rows (Item) field to be P4_ROWS_PER_PAGE.

Sorting

The Sorting section, shown in Figure 9-11, allows you to provide information that will be used when the user-initiated sorting feature is implemented. Use the Ascending Image and Descending Image fields to specify the image to be used to indicate when a column is sorted in ascending or descending order. Three default images are provided. They are easily selected by clicking on the image to the right of the field. You may also specify an image of your own. To do this, upload an image in the Image section of the application's shared components. Then reference the image in the image fields using the workspace image substitution variable (for example, #WORKSPACE_IMAGE#my_arrow.gif). The last two fields are used for specifying the attributes that will go into the HTML code for each of the images.

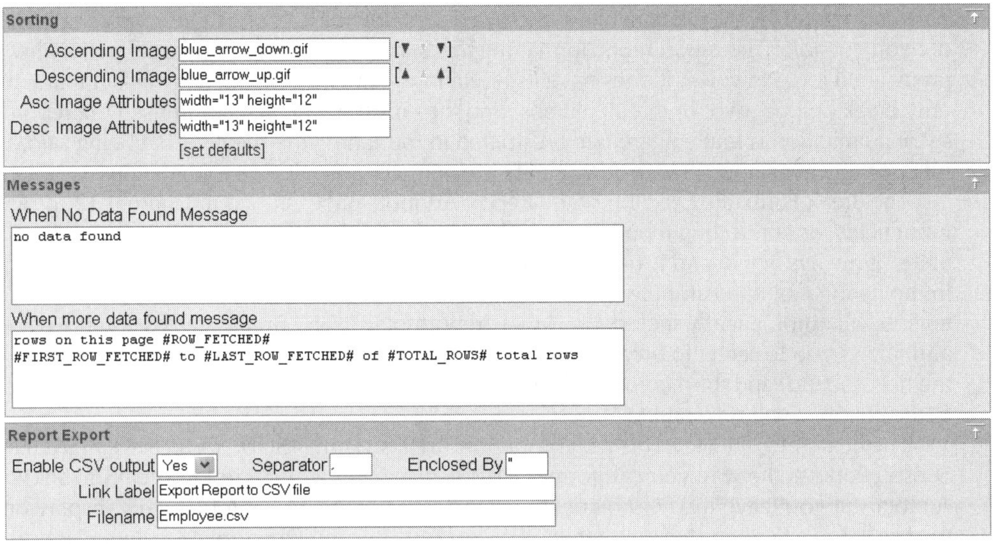

FIGURE 9-11   *Report Attributes page, part 2*

Messages

The Messages section contains fields for two messages. The field When No Data Found Message allows you to enter the text of the message that will be displayed when the query returns no data. The field When More Data Found Message allows you to specify a message when more data is found beyond what is specified in the Max Row Count field in the Layout and Pagination section. This area can be used as an alternative to pagination options. The Pagination substitution variables can be used in constructing the message. The variables are #ROWS_FETCHED#, #TOTAL_ROWS#, #FIRST_ROW_FETCHED#, #LAST_ROW_FETCHED#, #ROW_RANGES#, #ROW_RANGES_IN_ SELECTION_LIST#, and #INTERNET_PAGINATION#.

Report Export

This is a great example of how HTML DB makes things easy for you, the developer. By supplying a few pieces of information, you can provide your user a link that saves a copy of the current report to a delimited file on the user's machine. However, for this to work, your report template must include the #CSV_LINK# substitution variable in the After Rows section of the template. The exported file will contain all rows up to the Max Row Count specified. If no value is specified, it will only export the first 500 rows.

Selecting Yes for the Enable CSV output field enables the rest of the fields for data entry. The Separator field allows you to specify a character, normally a comma, to be used to separate the column values on each row of the output file. The character supplied in the Enclosed By field, normally double quotes, will be used on both sides of every field. This is done in case any of the fields being exported contain the character that is used to separate the column values. The text entered in the Link Label field will become an active link that brings up the Save File dialog box from your report page. The Filename field allows you to specify a default filename for the file that is going to be saved. If you don't supply a value here, it will default to the title of the report region with a .csv extension.

Break Formatting

The idea behind HTML DB is to allow you to create fairly robust applications with the least amount of effort possible. The report break formatting that's implemented as standard functionality does a pretty good job. However, it does have its limitations—the first of which is the fact that you can only break on one, two, or three columns, and they must be the first columns in the report. The second limitation is that you are fairly restricted in formatting the breaks. That being said, the functionality available allows you to create breaking reports with very little effort.

The Break Formatting section of the Report Attribute page, shown in Figure 9-12, provides the input fields for controlling report breaks. The first field, Display This Text When Printing Report Sums, is always active and is used whenever you select the Sum check box for a numeric column in the Report Column Attributes section. If you do not provide text in this field, the HTML DB engine will automatically include the label "report total:". The Breaks field defaults to No Breaks and allows you to select to break the report on the first column, the first and second columns, or the first, second, and third columns. Once you select a value other than No Breaks, the remainder of the columns will be enabled.

The next field, Display This Text on Report Breaks Using #SUM_COLUMN_HEADER# Substitutions, is the way you can format what is displayed when a report breaks to show subtotals. If you leave the field blank, the HTML DB engine will automatically display on the break rows "*columnheading* total:". For instance, for the Department column subtotals, it will display "Department total:". You can customize what is displayed using this field. Use the substitution variable #SUB_COLUMN_HEADER# to reference the header of the break column. Unfortunately, the current version does not allow you to reference the value of the break column.

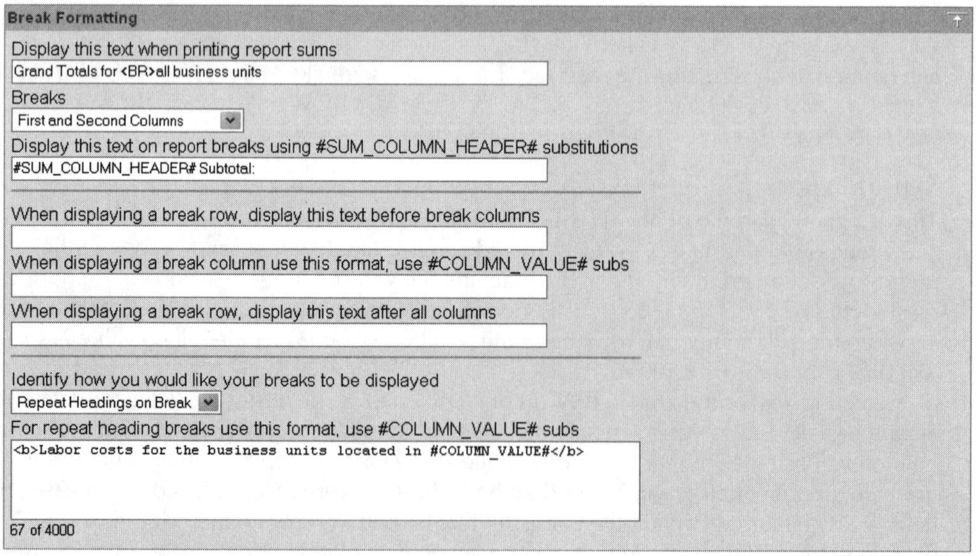

Break Formatting

Display this text when printing report sums
`Grand Totals for <BR>all business units`

Breaks
`First and Second Columns`

Display this text on report breaks using #SUM_COLUMN_HEADER# substitutions
`#SUM_COLUMN_HEADER# Subtotal:`

When displaying a break row, display this text before break columns

When displaying a break column use this format, use #COLUMN_VALUE# subs

When displaying a break row, display this text after all columns

Identify how you would like your breaks to be displayed
`Repeat Headings on Break`

For repeat heading breaks use this format, use #COLUMN_VALUE# subs
`<b>Labor costs for the business units located in #COLUMN_VALUE#</b>`

67 of 4000

FIGURE 9-12 *Report Attributes page, part 3*

The first and last field in the center section of the Break Formatting section can be used to format a row before and after the break row, respectively. Unfortunately, with the way they are currently implemented, you must provide the complete HTML code for the row. For instance, if your report has five columns, you would enter something like:

```
<tr><td>first col</td><td colspan="3"><td>last col</td></td></tr>
```

The center field is used to format the actual break column. The formatting entered needs to be the HTML for a column and can use the #COLUMN_VALUE# substitution variable, like this:

```
<td align=right>#COLUMN_VALUE#</td>
```

Note that all the columns in the row will have the formatting applied to them.

The final two fields provide you two different options for displaying the first column break. The field Identify How You Would Like Your Breaks to be Displayed has two possible values: Default Break Formatting and Repeat Headings on Break. The Repeat Headings on Break option causes the first breaking column to be reported as a heading with the column headings for all the remaining columns repeated after each break. Figure 9-13 shows the report generated based on

Wages

Labor costs for the business units located in NEW YORK

Department	Employee	Job	Salary	Commission
ACCOUNTING	KING	PRESIDENT	$5,000.00	$0.00
	CLARK	MANAGER	$2,450.00	$0.00
	MILLER	CLERK	$1,300.00	$0.00
Department Subtotal:			$8,750.00	$0.00
OPERATIONS	RUBBLE	MANAGER	$3,500.00	$0.00
	FLINSTONE	CONSULT	$2,100.00	$0.00
	SLATE	ASSIST	$1,900.00	$0.00
Department Subtotal:			$7,500.00	$0.00
Location Subtotal:			$16,250.00	$0.00

Labor costs for the business units located in DALLAS

Department	Employee	Job	Salary	Commission
RESEARCH	JONES	MANAGER	$2,975.00	$0.00
	FORD	ANALYST	$3,000.00	$0.00
	SMITH	CLERK	$800.00	$0.00
	SCOTT	ANALYST	$3,000.00	$0.00
	ADAMS	CLERK	$1,100.00	$0.00
Department Subtotal:			$10,875.00	$0.00
Location Subtotal:			$10,875.00	$0.00

Labor costs for the business units located in CHICAGO

Department	Employee	Job	Salary	Commission
SALES	BLAKE	MANAGER	$2,850.00	$0.00
	ALLEN	SALESMAN	$1,600.00	$350.00
	WARD	SALESMAN	$1,250.00	$500.00
	JAMES	CLERK	$950.00	$0.00
	MARTIN	SALESMAN	$1,250.00	$1,400.00
	TURNER	SALESMAN	$1,500.00	$0.00
Department Subtotal:			$9,400.00	$2,250.00
Location Subtotal:			$9,400.00	$2,250.00
Grand Totals for all business units			$36,525.00	$2,250.00

FIGURE 9-13 *Break Formatting example*

the settings displayed in Figure 9-12. The first column was Location, which is used in the header. You can see that by using the #COLUMN_VALUES# substitution variable you are able to reference the actual values of the breaking column (in this case, the names of the cities). If the Default Break Formatting option was selected, the first column would be displayed in position next to the other columns, with its header displayed and its value displayed each time a new value is encountered.

Editing Column Attributes

The Column Attributes page allows you even more control over individual report columns. You navigate to the page via the pencil and paper edit icon for a specific column on the Report Attributes page, shown earlier in Figure 9-10. Like with many of the longer HTML DB pages, you can use quick links to navigate to any one of the six sections on the Column Attributes page. Along with the standard Cancel and Apply Changes buttons at the top, you will find left and right arrows that allow you to navigate to the previous and next Column Attributes pages. When you use these arrows, any changes you made to the current page will be saved before navigating to the next column.

Column Definition

The Column Definition section allows you to edit many, but not all, of the same column attributes contained in the table in the first section of the Report Attributes page. You may set the column heading, the column and heading alignments, and whether the column will be displayed, sorted, and/or summed. Refer to the "Report Attributes Page" section earlier in this chapter, for more details on these settings.

Column Formatting

The Column Formatting section, shown in Figure 9-14, allows you to further control the formatting of individual columns. Without any entries in this section, your column will be formatted according to the formatting applied to the columns in the report template. The Number/Date Format field allows you to enter any valid PL/SQL format for a number or a date. The arrow next to the field pops up a small window from which you can select a number of predefined formats. You may also take advantage of Cascading Style Sheets by simply entering the name of a CSS class or style in the fields provided.

The Highlight Words field allows you to enter a single word (or a comma-delimited list of words) that will be highlighted if it is contained in the value of the column. The word does not have to be a whole word. The functionality will highlight a portion of the word if a match is found. You can also reference a page item using the "&ITEMNAME." syntax and highlight words that match the contents of the page item. This is most frequently used in a search function to highlight the word you are searching for. The following table shows the basic steps for implementing a search-and-highlight functionality. Some of the items in these steps are concepts that have not yet been covered. Refer to later chapters for more details. The results should look something like what is shown next.

Steps for Implementing a Search-and-highlight Functionality

1. Create a page item of type Text Field (always submits a page when ENTER is pressed) named P4_JOB, positioned at the top of your report region, and give it no default value and a label of Find All Jobs.

2. Create a Go To Page branch that unconditionally branches back to the same page number on which you are implementing the report.

3. Modify your report query and add the following to the WHERE clause:

```
upper(emp.job) like '%'||upper(:P114_JOB)||'%'
```

4. Set the Highlight Words field for the Job column to **&P4_JOB.** (note that the syntax includes a trailing period).

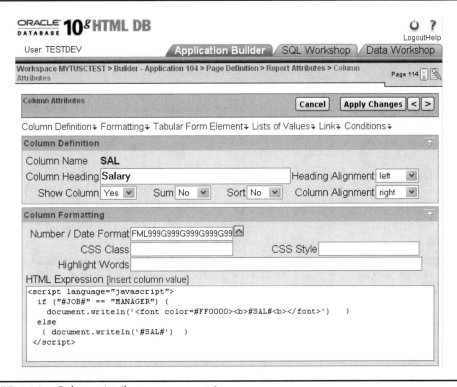

FIGURE 9-14   *Column Attributes page, part 1*

The HTML Expression field allows you to enter a valid HTML expression for the column. In constructing the HTML expression, you can reference the value of any column. In the example in Figure 9-14 for the Sal column, the JavaScript looks to see if the value for the job field for the current row is equal to MANAGER. If it is, it highlights the salary. A more useful function would have been to highlight the salary if the salary were greater than some value. However, in this example, this could not be done because of the formatting being applied to the column. You would end up with an expression like $2,500 > 2000, which would not work. A workaround to this would be to have another column that also contains the salary but it is not formatted and is not displayed.

Tabular Form Element

A report can actually be turned into a multirow editing form like the one shown in Figure 9-15. With the fields in the Tabular Form Element section, we can turn a displayed column into a text field, text area, select list, or date picker, but before any updates can actually be made to the database, a multirow update process must be defined or a PL/SQL process implemented to process the changes. HTML DB provides wizards to create tabular forms, which are actually implemented as a report with a process to handle the database inserts/updates and deletes. This section will be covered in depth in Chapter 10.

The Display As field allows you to select from all the different types of fields available, which are detailed in the following table. Most types are for use in tabular edit forms, but several are for use in normal reports. Whether or not the Display As type saves the state of the field is what determines whether it is for a normal report or a multirow update form. In Chapter 8, we discussed the topic of session state management, which is the mechanism that HTML DB uses to maintain information from page to page so it can be processed.

Display As Type	Saves State	Comments
Standard Report Column (display only; does not save state)	No	Default type for all report columns.
Display as Text (based on LOV; does not save state)	No	Used with reports; takes the key from the source table and looks up the corresponding value. For example, dept_no in the source table displays Department name from the LOV.
Display as Text (saves state)	Yes	Used with update forms; allows the display of a value that you don't want the user to be able to edit.
Display as Text(escape special characters; does not save state)	No	Used with reports. Used to display special characters that might be interpreted as part of HTML. Ex. column contains <td>Weld</td> and you want to display <td>Weld</td>.
Date Picker	Yes	Used with update forms. Implements a JavaScript calendar to select dates.
Text Field	Yes	Used with update forms. Normal HTML text field.
Text Area	Yes	Used with update forms. Normal HTML text area.
Select List (static LOV)	Yes	Used with update forms. HTML select list based on an LOV made up of static values.

Display As Type	Saves State	Comments
Select List (named LOV)	Yes	Used with update forms. HTML select list based on a named LOV from the application's shared components.
Select List (query-based LOV)	Yes	Used with update forms. HTML select list based on an LOV from a SQL query.
Hidden	Yes	Used with update forms. HTML hidden item. Used to pass on values that don't need to be seen.
Popup LOV (named LOV)	Yes	Pops up a separate small window with values from a named LOV from the application's shared components
Popup LOV (query-based LOV)	Yes	Pops up a separate small window with values from a named LOV SQL query.

When you specify a column as a Display As type of Date Picker, the Number/Date Format field in the Column Formatting section will be disabled and the Date Picker Format Mask field, shown in Figure 9-16, is enabled. The Date Picker Format Mask field allows you to select the way the date will be displayed in the field. The Element Width field allows you to specify the width of a form item, whereas the Number of Rows field is used to set the number of rows for a text area.

The Element Attributes field is supposed to be for adding a style or standard HTML form element attributes. However, the style is taken care of in the CSS style field in the Column Formatting section. As for the standard HTML form element attributes, you would never want to specify the type="", value="", and name="" attributes because the HTML DB engine is already taking care of these. The size="" attribute is handled by the Element Width field. The one HTML attribute you might want to put here is maxlength="", but the HTML DB engine is already putting in maxlength="2000", so the one you enter will have no effect. You could enter a maxlength="" anyway, assuming that the bug will be fixed in a future release, thus allowing you to control the maximum input length for a text field in a tabular edit form.

Wages

Find all Jobs [man]

Location	Department	Employee	Job	Salary	Commission	Hiredate	Temp
NEW YORK	ACCOUNTING ▾	CLARK	MANAGER ▾	$2,450.00	$0.00	09-JUN-81	☐
NEW YORK	OPERATIONS ▾	RUBBLE	MANAGER ▾	$3,500.00	$0.00	08-JAN-83	☑
DALLAS	RESEARCH ▾	JONES	MANAGER ▾	$2,975.00	$0.00	02-APR-81	☐
CHICAGO	SALES ▾	BLAKE	MANAGER ▾	$2,850.00	$0.00	01-MAY-81	☐
CHICAGO	SALES ▾	ALLEN	SALESMAN ▾	$1,600.00	$350.00	20-FEB-81	☐
CHICAGO	SALES ▾	WARD	SALESMAN ▾	$1,250.00	$500.00	22-FEB-81	☐
CHICAGO	SALES ▾	MARTIN	SALESMAN ▾	$1,250.00	$1,400.00	28-SEP-81	☐
CHICAGO	SALES ▾	TURNER	SALESMAN ▾	$1,500.00	$0.00	08-SEP-81	☐

FIGURE 9-15 *Sample tabular edit report/form*

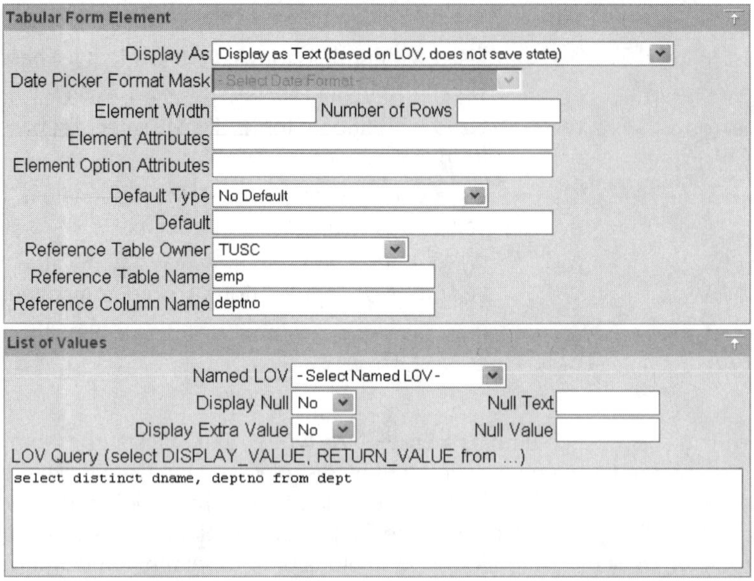

FIGURE 9-16 *Column Attributes page, part 2*

The Element Option Attributes field is supposed to be for items in a radio group or check box; however, those options are not available in the Display As field. Radio groups and check boxes can be implemented with the HTMLDB_ITEM package (see Appendix I). The Default Type field and Default field are used to add new rows to a form. The HTML DB engine uses their settings to determine the default values for the column. Without them, the column is defined as NULL. This is part of the tabular form and will be covered more in Chapter 10. Likewise, the Reference Table and Column fields are used with tabular forms.

List of Values

The Lists of Values section is used to define the list of values that will be used with the current column if it is one of the Display As types that require an LOV. This can also be used with a straight report to display values that normally would have to be obtained via a join. Figure 9-16 shows an example where the department number will be used against the LOV to display the department name in the report.

The Named LOV field allows you to select from a list of existing LOVs. These are created and maintained from the application's Shared Components section. If you do not have an existing named LOV, you can specify a query in the LOV Query text area. You must select two columns—the first is the value that will be displayed in the report, and the second is the value that will correspond to the value in the report's query.

The fields dealing with null values have no effect on regular reports. If your report query returns columns that are being displayed through an LOV, rows that contain null values in the LOV column will not be displayed. However, if the report query returns values other than null that are not in your LOV, the actual value of the column will be displayed regardless of the value of the Display Extra Values field.

Column Link

The Column Link section allows you to make a column in your report an active link to another page in your application or any page accessible with a URL. You have seen this several times before. In Chapter 8, we created a report and edit page that has a column in the report that contains an icon that navigates to the edit page for that particular row.

Earlier in this chapter, we created a report for the Contacts table. In the next chapter, we will create an edit form for Contacts table. We will want to be able to navigate from our Contacts report to our Contacts edit form. If you edit the Column Link fields for the ContactID column, as shown in Figure 9-17, you will have enabled an active navigational link. The following paragraphs discuss each field shown.

What the Column Link section is really doing is building an "f?p" syntax URL behind the scenes. In fact, if you want to see the URL that is constructed from your inputs, return to this section after applying the changes and change the Target field from Page in This Application to URL. A URL field will appear at the bottom of the section that contains the generated URL in the f?p syntax. This syntax is discussed in detail in Chapter 11.

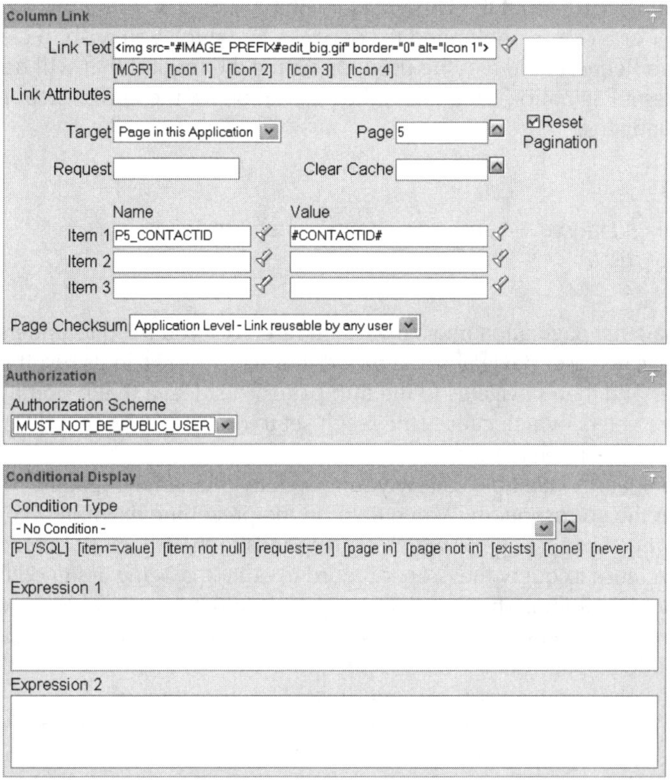

FIGURE 9-17 *Column Attributes page, part 3*

Whatever you enter into the Link Text field will be displayed in the column in the report and will be an active link. HTML DB provides you with five quick-fill links below this field. The first populates the field with the #ALIAS# syntax variable for the current column so the value of the column will be displayed as a link. As you hold your mouse over the next four quick-fill links, their corresponding icon will be displayed in the box to the right of the field. Click on any one of the quick-fill links and the complete HTML <img> tag to display the icon will be populated into the Link Text field. The flashlight icon next to the Link Text field pops up a small window that lists the rest of the columns in the report as active links. Clicking on one of the column links will return, to the Link Text field, the column in its #ALIAS# syntax, allowing you to reference the value of any other column in the Link Text field.

The Link Attributes field is for entering any additional HTML attributes or CSS styles or classes that you want included in the generated <a href> tag. For instance, you could include target="new" so that the navigation would open a new browser window instead of replacing the existing page. The Target field defaults to Page in This Application. If you change it to a URL, all the fields below it will be disabled and a URL field will be added at the bottom of the section where you can enter any valid URL, including your own f?p syntax URL.

In the Page field, you specify the number of the page you wish to navigate to. You can select from a list of page names by clicking on the arrow icon next to the field. To fully understand the following fields, read about the f?p syntax in Chapter 11. Enter into the Clear Cache field a single page number or a comma-delimited list of pages for which you wish to clear the cache when you navigate. The Request field may be used for setting the request that will be used in the link. If you check the Reset Pagination check box, the pagination for the current report will be reset when navigation happens.

NOTE
Report pagination can cause some unexpected behavior
if it is not reset.

Not to say that pagination must always be reset, but you need to understand what can happen. For instance, say a user navigates to a report that has 50 rows in its result set paginated into five logical pages and then navigates to the fifth page. They leave that report and later return to it with different parameters, which causes the result set to only have 20 rows. It will attempt to go to the fifth page, which will be blank.

The Name and Value fields allow you to specify the name of page items that will be assigned the values in the corresponding Value field. In the preceding example, P5_CONTACTID is a page item on the target page, page 5, which corresponds to the ContactID column and will be used in the WHERE clause to query the proper record to edit. It is being assigned the value of the current row's ContactID column. The flashlight icons next to the Name fields allow you to select from a list of existing page items for the page specified in the Page field. If no page has been entered, the list will include all page items in the application. The flashlight icons next to the Value fields allow you to select from a list of columns from the current report.

The final field in the Column Link section is new to version 2.0. The Page Checksum field allows you to specify whether a checksum will be added to the generated URL, which will make the URL unusable. The default value will make it unusable in any session other than the current one. The Workspace Level option allows the URL to be reused by any authenticated user. The User Level option allows the URL to only be reused in any session by the same authenticated user.

The remaining sections in the Column Attributes page—Authorization and Conditional Display—are common to most HTML DB elements. Authorization can be used to display a column only to users who meet the authorization scheme. Authorization is discussed in Chapter 16. Conditional Display can also be used to dynamically control whether a column is displayed. Conditional Display uses the same conditions as Conditional Processing, which was discussed in Chapter 8.

Structured Query Attributes

If a report is created using the Structured Query Wizard, an additional tab titled Query Definition will appear on the Region Definition page or the Reports Attributes page, as shown in Figure 9-18. This page allows you to modify the query you built in the wizard during report creation.

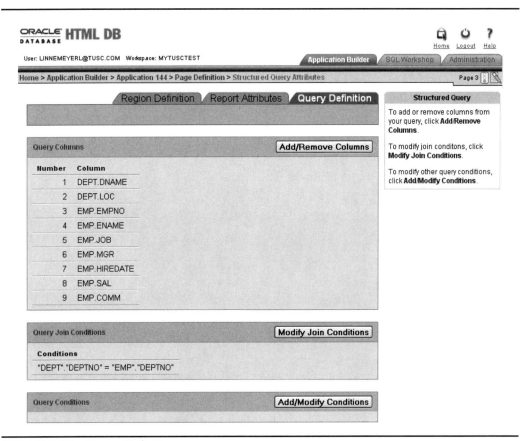

FIGURE 9-18 *Query Definition page*

The functionality of the first two sections is identical to the functionality in the Report Wizard. If you click on the Add/Remove Columns button, you will be taken to a screen where you can specify the source tables and columns for the query. The screen will look and behave just like the one shown in Figure 9-4. Likewise, the Modify Join Conditions button will take you to a page to specify the join conditions if you specified more than one table. This page looks and behaves just like the one in Figure 9-5.

If you click on the Add/Modify Conditions button, you will be taken to a screen where you can create additional conditions aside from the join conditions for the WHERE clause of the generated query. For example, you could add a condition like EMP.COMM IS NOT NULL.

CHAPTER
10

Defining and
Processing Forms

TML DB uses forms as the mechanism for users to enter and edit data from the database. In Chapter 8, we created a report and a corresponding form to display and edit the data contained in the Calls table. The form page produced, shown in Figure 10-1, is a typical example of a single-record HTML DB edit form.

The same form page can be used to insert, update, and delete records from a table. Different buttons can be presented to the user depending on the action that caused the navigation to the page. If the action was caused by an Edit link, the Cancel, Delete, and Save buttons will be available. If it was caused by a Create link, only the Cancel and Create buttons are displayed. Although the form in Figure 10-1 only allows the user to edit a single row at a time, forms can be easily created that allow the editing of multiple records at the same time.

In this chapter, we will look into the wizards that HTML DB provides to the developer for quickly creating different types of form pages. We will also dig into the workings of a form page and learn how to enhance the actions provided in a wizard-created form.

The Form Wizard

Once again, the HTML DB development environment provides tools to enable the developer to quickly create the elements needed for a fully functional application. Forms like reports are regions upon a page. You may remember when we covered the types of regions in Chapter 8 that we did not see the region type Form. Forms are actually built in an HTML region. Also like with reports, HTML DB has wizards to help you create forms. Two different wizards can be use to create a form. Once you get into the form-building section of each of these wizards, they are very similar.

- **Create Page Wizard (Page with Component option, Form option)**   Create Page Wizard is started from the Create Page button on Application Builder main page or the Create button on any Page Definition page.

- **New Component Wizard (Region on This Page option, Form option)**   The New Component Wizard is started from the Create link on the Developer's Toolbar.

Print Logout

Home | Reports | Edits

Contact Edit [Call Edit] LookUp Edit

Calls   Cancel | Delete | Apply Changes

Contactid 1
Calldate   11/21/1999
Calltime   1/0/1900
Subject   Buy flavored coffees.
Notes   Mike told me about their blends. Thin|

TESTDEV

Edit Application | Edit Page 6 | New | Session | Debug | Show Edit Links

---

FIGURE 10-1   *Calls edit page*

In Chapter 9, we manually created a report for the Contacts table for the application that we have been building. We also looked at how we would link that report to an edit form for the contacts. We will now build a form for editing a single Contacts record. Recall in Chapter 5 when we created the shell for the application we created a page for the edit form for contacts.

From the Application Builder main page for the Contacts application, click on the run icon for the Contacts edit page. This will run the page for you. You may have to log in before the page is displayed. The page should be nearly blank, consisting of only the page headers and footers, which include the tabs. The Developer's Toolbar should be displayed below the footer. Click on the Create link. Select the Region on This Page option and click on Next. Then select the Form option and click on Next. The next page, shown in Figure 10-2, will provide you with all the options for creating a form. These options are detailed in the following table:

Form Option	Description
Table	This option creates a form based on a single table that you select. It creates edit fields for every column except the primary key column. The fields will be for a single table record presented in a form style. This option also creates a Cancel button and optionally Create, Save, and Delete buttons. It implements the processes to fetch the records and to process inserts, updates, and deletes for a single record.
Tabular Form	This option creates a form based on a single table that you select. It creates edit fields for every column except the primary key column. It displays the fields in a columnar report. This option also creates a Cancel button and optionally Create, Save, and Delete buttons. It implements the processes to fetch the records and to process inserts, updates, and deletes for multiple records.
Procedure Arguments	This option creates a form based on a stored procedure that you select. One text field will be created for each procedure parameter and will be presented in a form style. It also creates a Submit and Cancel button and a process that will execute the specified stored procedure. When the Submit button is clicked by the user, the values entered into the text fields will be passed in as parameter values to the stored procedure.
Form with Report	This option creates a report page and a form page based on a single table that you select. The report will be a columnar report on every column specified with an Edit button to link to the edit page. The edit page is just like the edit page described in the Table option.
SQL Query (Fetch Row)	This option creates a form with a field for every column in a SQL query you provide. It also creates buttons for Create, Save, Delete, and Cancel. This option will *not* create a process to query, update, insert, or delete from the database. These processes have to be manually created by the developer.
Display Only on Exiting Items (Summary)	This page is generally used as a confirmation page at the end of a wizard. It creates a read-only form based on items on exiting pages.

Form Option	Description
Master Detail	This option is for editing two tables in a master detail relation based on two related tables you select. It creates two pages. The first is a columnar report page on the master table with an Edit link for each column. The second page contains a single-record edit for the master table at the top of the page and a columnar edit for multiple records in the details table. It creates all the processes to perform the inserts, updates, and deletes on both tables.
Form on Web Service	This option creates a form based on a web service reference. Use this option for a web service that returns a single value. The form provides fields for all the web service inputs and a field for the web service's return value. This option also creates a Submit button and the process to submit the web service.
Form and Report on Web Service	This option creates a form based on a web service reference. Use this option for a web service that returns multiple values. The form provides fields for all the web service inputs and a report for the web service's return values. This option also creates a Submit button and the process to submit the web service.

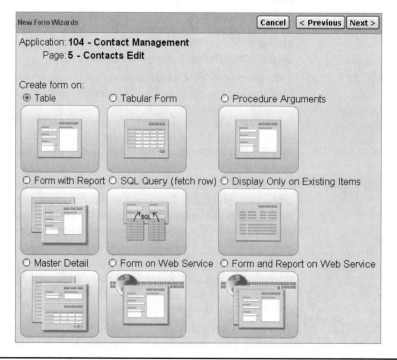

FIGURE 10-2 *Create Form Wizard*

We will use the Table option because we want to edit a single record as selected from the Contacts report page. Select the Table option and click on Next. This will start the Form on Table Wizard. In the first step of the wizard, you select the schema or table owner. The next step allows you to type in the name of a table, view or select a table, or view from a pop-up list. Enter **CONTACTS** and click on Next.

Figure 10-3 illustrates the next step in the wizard, where you specify the page and region attributes. Select the radio button to use the user interface defaults. Remember, these are the user-friendly names and other attributes that we gave to the table when we imported it from a spreadsheet. Because we are creating this region on an existing page, the Page and Page Name fields are already populated. You could enter a new page number to create the new page. The Region Title field will be what is displayed at the top of the region if the region template selected contains a #TITLE# substitution variable. The Region Template field will be set to the Themes default region template. You may select another template from the list of values. Click on the Next button to navigate to the next step.

Because we are creating this region on an existing page for which we have already specified tabs, the wizard will skip over the step to select tabs and go directly to the step to specify the column for the primary key. In that step, you select the column for the primary key from the list of values and then click on Next. In the following step, you specify the source for populating the primary key for new rows to be either an existing trigger, a custom PL/SQL function, or an existing sequence. The tables created from the spreadsheet have triggers created to populate the primary key, so select Existing Trigger and click on the Next button.

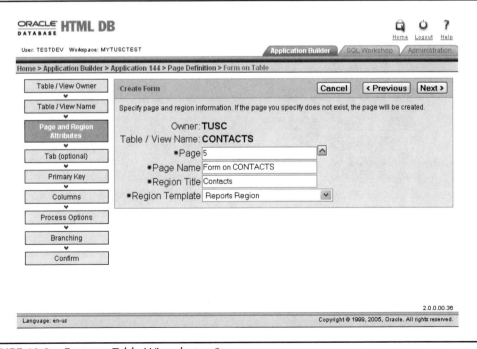

FIGURE 10-3   *Form on Table Wizard, step 3*

The next step allows you to select the columns you want to include; by default, they will all be selected in the pick list. Therefore, just click on Next to move to the next step. The next step allows you to select which processing functionality will be implemented. The labels for the buttons contain default text, but you may change this text if you so desire. The Cancel button and action are always created. The Create, Save and Delete buttons and their corresponding processes are only created if you select their respective Yes values, as shown in Figure 10-4. Select Yes for all buttons and then click on the Next button.

The last step before the final confirmation is where you specify the pages to which the user will navigate after processing an insert, update, or delete. You also specify the destination after the Cancel button is clicked. We will be navigating to this page from the Contact report page and would like to return to that page in both instances. Use the arrow button next to one of the fields to pop up the list of values and then select the Contact Report page. This will populate the page number in the field. You can then just type the same number in the other box and click on the Next button. The destinations that you specify will be used in the navigations that are created for the buttons. The Cancel button will actually be a redirect, whereas the other buttons will use the same post-processing branch.

The final step allows you to review the entries you have made so far. At this point, or any point before, you can always use the Previous button to step back in the wizard to make changes. Clicking on the Finish button will cause the HTML DB engine to generate all the metadata for the form region based on the values you entered. The following confirmation page allows you to run the page or edit the page. If you run the page, you should have a result similar to that shown in Figure 10-5. Notice that all the fields in the form are plain-text fields except the Contacttypeid and Title_Id fields. These fields were automatically created as pick list fields because a lookup table was defined for them. This was done in Chapter 5.

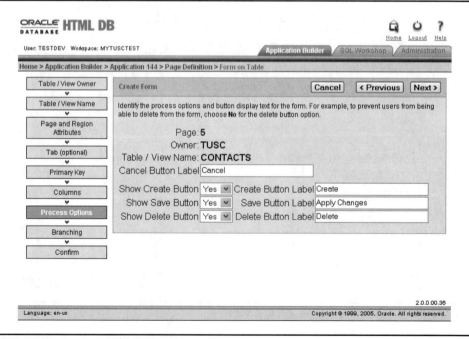

FIGURE 10-4 *Form on Table Wizard, step 8*

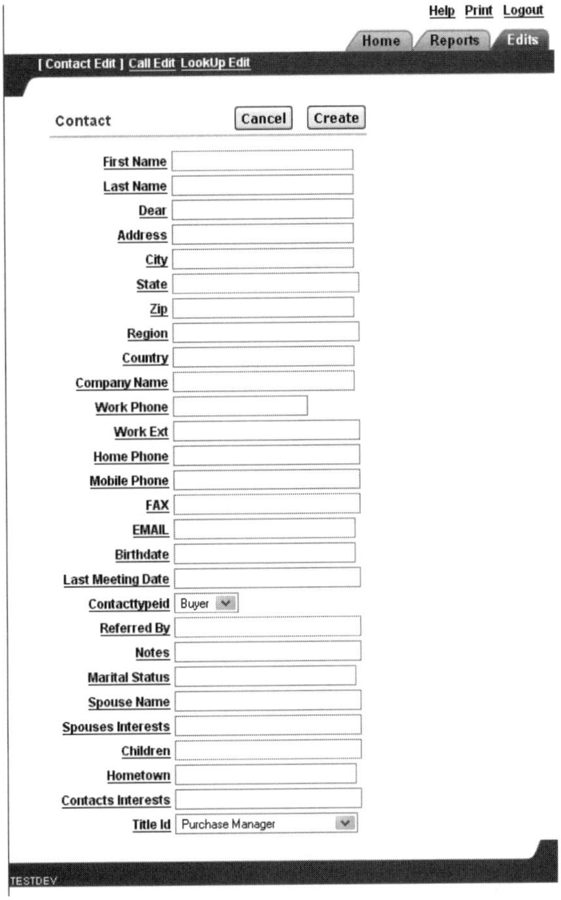

FIGURE 10-5 *Contact edit page*

Form Components

Navigate to the Page Definition page by clicking the Edit link in the Developer's Toolbar. We can now look at everything that was created for us by the Form Wizard. Prior to the wizard running, there were no values in either the Page Rendering column or the Page Processing column. As you can see in Figure 10-6, a large number of items were created. The wizard created a region in which it placed items for all the columns and buttons to initiate processing. It also created processes to retrieve a row into the fields and process the row after creation or editing. Also, two types of navigation were created—one of the buttons does a redirect and a branch was created for after the processing.

Regions

The first thing created for this form was the HTML region, which acts as the container for the other items. If you look at the subheadings in the Buttons and Items sections, you will see "Region" and the name of the HTML region. This shows that all the buttons and items are

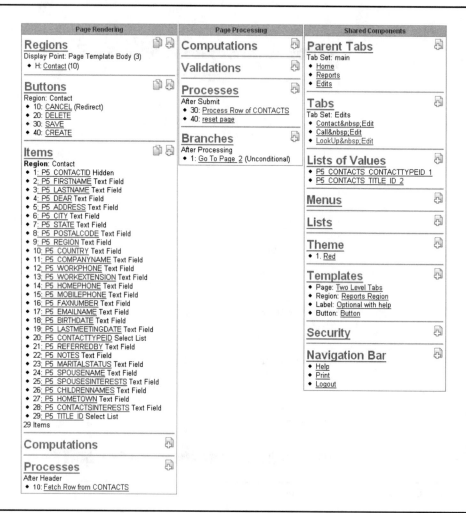

FIGURE 10-6 *Definition page for the Contact edit page*

associated with that region. You can have more than one region on a page and associate items to different regions.

If you click on the name of the region, you will go to the Edit Page Region page. In Chapter 8, we covered the majority of the sections contained in the Edit Page Region page because they are common no matter what type of region the page is for. The main area that differs from region type to region type is the Source section. Most forms use an HTML type region, and you will find the region source to be empty. The items that are placed in the region are generated as HTML and placed in the region when the page is rendered. You can enter HTML in the Source section and it will show up at the bottom of the section after all the items have been placed in the section.

The wizard for a tabular form actually creates a special type of SQL Query report region just for an updateable report. The Source section for this region contains the query to populate the tabular form. We will cover that type of form later in the chapter.

Items

Items make up the majority of a form. A item displays the value of a current field and allows the user to make changes to that value. If you look in Figure 10-6, you will see all the items listed that were created with the Contacts form. The standard naming convention for items created by the wizards is to precede the column name with a *P* and the page number on which the item is being created. Because you can reference page items from other pages, it is a good idea to stick with this naming convention when you create your own items. This enables you to quickly tell the location of an item being referenced.

The listing of items contains several pieces of information. The number that precedes the name is the sequence number assigned to the item. The sequence number determines the order in which the items will be rendered on the page. The name identifies the item and is also a link to the Edit Page Item page. Following the name of each item is the item's type. As you saw in Figure 10-5, the majority of items are text fields, but the Contacttypeid and Title_Id fields are pick lists. If you look at Figure 10-6, you see that the P5_CONTACTTYPEID and P5_TITLE_ID types are Select List and that the first item, P5_CONTACTID, is a Hidden type field.

P5_CONATACTID was created as a hidden field because it was specified as the primary key for the table. For new records, we specified that it be populated based on a trigger on the table. For existing records, it will be used to query the existing record, and you would not want to allow the user to edit this field. Recall in the last chapter when we created the link on the ContactID column. In doing so, we specified the P5_CONTACTID field to be populated with the value of the ContactID from the link's row. When navigation from the Report link occurs, P5_CONTACTID will be populated and the Automated Row Fetch process will use the value to query and populate the remaining page items.

Item Types

We have seen three different item types. However, many more types are available, not all of which can be used in a form that queries and processes a row of data from the database. Some you might use in a form for which you create the processes, like a multistep wizard. When you click on the create icon in the upper-right corner of the Items section, you start the Create Item Wizard. The first step of the wizard, shown in Figure 10-7, displays all the different item types. At this point, we are not going to create any new items, just review the types available.

As stated previously, not all these items would be used with a form that queries and processes a row of data from the database—these include the File Browser, List Manager, and Multiple Select types. All the others could be used. Most of the types correspond directly to an HTML form input element type. However, some of them are implemented as HTML text input types with added functionality from the HTML DB engine implemented in JavaScript, such as the Date Picker and Pop List of Values types.

Several of our fields would be better served by different types. The P5_NOTES field can contain a lot of data and is therefore a good candidate for a Text Area type. The P5_MARITALSTATUS field contains only two values and could easily be implemented as Radio buttons. We will make these changes and several other minor changes to enhance the usability of our form. In the rest of this section, we will look in detail at the Edit Page Item page, which allows us to change attributes of the individual items. With a full understanding of these attributes, you should be able to alter the items on the page so that it looks similar to the page shown in Figure 10-8.

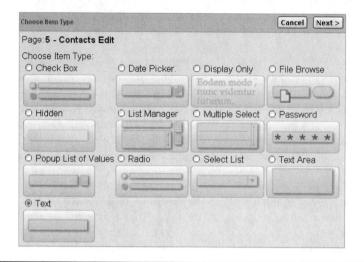

FIGURE 10-7 *Item types*

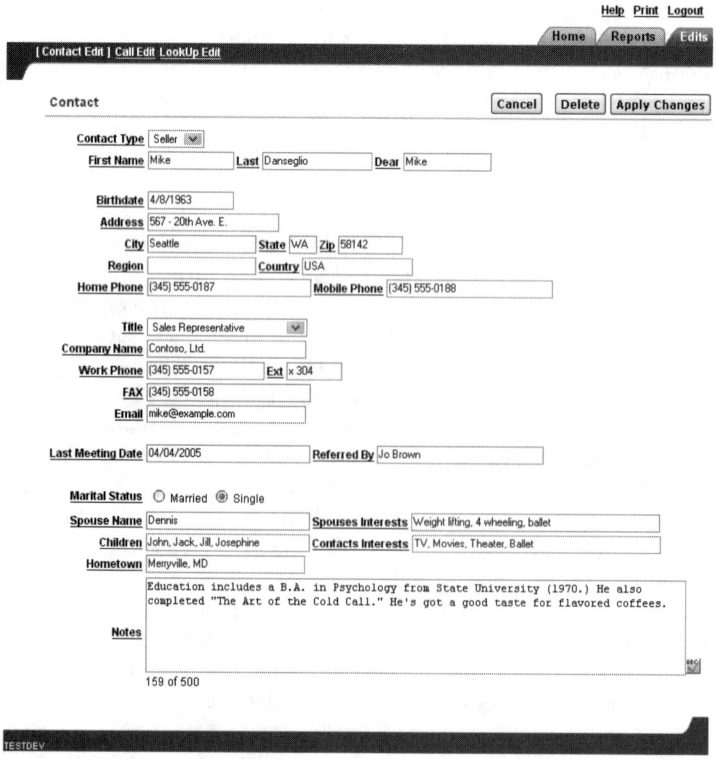

FIGURE 10-8 *Contact edit page, revised*

Edit Page Item Page

Navigate to the Edit Page Item page by clicking on a name of an item. The Edit Page Item page has many similar features to other edit pages we have looked at. On the top of the page you will find action buttons. The Cancel button allows you to discard any changes you have made and return to the Page Definition page. The Delete button deletes the current page item after you confirm you wish to delete it. The Apply Changes button saves any changes you have made and returns to the Page Definition page. Note the check box to the side, labeled Return to Page. If this check box is checked and you apply changes, you will remain on the Edit Page Item page. Next to the Apply Changes button may be left and right arrow buttons, depending on whether there are items with sequence numbers before and after the current item. Using these navigation buttons will commit any changes that you have made to the current item. Just below the buttons you will find the normal quick links that allow you to jump directly to any section on the page.

Name Section   The first section is where you can change the name of the item. Remember, the name you specify can be used to reference the value of the item. The Display As field is where you specify the type of item from the list of values. It is possible to change an item to almost any other type of item. This is where you would change the P5_NOTES item to a Text Area type, and P5_MARITALSTATUS to a Radio type. You may also change the type by clicking on one of the quick-fill links directly below the Display As field.

Over 50 different options appear in the Display As list of values. They are made up of variations of the 13 types shown in Figure 10-7. For example, there are nearly 20 variations of the Date Picker type, each with a different date format. The other main variation is whether or not the item's value will be maintained in the session. Remember, the session is a logical construct that HTML DB uses to allow the values of items on one page to be referenced on another page. Some of the items also offer variations with extra functionality, such as a spell checker, a calculator, and a character counter. Also provided is the ability to submit the page when the item value is changed or when the ENTER key is pressed from the item.

Displayed Section   The Displayed section, shown in Figure 10-9, allows you to control where and how an item is displayed. The value in the Sequence field determines the order in which the items contained in the same region will be rendered on the page. It also changes the order they are displayed in the list on the Page Definition page. Sections of an HTML DB page are rendered as HTML tables. Page items by default are placed as a single table cell in a table row within that HTML table. The remaining fields in the Display section give you some control over the HTML table rows. If you set the Begin on New Line field to No, that item will be placed in the same HTML table row as the item that precedes it. If you set the Begin on New Field field to No, the item will be placed in the same HTML table cell as the previous item. A number of fields displayed in Figure 10-8 have both of these fields set to No. If you set the New Line field to No and the New Field field to Yes, there will be considerably more space between them. The other fields allow you to set values for the ColSpan and RowSpan table cell attributes.

Label Section   The Label section allows you to control attributes of the item's label. The Label field is the text that will be displayed. You control the placement and alignment of the label with the Horizontal/Vertical Alignment field. With the different options available in the pick list, you can place the label above, below, to the left, or to the right of the item. You can also choose the alignment within those placements. The Template field allows you to select a template for the label from existing label templates for the current theme. Typically, different templates will be used to indicate required fields and nonrequired fields. Additionally, the template may allow for help on the item. A label with help will be an active link to pop up help specific to the label's

Page Item			Cancel	Delete	Apply Changes	<

Name↓ Displayed↓ Label↓ Element↓ Source↓ Default↓ LOV↓ Security↓ Conditions↓ Read Only↓ Help↓ Configuration↓ Comments↓

Name

Page: **6 Call Edit**

*Name P6_NOTES

Display As Textarea with HTML Editor ▾

[Text] [Text Area] [Select List] [Radio] [Popup List of Values] [Checkbox] [Date] [Hidden]

Displayed

*Sequence 60

*Region Calls (1) 10 ▾

Begin On New Line Yes ▾ ...Field Yes ▾ ColSpan 1 Row Span 1

Label

Label Notes

Horizontal / Vertical Alignment Right ▾

Template Optional with help ▾

HTML Table Cell Attributes nowrap="nowrap"

Post Element Text </td></tr><tr><td>

FIGURE 10-9 *Edit Page Item page, part 1*

item. The HTML Table Cell Attributes field allows you to enter any additional table cell attributes, such as nowrap. The Post Element Text field provides a means for placing additional text after the field. This text is placed before the </td> tags after the item. You can reference the name of the current HTML form element and the name of the current item with #CURRENT_FORM_ELEMENT# and #CURRENT_ITEM_NAME#. You can also use this field to add another blank table row after the current field by closing out the current row and opening another, as shown in Figure 10-9. Although you can do this, a better way would be to create a display-only field with a static text source of " " and place it on a new line after the field where you want the break.

Element Section   The Element section, shown in Figure 10-10, allows you to control attributes of the individual item. The value in the Width field specifies the length in characters of the form element. Notice the many different lengths of fields in the example in Figure 10-8. The Maximum Width field is used to set the HTML maxlength attribute, which controls the maximum number of characters that can be entered into a field. The Height field is used to specify the height in lines for text areas and multiselect lists, such as the Notes field in the Figure 10-8. The next three fields are used to place additional attributes within the HTML tags that are used with the element. The HTML Table Cell Attributes field's value is placed in the <td> tag, which is the HTML table cell tag. An example would be bgcolor='blue'. Depending on the type of item, the HTML Form Element Attribute field's value is placed in the item's corresponding HTML form element tag, which could be <input>, <select>, or <textarea>. This is most often used to add JavaSript using an onFocus or onBlur attribute. The Form Element Option Attributes field's values will be placed in the <option> tags for those HTML form elements that use them.

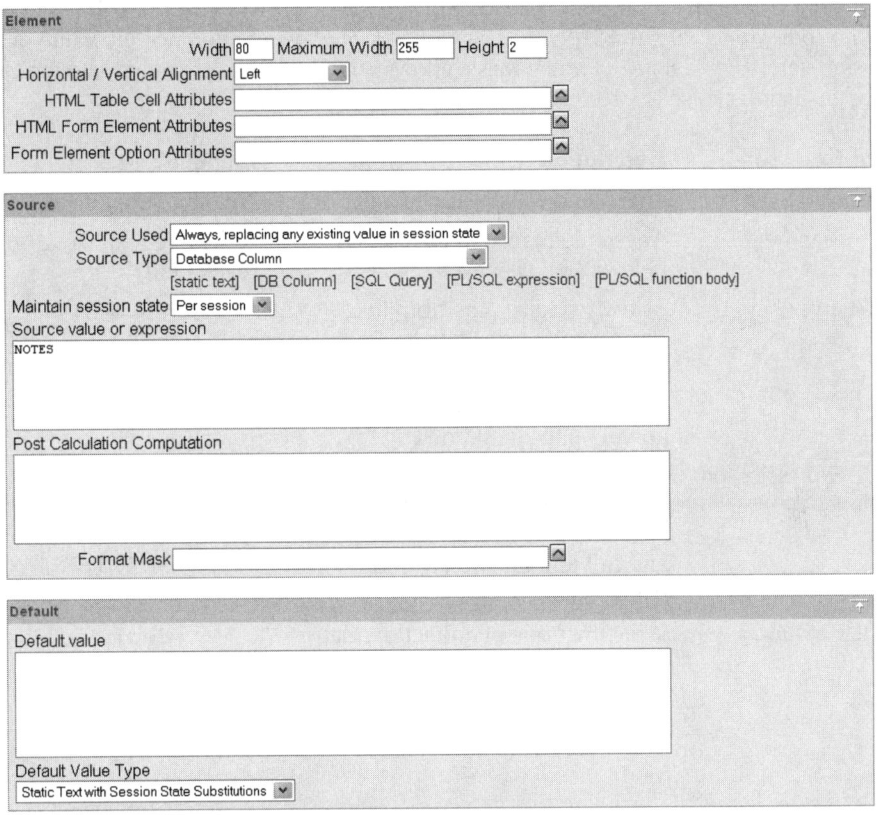

FIGURE 10-10 *Edit Page Item page, part 2*

Source Section   The Source section is used to specify information about the source for the value of the item. The Source Used field has two possible values:

■ Only when current value in session state is null

■ Always, replacing any existing value in session state

This tells the HTML DB engine whether it should use the source to populate the item or not. For items that come from a database column, you will always use the Always option. The Replace Only option is typically used for preferences. Remember, preferences are maintained per user, so when they end a session and come back, the value is still available in the new session. This is controlled with the Maintain Session State field, which has two possible values: Per Session and Per User.

The Source Type field is where you specify the source for the value of the item. For a form created from a table, all the type fields will be set to Database Column. Keep in mind that items can be used for many other things besides displaying and updating columns from the database. The other source types are listed in the following table. The examples shown would be entered into the Source Value or Expression field. The next field in the Source section is the Post Calculation

Computation field. This field can be used to modify the source after it is returned. You may use a SQL or PL/SQL expression, such as UPPER(:P4_COMPANY), or you can call a function such as return some_func(:P9_SALESAMOUNT). Notice that you can reference the value of any item in session state. The final field, Format Mask, allows you to apply a format mask to the value returned. Use the pick list to select from some predefined format masks.

Source Type	Description	Example
Always Null	The source will always be null.	Nothing entered
Static Assignment	Any value placed in the Source field will be displayed.	Any static text, `or  ` - for a blank field
SQL Query	Select a single value from the database. You can reference other page items with the ??? syntax.	`select name from employee where empno = :P2_EMPNO`
ITEM	Either an application-level item or another page item.	`P3_COMPANY`
PL/SQL Expression or Function	Use any valid PL/SQL expression that you could place on the right side of an assignment operator, or any call to a function stored in the database.	`:P12_SALARY * 1.1 + :P12_COMMISSION` or `Calc_Cost(:P12_SALARY, :P12_COMMISSION)`

PL/SQL Function Body	Write the body of a function that returns a value.	`declare`
		`avar number;`
		`begin`
		`avar := :P12_SAL * 1.1;`
		`return avar + :P12_COMM;`
		`end`

Database Column	Used when doing an Automated Row Fetch process. Simply enter the name of a column.	`LASTNAME`
Preference	Preferences must be set programmatically with the HTMLDB_UTIL.SET_PREFERENCE procedure (see Appendix A). Simply reference the name of the preference assigned.	`app104_show_extras`

PL/SQL Anonymous Block	This source type can only be used with an item type of Display as Text (based on PL/SQL; does not save state). You can build a dynamic display for this field using the PL/SQL Web Toolkit (see Appendix B).	`begin`
		`  htp.fontOpen('RED',`
		`'ARIAL', '7', '');`
		`htp.print('This is just a test');`
		`  htp.fontclose();`
		`end`

Default Value   The default value is used when the item's value is not derived from session state and the value of the source specified is null. The Default Value Type field can be one of the following:

- Static Text with Session State Substitutions

- PL/SQL Function Body

- PL/SQL Expression

Select a type and place the source in the Default Value field.

List of Values   The List of Values section, shown in Figure 10-11, is used when the current item type is one of the ten that are based on an LOV. The Named LOV field contains an LOV of all the named lists of values that were created in your application's Shared Components section (see Chapter 4). You may select a named list of values or you can specify the source of one in the List of Values Definition field. The source can be dynamic, where values are supplied by a SQL query, or the source can be static. The SQL query must return two columns—the first being the displayed value and the second being the returned value. This way, if you have a column that is a lookup code such as department ID, you can query to display the department name and return the department ID. Here's an example:

```
Select dept_name d, dept_no r
   from departments
```

For a static list, click on the Create or Edit Static List of Values link. This will take you to a page with two columns where you can fill in corresponding display and return values. When you are finished, it will return a string such as the following:

```
STATIC:Red;1,Blue;2,Green;3,Orange;4,Yellow;5
```

When the Display Extra Values field is set to Yes and the current session value of the field is not in the list of values, the value will be displayed. If it is set to No, the first value in the list is displayed. The Columns field is used with radio groups and check boxes that are based on an LOV. It defines the number of columns the values will be displayed in, the default being one. The Marital Status field in Figure 10-8 was altered to be a radio group with two columns. The Display Null field specifies whether or not the list of values for this item should display a NULL value. The Null Display Value field is used to specify a display value for the null row in the LOV; this is especially useful when you are using a radio group. Likewise, the Null Return Value field allows you to specify the value that will be returned for null, the default is %null%. If the values can be dynamically translated and dynamic translations are set up in the application's shared components, then set the Dynamic Translation field to Yes. This only works with LOVs based on a SQL query.

Security Section   The authorization scheme can be set to conditionally display the current item based on a user's authorizations. Authorization schemes are covered in Chapter 16. Setting the Cross-Site Scripting Protection field to Yes will cause values passed for this item into the application to be escaped when they are saved into session state. Additionally, values that are submitted and processed for this item will also be escaped when they are saved into session state. The Session State Protection field must be set to Unrestricted for any item that is a user input field, or whose value will be set from within the URL. The Restricted setting would be used on items that are only set by internal processes. See Chapter 16 for more details on security.

Conditional Display and Read-Only Display Settings Sections   The Conditional Display section and the Read-Only Display Settings section work just like the Conditional Processing section described in detail in Chapter 8. They allow you to set different types of conditions. Based on the

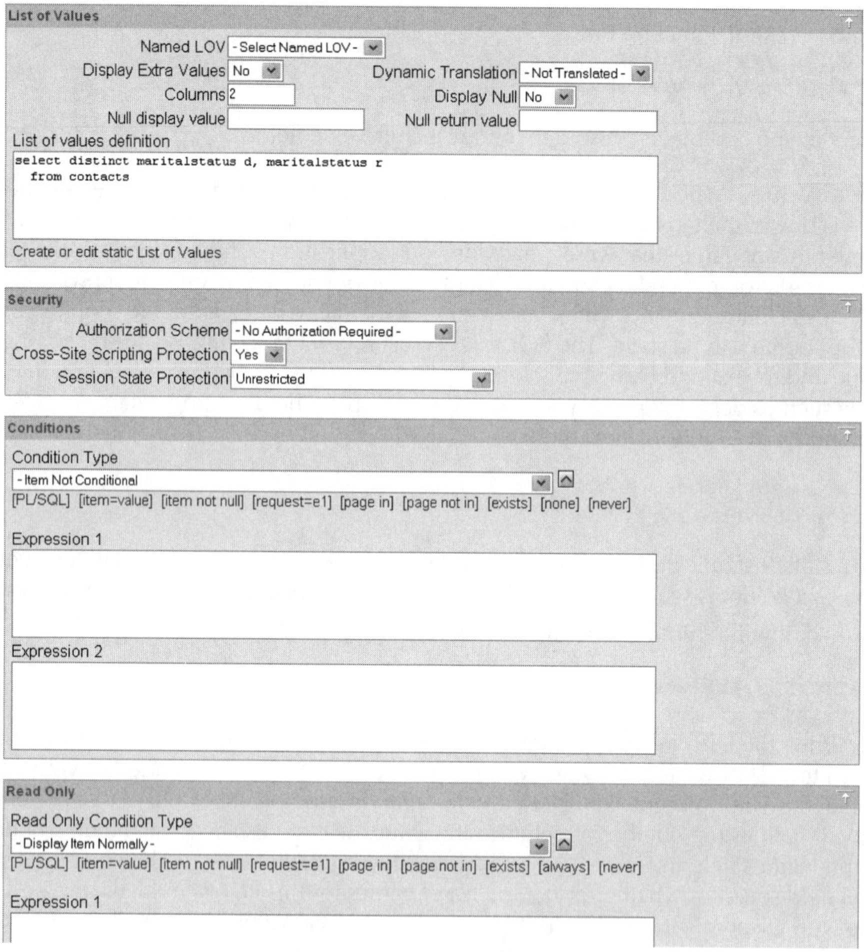

FIGURE 10-11 *Edit Page Item page, part 3*

result of the condition, the current field will not be displayed (Conditional Display section) or may be displayed as a read-only field (Read-Only Condition).

Help Text Section The Help Text section allows you to specify context-sensitive text for each individual field on your page. In order for the text that you type into the field to be displayed, the label of the item must have a template specified that supports help text (see the "Label Section," earlier in this chapter). See the "Page Items Page" section for additional information about editing help text.

Configuration Section The Build Option pick list in the Configuration Management section allows you to select a build option for the item. Build options are typically used to include/ exclude debug items or to separate normal functionality from premium functionality. Build options are discussed in further detail in Chapter 4.

Comments Section   Use the Comments section to note any peculiarities about this item to any other developers. If you used strange logic or an abnormal procedure, it is a good idea to document it here. This makes maintaining an application much easier. After all, how many times have you returned months later after developing something only to ask yourself, What was I thinking?

Page Items Page

Now that we have seen how to edit items one at a time, you might be wishing that you could edit more than one item at a time. HTML DB provides the Page Items page to allow you to edit some of the properties for all the items at the same time. Figure 10-12 shows a small portion of the page. You navigate to this page by clicking on the Items section header on the Page Definition page. This page is ideal for reordering your columns within the page. The attributes available for editing on this page are primarily display-related attributes. Notice the sub-tabs across the top of the page. These will navigate you to several other useful pages for page items.

The page accessible via the Item Help sub-tab allows you to see the help text specified for all items on your page. From there, you can click on a field to display a pop-up window that allows you to change the help text and/or subscribe to the help text from another item within

Items   Item Help   Delete Multiple Items   History

Page 8   ⬦ Show Region(s) - All Regions -   ☑   [Go]   [Apply Changes] ◀ ▶

	Sequence ▲	Name	Prompt	Field Template	Region	New Line	New Field
▣	1	P8_CONTACTID	Contactid	1. Optional with help ☑	CONTACTS ☑	Yes ☑	Yes ☑
▣	2	P8_CONTACTTYPEID	Contacttypeid	1. Optional with help ☑	CONTACTS ☑	Yes ☑	Yes ☑
▣	20	P8_FIRSTNAME	Firstname	1. Optional with help ☑	CONTACTS ☑	Yes ☑	Yes ☑
▣	30	P8_LASTNAME	Lastname	1. Optional with help ☑	CONTACTS ☑	No ☑	No ☑
▣	40	P8_DEAR	Dear	1. Optional with help ☑	CONTACTS ☑	No ☑	No ☑
▣	41	P8_X		1. Optional with help ☑	CONTACTS ☑	Yes ☑	Yes ☑
▣	45	P8_BIRTHDATE	Birthdate	1. Optional with help ☑	CONTACTS ☑	Yes ☑	Yes ☑
▣	50	P8_ADDRESS	Address	1. Optional with help ☑	CONTACTS ☑	Yes ☑	Yes ☑
▣	60	P8_CITY	City	1. Optional with help ☑	CONTACTS ☑	Yes ☑	Yes ☑
▣	70	P8_STATEORPROVINCE	State	1. Optional with help ☑	CONTACTS ☑	No ☑	No ☑
▣	71	P8_POSTALCODE	Zip	1. Optional with help ☑	CONTACTS ☑	No ☑	No ☑
▣	90	P8_REGION	Region	1. Optional with help ☑	CONTACTS ☑	Yes ☑	Yes ☑
▣	100	P8_COUNTRY	Country	1. Optional with help ☑	CONTACTS ☑	No ☑	No ☑
▣	102	P8_HOMEPHONE	Homephone	1. Optional with help ☑	CONTACTS ☑	Yes ☑	Yes ☑
▣	104	P8_MOBILEPHONE	Mobilephone	1. Optional with help ☑	CONTACTS ☑	No ☑	No ☑
▣	106	P8_TITLE_ID	Title	1. Optional with help ☑	CONTACTS ☑	Yes ☑	Yes ☑
▣	110	P8_COMPANYNAME	Companyname	1. Optional with help ☑	CONTACTS ☑	Yes ☑	Yes ☑
▣	120	P8_WORKPHONE	Workphone	1. Optional with help ☑	CONTACTS ☑	Yes ☑	Yes ☑
▣	130	P8_WORKEXTENSION	Ext	1. Optional with help ☑	CONTACTS ☑	No ☑	No ☑
▣	160	P8_FAXNUMBER	Faxnumber	1. Optional with help ☑	CONTACTS ☑	Yes ☑	Yes ☑
▣	170	P8_EMAILNAME	Emailname	1. Optional with help ☑	CONTACTS ☑	Yes ☑	Yes ☑
▣	190	P8_LASTMEETINGDATE	Lastmeetingdate	1. Optional with help ☑	CONTACTS ☑	Yes ☑	Yes ☑
▣	191	P8_FOLLOW_UP_DATE	Follow Up Date	1. Optional with help ☑	CONTACTS ☑	No ☑	No ☑

FIGURE 10-12   *Page Items page*

your application. This way, if the same help text is needed in more than one place in your application, you only need to maintain it in a single location.

The Delete Multiple Items button takes you to a page where you can select page items by checking a box next to the items' names and then delete them all by clicking on the Remove Items button. The History button displays a report of the items that have been changed, the name of the developer who last changed them, and when the changes were made.

NOTE
Another very useful way to quickly modify items on a page is to run the page and then click on Show Edit Links on the Developer's Toolbar. This displays a small icon that looks like four dots after editable items. Click on the icon for a pop-up window of the Page Item Edit page, make changes, and click the Apply button and then the Cancel button. Then refresh the page that is displayed.

Buttons

Buttons are used within a form to initiate an action. The Form Wizard supplied four buttons for us in the form we just created. In insert mode, only the Cancel and Create button are displayed, while in update mode, the Cancel, Delete, and Save buttons are displayed. Clicking on each button will result in a different action. Buttons are similar to items in that they result in generated HTML items placed within a region. Buttons are not just another type of item because of the navigation associated with a button.

Two types of navigation happen as a result of clicking on a button in an HTML DB application. As you'll recall from Chapter 8, we looked at the complete cycle of an HTML DB page. The high-level steps are as follows:

1. The page is requested.
2. The HTML DB engine renders the page utilizing the metadata defined in the Page Rendering section of the Page Definition page, including regions, buttons, items, and processes.
3. The page is submitted back to itself.
4. The HTML DB engine processes the page utilizing the metadata defined in the Page Processing section of the Page Definition page, including computations, validations, and processes.
5. The HTML DB engine redirects to another page based on branch metadata defined in the Page Processing section of the Page Definition page.
6. Another page is processed.

The first type of navigation from a button is step 3, where the page is submitted back to itself. The Create, Delete, and Save buttons of our form are of this type. The second type of navigation occurs when a button redirects to another page or URL, in essence skipping directly from step 3 to step 6, thus ignoring everything defined in the Page Processing section of the Page Definition page. The Cancel button in our form is of this type, because we would want to discard any changes made. It is important to understand this concept. The mechanics of how each of these is accomplished is covered next.

Edit Page Buttons Page

If you click on the name of a button in the Buttons section of the Page Definition page, shown earlier in Figure 10-6, you will navigate to the Edit Page Buttons page. This page is very similar to the Edit Page Items page. On the top of the page you will find action buttons. The Cancel button allows you to discard any changes you have made and return to the Page Definition page. The Delete button deletes the current button after you confirm that you wish to delete it. The Apply Changes button saves any changes you have made and returns to the Page Definition page. Note the check box to the side, labeled Return to Page. If this check box is checked and you apply changes, you will remain on the Edit Page Buttons page. Next to the Apply Changes button may be left and right arrow buttons, depending on whether there are buttons with sequence numbers before and after the current button. Using these navigation buttons will commit any changes that you have made to the current button. Just below the buttons you will find the normal quick links that allow you to jump directly to any section on the page.

Name Section   The Button section allows you to set the button sequence, name, and label text. The value in the Sequence field determines the order in which the buttons contained in the same region and position will be rendered on the page. The value in the Button Name field is used as a reference to the button. When the page is submitted, the value of the REQUEST, a built-in application item, will be set to the button name. The value in the Text Label/Alt field will be used in one of two ways: If the button is an image, it will be used as the ALT value in the HTML image tag. Otherwise, the value will be used as the label in constructing the button.

Display Section   The Display section, shown in Figure 10-13, allows you to control the placement of the button. The Display in Region field determines which page region the button will be displayed in. Button Position is a pick list with a large number of values that allow you to control the placement of the button. Some of the choices are generic, such as Left of Page Title, Top of Region, and Top and Bottom of Region. Others refer to placements that are specifically referenced within the region template with substitution variables such as #CLOSE#, #HELP#, and #EDIT#. The Button Alignment field allows you to specify whether the button will be aligned left or right within the assigned position.

Attributes Section   How the button will be rendered is controlled from the Attributes section. The Button Style field is an LOV with three choices: HTML Button, Template Based Button, and Image. The HTML button will be a plain browser-generated button. If this option is selected, the Button Attributes field will be activated and you can add further attributes for the HTML button.

The Button Template field allows you to select the template for a template-based button and is usually constructed of three images—one each for the left and right side of the button and one very narrow image that is used as the background for the center of the button. The center image together with the label make up the middle of the button. This way, you can create variable-length buttons. Look at any one of the button templates that come with the preinstalled themes to see how this all comes together.

If you choose to use image-based buttons, the Button Image and Image Attribute fields will be enabled. With an image-based button, you must have a different image for each button. The actual label of the button will be part of the image. The pick list button next to the Button Image field brings up a list of images that have been imported into your workspace. The Image Attributes field is used to specify attributes of the <img> tag that will be generated.

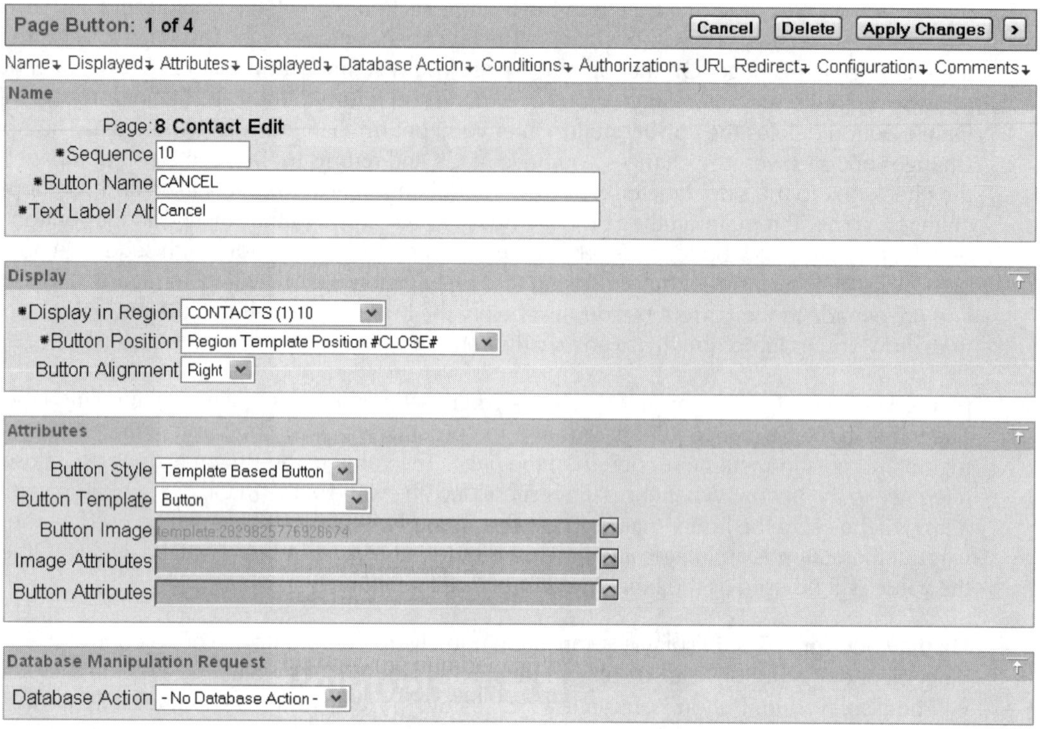

FIGURE 10-13 *Edit Page Buttons page, part 1*

Database Manipulation Request Section   Select a value for the Database Action field to trigger an insert, update, or delete SQL action when the button is clicked. These work in conjunction with the Automatic Row Processing process. We will cover this process later in this chapter. The example in Figure 10-13 is for the Cancel button, so no database action is associated with the button. The remainder of the buttons generated by the wizard have a database action associated with them.

Conditions Section   The Conditions section, shown in Figure 10-14, is often used with buttons because, depending on whether the form is being used for an insert or for modifying an existing record, you will want different actions/buttons available to the user. The Conditional Display section operates just like the Conditional Processing section described in detail in Chapter 8. Typically for a database row edit form, you will specify a condition type of "Value of Item in Expression 1 is NULL" or "Value of Item in Expression 1 is NOT NULL" and specify the field that contains the primary key in the Expression 1 field. Recall from Chapter 9 when we created the link from the Contacts report into the Contact edit form that we specified that the P5_CONTACTID field would be populated with the value of the CONTACTID field for the current row of the report. Whether the P5_CONTACTID field has a value or not determines if the form is in an insert or update "mode." Really the only difference between the two "modes" is the buttons displayed. Also, if the P5_CONTACTID field is null, then no row will be queried into the fields when navigation to the page occurs.

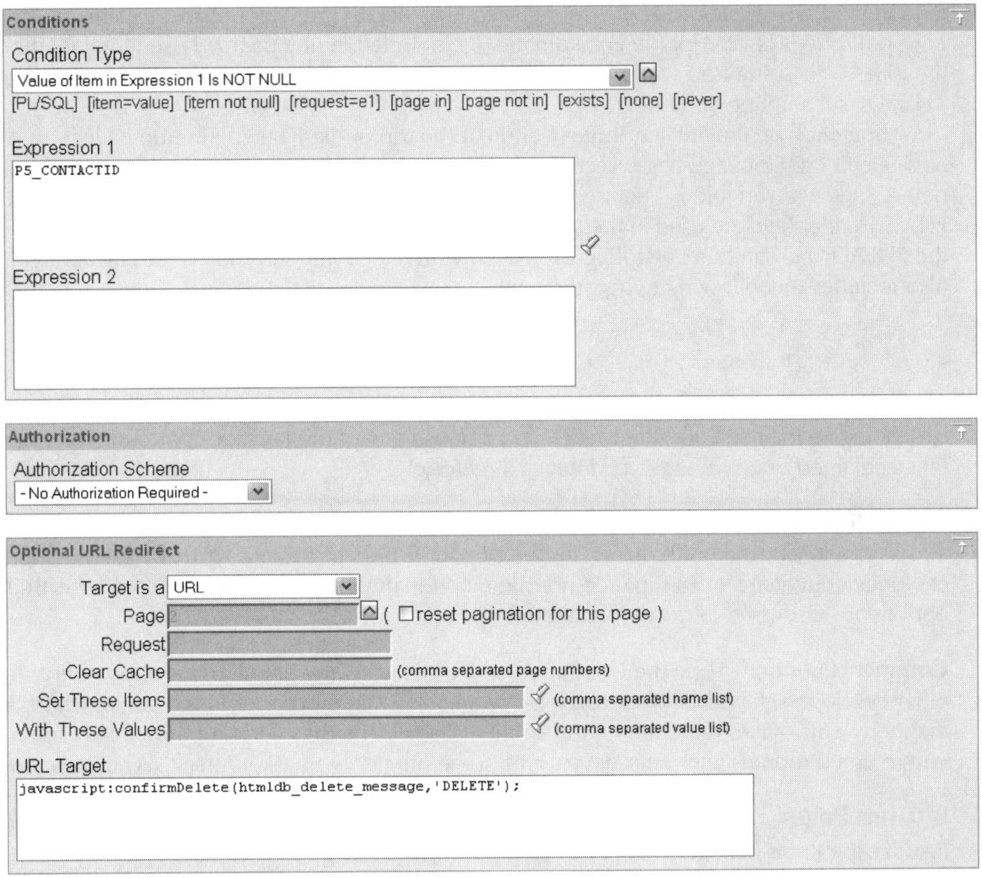

FIGURE 10-14   *Edit Page Buttons page, part 2*

Authorization Section   Authorization Scheme can be set to conditionally display the current button based on a user's authorizations. Authorization schemes are covered in Chapter 16.

Optional URL Redirect   Normally, a button will not use a redirect. If a redirect is used, the page will not get submitted and the computations, validations, and processes defined to be evaluated after the page is submitted will *not* occur. Remembering this fact can save you a lot of trouble in debugging your applications. In some instances, you will want to navigate to another page in the application or to a URL without doing any further processing on the current page. The Cancel button is implemented like this. It returns you to the Contact report page. With that being said, you may wish to use a redirect similar to the one used in Figure 10-14. This redirect, created by the Forms Wizard, executes a JavaScript function that pops up a confirmation message and then submits the page if the user confirms that they wish to proceed with the delete. This way, the computations, validations, and processes do occur because the JavaScript submits the page.

The JavaScript consists of a function, confirmDelete, that takes two parameters: one a JavaScript variable that passes in the message to use in the confirmation pop-up, and the other a string variable that will be the contents of the REQUEST, a built-in application item, if the page is submitted. The function can be found in the HTMLDBOracleHome\marvel\images\javascript\ core.js file. This JavaScript file is automatically included in any page whose template includes the #HEAD# substitution variable. All the page templates that come with HTML DB include the #HEAD# substitution variable.

If you click on the Edit Attributes button at the top of the Page Definition page, you will navigate to the Edit Page page. Look in the HTML Header field; you will see that the htmldb_ delete_message variable is declared in a small block of JavaScript code. The contents of the HTML Header field are used in the template for the #HEAD# substitution variable. Not only does the #HEAD# substitution variable get replaced with the contents of the HTML Header field, but it also includes the following two statements.

```
<script src="/i/javascript/core.js" type="text/javascript"></script>
<link rel="stylesheet" href="/i/css/core.css" type="text/css" />
```

You can reference any of the code included in the core JavaScript file or anything from the core Cascading Style Sheet. For that matter, you can use any of the JavaScript files or any of the CSS files contained under the marvel\images directory.

Configuration Section The Build Option pick list in the Configuration Management section allows you to select a build option for the button. Build options are typically used to include/ exclude debug items or to separate normal functionality from premium functionality. Build options are discussed in detail in Chapter 4.

Comments Section Use the Comments section to note any peculiarities about this button to other developers. If you used strange logic or an abnormal procedure, it is a good idea to document that here. This makes maintaining the application much easier. After all, how many times have you returned months later after developing something only to ask yourself, What was I thinking?

Buttons Page

Just like the Items header on the Page Definition page navigates to a page where you can edit all the page's items at the same time, the Buttons header presents a multirow edit page for the page's buttons. The attributes available for edit on the Buttons page are primarily display-related attributes, but the target URL is also shown if one exists. This page is not quite as useful as the one for items, but it could prove handy. Also, a History button is included at the top of the page to view the history of the last changes for buttons on every page in your application.

Processes

Processes play two roles in the edit form the wizard created for us. One process is responsible for populating the fields in our form from the database when we are editing an existing row. Two other processes will take care of the inserts, updates, and deletes of the row after the page is submitted. When you look at the Page Definition page, shown earlier in Figure 10-6, you will see one process listed in the Processes section of the Page Rendering column and two more processes in the Processes section of the Page Processing column. The first one is processed after the header is processed during the page rendering. The other two are processed after the page is submitted.

Edit Page Process Page

As with any other element on the Page Definition page, if you click on the name of a process, you will navigate to its edit page, in this case the Edit Page Process page. At the top of the page you will find action buttons. The Cancel button allows you to discard any changes you have made and return to the Page Definition page. The Delete button deletes the current process after you confirm that you wish to delete it. The Apply Changes button saves any changes you have made and returns you to the Page Definition page. Note the check box to the side, labeled Return to Page. If this box is checked and you apply changes, you will remain on the Edit Page Process page. Next to the Apply Changes button may be left and right arrow buttons, depending upon whether there are other processes on the page. This includes processes defined in both the Page Rendering column and the Page Processing column. Unlike with items and buttons, using these navigation buttons will *not* commit any changes you have made to the current process. Just below the buttons you will find the normal quick links that allow you to jump directly to any section on the page.

Name Section   The Name section allows you to identify the process. In the Page field, you can actually change the page the process is for. The Name field is just used to identify the process to developers. Therefore, you should make the name as meaningful as possible. The name can be almost as long as you like, but only the first 35 characters are displayed on the Page Definition page. The Type field is not a changeable attribute once the process is created.

Process Point Section   This section determines when and how often the process will be evaluated. The Sequence field controls the order in which the processes will be evaluated for the same processing point. Otherwise, it has no effect.

The Process Point field has a list of values to select from to set the point when the page will be processed. The three main points for processing are On New Instance, On Load, and On Submit. On New Instance happens after the authentication has taken place but before anything else happens. The six On Load options are further classified for evaluation before or after the header, regions, or footer. There are two choices for On Submit—either before or after computations and validations. Processes specified to process "on submit" will show up in the Page Processing column, and all the rest will show up in the Page Rendering column.

Figure 10-15 shown the two choices for the Run Process field. The default action is to evaluate the process once per page visit. However, you may choose to have a process that is evaluated only once per session or when the session is reset.

Source: Automatic Row Processing (DML) Section   The third section in the Edit Page Process page will vary depending on the type of process the edit page is for. Chapter 13 covers in detail the different types of processes you can add to a page. Of the three processes created for our page, the two that fetch and process the row of data have the Automatic Row Processing section as their third section. The Reset Page process has the Source section as its third section.

The Automatic Row Processing section contains the information about the table to be processed. The HTML DB engine creates the SQL statements to perform the insert, update, and delete actions. The Table Owner and Table Name fields identify the schema and table to be processed. Be careful: The table name is case sensitive, so unless you created your table with quotes, the name should be all uppercase. The next four fields allow you to provide information about the primary key on the table. The Item Containing Primary Key Column Value is used to specify the page item that contains the primary key, whereas the Primary Key Column field contains the name of the actual column in the table. Again, this field is case sensitive. There are two additional fields to specify both items for the secondary column in a primary key. If the primary key contains more than two fields, you will have to write your own SQL process to handle the row processing.

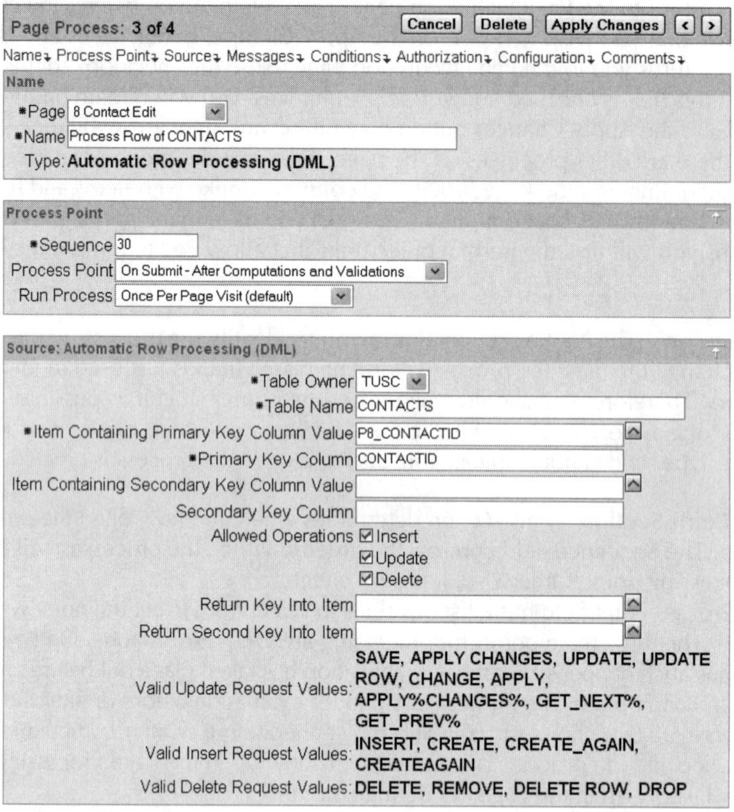

FIGURE 10-15 *Edit Page Process, part 1*

The Return Key Into Item fields allow you to have the first and second column of the primary key returned into page items. If your table is using a database trigger to populate the primary key on inserts, this allows you to have that value returned to you so you can further use it. The values shown in the three Valid Request Values fields are values the request can be set to that trigger the corresponding database action. When a form is created for you, so are the buttons and their names. However, you may add additional navigational methods. If the additional navigation methods set the request to one of these values, the navigational methods can also trigger database actions.

All the fields already addressed for the Automatic Row Processing section are common to both of the processes created for our form. Figure 10-15 shows the section for the process that handles the insert, update, and delete operations for the row of the Contacts table. As you can see in the figure, three check boxes allow you to add or remove any of those functionalities from the generated process. Recall in the Form Wizard that we selected whether or not to display the Create, Save, and Delete buttons (refer to Figure 10-4). This corresponds to these check boxes. If you had not selected to display one of the buttons at creation time, you could now enable the process here. However, if you do not select the option at creation time, the button will not be created, so you will have to create it yourself if you wish to add the functionality.

The Automatic Row Processing section for the Automatic Row Fetch process has two radio buttons instead of the three check boxes. The two radio buttons allow you to select either to set the value of the fetched row to the in-memory session state at the time the row is fetched or to wait and place the value in the in-memory session only when and if the item is rendered. The default and preferred mode is to have values saved when they are fetched. This allows you to reference the values of the page items using the v('ITEM_NAME') syntax in any computations or processes that are evaluated prior to the page being rendered. Only use the other option if your page logic requires values not to be placed in the in-memory session state until they are rendered.

Messages Section   The Messages section allows you to specify the messages that will be displayed on the next page after the process runs. That page's template must contain the #SUCCESS_MESSAGE# substitution variable for these messages to be displayed.

The Process Error Message field allows you to specify the message that will be displayed to the user if any unhandled exception is raised during the processing. You can include the text of the SQL error message by using the #SQLERRM_TEXT# substitution variable. Although the #SQLERRM# substitution variable is available to display the SQL error message, this is not really necessary because the message will automatically be displayed at the bottom of the page.

The Process Success Message field, shown in Figure 10-16, allows you to specify the message that will be displayed to the user when the process runs without generating an error. If this process is a multirow process, you can use #MRU_COUNT# to display the count of rows updated or #MRI_COUNT# to display the number of rows inserted.

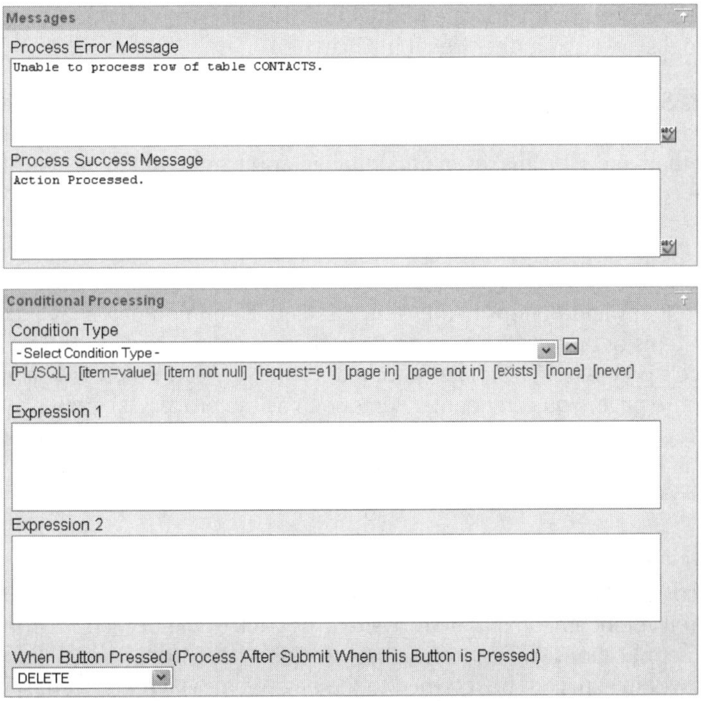

FIGURE 10-16   *Edit Page Process, part 2*

Conditional Processing   The Conditional Processing section is just like the many conditional sections you have seen thus far. See the "Conditional Processing" section in Chapter 8 for more details on the types of conditions and how to use them. The one additional field available in this Conditional Processing section that is not available in the other Conditional Processing sections is the When Button Pressed field (see Figure 10-16). This allows you to associate a process with the click of a specific button. The list of values for the field contains the names of all the buttons on the page. This process will only be evaluated if the button submits the page, as opposed to redirecting to a URL. Remember the little JavaScript function we looked at earlier in the URL Target field of the Delete button? Recall that one of the parameters passed in was the string variable 'DELETE' and that this value would be place in the REQUEST, a built-in application item, when the page is finally submitted. This is how the process knows which button is clicked. If the JavaScript function is not used and the button has no Target specified, the page will be submitted and the name of the button will be placed in the REQUEST.

NOTE
You can use a When Button Pressed condition along with a regular condition specified in the other fields.

Authorization Section   The Authorization Scheme can be set to conditionally evaluate the current process based on a user's authorizations. Authorization schemes are covered in Chapter 16.

Configuration Section   The Build Option pick list in the Configuration Management section allows you to select a build option for the process. Build options are typically used to include/ exclude debug items or to separate normal functionality from premium functionality. Build options are discussed in further detail in Chapter 4.

Comments Section   Use the Comments section to note any peculiarities about this process to any other developers. If you used strange logic or an abnormal procedure, it is a good idea to document that here. This makes maintaining an application much easier. After all, how many times have you returned months later after developing something only to ask yourself, What was I thinking?

Page Processes Page

Just like the Items and Buttons headers on the Page Definition page navigate to a page to edit all the page's items or buttons at the same time, the Processes header presents a multirow edit page for the page's processes. This page is not real useful, but it does provide a look at all the processes on your entire page. You can change items such as the processes' sequence number, evaluation point, name, and When Button Pressed condition. You can also see if the process is conditional and when it was last updated. Like the other multiedit pages, this page provides a History button at the top so you can see a report of the last changes to the processes.

Branches

Branches control the flow of the application after a page has been processed. The form we created is simple in its branching in that it always returns back to the Contacts report page. Seldom are production applications so simple. You may access a page from several different locations, and your users would expect to be returned to the page from which they came. Therefore, HTML DB gives us the ability to be just as flexible as we need to be in controlling the flow of the application.

All of Chapter 11 will be spent on the topic of navigation between pages, but to close out our discussion of our wizard-generated form, we will look at the single branch that was created.

All the branches on a page will be listed in the Page Processing column under the Branches section. The branches are listed in groups by the point at which they will be evaluated. It is possible to have a branch that happens before the page is rendered. As with all the other elements listed on the Page Definition page, the name of a branch is an active link that will take you to the Edit Branch page. To the left of the branch name is its sequence, and on the right of the branch is the number of the page it branches to. This page number is an active link that navigates to the Page Definition page for this page. If the branch has no conditions defined for it, the word "Unconditional" will appear to the right of the branch name.

Edit Branch Page

As with the other elements, clicking on the name of a branch will take you to the Edit Branch page. At the top of the page you will find action buttons. The Cancel button allows you to discard any changes you have made and return to the Page Definition page. The Delete button deletes the current branch after you confirm that you wish to delete it. The Apply Changes button saves any changes you have made and returns you to the Page Definition page. Next to the Apply Changes button may be left and right arrow buttons, depending on whether there are other branches on the page. Unlike with items and buttons, using these navigation buttons will *not* commit any changes you have made to the current branch. Just below the buttons you will find the normal quick links that allow you to jump directly to any section on the page.

Point Section   The Point section defines the branch, the point at which the branch will be evaluated, and the sequences in which it will be evaluated. Unlike all the other elements on a page, you do not name branches. The name of a branch displayed on the Page Definition page is actually generated by the action of the branch and its destination. The branch type is specified at the time the branch is created and cannot be changed.

The Branch Point field, shown in Figure 10-17, is a pick list that allows you to change the point in the page process where the branch will be evaluated. Branches are evaluated either "on load" before the header is rendered or after the page has been submitted. There are four points after the page has been submitted at which a branch can be evaluated. Three things happen after a page is submitted: computations, validations, and processes, and they happen in that order. The four places that branches are evaluated are before, between, and after these three items. The Sequence field determines the order in which the branches will be evaluated within the same branch point.

Action Section   Depending on the type of branch, the Action section will contain different fields. All the different types of branches will be covered in the next chapter. The most common branch types are those that branch to another page in the application. The Action section shown in Figure 10-17 is the one you are likely to see most often.

The Target Type field allows you to select a page in this application or a URL. The two check boxes stay active for both target types. Selecting the URL type will disable the rest of the fields except for the URL Target field. The Page in This Application option will look like the example in the figure.

The Page field can contain the page number or the alias for the page. Using the alias makes it a little easier to tell the destination of the branch. The Reset Pagination for This Page check box, if selected, will cause the pagination on this page to be reset upon navigation. Recall from the last

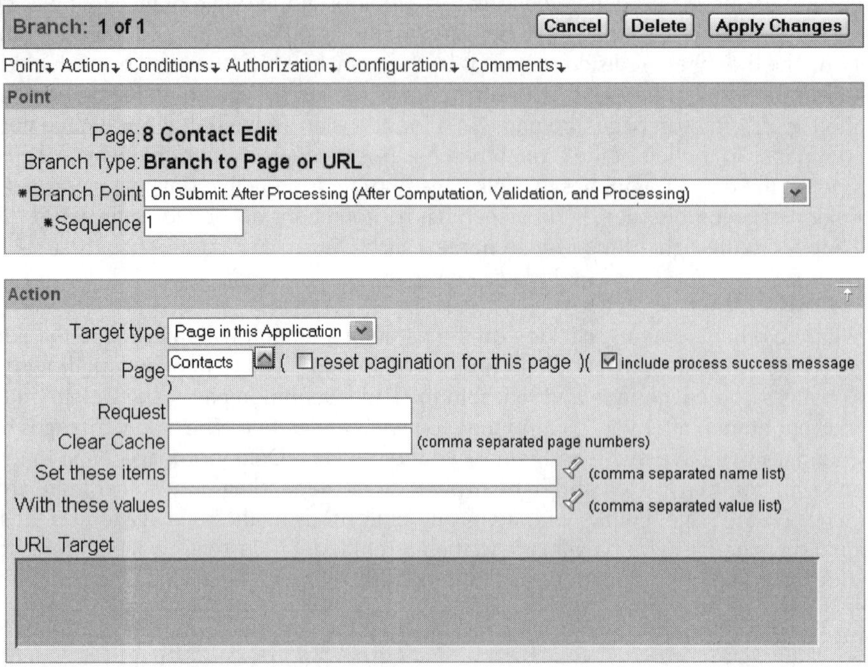

FIGURE 10-17 *Edit Branch page*

chapter the importance of resetting pagination on report pages. The Include Process Success Message check box, when checked, will cause the HTML DB engine to include the text of the error or success message that was defined for the process so that it can be displayed on the next page (see the "Messages Section" earlier in the chapter).

The Request field's value will be placed into the REQUEST, a built-in application item, and will be available on the next page. Recall that the name of a button when it is clicked is placed into the REQUEST and is used by the conditions to tell which button has been clicked. The Clear Cache field can contain one or more page numbers, separated by commas, for which you want the items cleared out of the session cache. Unlike with the Page field, you may not use page aliases in place of the page numbers.

The Set These Items field and the With These Values field work together to set page or application items with values of other items upon navigation. Use either one of the flashlight icons to pop up a small window where you can select multiple items to be set and multiple values to set them with. When completed, the window will close and populate the two fields with the items in the proper syntax.

For a URL target type, the URL Target field will be active. You may enter in any valid URL, including an f?p syntax URL to direct to a page in the application. HTML DB engine uses the values in the other fields when the target type is not URL to construct an f?p syntax URL for you. This syntax will be covered in great detail in the next chapter.

Conditions Section   The Conditional Processing section is just like the many Conditional Processing sections you have seen thus far. See the "Conditional Processing" section in Chapter 8 for more details on the types of conditions and how to use them. Note that this Conditional Processing section also has the additional When Button Pressed field, which allows you to associate a branch with the click of a specific button. The list of values for the field will contain the names of all the buttons on the page. You can use a When Button Pressed condition along with a condition specified in the other fields.

Authorization Section   The Authorization Scheme can be set to conditionally process the current branch based on a user's authorizations. Authorization schemes are covered in Chapter 16.

Configuration Section   The Build Option pick list in the Configuration Management section allows you to select a build option for the branch. Build options are typically used to include/ exclude debug items or to separate normal functionality from premium functionality. Build options are discussed in detail in Chapter 4.

Comments Section   Use the Comments section to note any peculiarities about this branch to other developers. If you used strange logic or an abnormal procedure, it is a good idea to document that here. This makes maintaining an application much easier. After all, how many times have you returned months later after developing something only to ask yourself, What was I thinking?

Multirow Edit Form

Everything we have looked at to this point in this chapter has been on forms for a single row of a table. In Chapter 9, we hinted at a way a report could be used as a multirow editing form. Due to space constraints, we will walk quickly through another wizard. This wizard creates a page with a multiple-record edit form for the Calls table. When we are done, we will have a form that looks similar to the one shown in Figure 10-18. Then we will look at a few of the items created by the wizard.

Multirow Edit Form Wizard

Follow these steps to create a page with a multiple-record edit form for the Calls table:

1. From Page Definition page, click on the Create button (in upper-right corner) to start a new page wizard.

2. Select the New Page option and then click on the Next button.

3. Select the Form option and then click on the Next button.

4. Select the Tabular Form option and then click on the Next button.

5. Select the schema that contains the Calls table and then click on the Next button.

6. Select the Calls table and then click on the Next button.

7. Select all columns and then click on the Next button.

8. Accept the defaults for Callid as primary key and then click on the Next button.

9. Accept the primary key source of Existing Trigger and then click on the Next button.

10. Select all columns and then click on the Next button.

11. Accept the defaults and then click on the Next button.

12. Select to use an existing tab set and create a new tab within the existing tab set, select the Edits tab set, and specify **Multi Edit** for the new label. Click on the Next button.

13. Accept the default labels for the buttons and then click on the Next button.

14. Accept the default for the "After Page Submit and Processing Branch to Page" choice, use the pick list to select the page number for the Call Report page for the "When Cancel Button Pressed Branch to this Page" field, and then click on the Next button.

15. Click on the Finish button.

16. Click on the Run Page icon.

The edit form created will not be quite like the one shown in Figure 10-18, but rather will look more like the one shown in Figure 10-19. The contact ID will be displayed instead of the contact name, the Notes field will be just a text field and not a text area, the Calldate field will not be a date picker, and the remaining fields may be too small or too large.

A Look Under the Hood

When you compare what was created for this form (see Figure 10-20) versus what was created for the single-row edit form (refer back to Figure 10-6), you will immediately notice some differences—the largest of which is that no items were created. This is because the region type is SQL Report,

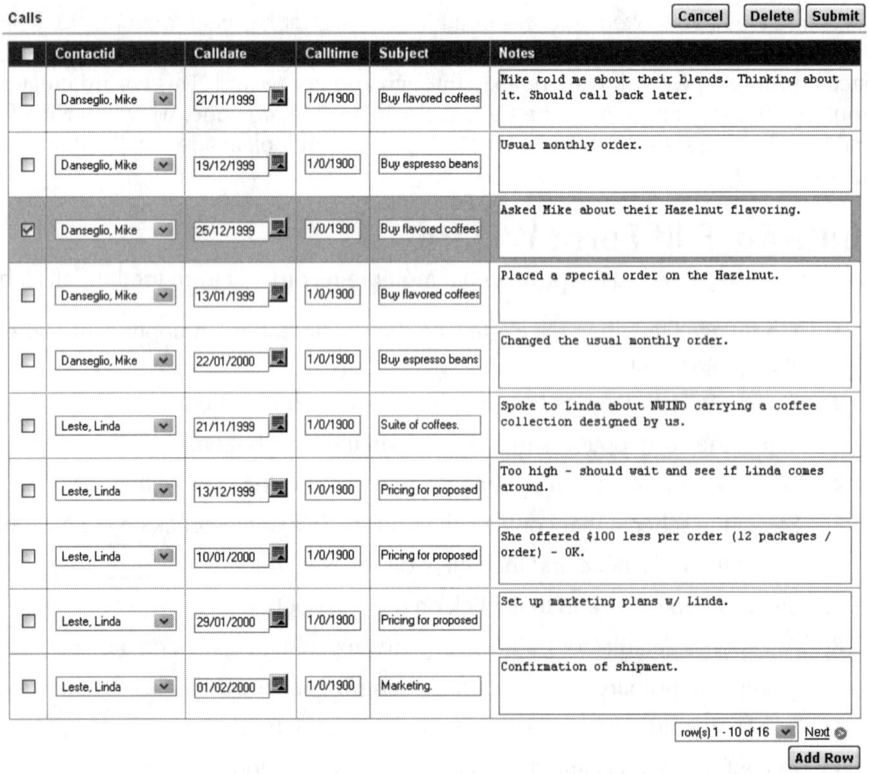

FIGURE 10-18   *Multirow Calls edit form*

Tabular Form   Cancel   Delete   Submit

☐	Callid	Contactid	Calldate	Calltime	Subject	Notes
☐	1	1	21-NOV-99	1/0/1900	Buy flavored coffees	Mike told me about t
☐	2	1	19-DEC-99	1/0/1900	Buy espresso beans	Usual monthly order.
☐	3	1	25-DEC-99	1/0/1900	Buy flavored coffees	Asked Mike about th
☐	4	1	13-JAN-99	1/0/1900	Buy flavored coffees	Placed a special ord
☐	5	1	22-JAN-00	1/0/1900	Buy espresso beans	Changed the usual r
☐	6	2	21-NOV-99	1/0/1900	Suite of coffees.	Spoke to Linda abou
☐	7	2	13-DEC-99	1/0/1900	Pricing for proposed	Too high - should wa
☐	8	2	10-JAN-00	1/0/1900	Pricing for proposed	She offered $100 les
☐	9	2	29-JAN-00	1/0/1900	Pricing for proposed	Set up marketing pla
☐	10	2	01-FEB-00	1/0/1900	Marketing.	Confirmation of shipr

row(s) 1 - 10 of 16 ▾   Next ⊘

Add Row

FIGURE 10-19   *Multirow Calls edit form before modifications*

and the report contains columns for all the items. If you were to look at the individual columns in the report on their corresponding Column Attributes pages, you would see that the Display As type is defined as Text Field for almost all of them. The buttons are just the same—the Cancel button redirects the page, whereas the others submit the page and rely on the After Processing branch for navigation.

You will also notice the lack of an After Header process to fetch the row and populate the items—this is also handled by the Report region. As for After Submit processes, there is now one each to handle inserts, updates, and deletes. These are special multirow built-in processes. In Chapter 13, we will look at creating our own multirow process to handle something more complex than a single table. There is an additional process for adding blank rows to your form so new records may be inserted. Again, this is a special process created just for adding columns to a tabular form. Take a little time to explore each of these processes in light of what was covered earlier in the chapter concerning processes. We will dig further into processes in the next chapter.

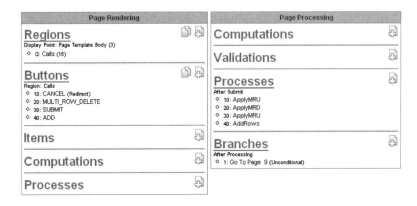

Page Rendering	Page Processing
Regions 📄 📑	**Computations** 📑
Display Point: Page Template Body (3)	
◦ Q: Calls (16)	**Validations** 📑
Buttons 📄 📑	**Processes** 📑
Region: Calls	After Submit
◦ 10: CANCEL (Redirect)	◦ 10: ApplyMRU
◦ 20: MULTI_ROW_DELETE	◦ 20: ApplyMRD
◦ 30: SUBMIT	◦ 30: ApplyMRU
◦ 40: ADD	◦ 40: AddRows
Items 📑	**Branches** 📑
	After Processing
Computations 📑	◦ 1: Go To Page 9 (Unconditional)
Processes 📑	

FIGURE 10-20   *Page Definition page for the multirow edit form*

If you look at the Edit Page Region page, you will notice that it looks just like a SQL Report region, except the type is SQL Report (updateable report). A quick look at the Report Attributes page will show it to look just like any other SQL report, except that most of the columns are marked as "Edit" because of their Display As type. Also, there is a special column with the alias "[row selector]" that provides a check box to specify multiple rows to be deleted. The main difference between this SQL report and a normal one is that the individual columns are defined as editable types, which can be modified to make the form even more useful.

Modifications, Step by Step

For the following modifications, we will assume you can navigate to the Page Definition page, Navigate to the Report Attributes page via the Q next to the region name, and then navigate to the Column Attributes page for each of the columns we are about to edit. The Column Attributes page was covered in detail in Chapter 9.

Callid Column

Notice the callid and callid_display columns. The callid column is a hidden column; the other is so the callid column can be displayed. Because we don't really need to show the primary key column, mark it so that it will not be displayed. This can be done from the Report Attributes page as well as from the Column Attributes page for that column.

ContactID Column

Make the following changes for the ContactID column:

1. Change the Display As type to Select List (query-based LOV).
2. Enter the following query in the LOV Query field:

    ```
    select lastname||', '||firstname d, contactid r
    from contacts
    ```

3. Set Display Null to No and Display Extra Value to Yes.
4. Change Element Width to 25.
5. Apply these changes and run the page. Make any adjustments necessary.

Calldate Column

Make the following changes for the Calldate column:

1. Change the Display As type to Date Picker.
2. Select a date picker format mask.
3. Set Element Width wide enough to handle the format mask you selected.
4. Apply these changes and run the page. Make any adjustments necessary.

Notes Column

Make the following changes for the Notes column:

1. Change the Display As type to Text Area.
2. Set Element Width to 45.
3. Set Number of Rows to 2.
4. Apply these changes and run the page. Make any adjustments necessary.

Your form should now look similar to the one shown in Figure 10-18. As you can see, it is relatively simple to change the type of HTML form element that each column will use.

If you have followed the chapters through to this point, you should be starting to really understand the elements that make up most pages and the process that the HTML DB engine goes through to render and process these pages. We still have a couple more subjects to explore before you will feel comfortable manually creating all the pieces of a page.

Manually Creating Forms

The forms we have created so far have been with the assistance of the wizards. However, when you use the wizards, you are limited to querying and updating a single table. How often does a real-world application query and update only a single table? It happens occasionally, but more often not. Fear not: You can easily create your own forms and the processes to populate them and process the changes. In this section, we will take a quick look at manually creating forms.

Single-row Form

Before we discuss the multirow edit form, let's address a single-row edit form. As you'll recall, the single-row edit form is made up of an HTML type region, with one item for each of the columns in a table, along with a couple buttons to control actions. There is also a process to query data into the items, a couple processes to handle the page once the user submits changes, and finally a branch for navigation.

In this chapter and the last one, we looked in detail at the attributes of regions, items, and buttons. With that in-depth knowledge, you can easily create regions, items, and buttons from scratch. Actually, it really isn't from scratch because HTML DB provides wizards for these items, too. To create regions, items, or buttons, you click on the Create icon (the one with the plus sign on a page), which appears in the upper-right corner of each of the regions on the Page Definition page. Each wizard will have a series of pages that help you fill in the minimum attributes for each element. The attributes will be the same ones that appear on the edit pages we have looked at in depth.

In Chapter 13, we will look at manually creating processes, so for now the following high-level steps would be used to create the shell of a single-row edit form:

1. Use one of the previously defined methods for creating a new blank page—either the Create Page button on the Application Builder page, the Create button on the Page Definition page, or the New link on the Developer's Toolbar.

2. On the new page, create a new HTML region, leaving the source blank.

3. Create an item for each of the elements you want to edit, arranging them as you desire on the HTML region.

4. Create a button on the HTML region for each of the actions. You will probably want Create, Save, Delete, and Cancel buttons. Recall that the Cancel button usually performs a redirect to the calling page, whereas the others rely on post-submit branches for their navigation.

These steps provide the shell for the single-row edit page. After reading the chapters on navigation and processes, you will be able to complete the other pieces needed for your manually created page.

Multirow Form

You have seen that the multirow form is actually a SQL report where the individual column attributes have been set so that the Display As type is one of many editable HTML form elements—Text Field, Text Area, Select List, and so on. These Display As types were covered in Chapter 9. A multirow form, like the one shown in Figure 9-21, can be created by another method where you create a SQL report and query the columns using the HTMLDB_ITEM package.

The HTMLDB_ITEM package is covered in more detail in Appendix A. The form shown in Figure 10-21 was created with the following query:

```
select htmldb_item.hidden(1,empno) ||
        htmldb_item.text(2,ename,10,20) Name,
        htmldb_item.select_list_from_query(3,job,
                    'select distinct job from emp order by 1') job,
        htmldb_item.select_list_from_query(4,mgr,
                    'select ename, empno from emp order by 1') manager,
        htmldb_item.text(5,hiredate,10,20) hiredate,
        htmldb_item.text(6,sal,6,10) salary,
        htmldb_item.text(7,comm,6,10) comission,
        htmldb_item.select_list_from_query(8,deptno,
                    'select dname, deptno from dept order by 1') department
    from emp
```

Creating a form with this method and processing its data are covered in detail in Chapter 13.

Employees

NAME	JOB	MANAGER	HIREDATE	SALARY	COMISSION	DEPARTMENT
KING	PRESIDENT		17-NOV-81	5000		ACCOUNTING
BLAKE	MANAGER	KING	01-MAY-81	2850		SALES
CLARK	MANAGER	KING	09-JUN-81	2450		ACCOUNTING
JONES	MANAGER	KING	02-APR-81	2975		RESEARCH
SCOTT	ANALYST	JONES	09-DEC-82	3000		RESEARCH
FORD	ANALYST	JONES	03-DEC-81	3000		RESEARCH
SMITH	CLERK	FORD	17-DEC-80	800		RESEARCH
ALLEN	SALESMAN	BLAKE	20-FEB-81	1600	300	SALES
WARD	SALESMAN	BLAKE	22-FEB-81	1250	500	SALES
MARTIN	SALESMAN	BLAKE	28-SEP-81	1250	1400	SALES
TURNER	SALESMAN	BLAKE	08-SEP-81	1500	0	SALES
ADAMS	CLERK	SCOTT	12-JAN-83	1100		RESEARCH
JAMES	CLERK	BLAKE	03-DEC-81	950		SALES
MILLER	CLERK	CLARK	23-JAN-82	1300		ACCOUNTING
LEWIS	WRITER	KING	07-SEP-05	5500	0	ACCOUNTING

1 - 15

FIGURE 10-21 *Multirow form created using HTMLDB_ITEM*

CHAPTER
11

Navigating Between Pages

he logical flow of an application and the ability for a user to quickly and easily navigate within your application are both controlled by the navigational features available in the HTML DB environment. Figure 11-1, which is the Application Builder main page, contains most of the navigational elements available in HTML DB, which are listed here:

- Embedded URLs using f?p syntax
- Navigation bar
- Tabs
- Breadcrumb menus
- Lists
- Trees

FIGURE 11-1 *Navigational elements on the Application Builder main page*

The HTML DB development environment is itself an HTML DB application and a great example for the use of available navigational elements. Look at the Application Builder main page, shown in Figure 11-1. The Home, Logout, and Help text and icons in the upper-right corner comprise an example of a navigation bar. The three main tabs are, of course, an example of tabs. The navigation trail, Home>Application Builder>Application 144, directly below the tabs is an example of a breadcrumb menu. Also, the link items contained in the Tasks panel are an example of a List navigational item. There are many examples of embedded URLs. The small and large icons on the page all have embedded URLs. Also, each page name in the Pages report section is an active link. The only navigational element not demonstrated on this page is the tree.

In this chapter, we will look at the details behind each of these navigational elements and how to implement them. By the end of the chapter, you should feel comfortable enough to know when and how to use each type of navigation.

Understanding f?p Syntax URL

Behind the implementation of almost every type of navigation in an HTML DB application lies a URL in what is know as the f?p syntax. If you place your cursor over any of the navigational elements on the Application Builder main page and look at the target displayed at the bottom of your browser, you will see a full URL, something like http://srvr.com:80/pls/htmldb/f?p=4000:415 0:2340950924::NO::P9_EMPID:8. This is the f?p syntax URL. Most of the time, you will not have to manually create the f?p syntax, but you may need to occasionally, so it is important to understand this syntax. The breakdown of the URL is shown in the following table:

http://srvr.com:80	The server and HTTP server port
/pls	Tells the Apache web server to fire off the PL/SQL module
/htmldb	The Database Access Descriptor (DAD)
/f	The main entry point to the HTML DB engine
?p=x:x:x:x:x:	A single HTML parameter that is evaluated as a colon-separated list of parameters by the HTML DB engine

The parameters contained in the colon-delimited list are f?p=App:Page:Session:Request:Debug: ClearCache:itemNames:itemValues:PrinterFriendly and are explained in the following table. Note that when you are constructing an f?p syntax URL, it is not necessary to include all the parameters. You may stop at any point, but you may not skip any of the parameters. If you don't need to supply a value for one of the parameters, just include the colon. The following would be a valid URL:

```
f?p=104:4:&SESSION.:::::::YES
```

In this case, the App, Page, Session, and PrinterFriendly parameters are supplied.

Parameter	Description	Syntax for Referencing Value
App	References the application. This can be the application number or the application alias. Or, within an application, the current application can be referred to with a substitution variable. The least preferable method is the actual application number, because if the application is ported to another environment, the application number may change.	Substitution variable: `:APP_ID`
Page	The destination page, which can be the page number or the page alias.	
Session	Identifies the numeric value assigned to each individual session, which allows HTML DB to maintain session state. Reference using one of the syntaxes.	Substitution variable: `:SESSION` PL/SQL: `V('SESSION')` Bind variable: `:APP_SESSION`
Request	This parameter sets the value of REQUEST. Buttons will populate this parameter with the names of the buttons. The value of the request is referenced in the next page with one of the available syntaxes. You could use one of the syntaxes when constructing a URL to pass on the REQUEST that was passed to the current page.	Substitution variable: `:REQUEST` PL/SQL: `V('REQUEST')` Bind variable: `:REQUEST`
Debug	Sets the processing mode for the upcoming page. Valid values for this flag are YES and NO; if it is left blank it defaults to NO. When the debug flag is set, the HTML DB engine will display application processing details on the page. When constructing a URL, you could reference the current value of the debug flag to pass it on to the next page.	Substitution variable: `:DEBUG` PL/SQL: `V('DEBUG')` Bind variable: `:DEBUG`

Parameter	Description	Syntax for Referencing Value
ClearCache	The value placed in this parameter controls the clearing of items in the session (cache). Use a single page number or a comma-delimited list of page numbers to clear the session for all items on that page. The list can also contain the names of collections to be reset or the keyword RP, which will reset the region pagination for the following page.	
itemNames	This parameter can contain a comma-delimited list of the names of page items or application items whose values you want to set in session with the values that will be specified in the next parameter.	
itemValues	This parameter can contain a comma-delimited list of values for each of the items listed in the previous parameter. The items cannot contain any colons. Also, if they contain commas, they must be enclosed with backslashes (for example, : Fred,\Wilma,Dino\).	
PrinterFriendly	This flag tells the HTML DB engine to render the page in a printer-friendly mode. Valid values are YES and NO (the default is NO). The HTML DB engine will not display navigation elements, and all items will be displayed as text instead of form elements. You can reference the value of the PrinterFriendly flag in elements conditional definition.	PL/SQL: `V('PRINTER_FRIENDLY')`

Although it is good to understand the workings of the f?p syntax URL, you will probably not create it that often because the HTML DB wizards usually do it for you. However, when you want to dynamically create URLs that vary based on values queried or values entered by the user, the power and flexibility of the f?p syntax comes in real handy. For example, the following query was used in a testing application with a report region based on a SQL query to make the column that displays the person's name into an active link to a report page that provides details for that person and particular test.

```
select t.test_no, p.person_no, t.test_n,
         '<a href="f?p=&APP_ID.:303:&SESSION.:::::P303_P_NAME,P303_P_NO,P303_TEST_NO:'||
                      person_name||','||person_no||','||test_no||'">'||
                      person_name||'</a>' person_name,
              test_name,
              rating,
       from person p, questions q, tests t, test_results r
      where p.person_no   = r.person_n
        and r.question_no = q.question_no
        and t.test_no     = q.test_no;
```

Navigation Bars

A navigation bar is typically used for standard navigational items that are available on every page, such as Logout, Print, and Help. The location of the navigation bar on a page is dependent on the current page template and where the #NAVIGATION_BAR# substitution variable is used.

Each application can have only one navigation bar. However, because each element in a navigation bar can be conditionally displayed, it could appear that there is more than one navigation bar in an application. An application's navigation bar is created and maintained from the Navigation Bar Entries link under the Navigation section of the application's Shared Components page, as shown in Figure 11-2, or through the drop-down menu off the Shared Components icon on the Application main page, or by clicking on the Navigation Bar header on any Page Definition page.

The Navigation Bar Entries page, shown in Figure 11-3, provides an overview of the existing entries in an applications navigation bar. The child tabs allow you to navigate to a grid edit page where you can edit some of the attributes of each of the elements in a navigation bar. Additionally, if the navigation bar is subscribed to a master navigation bar, the Subscription child tab navigates to a report on subscriptions. Finally, there is a link to view the history of the last changes to be made to elements in the navigation bar.

When you create a new navigation bar entry with the Create button, you will be given the option of creating from scratch or copying from another application and subscribing to the master entry.

Navigation

- Breadcrumbs
- Lists
- Navigation Bar Entries
- Tabs
- Trees

FIGURE 11-2 *Navigation section from the Shared Components page*

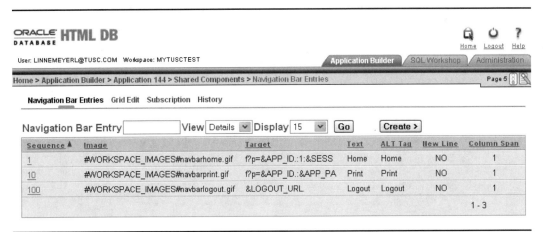

FIGURE 11-3   *Navigation Bar Entries page*

Edit Navigation Bar Entry Page

Clicking on the sequence number of a navigation bar entry will open the Edit Navigation Bar
Entry page for that entry. This edit page is very much like all the other edit pages we have covered
to this point. Therefore, we will not go through each and every section as we have done so far.
The common sections on this edit page you should be familiar with by this point are the Conditions,
Authorizations, Configuration, and Comments sections.

Sequence Section

The first section is the Sequence section. Here, you assign a sequence number in the Sequence
field that determines the order in which the entries are evaluated to be included on the navigation
bar. Additionally, this section contains a Begins on New Line field and a Cell Column Span field
that place the entry on a new line and set its COLSPAN property.

Subscription Section

The Subscription section here is similar to the same section in the template edit page. Because
there is a bug in the Copy and Subscribe functionality, this is the only way that a navigation bar
entry can subscribe to another in a different application. This way, when changes are made to the
master, they can be propagated to the subscribing entries with the Publish NavBar button that is
present only when the current entry is a master to other subscriptions, as shown in Figure 11-4. If
the entry is subscribed to another, a Refresh NavBar button will appear.

Image Attributes

If you want your navigation bar's entries to have icons, all the information will be supplied in this
section. Select an image from the pick list on the Image field, which will list all the workspace and
application images that have been uploaded in the Shared Components part of your application.
You can also reference all the images that come with HTML DB and are located in the HTMLDB_
ORA_HOME\marvel\images directory using the virtual path defined for the image directory (for

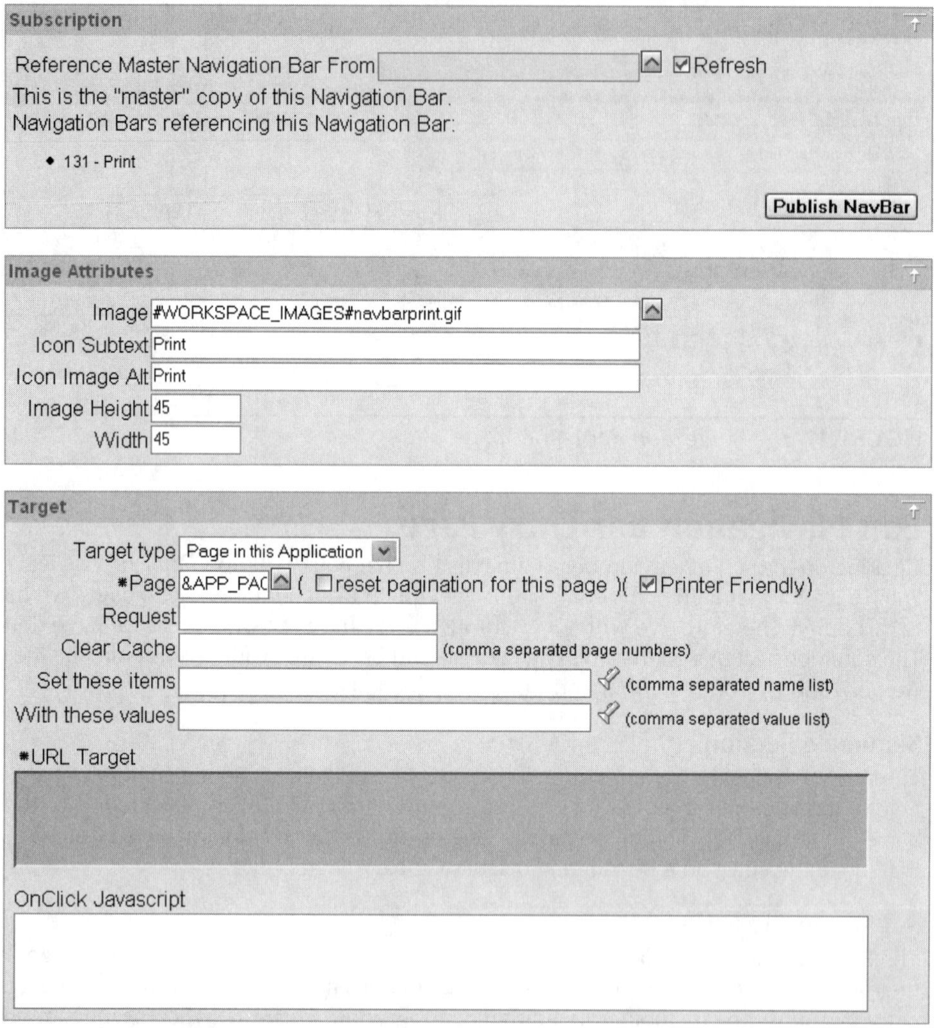

Subscription

Reference Master Navigation Bar From [⌃] ☑Refresh
This is the "master" copy of this Navigation Bar.
Navigation Bars referencing this Navigation Bar:

- 131 - Print

[Publish NavBar]

Image Attributes

Image [#WORKSPACE_IMAGES#navbarprint.gif] [⌃]
Icon Subtext [Print]
Icon Image Alt [Print]
Image Height [45]
Width [45]

Target

Target type [Page in this Application ▼]
*Page [&APP_PAC ⌃] (☐reset pagination for this page)(☑Printer Friendly)
Request [ ]
Clear Cache [ ] (comma separated page numbers)
Set these items [ ] (comma separated name list)
With these values [ ] (comma separated value list)
*URL Target

OnClick Javascript

FIGURE 11-4   *Edit Navigation Bar Entry page (partial)*

example, /i/navbarprint.gif). If you don't have an image, or if you want text and an image together, you need to supply the text to be seen in the Icon Subtext field. The Icon Image Alt field's value can be used in the image's alt attribute as well as its title attribute. Finally, you can supply values for the Image Height and Width fields.

If you try all of this and no image is displayed, look at the page template you are using. Make sure the Navigation Bar Entry field on the page template contains something similar to the following:

```
<a href="#LINK#" class="t1NavigationBar"><img src=#IMAGE# width=#WIDTH#
    height=#HEIGHT# alt=#ALT# title=#ALT# >#TEXT#</a>
```

Notice that the #ALT# substitution variable is used twice—once for the alt attribute and once for the title attribute. The title attribute provides a text flyover on the image. The help text for the Navigation Bar Entry field states that the #IMAGE# substitution variable will supply all the entries for height, width, and alt, but this does not prove to be true.

NOTE
Using the View Source option on a browser to look at the final HTML code that is produced by the HTML DB engine is a great way to gain insight into what is happening.

Target Section

The Target section for a navigation entry is similar to the Action section in Branches and the Optional URL Redirect section in Buttons. You will see this section in every type of navigational element.

The Target Type field allows you to select a page in this application or a URL. The two check box fields stay active for both target types. Selecting the URL type will disable the rest of the fields except for the URL Target field and the OnClick JavaScript field. The Page in This Application option is shown in Figure 11-4.

The Page field can contain the page number, the alias for the page, or the "&APP_PAGE_ID." substitution variable. Using the alias makes it a little easier to tell the destination of the branch, whereas the substitution variable will be replaced with the current page, so it is very useful in entries such as Print where you want the current page. The Reset Pagination for This Page check box, if selected, will cause the pagination on this page to be reset upon navigation. Recall from Chapter 9 the importance of resetting pagination on report pages. The Printer Friendly check box, when checked, will cause the HTML DB engine to include the YES value for the PrinterFriendly flag in the generated f?p syntax URL.

The Request field's value will be placed into the REQUEST, a built-in application item, and will be available on the next page. Recall that the name of a button, when the button is clicked, is placed into the REQUEST and is used by the conditions to tell which button has been clicked. The Clear Cache field can contain one or more page numbers, separated by a comma, for which you want the page's items cleared out of the session cache. Unlike with the Page field, you may not use page aliases in place of the page numbers, but you can still use the substitution variable.

The Set These Items field and the With These Values field work together to set page or application items with values of other items upon navigation. Use either one of the flashlight icons to pop up a small window that allows you to select multiple items to be set and multiple values to set them with. When completed, the window will close and populate the two fields with the items in the proper syntax.

For a URL target type, the URL Target field will be active. You may enter in any valid URL, including an f?p syntax URL to direct to a page in the application. The HTML DB engine uses the values in the other fields when the target type is not URL to construct an f?p syntax URL for you. Recall that you can also put JavaScript in the URL Target field if it will accomplish the navigation you want.

The OnClick JavaScript field is supposed to allow you to enter code for a JavaScript OnClick action, but if you follow the directions in the help text, nothing is done with the text entered into the field.

Tabs

Tabs are probably the most prominent type of navigation within many applications. The sample application we began building in Chapter 5 was created with two levels of tabs. The parent level is defined with tabs for Home, Reports and Edits. The Reports and Edit tabs are defined to each contain standard tabs for Contacts, Calls, and LookUps. Any wizard that creates a new page allows you to add that page to an existing tab or provides you several options in creating new tabs. Therefore, you could build an entire application without ever using the tab edit pages.

Tabs are said to be current or noncurrent. The difference is the way they are displayed and whether they are an active link or not. The current parent tab may be a bright color and not an active link, whereas noncurrent tabs are a subdued color and are active links. The current standard tab may be bracketed text, and the noncurrent standard tabs are underlined active links. The appearance of the tabs is generally controlled in the page template, although it is possible to define each tab as two individual images—one current, one noncurrent. Typically, template tabs are created with three images for the current tab and three images for the noncurrent tab—one for the left side of the tab, another for the right side of the tab, and the third used in conjunction with the tab's label to make dynamic-length tabs.

Like Navigation Bar Entries and most of the other navigational elements, you access the tab definition page through the Navigation section of the application's Shared Components. You can also click on the Parent Tab or Tab header on any Page Definition page.

The main Tabs page, shown in Figure 11-5, is a graphical representation of your application's tabs as they are currently defined. From this page, you initiate any changes that you would like to make to your tabs. Across the top of the page, just below the breadcrumb menu, is a standard set of tabs for navigation to two tab edit pages and two tab report pages. HTML DB refers to the child-level tabs as *standard* tabs and the main-level tabs as the *parent* tabs, which are associated with a set of standard tabs. If your application has only a single set of tabs, there will be one pseudo-parent tab and the others will be defined as standard tabs.

Although you can't make any changes on the main tabs page, you can use it to see details about all your defined tabs. The representation shows you a current parent tab, indicated by the edit icon next to its name, and all the standard tabs associated with that parent tab. One of the standard tabs will also be current, indicated by the edit icon next to its name. Below the standard tabs you will see page numbers and names for all pages that are currently associated with the active standard tab. Clicking on any parent or standard tab makes it the current tab and updates the display.

As you can see in Figure 11-5, it is possible to have more than one page associated with a standard tab, although only one page will be the target of that tab's navigation. The first page, page 5 in this example, is the main page associated with and the target for the navigation of that tab. When that tab is not the current tab and it is clicked on, the first page is the page that the user will navigate to. The other pages are listed because when they are displayed, the tabs are still displayed just as they are for the first page. A good example of where you might have a number of pages associated with the same tab would be a wizard. The first page is the start of the wizard, and the rest of the pages are those you step through in the wizard. As the user goes through the wizard, the tab display remains the same.

The main Tab page, shown in Figure 11-5, is full of navigation options, many of which accomplish the same thing in a slightly different manner. It can be a little confusing knowing which options to use. Get familiar with the basic ones and then explore the others. The two tab edit pages available from the standard tabs—Edit Standard Tabs and Edit Parent Tabs—are

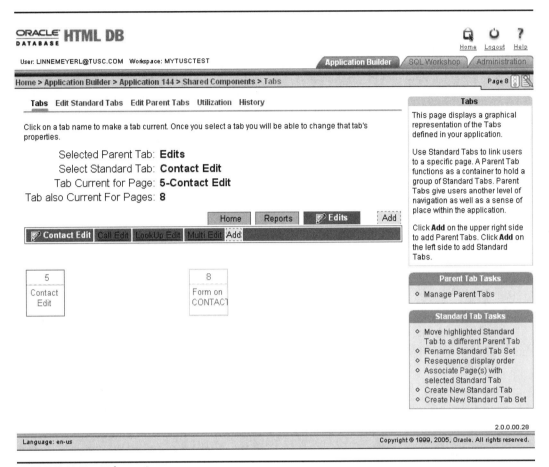

FIGURE 11-5 *Tabs main page*

multirow edit pages for the current application's parent and standard tabs. These multirow edit pages allow you to make changes to certain attributes for either the parent or standard tabs. Each row on the multirow edit page for the standard tabs contains an edit icon that takes you to an edit page for an individual standard tab. You can navigate directly to the individual parent or standard tab edit pages with the edit icons next to the active tabs on the main Tab page.

You need to understand that *all* tabs belong to a tab set. Typically, an application will only have a single parent tab set to which all parent tabs in the application belong, although it is possible to have more than one parent tab set. Standard tabs are grouped together into tab sets. A parent tab is associated with a standard tab set and will show as current whenever the user is on a page associated with one of the standard tabs in the associated standard tab set.

Standard Tabs

When an application uses only one level of tabs, these are implemented as standard tabs. If an application has two levels of tabs, the standard tabs are the tabs subordinate to the parent tabs.

Edit Standard Tabs Page

The multirow edit page for standard tabs, shown in Figure 11-6, allows you to edit a few attributes of your standard tabs. This page is most useful for adjusting the display order of the tabs. The Sequence field controls the order in which the tabs will be displayed within their tab set. The Name field simply provides a unique name for the tab. The Label field changes the text that is displayed for a tab. You may see labels that include " ", which is HTML for a space that was put in there during creation of the tab by a wizard. You may remove it and replace it with a single space. The Also Current Pages field contains a comma-delimited list of pages for which the tab is current for other than the main target page, which is listed in the Page field. The Tab Set field contains the name of the standard tab set to which the tab belongs. A tab set will be associated with a parent tab, so in essence the Tab Set field tells you what parent tab is for the current tab. An application can have more than one set of parent tabs, so the Parent Tab Set field tells you which parent tab set the tab belongs to. The icon in the Edit column navigates to the Edit Standard Tab page for the corresponding tab.

Edit Standard Tab Page

Standard tabs, like all other components in HTML DB, have their own edit page that contains some common sections found in other components' edit pages and some sections specific to the standard tab alone.

Common Sections   The Edit Standard Tab page allows you to edit attributes for a single standard tab. Like many of the edit pages we have looked at, this one contains several of the common sections addressed in previous chapters. These sections include Conditional Display, Authorization, Configuration, and Comments.

Name Section   The Name section, shown in Figure 11-7, allows you to edit the Tab Name, Tab Label, and Sequence fields, just as you could on the multirow edit page. The Standard Tab Set

Tabs   **Edit Standard Tabs**   Edit Parent Tabs   Utilization   History

Standard Tab Set [- All Tab Sets - ▾]   Display [20 ▾]   [Go]   [Apply Changes]

Edit	Tab Set ▲	Sequence	Name	Label	Page	Also Current Pages	Parent Tab Set
📝	Edit Forms	5	T_CONTACT_EDIT	Contact Edit	5	11	main
📝	Edit Forms	6	T_CALL_EDIT	Call Edit	6		main
📝	Edit Forms	7	T_LOOKUP_EDIT	LookUp Edit	7		main
📝	Edit Forms	17	T_MULTI_EDIT	Multi Edit	9		main
📝	Home	1	T_HOME	Home	1		main
📝	Reports	2	T_CONTACTS	Contacts	2		main
📝	Reports	3	T_CALLS	Calls	10		main
📝	Reports	4	T_LOOKUPS	LookUps	4		main
📝	T_TESTING	10	T_TEST	Test	8		Others

FIGURE 11-6   *Edit Standard Tabs page*

field allows you to change the tab set to which this tab belongs, in essence changing the parent tab to which it belongs. Care should be taken when doing this with a tab that has pages already associated with it. There is an attribute associated with a page that does not always get updated when this is changed. If you change this and experience strange behavior, edit the page's attributes through the Edit Attributes button on the top of the Page Definition page. There is a Standard Tab Set attribute which may contain an invalid value, update to the proper set and it should work fine. Also note there is a field farther down the page for the Parent Tab Set; if the tab set that you change to belongs to a different tab set, you will also want to change that field.

Current for Pages Section   This section allows you to define the target and other pages for which the tab will show as current. The Tab Page field can be populated with the pop-up list of current pages if you can't recall the page number for your target page, or you may type the page number in directly. The Tab Also Current for Pages field may contain a single page number or a comma-delimited list of page numbers for which the tab should display as current. When these fields are changed, the page attribute Standard Tab Set, discussed previously, gets updated for the pages listed. The application just seems to get confused when the Standard Tab Set attribute is changed for a tab, and you may have to go to each page for this tab. Click on the Edit Attributes button and make sure the Standard Tab Set field is correct.

Images Section   The Images section allows you to specify individual images to be displayed for a tab. As discussed earlier in the introduction to tabs, the appearance of tabs is generally controlled by the page template, which can create dynamic-length tabs. However, if you want to

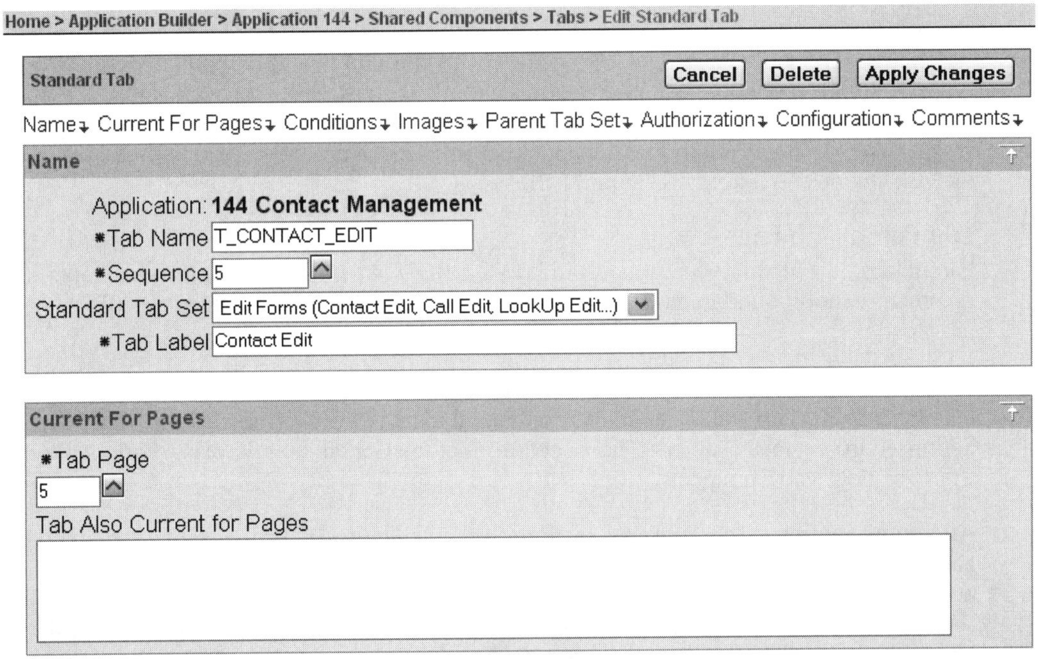

Home > Application Builder > Application 144 > Shared Components > Tabs > Edit Standard Tab

Standard Tab   Cancel   Delete   Apply Changes

Name↓ Current For Pages↓ Conditions↓ Images↓ Parent Tab Set↓ Authorization↓ Configuration↓ Comments↓

Name

Application: **144 Contact Management**

*Tab Name   T_CONTACT_EDIT

*Sequence   5

Standard Tab Set   Edit Forms (Contact Edit, Call Edit, LookUp Edit...)

*Tab Label   Contact Edit

Current For Pages

*Tab Page
5

Tab Also Current for Pages

FIGURE 11-7   *Edit Standard Tab page (partial)*

create two images for each of your tabs, this is where you use them. The Current Tab Image field contains the image to be used when the tab is displayed as current. The Non Current Tab Image field is used when the tab is not current. The Image Attributes field allows you to specify attributes, such as height, width, alt, and title for the image.

Adding Standard Tags

Although several links in the side panels of the main Tab page allow you to create a new standard tab, the cleanest way is with the Add link on the graphical representation of your tabs. Make sure that the parent tab, under which you want to create the new standard tab, is the current tab. If you want to create the tab under a new parent tab, you need to create that tab first. Clicking on the Add link will jump you into the Create Standard Tab Wizard, which allows you to set most of the attributes that are shown on the Edit Standard Tab page.

Parent Tabs

An application with only one level of tabs will still contain a single pseudo parent tab that is not editable by the developer. Applications with two levels of tabs will have one or more parent tabs. Changes to these tabs are made on their corresponding edit pages.

Edit Parent Tabs Page

The multirow edit page for parent tabs, shown in Figure 11-8, allows you to edit a few attributes of your parent tabs. This page is most useful for adjusting the display order of the tabs. The Sequence field controls the order in which the tabs will be displayed within their tab set. The only way to see which tab set a parent tab belongs to is to limit the report with the Tabset pick list and the Go button. The Name field simply provides a unique name for the tab. The Text field changes the text that is displayed for a tab if it is not an individual image. The Target field is the destination URL for when the tab is noncurrent. If you don't want to manually create the f?p syntax URL, the individual edit page has a section that constructs it for you. Unlike the multirow edit page for the standard tabs, this one does not have a link to the individual Parent Tab Edit page. To get there, you must return to the main tab page, select a parent tab you wish to edit, and use the Edit link next to it (refer to Figure 11-5).

Edit Parent Tab Page

Parent tabs, like all other components in HTML DB, have their own edit page that contains some common sections found in other component's edit pages and some sections specific to the parent tab alone.

Common Sections   The Edit Parent Tab page allows you to edit attributes for a single parent tab. Like the Edit Standard Tab page, it also contains several of the common sections already addressed in previous chapters. These sections include Conditional Display, Authorization, Configuration, and Comments.

Attributes Section   The Attributes section, shown in Figure 11-9, allows you to edit the Name, Label, and Sequence fields, just as you can on the multirow edit page. The Parent Tab Set attribute is displayed, but you cannot change it—once in a parent tab set, always in a parent tab set. The Current On Standard Tab Set field is where a parent tab is associated with standard tabs. This parent tab will be displayed as current when the current page is associated with a standard tab that is in the listed standard tab set.

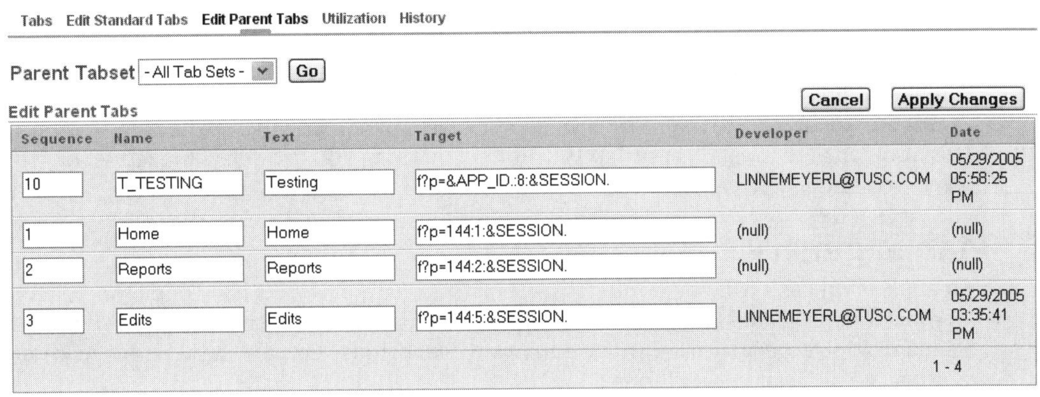

Tabs   Edit Standard Tabs   **Edit Parent Tabs**   Utilization   History

Parent Tabset - All Tab Sets - ⌄   [Go]

Edit Parent Tabs   [Cancel] [Apply Changes]

Sequence	Name	Text	Target	Developer	Date
10	T_TESTING	Testing	f?p=&APP_ID.:8:&SESSION.	LINNEMEYERL@TUSC.COM	05/29/2005 05:58:25 PM
1	Home	Home	f?p=144:1:&SESSION.	(null)	(null)
2	Reports	Reports	f?p=144:2:&SESSION.	(null)	(null)
3	Edits	Edits	f?p=144:5:&SESSION.	LINNEMEYERL@TUSC.COM	05/29/2005 03:35:41 PM
					1 - 4

FIGURE 11-8   *Edit Parent Tabs page*

Tab Target Section   The Tab Target section builds the URL displayed in the multirow Edit Parent Tab page. The fields in this section are identical to the Target section for the Navigation Bar Entry covered earlier in the chapter.

Image Section   The Image section for parent tabs is just like the Image section for standard tabs. It allows you to specify individual images for displaying the current and noncurrent tab.

Adding Parent Tags

Although several links in the side panels of the main Tab page allow you to create a new parent tab, the cleanest way is with the Add link on the graphical representation of your tabs if you want

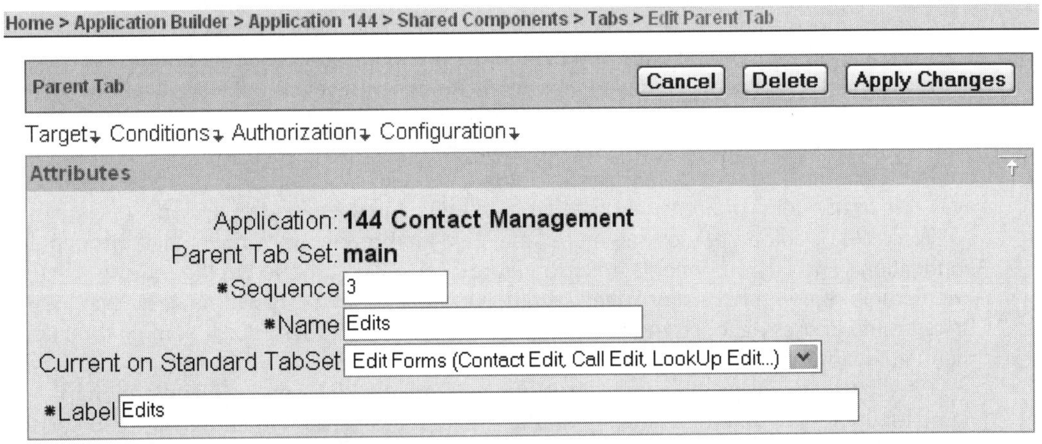

Home > Application Builder > Application 144 > Shared Components > Tabs > Edit Parent Tab

Parent Tab   [Cancel] [Delete] [Apply Changes]

Target↓ Conditions↓ Authorization↓ Configuration↓

Attributes   ⬆

Application: **144 Contact Management**
Parent Tab Set: **main**
* Sequence 3
* Name Edits
Current on Standard TabSet Edit Forms (Contact Edit, Call Edit, LookUp Edit...) ⌄
* Label Edits

FIGURE 11-9   *Edit Parent Tab page (partial)*

to create one in the default parent tab set. Click on the Add link to the right of your existing parent tabs. This starts the Create Parent Tab Wizard, which collects some basic attributes for the tab. It just won't let you select a tab set.

If you want a new parent tab in a tab set other than the default tab set, follow the Manage Parent Tabs link in the Parent Tab Tasks panel on the main Tab page. This will take you to the Parent Tab Report page, which contains another Tasks panel. Use the Create New Parent Tab link. This also starts the Create Parent Tab Wizard, but this time you can select the tab set or specify a name to create a new parent tab set. The remainder of the wizard is as before.

Tab Summary

An application can have one or more parent tab sets. Parent tab sets have one or more parent tabs that are associated with the set. An application can have one or more standard tab sets. Standard tab sets are associated with a parent tab. Standard tab sets also have one or more standard tabs that are associated with the set.

Parent tabs have a target that can be any URL, but it's usually a specific page within an application. Parent tab targets can also contain attributes found in standard links, like clearing cache or setting the value of items. Standard tabs also have a target that is a page within the application, but unlike parent tabs, standard tabs do not have the ability to set the other properties of a link, like clearing cache or setting item values. Other pages can be associated with a standard tab, but they are not the target. The tab will only show as the current tab when the page is current. Pretty simple, isn't it?

Breadcrumb Menus

Hansel and Gretel left a trail of breadcrumbs as they walked through the forest so they could retrace their steps—which would have been a good idea if it weren't for all the little critters around that like to eat bread. Breadcrumb menus get their name from Hansel and Gretel's half-baked idea, but ours are not likely to be eaten. Applications that are complex and hierarchical in nature are well suited for a breadcrumb menu. A breadcrumb menu allows users to navigate directly back to a higher-level page with a single click, skipping any pages in between.

Applications can have one or more breadcrumb menus, depending on how complex they are. If an application has a home page and everything branches off from there and doesn't go more than five or six levels deep, a single menu might suffice. However, if the application has hundreds of pages and goes many levels deep, you might want to design several menus. The Contact Management application we have been building is by no means a complex application, but it could benefit from a breadcrumb menu. Not that this will be adding navigation that isn't already available in one form or another—just that it will give the user another option.

To create or edit a breadcrumb menu, navigate the Breadcrumbs main page through the application's shared components (refer to Figure 11-2). You can also get there by clicking on the Breadcrumb region title on any Page Definition page, although this will navigate you to the Breadcrumb Entries page. From there, simply click on the Breadcrumbs link in the breadcrumb menu at the top of the page.

On the Breadcrumbs main page, create a menu by clicking on the Create button, providing a name for the menu, and then clicking on the Create button. You will end up at the Breadcrumb Entries page, shown next. We now have a menu, but the menu has no entries. You will have to create an entry for every page on which you want the breadcrumb menu to be displayed.

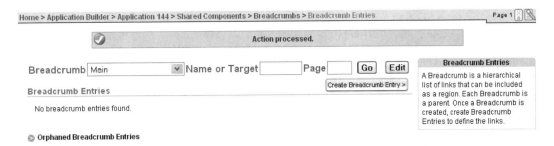

Breadcrumb Menu Creation

When you create a breadcrumb menu you are actually creating two things, the menu itself created above (which is a container for the menu items) and each individual menu entry.

Create/Edit Breadcrumb Entry Page

The generic hierarchical structure of our menu will be Home > Report Page > Edit Page. We will repeat this for the contacts, calls, and lookups. The easiest way to create a breadcrumb menu is from the top down. Clicking on the Create Breadcrumb Entry button takes you to the Create/Edit Breadcrumb Entry page, shown in Figure 11-10. This page, like many other edit pages, contains some common sections. Those that you should already be familiar with are Target, Conditional Display, Authorization, and Configuration.

FIGURE 11-10   *Create/Edit Breadcrumb Entry page (partial)*

Breadcrumb Section The Breadcrumb field is where you select which breadcrumb menu this entry will belong to; if only one exists, it will default to that menu. The Page field is where you specify the page number of the page to which this breadcrumb entry will belong. If you navigate to the breadcrumb-creation page from a Page Definition page, that page's number will be a quick fill link below the Page field. This feature makes it very easy to jump in and create the breadcrumb entries as you create pages or as you edit existing pages.

Entry Section The Entry section contains the field to specify display elements of the entry. The Sequence field help states that this field determines the order of evaluation; however, it apparently has no effect because it is not possible to create two items for the same page. Also, it does not influence the order in which the entries are displayed in the list of breadcrumb entries. The Parent Entry field is where you specify the entry for the page that precedes this entry. For the base level of our Home entry, this will remain unselected. Both the Short Name field and the Long Name field values are available to the menu template as substitution variables. The need to supply the long name will depend on the template you use, but the short name is required.

Target Section The Target section is just like previously covered Target sections. Almost always the target will be the same page in the application for which the entry is being created. The exception to this would be a case where you want to show this page in the trail, but if it is selected, you want to navigate the user back even further in the chain. This might be used in the case of a wizard.

Once you complete creating breadcrumb elements for all the pages in your application, the report on the Breadcrumb Entries page should look similar to that shown next. Note that each name in the report is an active link to that entry's edit page and that each page number is an active link to that page's Page Definition page. Also, Orphaned Breadcrumb Entries can be expanded to show any orphaned breadcrumbs.

Breadcrumb Entries

Name	Sequence	Page
Home	10	1
Calls	20	10
Call Edit	10	6
Contacts	10	2
Contact Edit	10	5
Lookups	1	4
Lookup Edit	10	7
row(s) 1 - 7 of 7		

▼ **Orphaned Breadcrumb Entries**

No orphaned breadcrumb entries found.

Displaying Breadcrumb Menus

Once the navigation bar is defined, it is automatically displayed on every page as long as the template for the page includes the proper substitution variable. Once tabs are defined and associated with pages, they are also automatically displayed as long as the template for the page included tabs. However, this is not the case with breadcrumb menus. Even though every breadcrumb menu entry is associated with a page, that page must contain a breadcrumb region.

Although it is possible to create a region and then copy that region from one page to another, that still seems like a lot of work if you have several hundred pages in your application. Wouldn't it be great if HTML DB provided you with a place where you could put something on every page? You might be saying to yourself, "Well, it does. It's called a page template." However, in this case that does not work because the element you want to duplicate on every page has to be a region, which will be placed in one of the page template's region areas. Once again, HTML DB comes through; it provides something called "page zero."

Before we address page zero, just a few quick notes on templates used with breadcrumb menus and regions. Most of the themes supplied by HTML DB use a standard approach when it comes to menus. Most of the page regions define Region Position 1 in the best place to display a breadcrumb menu. The themes will also have a region template for a breadcrumb menu. Also, the themes come with two menu templates. The first is a breadcrumb template that displays the menu entries in a line (for example, Home > Contacts > Contact Edit). The other menu template places the entries in a standard HTML unordered list.

Page Zero

Page zero is a special page where you can define elements that will appear on every page. To create page zero, follow these steps:

1. Click on the Create button on the Application Builder main page.
2. Select Blank Page and click on the Next button.
3. Fill in the value 0 for the Page field and click on the Next button.
4. Give the page a name and click on the Next button.
5. Select to use no templates and click on the Next button.
6. Click on the Finish button.

From the confirmation page, select to edit page zero. Page zero's Page Definition page only contains the Page Rendering column with its normal sections. The Regions, Buttons, and Items sections are the only sections to which you can add elements. The Computations and Processing sections are disabled. Any computations and processes that you need on every page should be handled as application-level computations and processes.

Creating a Breadcrumb Region A breadcrumb region is a typical use for page zero. The HTML DB sample application also uses page zero to place a list region on three different pages. Because regions, like almost every other element, have a Conditional Display section, you can define a region on page zero but specify a condition so that it will only display on certain pages. This approach can be taken with anything created on page zero.

To create the breadcrumb region on page zero, follow these steps from page zero's Page Definition page:

1. Click on the Create icon in the Regions section.
2. Select the radio button for the Breadcrumb region type. Click on the Next button to start the Create Breadcrumb Region Wizard.

3. The next step's default values will probably be okay. If you are using an HTML DB-supplied theme, there should be a Breadcrumb Region template. Also, you want to select Page Template Region Position 1 for the Display Point field. Click on the Next button.

4. If you only have one breadcrumb menu defined, it will be the default in the Breadcrumb field. If you have more than one breadcrumb menu, the page zero option will only work for one, and you will have to conditionally display it where appropriate.

5. Select the appropriate Breadcrumb template in the Breadcrumb Template field and click on the Next button.

6. If you are creating this region on a normal page that already has a breadcrumb menu element defined for it, the next step of the wizard would display the short name specified for the breadcrumb entry and the parent specified. For page zero, the Breadcrumb Entry Label field will default to the name of page zero and the Parent Entry field will default to "-No Parent-". Accept these defaults and click on the Next button.

7. Click on the Finish button on the final confirmation step.

After creating the breadcrumb region on page zero and defining breadcrumb entries for each of the pages, we now have a fully functioning breadcrumb menu on each of our pages.

Lists

A list is a group of links. The HTML DB development environment frequently uses lists to display side panels of tasks, as shown in Figure 11-11. Lists can also be used to show progress as you move through a wizard because a list element can be defined to be either current or noncurrent for specific pages. Version 2.0 adds another advance feature to lists—the ability to have dynamically displayed sub-lists, such as the menus displayed off of the main icons on the main Application Builder page, also shown in Figure 11-11.

The look and feel of lists are controlled by a list template. Although a list is placed in a region that has a template to control the title and border for the list, the list template controls the attributes of the individual list entries. This allows you to specify the look of the current and noncurrent elements. Additionally, version 2.0 list templates include sections for defining the dynamic actions of the sub-lists, as shown in Figure 11-11. Not all the themes that come with HTML DB include list templates with the sub-list feature implemented. Look at Theme 8 (Gray and Orange) for examples of these templates.

Lists are similar to menus in that a region must be defined on a page to hold a list. Most of the HTML DB themes have a large variety of predefined list templates. As with the other navigation types, you navigate to the Lists main page through the application's shared components, shown earlier in Figure 11-2. You can also get there by clicking on the Lists region title on any Page Definition page. Like breadcrumb menus, lists have a main piece to which you add list entries.

List Creation

At this point, the Home page of our application is empty, with the exception of the headers, footers, tabs, and breadcrumb menu. We could add a couple lists—one for reports and one for edit pages. Each list could contain a corresponding link for the Calls, Contacts, and Lookup pages.

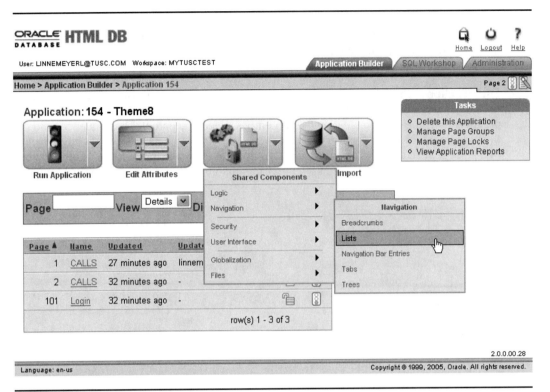

FIGURE 11-11   *List as a dynamic menu*

Navigate to the Lists main page. This page will show any existing lists or, if none exist, just the Create button. The following steps are used to create a list:

1. Click on the Create button.
2. Provide a name for the list, such as **Reports**.
3. For the list template, select Vertical Unordered List with Bullets from the list that contains various different types, including vertical, horizontal, dynamic lists with sub-lists, trees, and wizard progress templates.
4. Leave the Build Option field as no build option.
5. Click on the Create button.

You will end up on the Lists Entries page for the list you just created. Now we must add list entries for each of the pages. Clicking on the Create List Entry button takes you to the Create/Edit List Entry page.

Create/Edit List Entry Page

The Create/Edit List Entry page is no different from other edit pages we have looked at so far, in that it has some common sections. The sections you will recognize are the Target, Conditional Display, Authorization, and Configuration sections.

Entry Section The Entry section, shown next, allows you to enter display information about the list entry. The Parent List Entry field is used when defining a list with sub-lists. First, create the parent entries; then, when creating the sub-entries, select the parent. The Sequence field controls the order in which the list entries are displayed. If the list is to have images, specify which image in the Image field and any applicable HTML <img> attributes in the Attributes field. You must supply a label for the entry in the List Entry Label field. How this label is used is dependent on the template.

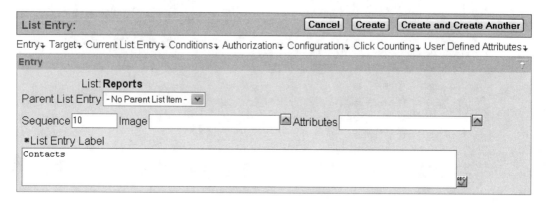

Target Section The Target section is just like the other Target sections in that it is used to specify the target of the link, which can either be a page in the application or any valid URL. If you are creating a list with sub-lists, the parent elements need not have a target. In order to do this, select URL as the Target Type and then leave the URL Target field blank.

Current List Entry Section The Current List Entry section allows you to specify a condition that will determine whether this list entry displays as current or noncurrent. If the condition is true, the current template will be used; otherwise, the noncurrent template will be used. The List Entry Current for Pages Type field specifies the type of condition. The options are Always, Never, Colon Delimited Page List, Exists SQL Query, Not Exists SQL Query, and a PL/SQL Expression.

The Always and Never types are definitive true/false Booleans and do not require an entry in the List Entry Current for Condition field. For the Colon Delimited Page List option, you can enter either a colon-delimited list of page numbers or a comma-delimited list. You may not use page aliases. If the current page is in the list, the condition is true. For the SQL query options, enter a valid query in the List Entry Current for Condition field. The condition is true for the Exists type and false for the Not Exists type if the query returns one or more rows, and it's false for Exists and true for Not Exists if no data is found with the query. For the PL/SQL expression type, simply enter a PL/SQL expression that will evaluate to true or false. You are permitted to reference application and page items in your PL/SQL expression or queries.

Click Counting Section   If the target for this list entry is an external URL, HTML DB provides a utility to count the number of times this link is clicked on. The results of the counts can be seen through the administrative logs, as discussed in Chapter 17. The Count Clicks field specifies whether or not to count clicks. The Click Count Category field's value is used to classify the counts into categories that are seen in the logs. This whole functionality is implemented through the HTMLDB_UTIL.COUNT_CLICK function, which is well documented in the HTML DB online help.

User Defined Attributes Section   The User Defined Attributes section contains ten fields that allow you to pass "attributes" to the list template. Fields 1–10 have corresponding substitution variables, #A01# through #A10#, that make the values entered into these fields available in the templates.

　　If you have not already, finish creating two lists—one for Reports and one for Edits—each containing a link entry for the Calls, Contacts, and Lookup report or edit pages, respectively. The List Entry pages should look similar to Figure 11-12. Notice on the List Entries page the Grid Edit button. This button allows you to edit certain attributes of all the entries in the current list. This is a good place to rearrange the sequences or adjust the link text.

Displaying Lists

Like breadcrumb menus, lists will not be displayed on a page until a list region is placed on the page to contain the list. As mentioned in the section on page zero, you could use page zero to create a region to display a list on every page. Or, if conditions are specified for the region, it could be used to display on only a list of pages. In our case, we only want them displayed on our home page, so we will create regions on our home page.

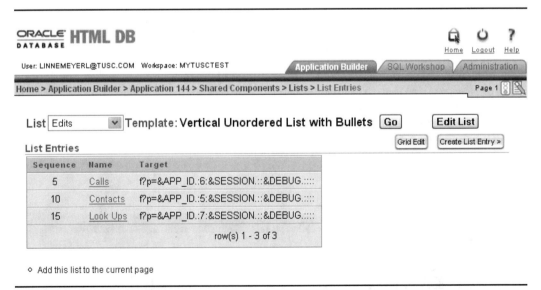

FIGURE 11-12　*List Entries page*

You have two methods for adding a List type region to your page. Starting from the Page Definition page for the page to which you wish to add the region, click on the Add icon in the region's section and then select List as the type of region you wish to create. The other option is available when you are on the List Entries page and the last page edited was your target page, as indicated by the page number just below the Administration tab. In Figure 11-12, you can see that Page 1 was the last page, which happens to be the page we want to add the region to. Also, notice in Figure 11-12 below the List Entries report that there is an Add This List to the Current Page link. This link will jump into the Region Creation Wizard, having already defined the type as a List region. Either method will get you to the third step in the wizard, shown here.

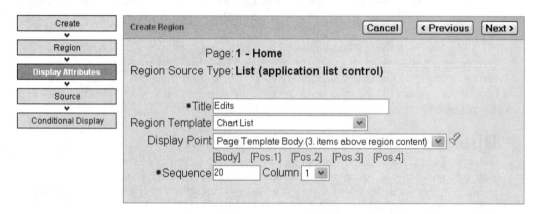

Remember that the attributes in the creation wizards are the same attributes we have already looked at in the Region Edit page. Therefore, if you have any questions, refer back to Chapter 8. Specify the region titles Edits and Reports, respectively, for each one you create. Select a template in the Region Template field. The Red theme we are using has the Report List and Chart List template types. Use Report List for the region to contain the Report lists and use Chart List for the region to contain the Edits list. For both regions you will create, use the same display point and the same sequence. However, place Reports in column 1 and Edits in column 2. Click on the Next button.

The next step in the wizard allows you to select the list that will be displayed in this region. If you started the wizard from the List Entries page, shown in Figure 11-12, this field will already be selected. If you wanted to conditionally display the region, you would click on the Next button. However, we clicked on the Create List Region button. After you create both regions, your home page should look similar to the one shown here.

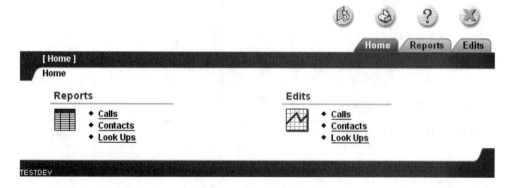

Trees

HTML DB provides the ability to create a graphical representation of hierarchical data through a navigational structure known as a tree. Everyone who has used Windows is familiar with the functionality of a tree, because that is how the Windows Explorer is implemented. Oracle had the ability to use trees in Oracle Forms as well. Unfortunately, the functionality of trees in HTML DB is not nearly as robust as it is in Oracle Forms.

The source of trees in HTML DB is limited to tables where you are able to use a self-joining connect by query. The example of this that most developers are familiar with is the EMP table, where you select the hierarchical structure of managers and employees. This is possible because managers are also employees, and each employee has a manager number that refers back to the employee number of the manager.

Trees are classified as navigational items because you can make the element that is displayed on the tree nodes an active link. For instance, the tree shown in Figure 11-13 displays the hierarchical structure of managers and employees and has the employee name displayed on each branch. Each employee name is an active link to an edit form for the employee.

Trees are a unique navigation type. Some of the navigational items show up on pages, once defined; others require the creation of a region in which to display the navigational item. When a tree is created, not only is the tree object created, but a page with several regions, buttons, items, and branches. The process that populates the tree is handled internally with the tree item and is not seen as a process on the page. Another unique feature of trees is that their template is actually part of the tree item.

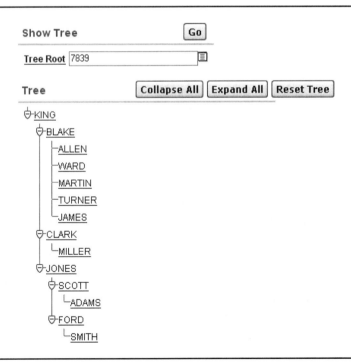

FIGURE 11-13 *Manager/Employee tree*

Tree Creation

Like the rest of the navigation item types, you navigate to the Tree main page through the application's shared components (refer to Figure 11-2). The Trees main page will display any existing trees and provide a Create button to start the Create Tree Wizard.

The first steps of the wizard are similar to other wizards we have worked with. The first step collects page and region attributes—as you create a tree for the first time, you can just accept the default values. The next step is for the page's tabs. Again, you have seen this before. The first tree-related step allows you to specify a name for the tree and two other important attributes.

The first attribute is the Default Expanded Levels field, which contains a numeric value. The number is the number of levels that will be expanded when the tree is first rendered. As an example, the tree in Figure 11-13 was set to expand to five levels. This is an acceptable approach if your entire hierarchical structure is not that large. If you are dealing with a very large hierarchical structure, like all the folders and files on your hard drive, you probably only want to expand the tree to one level.

The next attribute allows you to specify the source for the start of the tree. The three options are Static Value, SQL Query, and LOV. The start of the tree is the tree's root node, the uppermost parent that will be displayed. With a static value, which you provide at development, the tree will always start with the same value. When the start of the tree is based on a SQL query, the tree may vary each time the page is visited, depending on whether the query returns a different value. As with all queries, the WHERE clause can reference an application or page item. Basing the tree start on a new item with a pop-up list of values is the only way you will be able to let the user directly select a tree base and populate the tree. Figure 11-13 shows an example of this. Notice the Go button above the select list. The user can select a different tree start and then redisplay the tree with the Go button.

The next step allows you to select one of three possible templates. Each of the templates contains the standard plus and minus icons next to any tree node that has child nodes. One template adds a folder icon next to each node, one has an information icon next to each node, and the standard template adds nothing next to the node.

Based on the source type you selected for the start of the tree, the next step allows you to specify that source. The query you specify for an item with an LOV must have two columns—one will be the value returned, and the other will be the item the user selects. As you can see in Figure 11-13, the employee number is returned, but the pop-up list displayed contains the employee name. It is based on a query like the following:

```
select ename, empno from emp order by ename
```

The next step allows you to specify whether the Collapse All, Expand All, and Reset Tree buttons will be displayed as they are in Figure 11-13. In the next two steps, you specify the table/view owner and name. After that, you must select an ID, parent ID, and leaf node text from the lists of values that contain the columns of the table or view you just specified, as seen next. The only real flexibility you have that can increase the usefulness of trees is your ability to create views. If the tree is going to be used for navigation, you can only specify that it be used to navigate to an existing application item. The value of the ID field will be placed in an exiting application item, just like a link from an item in a report. That item can be used to populate an edit form.

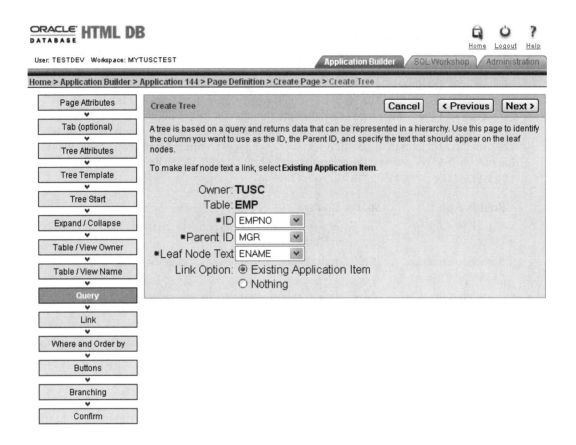

The next step will be skipped if you did not choose to implement a link. The step allows you to select the page you will link to and the item that will be populated with the value of the ID field. The next step allows you to specify a WHERE clause and an ORDER BY clause that will be used on the query that populates the tree. You can view the current query at the bottom of the screen.

The final steps before the confirmation allow you to specify the text used in the Go button, shown in Figure 11-13, and the page to branch to after processing. This will normally be the page you are creating. After you confirm the information entered and click on the Finish button, the HTML DB engine will create the page and all related elements.

The Page Definition page for the page containing the tree will have a region of type Tree. If you click on the Tree region type, not the name, you will be taken to the Edit Tree page. You can also get there through the shared components, as described earlier, and then click on the name of the tree you wish to edit.

The Edit Tree page contains the query used when rendering the tree and all the template elements used when rendering the tree. There is very little you can do to edit a tree once it is created. You are better off just creating a new tree. If you really wanted to, you could make changes to the template to customize the display of the tree, but this is not recommended.

Buttons and Branches

In Chapter 10, we looked at buttons and branches as they were used in the edit forms. We looked in depth at their corresponding edit pages. The various wizards in HTML DB often create branches that are used conditionally based on the button that was clicked to submit the page. Most of those branches created by the wizards are a branch type of Branch to Page or URL.

Recall that the branch type is an attribute that cannot be changed; it can only be set when the branch is created. You can create and use a number of other types of branches. To create a branch, click on the Add icon in the Branch section of the Page Definition page where you want to create the branch. You will select a branch point and a branch type; then, depending on the type selected, you will enter a source (see the following table).

Branch Type	Source Content
Branch to Page or URL	The Source section for this branch will be the typical Target section shown in Figure 11-4.
Branch to Function Returning a Page	PL/SQL function body that returns a page or a page alias.
Branch to Function Returning a URL	PL/SQL function body that returns any valid URL. Commonly used to dynamically construct an f?p syntax URL.
Branch to PL/SQL Procedure	The name of a stored PL/SQL procedure. This procedure will ultimately render a page. This is typically accomplished with the PL/SQL Web Toolkit (see Appendix B).
Branch to a Page	A page number.
Branch to a Page Accept Processing (Not Common)	A page number and a value for the request. This will branch to the Processing section of the page specified. A typical place this branch type would be used is in a wizard, where after several steps the user can either finish or move to the next step. The Finish button will typically submit to the Processing section of the confirmation page.
Branch to Page Identified by Item (Use Item Name)	The name of an item (for example, P12_PAGE), whose value will be either a number or an alias that identifies the page.
Branch to URL Identified by Item (Use Item Name)	The name of an item (for example, P12_PAGE), whose value will be a valid URL.

As you develop your applications, you may want to change some of the branches created by the wizards. The logic of your application may require a more dynamic branching type to be used. Because the branch type cannot be changed, you may end up creating another branch to replace one originally created through a wizard.

The purpose of the HTML DB development environment is to allow the developer to create full-featured applications without having to manually do all the repetitious coding. One thing that makes an application more user friendly is the ability for the user to move quickly and efficiently throughout the application. However, this often means a lot of repetitious coding. In this chapter, we have covered all the different types of navigation available in HTML DB that can be easily created within your applications, while HTML DB takes care of all the code behind the scenes.

CHAPTER
12

Building Other
Components

n previous chapters, we looked at reports and forms, which are the most frequently used elements in HTML DB. In this chapter, we will look at some of the less frequently used elements, such as calendars, charts, wizards, shortcuts and lists of values (LOVs).

Lists of Values

Of the items we will cover in this chapter, lists of values are probably the most frequently used. A list of values is just what its name implies. The values can be static values or they can be dynamically created from a query. A list of values normally includes a displayed set of values, such as contact names, and another set of values used behind the scenes, such as contact IDs.

In Chapter 9, when working with reports and column attributes, we looked at the List of Values section on the Column Attributes page. Figure 9-16 showed an example of entering a query for a list of values to be used as part of the source for a column. You will also see this List of Values section on the Edit Page Item page. In these sections, you can either enter the attributes of an LOV or select from a named LOV. If you use a named LOV, it only has to be maintained in one place, but can be used in many. Let's look at how to create a named LOV.

Creating Lists of Values

Named lists of values are application shared components and can be accessed through the User Interface section of Application Shared Components from an application's main builder page or from the Lists of Values section header in the Shared Components column of any Page Definition page.

The Lists of Values page will contain a listing of all existing LOVs and a Create button. You can edit any existing LOV by clicking on it, or you may create a new one by clicking on the Create button.

The Create button starts a short wizard whose first step allows you to choose to create an LOV as a copy of an existing LOV or to create one from scratch. When you create an LOV as a copy, you can copy LOVs from any application in the workspace. Not only can you copy an LOV, but you can subscribe to the LOV so that when any changes are made to the master LOV, they are pushed down to any subscribing LOVs.

On our Calls Edit page, we display the contact ID. IDs generally are meaningless to users. Therefore, let's create an LOV to use with the field so the users will see the contact's name rather than the ID. Start the LOV creation wizard by clicking on the Add icon in the Lists of Values section in the Shared Components column on the Page Definition page for Calls Edit. Then select Create From Scratch.

In the next step of the wizard, you can provide a name and specify whether the LOV is to be static or dynamic. Use static LOVs when you have a list of values that will not change and the data is not available as a query from the database. In the Name field, provide a meaningful name such as Contact Names. We will want the list type to be dynamic because users can always add more contacts. Click on the Next button.

If we had selected the type to be static, the final step of the wizard would provide a list with two columns—one for the display value and one for the return value. The creation wizard only allows you to enter up to 15 values. If you have the need to create a static LOV with more than 15 values, create the first 15 values in the creation wizard and then edit the LOV to add the remaining values. When you're using LOVs with list type items, the display value is shown to the user whereas the return value is used when populating the field and is returned as the actual value of the field for processing. If the display value is the same as the return value, you only need to fill in the display value column.

Because we selected the list type to be dynamic, the final step in the wizard provides a field to enter the query to be used when populating the LOV, as shown here. Even though this is a generic definition of an LOV that can be used in different places, it can still reference application items or page items. For instance, an application item might be populated at the start of the application with the user's department, and you could limit the LOV by including the following in the WHERE clause:

```
deptno = :user_deptno
```

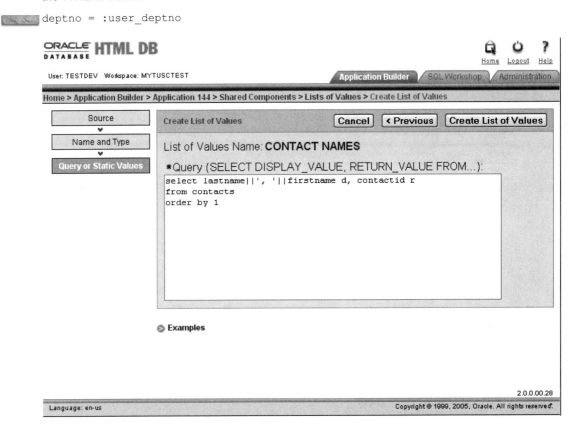

The first column selected in the query is used for the display value, whereas the second column in the query is used as the return value. You can select the column twice to use the same value for both, but make sure to include column aliases. For our LOV, enter the following query:

```
select lastname||', '||firstname d, contactid r
from contacts
order by 1
```

The source for the query can also be a function body that returns a query, so the dynamic query could be dynamically constructed. The function body would be structured as follows:

```
if :user_dept = 'Accounting' then
    return 'select ename, empno
            from emp order by 1';
else
    return 'select ename, empno
            from emp
          where deptno = :user_deptno
          order by 1';
end if;
```

When you click on the Create List of Values button, the query will be validated. If it is valid, you will be returned to the Lists of Value page, shown next, where you will see the new LOV with any others.

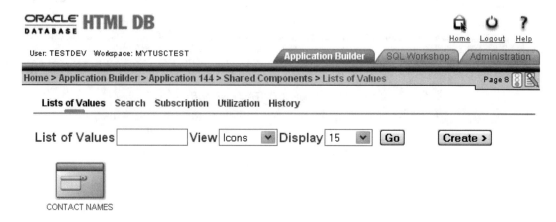

From the Lists of Values page, you can access several other pages that provide information about your LOVs. The Search page allows you to search the queries of all existing LOVs for a specified value. The Subscription page allows you to see details about your application's LOVs that are subscribed to other LOVS. The Utilization page displays a report that summarizes how many items, report columns, and page references each LOV has. Finally, the History page reports when each LOV was last updated and the username of the developer who made the change.

Using Lists of Values

Any element in your application that has a List of Values section in its edit page will now have access to the LOV we just created. The first field in a List of Values section is the Named LOV field, which is itself a list of values of all LOVs in the current application.

In Chapter 8, we created a page to report on Calls and a page to edit Calls. The Calls table only contains the contact ID and not the contact name, so the contact ID is all that is displayed on both the report and edit page. We can use the LOV that we just created in the report and on the edit page.

Navigate to the Page Definition page for the Calls report. In the Regions section, click on Query, which is the report type. This will take you to the Reports Attribute page, where you need to click on the Edit icon for the ContactID column. Make sure the Column Heading field in the Column Definition section contains Contact and not ContactID. In the Tabular Form Element section, change the Display As field to "Display as Text (based on LOV, does not save state)." This type uses the value in the report column ContactID to match a return value in the LOV and display its corresponding display value. Finally, select the LOV we just created from the list of values for the Named LOV field in the List of Values section. Click on the Apply Changes button and run the page. The only other thing you might need to do is update the column

Navigate to the Page Definition page for the Call edit page. Click on the ContactID item to navigate to the Edit Page Item page. Change the Display As field to Select List. Make sure the Label field in the Label section contains Contact and not ContactID. Finally, select the LOV we just created from the list of values for the Named LOV field in the List of Values section. Click on the Apply Changes button and run the page. Your edit page should now look similar to the one shown here.

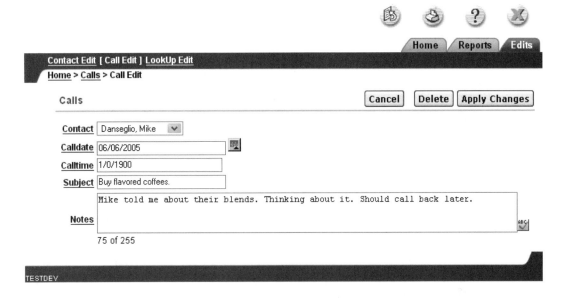

NOTE
If you have two fields on a page that are both LOVs and the second LOV needs to be limited by the selection made in the first (that is, it references the value of the first in its WHERE clause), you must use a display as type of Select List with Submit.

Shortcuts

Shortcuts are a mechanism HTML DB provides developers to help eliminate repetitive code. Various types of shortcuts can be created and then referenced numerous times throughout the application. The syntax for referencing a shortcut is simply the uppercase name of the shortcut in quotes (for example, "EXAMPLE_SHORTCUT"). Although shortcuts can be used to eliminate duplication of code, they can also be used to centralize help text, static display messages, and static error messages. Another great advantage of shortcuts is that copies of shortcuts in other applications can subscribe to a master shortcut, so when changes are made to the master they can easily be pushed out to all copies.

Shortcuts such as LOVs are found in the User Interface section of an application's shared components. The Shortcuts page, shown next, lists any existing shortcuts and provides a Create button to create new shortcuts. From here, you can also access a report about shortcuts in the current application that subscribe to other shortcuts as well as a report about the last time a shortcut was changed.

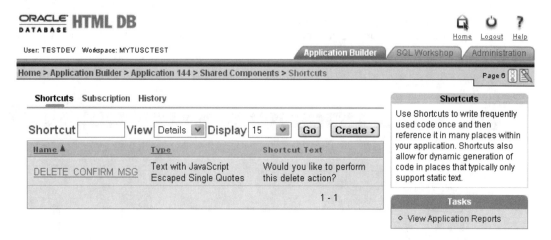

Creating Shortcuts

Like almost everything else in HTML DB, a wizard is provided for creating shortcuts. Start the wizard with the Create button on the Shortcuts page. The wizard has only a couple steps. The first step allows you to choose whether to create a shortcut from scratch or as a copy of an existing shortcut. Remember, shortcuts can be copied from other applications within the workspace.

If you choose to copy shortcuts, you will first select the application from which you wish to copy. In the final step, you select which shortcuts you wish to copy from a list of all shortcuts from the selected application. It is possible to copy all shortcuts at the same time; this makes it convenient if you have a large number of shortcuts in a master application.

If you choose to create a shortcut from scratch, the last step in the wizard looks just like the Edit Shortcut page, shown in Figure 12-1, minus the Subscription section. The Name field must contain a unique name in all uppercase. It identifies the shortcut and is used to reference the shortcut throughout the application.

The shortcut in the example, DELETE_CONFIRM_MSG, is created by the Edit Form Wizard whenever a Delete button is involved. Recall the use of JavaScript in the URL target of the Delete button:

```
javascript:confirmDelete(htmldb_delete_message,'DELETE');
```

This JavaScript references the JavaScript variable htmldb_delete_message, which is declared in the HTML Header section of the edit page for the page that contains the Delete button. It looks like this:

```
<script language="JavaScript" type="text/javascript">
<!--
 htmldb_delete_message='"DELETE_CONFIRM_MSG"';
//-->
</script>
```

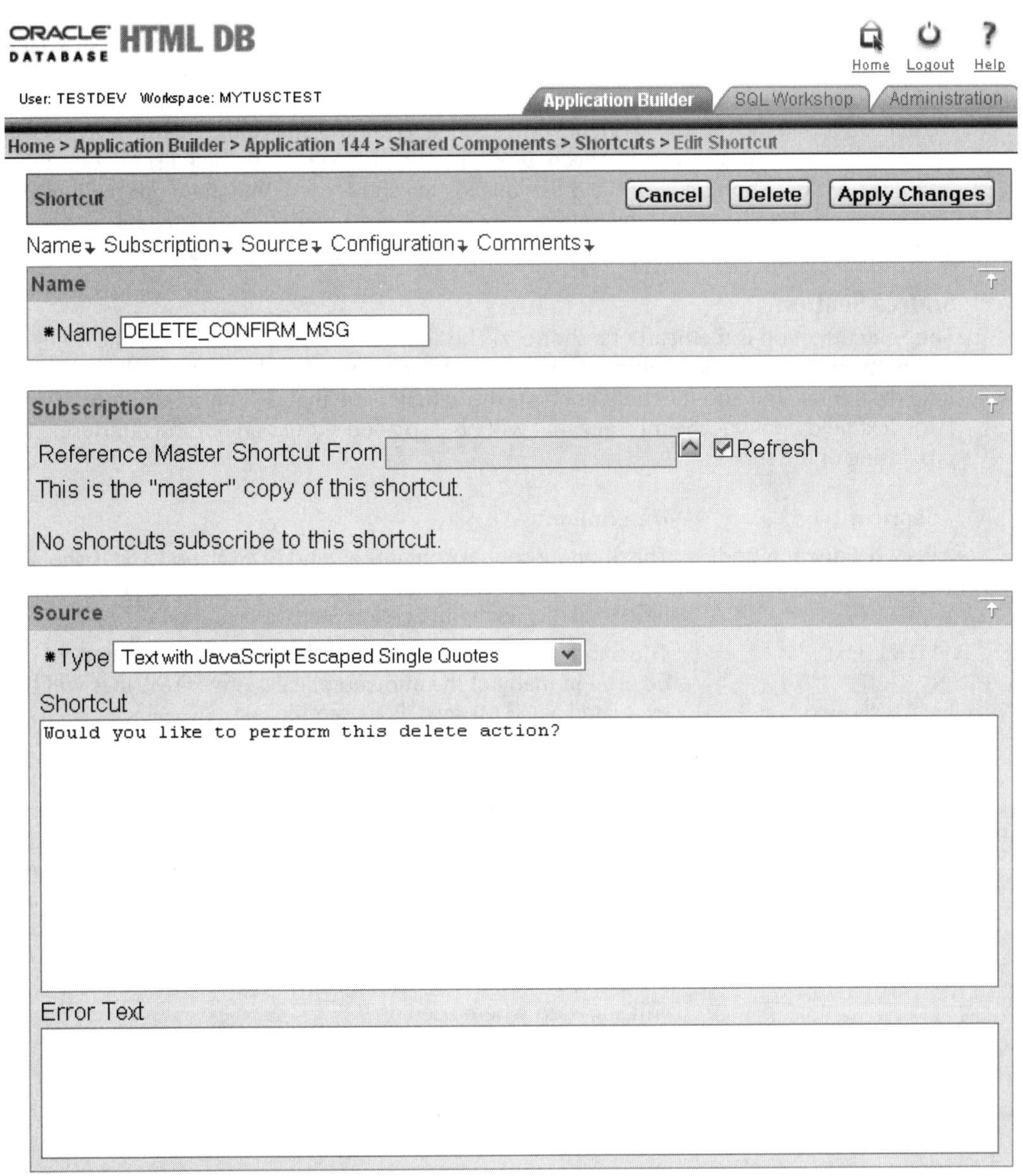

ORACLE HTML DB
DATABASE

Home   Logout   Help

User: TESTDEV Workspace: MYTUSCTEST   **Application Builder**   SQL Workshop   Administration

Home > Application Builder > Application 144 > Shared Components > Shortcuts > Edit Shortcut

| Shortcut | Cancel | Delete | Apply Changes |

Name↓ Subscription↓ Source↓ Configuration↓ Comments↓

Name

* Name DELETE_CONFIRM_MSG

Subscription

Reference Master Shortcut From [   ] ☑Refresh
This is the "master" copy of this shortcut.

No shortcuts subscribe to this shortcut.

Source

* Type Text with JavaScript Escaped Single Quotes

Shortcut

Would you like to perform this delete action?

Error Text

FIGURE 12-1 *Edit Shortcut page*

Here, the JavaScript variable is assigned a value using the shortcut. Notice the single quotes and the double quotes. The double quotes are part of the reference to the shortcut. Once the substitution is made, you will see the following line in the source of the rendered HTML page:

```
htmldb_delete_message='Would you like to perform this delete action?';
```

Subscription Section

The Subscription section, shown in Figure 12-1, is not present in the Create Shortcut Wizard. It appears when you subsequently edit a shortcut. It allows you to see any current subscriptions associated with this shortcut—both the other shortcuts subscribed to the current shortcut and the master shortcut if the current shortcut is subscribed to another shortcut. This section also allows you to reference a master shortcut even after it has been created. The pick list button next to the Reference Master Shortcut From field lists all existing shortcuts within the workspace. If you select a shortcut to subscribe to and the Refresh box is checked, when you apply changes the Source section and the Comments section of the master will be copied to the shortcut.

Source Section

The Source section is the heart of a shortcut. The shortcut Type field determines how the shortcut will be used. The following table lists the seven different types of shortcuts; each one behaves a little differently. The Shortcut field contains the actual value that will be substituted, whereas the Error Text field contains the message that will be displayed should an error occur during the processing of the shortcut.

Shortcut Type	Description
PL/SQL Function Body	The Shortcut source contains a valid PL/SQL body. This shortcut can be used in an item's default value. Set the item's Default Value Type field to Static Text with Session State Substitutions.
HTML Text	The Shortcut source contains valid HTML text. This shortcut can be used in many of the allowed places. Any HTML tags will be evaluated as HTML tags. For example, `<a href='http://google.com'> Google </a>` will show up, where used, as the active link <u>Google</u>.
HTML Text with Escaped Special Characters	The Shortcut source contains HTML text. This shortcut can be used in many of the allowed places. Any special characters contained in the text will be escaped, so the shortcut shows up, when used, exactly as typed in. For instance, the greater-than and less-than signs used in the following examples would be escaped to ">" and "<" respectively: `<a href='http://google.com'> Google </a>` will show up where used as `<a href='http://google.com'> Google </a>`

Shortcut Type	Description
Image	The Shortcut source contains the name of an image in the HTML DB default image directory or one of its subdirectories. The shortcut will be translated into an HTML <IMG> tag. It will prefix the image name with the image directory alias /i/, so if you enter **themes/ theme_1/report.gif**, the end result where the shortcut is used will be the following: `<IMG SRC="/i/themes/theme_1/report.gif">`
Text with JavaScript Escaped Single Quotes	The Shortcut source contains straight text. If the text contains single quotes, they will be escaped for use in JavaScript. For example, Quote 'THIS' will be escaped to Quote \'THIS\' so when it is used in a JavaScript message, it will show up as Quote 'THIS'.
Message	This shortcut type does not have a Shortcut source. Rather, the name of the shortcut must match the name of a translatable message. At run time, the shortcut expands to the text of the translatable message in the application's current language.
Message with JavaScript Escaped Single Quotes	Just like the Message type, except this type will be used within JavaScript so any single quotes in the translated message will be escaped with \'.

Configuration Section

The Build Option pick list in the Configuration Management section allows you to select a build option for the shortcut. Build options are typically used to include/exclude debug items or to separate normal functionality from premium functionality. Build options are discussed in further detail in Chapter 4.

Comments Section

Use the Comments section to note any peculiarities about this shortcut to any other developers. If you used strange logic or an abnormal procedure, it is a good idea to document that here. This makes maintaining an application much easier. After all, how many times have you returned months later after developing something only to ask yourself, What was I thinking?

Using Shortcuts

Using shortcuts is simple; in a place where they are allowed to be used, just reference the shortcut name in capital letters within double quotes (for example, "EXAMPLE_SHORTCUT"). You are allowed to use shortcuts in the following places:

- In regions of type HTML_WITH_SHORTCUTS (the Region source may contain shortcuts)
- Item labels
- Item default values
- Region templates
- Region headers and footers

- Item post element text
- HTML header of a page
- Help pages

Working with Graphs

Sometimes it is nice to give users a graphical representation of data. HTML DB provides you with the ability to create a number of different graphs. You can produce two types of graphs—plain HTML graphs, which are bar graphs created with images of different colors, and Scalable Vector Graphics (SVG) graphs. Scalable Vector Graphics is an XML-based language for creating graphics for web browsers. SVG graphs have a nicer look than the HTML graphs, but they require a plug-in for the browser.

The graphs available in HTML DB can be broken down into two categories—those that are created with only a single series of points, and those that can handle multiple series of points. An example of a single series would be total sales for the year displayed by month. An example of multiple series would be monthly sales, monthly expenses, and monthly profit for the year displayed by month.

Four types of graphs are available: line, bar, pie, and dial. They are further classified by whether they represent the points in relation to each other or whether they are represented as a percentage. Finally, the bar charts are divided by their orientation—some have horizontal bars and others have vertical bars.

Another feature of some of the graphs is the ability to make a point on a graph an active link so that the user can drill into detail about the point (for instance, from a monthly sales figure, you might drill to a sales report for that month). The following table describes the different types of graphs available. All but the HTML bar chart require the SVG browser plug-in.

Graph Type	Description	Number of Series of Points	Active Link Available
Bar (HTML)	Vertical or horizontal bar chart. Bar lengths are in relation to each other.	One	The labels for the bars can be active links.
Bar, Horizontal	Horizontal bar where bar lengths are in relation to each other.	One	Each bar can be an active link.
Bar, Vertical	Vertical bar where bar lengths are in relation to each other.	One	Each bar can be an active link.
Cluster Bar, Horizontal	Horizontal bars based on one or more series. The bars are clustered by their label. Their lengths are in relation to each other (see note below).	One or more	Each bar can be an active link.
Cluster Bar, Vertical	Same as the Cluster Bar, Horizontal but the bars are oriented vertically	One or more	Each bar can be an active link.

Graph Type	Description	Number of Series of Points	Active Link Available
Stacked Bar, Horizontal	Horizontal bars based on one or more series. The bars are stacked by their label and their lengths are in relation to each other. (See the following note.)	One or more	Each stacked section of the bar can be an active link.
Stacked Bar, Vertical	Same as Stacked Bar, Horizontal but the bars are oriented vertically.	One or more	Each stacked section of the bar can be an active link.
Stacked Percentage Bar, Horizontal	Same as the Stacked Bar, Horizontal except the bars are not in relation to each other. Rather, they are in relation to 100 percent.	One or more	Each stacked section of the bar can be an active link.
Stacked Percentage Bar, Vertical	Same as Stacked Percentage Bar, Horizontal but the bars are oriented vertically.	One or more	Each stacked section of the bar can be an active link.
Line	Standard line graph. Points are represented in relation to each other.	One or more	No link available.
Pie chart	3-D pie chart. Each wedge represents that point's percentage of the total.	One	Each pie wedge can be an active link.
Dial – Sweep	Sometimes referred to as a "speedometer." Represents a single point, either as a percentage of 100 or in relation to a high and low value. The sweep has a solid wedge up to the "needles" position.	No series, only a single point	No link available.
Dial	Same as the Dial – Sweep, but the point is represented just as a "needle" on the speedometer rather than a wedge.	No series, only a single point	No link available.

NOTE

For graphs that have more than one series, the labels for the series are taken from the first series defined. Also, the HTML DB engine is not smart enough to match up labels. If the first series has Jan, Feb, Mar and the second has Feb, Mar, Apr, the graph will display two points each for Jan, Feb, and Mar.

Creating Graphs

Charts are a type of region, so to create a chart use one of the three methods of creating a new region:

- Create a new page and select a page type of Chart.

- On an existing page, click on the Create icon in the Regions section and select a region type of Chart.

- While running a page, click on the Create button on the Developer's Toolbar, select either New page or Region on This Page, and then select a type of Chart.

Any one of these paths will place you into the Create Chart Region Wizard, where you can choose one of the 13 chart types outlined in the preceding table. In the next step, you will supply some general attributes for the region, including Title, Region Template, Display Point, Sequence, and Column. The next step is the heart of the chart region—the query that provides the points. Most of the chart types use the same query structure. The columns selected must be link, label, and value—in that order. If you don't want a link or the chart type does not support links, you can select Null for the first column. The following is a sample query:

```
select 'f?p=&APP_ID:6:&SESSION.:::::P6_EMPID:'||empno link,
       ename label,
       sal value
  from emp
```

The link uses the f?p syntax URL, discussed in Chapter 11, to link to page 6 of the current application and set the page item P6_EMPID to the value of the current empno. Typically you are going to populate an item on the target page so you can either report on or edit details of the column queried. Each query provides one series of points. Most of the wizards only allow you to add one series at the time the chart is created. Once the chart is created, it may be edited and more series can be added.

The two dial chart types take a different query structure. Dial charts can either represent a value as a percentage of a maximum value, as shown below in the sweep dial, where the indicator will show on the dial somewhere between 0 and 100 and the percentage is calculated by dividing the value by the maximum value.

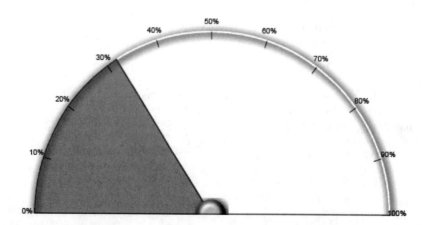

The second way a dial chart can be used is to show the report value in relation to a low value and a high value, as shown next. The query for a dial chart will return the columns value, maximum_value, low_value, and high_value—in that particular order. When the report is to be displayed as a percentage, low_value and high_value need not be queried. When a dial chart is first created, it defaults to a percent-type chart. If you wish to display it the other way, you must edit the chart after creation and change the Is Percentage field from Yes to No. The HTML DB help states that low_value and high_value set the lower and upper bounds of the dial display, which is not exactly true. They actually set where the lower and upper lines are displayed. The lower limit of the dial is always zero, and the upper bound is set by maximum_value.

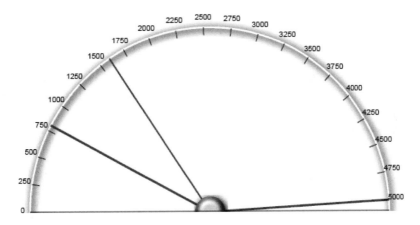

The following is an example of a query for a dial chart displayed as a percentage:

```
select sal val, max_value
  from emp a,(select max(sal)max_value from emp) b
 where a.empno = :p11_empno
```

This is an example of a query for a dial chart presenting a value between a high and low value. In this case, high_value will be the largest salary, so you can add the following bit to maximum_value so when the chart is drawn for the maximum salary, it does not peg out the dial:

```
select sal val, tmax+100 max_value, tmin low_value, tmax high_value
  from emp a,(select  min(sal) tmin, max(sal) tmax from emp) b
 where a.empno = :p11_empno
```

Due to space limitations, we cannot cover all the sections of the Chart Edit pages. The SVG and HTML charts have different edit pages. Each page allows you to control look-and-feel attributes for the charts, including colors and fonts. You are also able to provide additional series of points in the edit page. Note that Refresh is a section special to charts. It allows you to set the chart to refresh automatically at a set interval, so you can create a real-time dashboard that refreshes at a set interval.

Working with Calendars

Whenever you work with dates, users ask for calendars. HTML DB helps the developer in two ways. You have already seen how easy it is to add a date picker pop-up to any field that is a date data type. This is done by specifying Date Picker type when creating an item or editing a date item and changing the Display As type to Date Picker. HTML DB also provides a method to display a calendar and place items on the calendar based on dates queried from the database.

For our sample application, it would be nice to show a calendar that displays all our scheduled follow-up calls. I know, you are saying to yourself, What follow-up calls? We don't have a follow-up date. Well, you are correct, but we could add a field to the Contacts table to store a follow-up date. You can use the SQL Workshops Object Browser to add the new column.

Creating Calendars

As with everything else, calendars are created in HTML DB with a wizard. The wizard creates the necessary region, buttons, items, processes, and branches. Normally, you will create a calendar on a new page, but it is possible to create a calendar on an existing page. However, there can only be one calendar per page. Here are three ways to start the calendar-creation wizard:

- Use the Create Region icon in the Region section of a Page Definition page. Select Calendar for the region type.

- Use the Create page button, and select the New Page With Calendar option.

- Use the Create link on the Developer's Toolbar, select either the New Page With Calendar option or the Region On This Page option, and then select Calendar for the region type.

Once you get into the calendar wizard, you will proceed with either an Easy Calendar or a SQL Calendar. Both of these calendar types are based off of a query, but the Easy Calendar builds the query for you. The drawbacks with this are that the query has to be from a single table or view and the information displayed on the calendar can only be from a single column in that table.

For the Easy Calendar, after you supply a couple page attributes, the wizard allows you to select the table from which to build the calendar. Next, you select a date column from the selected table's date columns as well as a column to display on the calendar from the table's remaining columns. If all you need is a simple calendar, this path works fine.

From our Contacts table, for a calendar of next call dates, we want to display the contacts' last name, first name, and phone number. Therefore, we will want to use the SQL Calendar path in the calendar wizard. In the first step, you specify the normal page and region attributes. Then you may select two tabs for the page.

In the next step, you can specify the query from which the calendar will be constructed, as shown next. The columns do not need to be in a particular order like the chart queries. You may make the query as complex as needed. You will want to include a date column, a column or concatenation of columns to display in the calendar, and the individual fields you want to use in creating a link from the calendar.

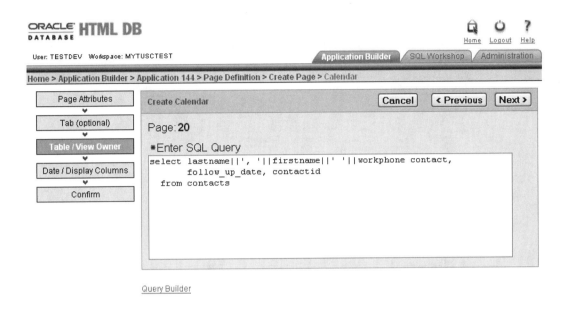

The next step allows you to choose the date column and the display column from LOVs derived from your previously entered query. After the confirmation page, the HTML DB engine will generate all the necessary elements to implement the calendar.

Editing Calendars

Once a calendar has been created, on the Page Definition page you will see a region, three buttons, one item, three processes, and a branch, all created by the wizard. To edit the calendar, you edit the region. The region name link will navigate you to the Edit Region page, shown in Figure 12-2, where you will find the query you entered (if you need to change it). The CAL region type link to the left of the region name will navigate you to the Calendar Attributes page. You can also navigate to the Calendar Attributes page from the Edit Region page with the Calendar Attributes tab.

Calendar Display Section

The Calendar Display section allows you to modify the choices you made for the template and which columns are used as the date column and the display column. Remember, what is available here is determined by the query you entered, which can be changed on the Region Definition page. This section also allows you to add further customization to the calendar.

The Display Type field can be changed from Column to Custom or No Display Value. If you select No Display Value, entries on the calendar will be indicated with ##. Not sure why you would want to do this (perhaps when using the small calendar template). The Column option just displays the value of the column in the Display Column field. Selecting Custom enables the Column Format field and gives you some room for creativity. In the Column Format field, you can

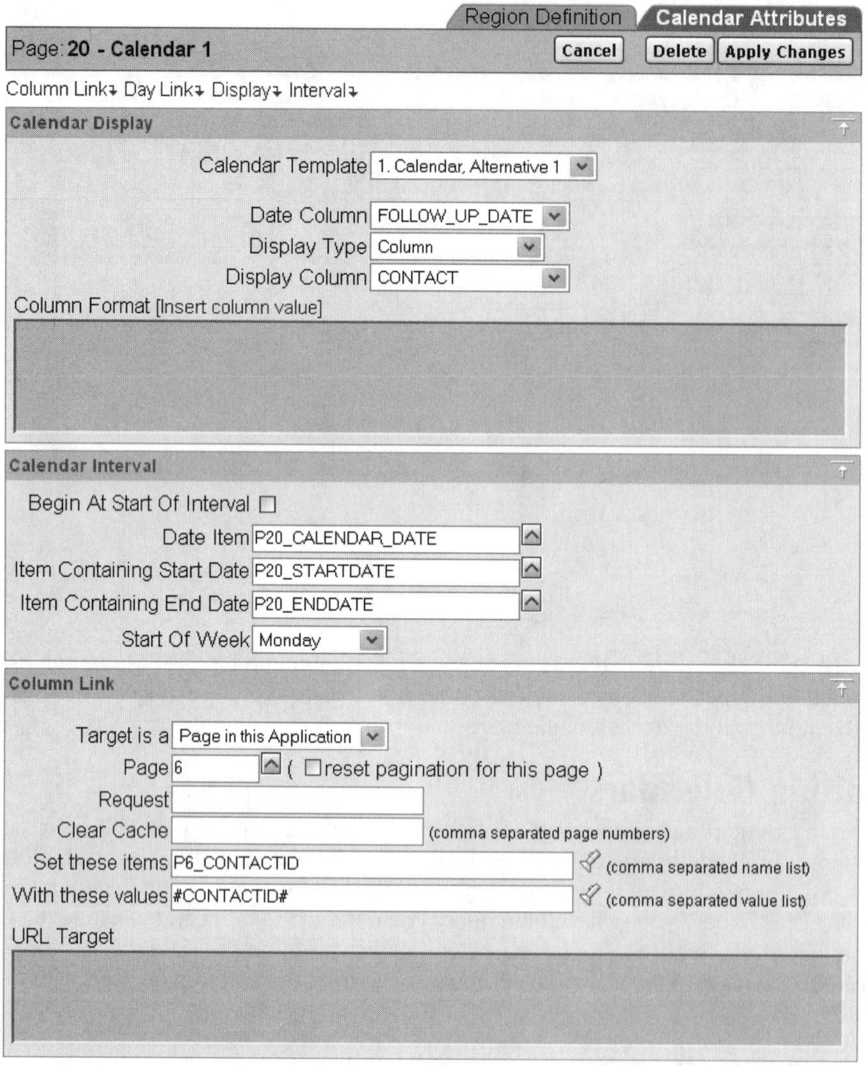

FIGURE 12-2   *Calendar Attributes page*

reference any column that you included in your query with the #COLUMN_NAME# syntax. In fact, if you click on the Insert Column Value link, a pop-up of the available columns will be displayed.

Now that you know this amazing fact, you are probably asking, What can I do with it? In your query, you might use a case statement to determine the priority of a follow-up call based on some logic. In that case statement, you could hard-code the name of several different workspace images based on the priority of the call, giving that field an alias of PRIORITY_IMAGE. Then you could enter something like the following in the Column Format field:

```
<img src=" #WORKSPACE_IMAGES##PRIORITY_IMAGE#">#CONTACT#
```

As long as you have workspace images that correspond to the names you put in PRIORITY_IMAGE, you will have an image followed by the name and number of the contact for each follow up call, as shown next.

Calendar Interval Section

The Calendar Interval section is supposed to give you control over how the calendar is displayed. The Date Item field contains the hidden item that was created by the wizard and defaulted to sysdate, which is the date the calendar will be based on. The Begin At Start of Interval check box, when checked, is supposed to start the calendar at the start of the month if the date in the Date Item is, say, the 15th of the month. However, it has no effect. Likewise, Item Containing Start Date and Item Containing End Date also have no effect. You are supposed to be able to enter a date in the format YYYYMMDD, and these settings will control the start and end date of the calendar. The Start of Week field controls which weekday will be on the left of the calendar. As you can see in Figure 12-2, this is set to Monday, which is the first day on the calendar above.

Column Link and Day Link Sections

The Column Link section and the Day Link section are like all the Target sections you have seen in the many previous edit pages. They allow you to specify the link for the display value and for each individual calendar date, respectively. The entries shown in Figure 12-2 branch to the Calls Edit page and set the contact ID. Because the call ID is not populated, the Call Edit page will be in "insert" mode so that the user can enter information for the follow-up call.

Wizards

Wizards are a series of pages used to collect information in small logical pieces, allowing the user to review and make changes prior to completing a process. You should be *very* familiar with wizards by this point, because the HTML DB environment uses them for almost everything.

Surprise, surprise. HTML DB also provides a wizard to build a wizard. You start the wizard by creating a new page and selecting a page type of Wizard. The wizard will walk you through a series of pages, where you can define a series of pages, including tabs and the number of items on each page. The wizard will handle navigation from step to step, but you will have to eventually create the process that uses all the data collected. It just so happens that the next chapter covers custom processes.

One other note about wizards: You know those nice step-by-step progress bars that HTML DB uses in its wizards? Those are implemented with lists, which are covered in Chapter 11. Remember that lists can be designated as current for a given page and that there are two display templates for the list items—one for a current item and one for a noncurrent item. Thus, the wizard progress bars are just lists without any links.

CHAPTER
13

Adding Computations, Processes, and Validations

alidations, computations, and processes are the mechanism by which the developer implements business logic. We have seen processes that have been created for us by the multitude of wizards within HTML DB—some to populate fields, some to process changes to a record, others to process multiple records.

Recall from Chapter 8 the method by which a page is rendered and then processed after it is submitted. Two main HTML DB engine processes are used for these two tasks: Show Page (rendering) and Accept Page (processing). Computations and processes can be used both in the rendering of a page and in the processing of a page. Validations are only used after a page has been submitted as a means to validate the data the user has submitted for processing.

In this chapter, we will look at validations, computations, and processes and how they greatly increase the functionality of an HTML DB application. We will explore the different types and when and where to use them. These three things allow you to bring together everything else we have covered to this point.

Validations

Validations are the method HTML DB provides to the developer to ensure the quality of data entered by a user prior to the data being submitted for processing. This is an important point to remember: if any part of your validation fails, no further processing will occur. This is not to say that the remainder of the validation will not occur, just that the processing will not occur.

Validations can be either item validations or page validations. Item validations are associated with a specific item on the page and check something specific about that item's value, such as if the item is null or if the item is greater than a certain value. Page validations are not associated with a specific item and may check a business rule that concerns several items on the page.

When a validation fails, the user is either returned to the page that was submitted or sent to an error page. One very good reason not to use the error page is that as soon as the validation process hits one failed validation, the user will navigate to the error page and see that single error message. Therefore, if they have several problems, they will make several trips to the error page. If you choose to display your error messages back on the submitted page, all the validations will occur and the user can see all the errors they must correct at the same time. The validation error messages, which are displayed back on the submitted page, can either be displayed in the submitted page's #NOTIFICATION_MESSAGE# section or presented next to the items with which they are associated, or both.

Creating Validations

Validations are created with a wizard, which is started by clicking on the Add icon in the Validations section on a page's Page Definition page. The wizard can be also be started while running a page and clicking on the Create link on the Developer's Toolbar and selecting to create a page control on this page and then choosing Validation. At the time this book was written, this second method of starting the wizard actually dropped you into the third step of the wizard, as shown here. Therefore, to specify the level of the validation and to select an item, you must use the Previous button to navigate back to the first steps in the wizard.

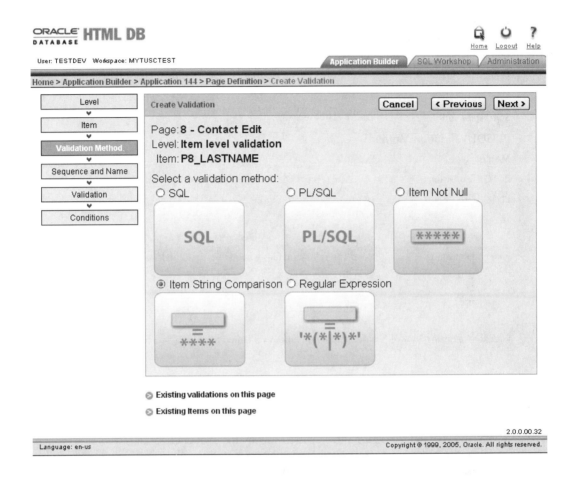

In the first step of the wizard, you choose the validation level, whether the validation is for an item or for the page. If you choose item-level validation, the next step allows you to specify on which item the validation will be created. Then you move on to the third step, where you select the method of the validation you wish to create.

As you can see, there are five major categories of validation methods. The SQL, PL/SQL, and Item String Comparison methods have further choices, where you specify a type within each method (see the following table for a further explanation of SQL and PL/SQL method types). The Item String Comparison types are fairly self-explanatory, so they will not be further explained.

SQL Validation Method

Method Type	Example
Exists	`select 1 from a_table where check_column = :p9_an_item`
Not Exists	`select 1 from a_table where check_column = :p9_an_item`
SQL Expression	`instr(:p10_email, '@')>0`

PL/SQL Validation Method

Method Type	Example
PL/SQL Expression	`to_char(:p9_start_date,'MON') != 'JAN'`

PL/SQL Error	`if to_char(:p9_start_date,'MON') != 'JAN' then`
	`  raise_application_error(-20001, 'Start Date must`
	`  be in January');`
	`end if;`

Function Returning Boolean	Note: The validation fails when false is returned.
	`if to_char(:p9_start_date,'MON') = 'JAN' then`
	`  return false;`
	`else`
	`  return true;`
	`end if;`

Function Returning Error Text	Note: return null for the validation to pass.
	`if to_char(:p9_start_date,'MON') = 'JAN' then`
	`  return null;`
	`else`
	`  return 'The Start date must be in January' ;`
	`end if;`

The next step in the wizard allows you to specify the sequence for the validation, which determines the order in which the validation you are creating will be evaluated among all validations. You must also provide a name. Try to make the validation names descriptive (for example, P8_LASTNAME_NOTNULL). This step is also where you specify the location in which the error message will be displayed. The choices are On an Error Page, Inline with Field, Inline with Notification, and Inline with Field and in Notification. Again, I would not recommend using the error page. Whether you want to display the error message inline with its associated field will depend on your page layout. If you have multiple items on a line, sometimes this method's results are not very appealing.

The next step is where you actually provide the implementation of the validation. It will be a little different depending on the method you selected to create. The following example shows the implementation of a Function Returning Error Text type of PL/SQL validation method.

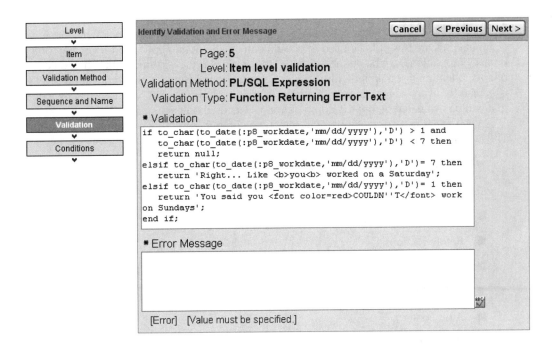

For some methods, you will supply an item and an expression; for others, you provide code for
the validation. For all types except Function Returning Error Text, you will also have to supply the
text of the error message to be displayed. As you can see in the example, you can use HTML tags
to spice up the display of your messages.

The final step in creating a validation is to specify the conditions under which this validation
is to be evaluated. If you do not specify any conditions, the validation will be evaluated whenever
the page is submitted. You can specify the validation to be evaluated when a certain button is clicked,
when a certain condition exists, or both. Using both comes in real handy when implementing a
multistep wizard. You would only want to evaluate your validations when the user clicks on the
Next button, and you might also want to add another condition, such as to evaluate a field only if
another field is a certain value.

Editing Validations

Validations can be individually edited by clicking on the name of the validation on the Page
Definition page. This opens the Edit Page Validation page, where you can edit the information
collected by the wizard when creating the validation. Additionally, the normal sections for
Authentication, Configuration, and Comments are available.

Clicking on the Validations title of the Validation section on the Page Definition page brings
up a page where you can edit the sequence, name, and display location for all your validations at
the same time. You can also see the validation type for each validation as well as if the validation
is conditional and when it was last updated.

Computations

Computations are bits of logic used to populate the value of an application-level item or a page item. Computations can be defined either at the application level through the shared components of an application or on an individual page. Computations defined at the application level will be executed for every page, but as with almost everything in HTML DB, you can specify a condition that will be evaluated before the computation is executed on each page.

When creating a computation, you select the computation point and the computation type. The available computation points are as follows:

- On New Instance (for example, On Login)

- Before Header

- After Header

- Before Regions

- After Regions

- Before Footer

- After Footer

- After Submit

Select the computation point that makes the most sense for the implementation of your business logic, the relationship of the item whose value you are calculating, and the other items that you might be using in the calculation. With the exception of the After Submit computation point, all the other points occur in the rendering of the page. The After Submit computation point is used for setting the value of items based on user input received from the page but prior to the execution of the page processes.

Creating Computations

Computations are created in two places. Application-level computations are created from the Application Computations link in the Logic section of the application's shared components. When creating an application-level computation, you are taken directly to the Edit Application Computation page. Page-level computations are created from the Add icon in either the Computation section at the bottom of the Page Rendering column or the Computation section at the top of the Page Processing column. Both of these will start the computation-creation wizard. This wizard can also be started through the Create link on the Developer's Toolbar and selecting the Page Control on This Page option.

The first step in the process is to select whether you want to calculate the value for an item on the same page, an item on another page, or an application-level item. Next, you select the item on which you want to create the computation from a pick list based on your first selection. You also specify the sequence for the computation. If there are multiple computations at the same processing point, they will be processed in the order of the sequence number. You also specify the computation point and the type of computation.

The six different types of computations offer the developer great flexibility in how the value of an item may be determined. Each type, along with an example, is shown in the following table.

Computation Type	Example
Static Assignment	5 or `completed`

PL/SQL Function Body	This is a simple example but it can be as complex as any function you would otherwise write including a declaration section.
	`if instr(upper(:p5_lastname),'DAN')>0 then`
	`  return :p5_notes||' it''s a Dan';`
	`else`
	`  return :p5_notes;`
	`end if;`

SQL Query	`select code_value`
	`  from code_table`
	`  where code = :p45_user_value;`

SQL Expression	`substr(:p5_name, instr(:p5_name, ',') + 1 )`
PL/SQL Expression	`nvl(:p5_country, 'Unknown')`
Item Value	`p5_other_field`

The last step in the wizard allows you to specify a condition that must be met before the computation will be executed. All the normal 60-plus condition types are available.

Editing Computations

To edit a page-level computation, click on the name of the computation to navigate to the Edit Page Computation page. In addition to the attributes entered in the wizard, you can specify an error message in case the computation fails. Additionally, the normal sections for Authentication, Configuration, and Comments are available.

When you click on the title of the Computations section, you will navigate to the Page Computations page, where you can edit the sequence and computation point of all your computations. You can also see the computation type, whether it is conditional, and when it was last updated.

To edit application-level computations, navigate to the specific computation through the Application Computations link in the Logic section of the application's shared components.

Processes

Processes are the heart of an HTML DB application when it comes to making the application more than just another HTML application. The primary purpose of processes is to interact with the database, but other types of processes are also available to the developer. Most of the time processes are defined at the page level, but you can also define application-level processes. Processes defined at the application level will be evaluated for every page of the application unless limited by their Condition section.

Like computations, processes can be defined to be evaluated either during the page rendering or during the page processing. Those done during page rendering are usually used to retrieve data from the database and populate items on the page. Those done during processing are often used to save the user-entered information into the database. If we look back at a form page we created using wizards, such as the one to edit CONTACTS, we see three processes—one to fetch a row from CONTACTS, one to process a row of CONTACTS, and one to reset the page. The first two are Data Manipulation type processes, whereas the last is a Session State type process.

Processes can both reference and set the values of any page-level or application-level item for the current application. The items will be referenced in different ways, depending on the type of processes you are defining. You will use one of the substitution variable syntaxes discussed in Chapter 6, but most often you will use the bind variable syntax (:P8_MY_ITEM), or in PL/SQL you might use the v() or nv() function.

Creating Processes

Processes, like almost anything else in HTML DB, are created with a wizard. The wizard for page-level processes is started either from the Add icon in one of the two Processes sections on the Page Definition page or through the Create link on the Developer's Toolbar (selecting the Page Control on This Page option and then the Process option). In the first step of the Create Page Process Wizard, you must select from one of the eight different types of processes available (see Figure 13-1).

The wizard for *application-level* processes is started with the Create button from the Application Processes section of an application's shared components. With application-level processes, you will not have to select a process type because the only type you are allowed to create as an application-level process is a PL/SQL type process. The eight different types of processes are

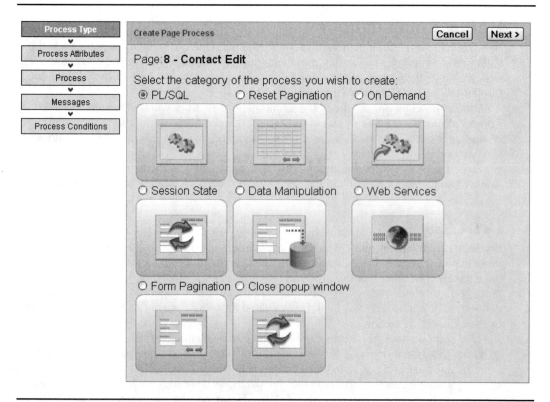

FIGURE 13-1 *Process types in the Create Page Process Wizard*

briefly described in the following table. The remaining steps in the process-creation wizard vary depending on the process type you select.

Process Type	Description
PL/SQL	This is a generic PL/SQL anonymous block of code, which could be as complicated as you would like to make it or could simply call a program unit that is stored in the database (for instance, a general API that is always used for access to a particular table).
Reset Pagination	This process type is used to reset the pagination of a report back to the beginning of the result set. This way, the next time the report is displayed, the items displayed will be the first part of the result set.
On Demand	The purpose of a page-level On Demand type process is to execute an application-level process that has been defined to have a processing point of On Demand. This way, a single process can be called from several different locations throughout the application. Use this process type if you have a generic process that must be executed at multiple locations in your application.
Session State	This process type is used to null out the values of existing session state items. It can be used to clear the cache for all workspace applications, for a selected workspace application, for the current session, for certain pages, or for particular items. This process type is also used to set the value of a user preference.
Data Manipulation	This process type is used for an automatic Data Manipulation Language (DML) process. The processes created by the wizards to do multirow or single-row form fetches, saves, updates, and deletes are of this type. Typically when you use this type of process, it will be created for you by a wizard.
Web Services	This process type is used to implement a web service. When this process is run, it submits a request to the web service provider.
Form Pagination	This process type is used with a master detail page. It is used to determine the next and previous master records and to display the master record positional count (for example, "3 of 4").
Close Popup Window	This process type is used to close a pop-up window and refresh the calling window. This process type is new to version 2.0—so new that as of the time of publishing this book, Oracle had not been able to provide instructions on how it refreshes the calling page.

The path of the wizard will vary depending on the type of process you choose to create. A number of fields will be entered for most processes. In the Name field, you provide a descriptive name of the process to give other developers an idea of what the process does. The value you enter in the Sequence field is used to determine the order in which processes will be evaluated within the same process point. The Point field is used to specify a point in page rendering or page processing at which the process will be evaluated. Here are the possible points:

■   On New Instance – After Authentication

- On Load – Before Header

- On Load – After Header

- On Load – Before Regions

- On Load – After Regions

- On Load – Before Footer

- On Load – After Footer

- On Submit – Before Computations and Validations

- On Submit – After Computations and Validations

In almost all the paths through the Create Page Process Wizard, after you select the type of process you want to create, as shown earlier in Figure 13-1, you will be presented with the process's Type field. The value of this field will be the type you selected. In most cases, you won't want to change its value. However, when you select to create a PL/SQL type process, this field will default to the value "PL/SQL anonymous block." You may wish to change the Type field to "PL/SQL DBMS JOB (runs anonymous block asynchronously)." This allows you to run the process in the background. This is ideal for long-running processes where the user does not need immediate feedback from the process.

The values entered into the Success Message field will be displayed if the process is evaluated successfully and the following page has the #SUCCESS_MESSAGE# substitution variable used in the page template. The value entered into the Failure Message field will be displayed if the process fails. You can make a process conditional by selecting a button for the When Button Pressed field and/or by selecting a condition type and specifying values for Expression 1 and Expression 2.

PL/SQL

PL/SQL processes offer you the most flexibility in what you can do with them—from a simple DML on a single table, to DML on multiple tables, to the most complex business logic. Aside from the common fields discussed previously, you will also have to enter an anonymous block of PL/SQL. One example might be to insert a row into a table with data collected in a wizard. As noted, you can create a normal PL/SQL process or one that runs in the background. Refer to Appendix A for details on the HTMLDB_PLSQL_JOB package.

The CONTACTS table we have been working with contains almost 30 columns, so it would be a good candidate for a wizard. Use the Create Page | Wizard option to create a wizard with four or five pages. Divide up the fields over three or four pages, leaving the last page for a confirmation page. On the final confirmation page you would have a Finish button. Also, you could display all the data collected so far in a Display Only on Existing Items type region. You then create a PL/SQL process that's conditional on the Finish button being clicked and inserts a record into the CONTACTS table. The PL/SQL for the process would look something like this:

```
insert into contacts (contact_id, firstname, lastname, dear, …
                       companyname, workphone, workextension, … )
        values (:p20_contact_id, :p20_firstname, :p20_lastname, …
              :p23_companyname, :p23_workphone, :p23workextension, … );
```

Another useful purpose for a PL/SQL process would be to process the contents of a custom multirow edit form. The wizards in HTML DB make implementing a multirow edit form very easy if it is for a single table. If you have the need to create a multirow edit form based on a complex query, you can create and process the form using two built-in packages: HTMLDB_ITEM and HTMLDB_APPLICATION. The form is constructed by creating a SQL Query–based report and using the HTMLDB_ITEM package in the query to generate the items. To illustrate the concept, the following is a simple query based on the EMP table:

```
SELECT empno,
        HTMLDB_ITEM.HIDDEN(1,empno),
        HTMLDB_ITEM.TEXT(2,ename,10,10) ename,
        HTMLDB_ITEM.TEXT(3,job,9,9) position,
        HTMLDB_ITEM.SELECT_LIST_FROM_LOV(9,mgr,'managers',null, 'NO') mgr,
        HTMLDB_ITEM.DATE_POPUP(4,rownum,hiredate,'Month dd, yyyy') hd,
        HTMLDB_ITEM.TEXT(5,sal,12) sal,
        HTMLDB_ITEM.TEXT(6,comm,12) comm,
        HTMLDB_ITEM.SELECT_LIST_FROM_LOV(7,deptno,'department',null, 'NO')
    deptno,
        HTMLDB_ITEM.CHECKBOX(8,empno,decode(temp,'Y','CHECKED',null)) temp
    FROM emp
    ORDER BY 1
```

A report created with the previous query produces a report like the one shown here:

Multi-Row Edit of the Emp table

Empno	Name	Position	Manager	Hire Date	Salary	Commission	Department	Temp
7369	SMITH	CLERK	FORD	December 17, 1980	800	200	RESEARCH	☐
7499	ALLEN	SALESMAN	BLAKE	February 20, 1981	1600	350	SALES	☑
7521	WARD	SALESMAN	BLAKE	February 22, 1981	1250	500	SALES	☐
7566	JONES	MANAGER	KING	April 02, 1981	2975		RESEARCH	☐
7654	MARTIN	SALESMAN	BLAKE	September 28, 1981	1250	1400	SALES	☐
7698	BLAKE	MANAGER	KING	May 01, 1981	2850		SALES	☑
7782	CLARK	MANAGER	KING	June 09, 1981	2450		ACCOUNTING	☐
7788	SCOTT	ANALYST	JONES	December 09, 1982	3000		RESEARCH	☐
7839	KING	PRESIDENT	FLINSTONE	November 17, 1981	5000		ACCOUNTING	☐
7844	TURNER	SALESMAN	BLAKE	September 08, 1981	1500	0	SALES	☐
7876	ADAMS	CLERK	SCOTT	January 12, 1983	1100		RESEARCH	☐
7900	JAMES	CLERK	BLAKE	December 03, 1981	950		SALES	☐
7902	FORD	ANALYST	JONES	December 03, 1981	3000		RESEARCH	☐
7934	MILLER	CLERK	CLARK	January 23, 1982	1300		ACCOUNTING	☐
8000	RUBBLE	MANAGER	KING	January 08, 1983	3500		OPERATIONS	☑

row(s) 1 - 15 of 17   Next⊙

Submit

To process the changes to this multirow edit form, you use a PL/SQL process like the following. The values of the items in a multirow edit form are passed in arrays that are available to the developer using the HTMLDB_APPLICATION package. Note the special treatment of the check box (item 8). The arrays for check box items only contain entries for those check boxes that are checked.

```
declare
        is_temp char(1);
begin
    for i in 1..htmldb_application.g_f01.count loop
        is_temp := 'N';
        for x in 1..htmldb_application.g_f08.count loop
            if htmldb_application.g_f01(i) = htmldb_application.g_f08(x)then
                is_temp := 'Y';
            end if;
        end loop;
        update emp
            set ename    = htmldb_application.g_f02(i),
                job       = htmldb_application.g_f03(i),
                hiredate  = to_date(htmldb_application.g_f04(i),'Month dd,
yyyy'),
                sal       = htmldb_application.g_f05(i),
                comm      = htmldb_application.g_f06(i),
                deptno    = htmldb_application.g_f07(i),
                temp      = is_temp,
                mgr       = htmldb_application.g_f09(i)
            where empno = htmldb_application.g_f01(i);
    end loop;
end;
```

The HTMLDB_ITEM and HTMLDB_APPLICATION packages are introduced in Appendix B and are covered in great detail in the HTML DB User's Guide. Note that the first parameter passed into the various HTMLDB_ITEM functions is a sequence number. This sequence number corresponds to the g_fXX functions in the HTMLDB_APPLICATION application that reference the arrays of data passed from the items.

These are just a couple examples of how a PL/SQL type process can be used. Its limitations lie only in your PL/SQL coding skills.

Reset Pagination
The Reset Pagination process does one and only one thing—it resets the pagination for the current page. After selecting the Reset Pagination type option in the Create Page Process Wizard, the only information you must provide is a name, sequence, processing point, and any conditions.

On Demand
On Demand processes allow you to write a single process that can be evaluated on multiple pages at different points. There are two parts to On Demand processes: the definition of an application-level On Demand process and page-level definitions of On Demand processes that call the application-level process. Like all application-level processes, an On Demand process is a PL/SQL type process.

If you have a process that needs to be evaluated at the same evaluation point on multiple pages, create an application-level process and limit its evaluation to the appropriate pages with the process's Condition section. However, if you need the same process to be evaluated by multiple pages at different points, you will want to create an application-level On Demand process and page-level On Demand processes on the appropriate pages for evaluation at the appropriate points.

Session State

Session State processes allow you to clear out the session state. Normally this type of process is used to clear out the cached values for the current session of the current user. You can clear out individual items by listing those items. You can clear out all items on individual pages by listing the pages, or you can clear out everything for the current session of the current user.

In addition to clearing items for the current session, this type process can also deal with the current user's preferences. Remember, preferences are values stored *per user,* so the next time the user returns, in a different session, the values are still available. With a Session State process, you can clear all the preferences for the current user or you can set the value of a certain preference based on the value of an item.

Finally, Session State processes can be used for managing sessions within the workspace. This is part of the administrative portion of an application. Remember, session states are stored in the database, and they don't go away until they are removed either through the Workspace Administration section available in the HTML DB development environment or through the HTML DB Administrator interface. The options available for this purpose are Remove All Session State for the Current Application and Remove All Session State for a List of Applications Within the Workspace.

Data Manipulation

The Data Manipulation type processes are called *declarative processes* because the HTML DB engine will create processes from declarations provided by the developer. These processes perform inserts, updates, and deletes without the developer having to write the actual DML statements. The actual code is generated based on information provided by the developer. These processes are then used with single-row form pages and multirow form pages.

There are several categories of Data Manipulation processes. With a single-row form page, you use an Automated Row Fetch category process to fetch rows and populate your fields on the rendering of the page. You use an Automated Row Processing (DML) category process when the page is submitted—to process inserts, updates, and deletes.

Multirow edit forms are implemented as a variation of a report, so the fetching of data into the form during the page rendering does not require a separate process; it is actually handled by the report region. Several categories of Data Manipulation processes are specifically designed for working with multirow forms. Two categories—Multi Row Update and Multi Row Delete—are used to perform just what their names imply: updates and deletes. The final category of Data Manipulation processes is used to add additional blank rows to the report so that new rows can be inserted into the table.

These processes are limited to operating on a single table or view. Additionally, the table can have at most a two-column primary key. If you are going to use this type of process, it is best to have the wizards create it for you. Invoke the wizards by creating a new page or a new region. If you need to deal with more complex structures than the wizards will allow, take the approach discussed earlier in the section on PL/SQL type processes.

Web Services

Web Services processes are used to submit parameters to and retrieve results from a Web Service Reference. Web Service References were covered in Chapter 7 as part of the shared components of an application. Once you have a valid Web Service Reference, you can create a process to utilize the web service.

Once again, although you can manually create a process for a web service, it is recommended that you use the wizards to create all the elements needed to use a web service. Once you finish creating a Web Service Reference, you will be given the opportunity to start a wizard either to create a form using the web service or to create a form and a report using the web service. You can also start the wizard by running a page and clicking on the Create link on the Developer's Toolbar, then selecting the Region on This Page option, selecting the Form option, and finally selecting either the Form on Web Service option or the Form and Report on Web Service option.

If the results of the web service will be single values, you want to use the just the form. If the results of the web service will be multiple rows of results, you want to use the form and report. The wizards will use the information in the Web Service Reference to create the required input fields, the required output fields or report, and the process to submit the input fields and display the output.

Manually Creating a Web Services Process   To create a Web Services process manually, after starting the Create Page Process Wizard, select the Web Services type. In the next step of the wizard, you will supply a name and a sequence. You can accept the defaults for the Type field and the Point field, which will be On Submit – After Computations and Validations.

Many web services offer different operations from the same Web Service Reference. For instance, a ZIP code web service may offer an operation to return the city for a ZIP code, an operation to return the city and state, or an operation to return the distance between two ZIP codes. In the next step of the wizard, you will select the Web Service Reference from an LOV and then a particular operation from an LOV, which will be based on the reference you selected.

When you select a particular operation, the wizard will provide two additional sections—one for the input parameters and one for the output parameters, as shown next. The source for the input parameter can be either a static value or an item on your page. Some web services are subscription services and you must provide a username and a password. For these, you use a static value that your users never see. For the remaining items—the ones you want your users to be able to enter values for—you will want to use page items. In the Value field, you either enter the static value or the name of the page item.

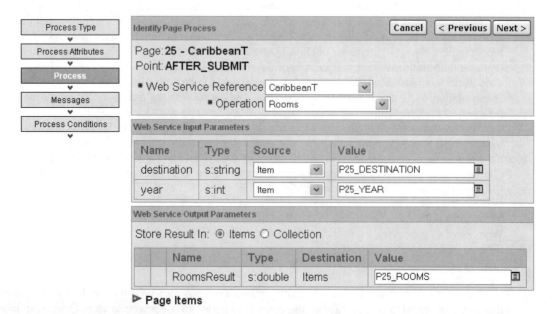

▷ **Page Items**

For the output parameters, you need to specify whether to use items or collections. Items are used for web services that return a single record. Collections are used for a web service that returns multiple records in the results. The two final steps in the wizard for a Web Services process allow you to enter success and failure messages and any conditions under which you want the process to be evaluated.

Form Pagination

The Form Pagination process is used with a master detail page. It determines the next and previous master records and populates a field to display the positional count of the current master record (for example, "3 of 4"). This particular type of process is created when you use the wizard to create a master detail form.

Most of the time when your application uses one of these type processes, it is created by the Master Detail Wizard. However, if you understand what the process does, you may find a time when you want to create a process of this type manually. For instance, you could use a Form Pagination process on a page that displays a single record from a table and the process would handle the next-record and previous-record navigation for that table.

The process operates on a single table and should usually be defined to be evaluated after the header when the page is being rendered. The process takes the current primary key and determines, based on a specified sort order, the primary keys of the records that are logically before and after the current record.

You must already have an item on your page where the primary key of the table will be stored. Creating a Form Pagination process not only produces the process but also creates the following:

- A hidden field to hold the value of the primary key for the next master record

- A hidden field to hold the value of the primary key for the previous master record

- A Previous button with conditions to display only if there is a value in the previous primary key hidden field

- A Next button with conditions to display only if there is a value in the next primary key hidden field

- A display field for the current master record count (for example, "3 of 4")

- A branch back to the same page, conditional on the Next button, that populates the item holding the primary key with the value from the item holding the primary key of the next record

- A branch back to the same page, conditional on the Previous button, that populates the item holding the primary key with the value from the item holding the primary key of the previous record

If you are manually using this processes, you would have a query whose WHERE clause references the item containing the primary key.

This explanation always refers to a single primary key on the table. However, the wizard and process can handle a primary key with two columns. In that case, the wizard would create two "next" and two "previous" hidden fields.

In the Create Page Process Wizard, after selecting the Form Pagination type process, you specify the table on which to base the process. Next, you specify the one or two columns that make up the primary key on the table and the existing page items where these keys will be. These items are the only ones that must exist prior to creating the process. Then, you must specify the region on your page where the wizard should create all the items specified previously. You will also specify one or two columns from the table that will be used to determine the ordering of the table. If you do not specify a column for ordering, the order will be determined by the primary key. Finally, you can specify a WHERE clause if you want to limit the records that will be included.

Close Popup Window

The final type of process, which is new to version 2.0, is the Close Popup Window type process. This process is used on a page that's the source for a pop-up window. The process, when executed, will close the pop-up window and according to the wizard refresh the calling window. You can successfully use this process to close a pop-up window if there is no branch defined; however, the refreshing of the calling window does not occur.

In the process-creation wizard, when you select to create a process of this type, all you have to specify is its name, a sequence, and the point at which the process will be evaluated. If you want to add a condition to the process, you must edit the process after it is created.

Editing Processes

To edit a process, click on the name of the process on the Page Definition page. This will open the Edit Page Process page. The Edit Page Process page is primarily the same for all types of processes; the biggest difference is the Sources section, which is dependent on the process type.

Most of the information entered in the process-creation wizards can be changed through the edit page. However, the one thing that can never be changed is the process type. In addition to the elements defined during creation are the standard sections for Authorization, Configuration, and Comments.

One attribute found in the Processing Point section, in addition to the sequence and the processing point, is the Run Process field. This field has two choices that allow you to specify whether the process should be run once per page visit, which is the default, or once per session or when reset. The latter option is very useful for tasks that only need to happen once per unique visit to the application.

PART
IV

Website and Application
Examples

CHAPTER
14

Building an Event
Scheduling Application

 ith most any technical book that you've read, you're likely always thinking how to relate your environment to what the author covers. You are typically dreaming of building a real-world application using the tools discussed. This chapter discusses how building an HTML DB app can provide real-world functionality and solutions to many everyday problems (or *opportunities* as I like to call them).

The Opportunity at Hand

To begin the process, you must assess the problem or task to be solved or simplified. For this chapter, I will use the Young Presidents Organization (YPO) RSVP or event-scheduling application as the example. YPO is a worldwide organization with about 9,000 members, each of which is a company leader. Your CEO may be a part of this group. Local areas have chapters of regional business leaders.

One of our local YPO chapters consists of a group of 50 CEOs and roughly 50 spouses. Throughout the course of a year, our chapter holds many different types of events: regularly scheduled monthly meetings, breakfast of champions (BOC), lunch of champions (LOC), spur-of-the-moment events, members-only events, joint chapter events, and more. The problem herein lies with handling the RSVPs for the group's many types of events. Collecting RSVPs can be a time-consuming, exhausting, and manually intensive process. Members may not respond in a timely fashion, forget to RSVP, or forget who they are supposed to respond to because a different person coordinates and is responsible for each event. A practical solution to this problem would be to create an automated RSVP process to eliminate inconsistencies in RSVP patterns and to allow people to use a self-service application any time of the day.

The Database

You can download the database definition and all the application files for this application at http://www.oraclepressbooks.com. As you'll see next, the application scope has branched beyond simple RSVP tallies to tracking members' information. This was taken into consideration at the time of the initial database design, as is shown in the entity relationship diagram in Figure 14-1. The primary application tables are the events and members tables. The RSVP table contains the RSVPs and attendance information for a specific event for a specific member. All the other tables are supporting tables for the application.

In the Beginning

As designed, the RSVP process begins with an initial, automated e-mail personally asking the member and spouse to please RSVP for a specific upcoming event. The initial e-mail invitations go out to the membership about one to two months in advance of the actual event. Besides containing the event details, the e-mail contains a simple set of directions on how to RSVP as well as a link, username, and password for the database. In this e-mail are also options to click on links that detail the attendees for the meeting. All the information the member needs is in one place, creating a simple beginning to the process. Figure 14-2 shows a sample e-mail that a member might receive for event.

The e-mail you see in Figure 14-2 is generated from a PL/SQL procedure (send_rsvp_letter) that is run manually or on a scheduled basis. The code for this procedure and the entire

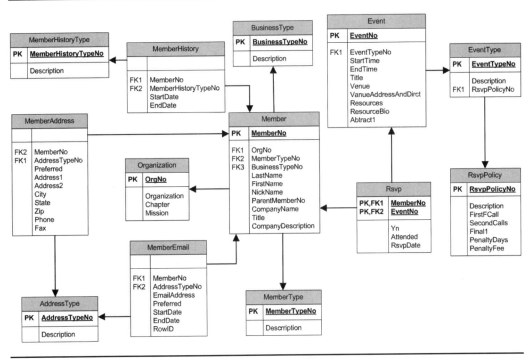

FIGURE 14-1   *Entity relationship diagram for RSVP application*

application can also be downloaded from http://www.oraclepressbooks.com. You'll see later in this chapter that administrators can manually ask for an RSVP request to be sent or the check_send_rsvp_letter procedure will kick this off on a daily basis as necessary. The send_rsvp_letter procedure has the capability of sending RSVP requests, e-mailing to those who are and are not coming to an event, invoicing no-shows, and much more. This procedure probably should have been renamed. It uses the send_e-mail_type procedure, which in turn calls the send_e-mail procedure.

As mentioned, this is where the application process begins—with a simple e-mail to each member in the organization.

Confirmation from E-mail

From the link area in the e-mail, the member or spouse clicks on the link that best describes who in their family will be attending the meeting. This link logs them into the RSVP web application. A browser starts on their machine, and they are directed to the application home page. Here, the member can securely enter the site with their username (e-mail address, which will automatically fill in) and password (which is in the e-mail in the event that they forgot it).

Once into the RSVP portion of the page, the member can review and change the events as well as change the RSVP notification. Regardless of the event registered for, after the information is entered, the member has to click on the Confirm button to set the RSVP. If the member has

From: Kathy Donnelly
Sent: Wednesday, March 09, 2005 9:48 AM
To: Brad Brown
Cc: Kristen Brown
Subject: YPO Lunch of Champions (LOC) Event - Stopping the Ultimate Bully RSVP Request - *** ACTION REQUIRED ***

Importance: High

Brad and Kristen,

We've likely all experienced bullies. I'd encourage you to come to this presentation to learn about a very effective way of reducing violence at your kids' schools. We're going to try out a new location, too. This is an LOC that you don't want to miss.

It is time to RSVP for an upcoming YPO event. Please RSVP by Tuesday, March 15, 2005 for the Thursday, April 14, 2005 Lunch of Champions event, from 11:30am to 1:00pm. Click on one of the links below the event information or cut and paste the link into a browser to RSVP. Log in using the username and password provided below, then click on CONFIRM. It's that simple!

Both of us will attend
Brad is attending without Kristen
Brad is attending, Kristen will RSVP on own
Kristen is attending without Brad
Kristen is attending, Brad will RSVP on own
Neither of us are coming

Event	Stopping the Ultimate Bully
Event Type	Lunch of Champions
Date	Thursday, April 14, 2005 from 11:30 a.m. Until 1:00 p.m.
Venue	Community Banks
Venue Info	6503 Hampden Ave Suite 206 Denver, CO 80224 the location is at Hampden and Monoco, just east of I25. It's 13 minutes from downtown, 3 from the tech center, and 8 from Cherry Creek.

FIGURE 14-2 *E-mail to a specific member and spouse*

Resource	Gary Ebel and Dave Jensen
Resource Bio	
Abstract	Have you or your kids ever experienced a bully? Gary Ebel and his family experienced the worst possible bully imaginable. Gary and Dave Jensen would like to share their perspective about teenager culture in the United States. Gary is going to share his journey to where he is today. Gary's organization, CETAV (Cameron Ebel Teens Against Violence) is available to visit the schools that our kids attend (at no cost to the schools). Teen violence has moved from the streets to our schools and now into our homes. These instances of teen violence happen across the country and are usually in one-off situations and are so spread out that the general public isn't aware of the vastness of the problem, and the overall impact on our country isn't felt or understood. CETAV has a comprehensive approach to dealing with teen violence - it starts when they are young. It's time that we rise up and work with our communities to help our youth develop strong core values. Gary and his wife have reduced bullying and violence by over 20% in the schools that they have attended. This is an LOC that you don't want to miss. The story that Gary will share is absolutely amazing - you won't believe it's possible. You'll learn a lot about yourself and how to protect your kids. You'll learn about bullies and how to protect your kids against them. Please attend this LOC!
Details	

Note:
To log into the YPO RSVP application to look up member addresses, events, and more, <u>Click here</u>
Brad's username/email address is: brownb@tusc.com and your password is: putithere
Kristen's username/email address is: brownk6483@hotmail.com and your password is: whynot

Thank you,

Tom and Jack Thompson (Day Chairs)

FIGURE 14-2   *E-mail to a specific member and spouse* (continued)

previously RSVPed for this event, that information will show also. The member also has an option to add the event to their personal calendar. Figure 14-3 shows the confirmation page for this event. The RSVP_ME procedure is called when the user clicks on Confirm.

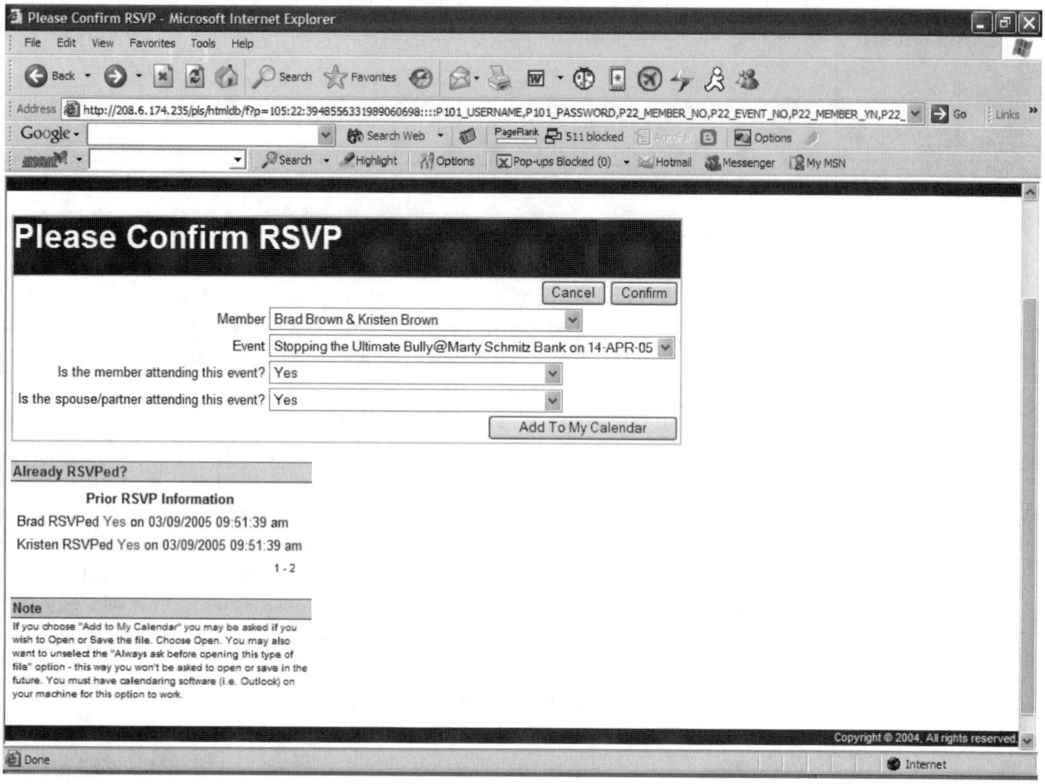

FIGURE 14-3 *Confirmation page*

After confirming the RSVP, members are taken to the main event page, which shows information about the specific event, an RSVP summary in graph and text form, along with a complete list of members who are planning to attend, who's not attending, and who still has not responded. Figure 14-4 shows the summary information from this page.

The RSVP_ME procedure sends the member and spouse a confirmation e-mail, along with one to the event day chair (the person responsible for the event), letting that person know someone else has RSVPed for their event. Figure 14-5 shows a sample e-mail.

Tracking Registrations

If an RSVP is not provided by the member, reminder messages are sent out on an escalating basis (one month before, two weeks before, one week before, every day thereafter). Once the member submits an RSVP, the e-mail reminders stop. As mentioned, the check_send_rsvp_letter procedure calculates when it's time to send another reminder for an event. This procedure is run via a dbms_job process that runs daily. The last call for an RSVP notice is sent two days prior to the event. If a member has still not provided an RSVP for the event, fines are queued for the member. A member also encounters a fine for accepting an invitation and not showing at the event or for showing without an invitation. Cost containment is important.

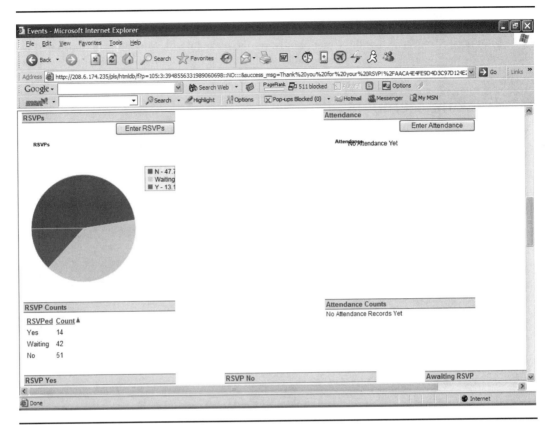

FIGURE 14-4   *RSVP summary information*

FIGURE 14-5   *Sample confirmation e-mail*

Members are able to check an event's status online at any time. Figure 14-6 shows a page where the members can see who will be attending the event, who cannot attend, and those who have not yet registered for the event (that is, public humiliation). After an event has been held, the attendance records are shown immediately below the RSVP information, along with no-shows and no-RSVPs.

Tracking Members

Another dimension to most organizations is the issue of maintaining current, precise information about the membership in a fashion that is user friendly to members, as well as to the multiple event coordinators. In this application, members are able to log on to the YPO site and update their information at any time. The chapter administrator and the board can manage any event and

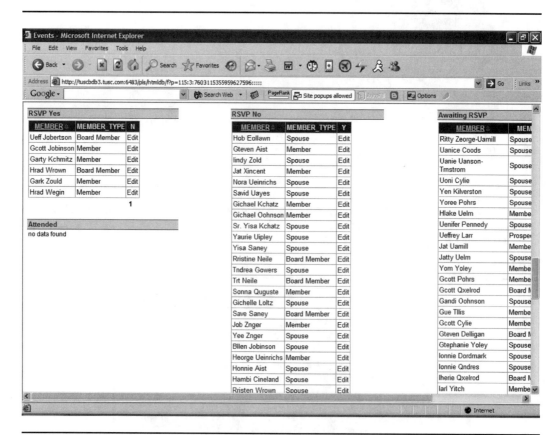

FIGURE 14-6 *Detailed RSVP information*

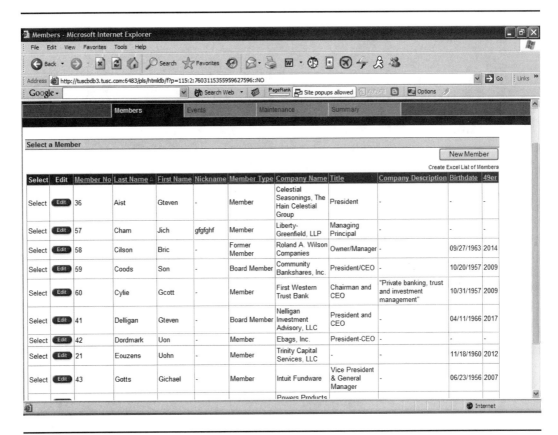

FIGURE 14-7   *Member-tracking page*

any member's information. The database contains information such as mailing and e-mail addresses, associates, demographics (age, sex, business type, 49er date), chapter history (board positions held, status), and so on. As shown in Figure 14-7, this information is available to all the YPO membership.

In addition to keeping personal information about the members, Figure 14-8 shows that this application keeps track of a person's history of attendance at all types of events, hosted events, as well as past mailing and e-mail addresses.

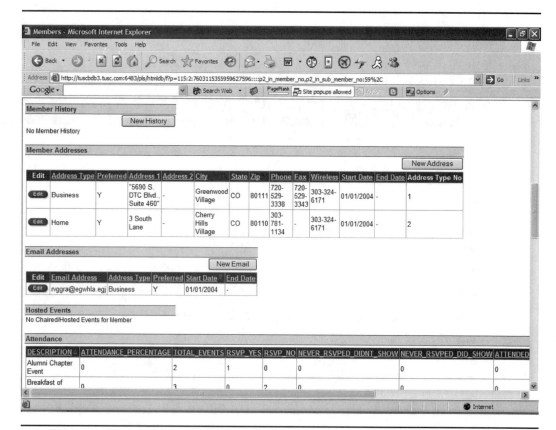

FIGURE 14-8 *Extra personal information*

Members may store information about an unlimited amount of associates within this database: other member names and their spouses, children, assistants, friends, and so on. As shown in Figure 14-9, a history of associate mailing and e-mail addresses as well as attendance at past events is also kept.

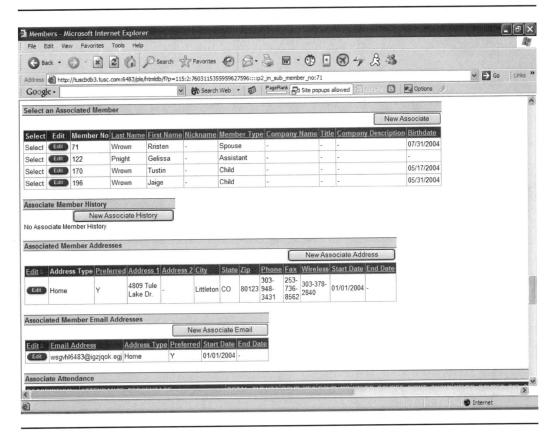

FIGURE 14-9 *Associates*

Attendance

Following the event, it is important for the coordinator to track the attendance and enter no-shows and so on. The events can be tracked by type, percentage of events made, number of events RSVP Yes, RSVP No, events not RSVPed to and showed, RSVPed and didn't show, events not RSVPed and didn't show, number of events attended, number not attended, no-shows, and no RSVPs. This process is made quick and easy using the designed database. The application contains a quick RSVP entry page as well as a quick attendance entry page, as shown in Figure 14-10.

In turn, the data entered can be programmed to produce graphs or charts for each event. For example, some information provided includes RSVP by member type, non-RSVP by member type, attendance by member type, and non-attendance by member type.

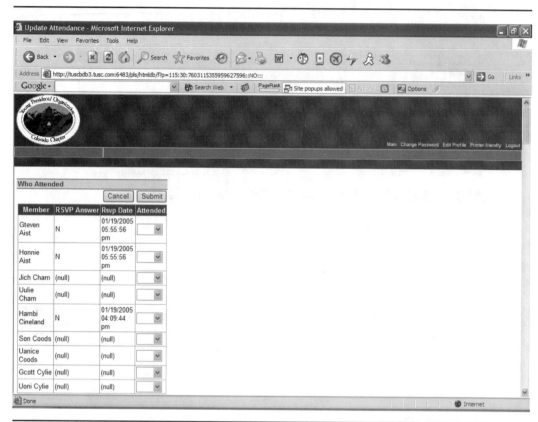

FIGURE 14-10 *Quick attendance-tracking page*

Statistics Everywhere

All the statistics are stored for each event and shown graphically in the event page, as shown in Figure 14-11.

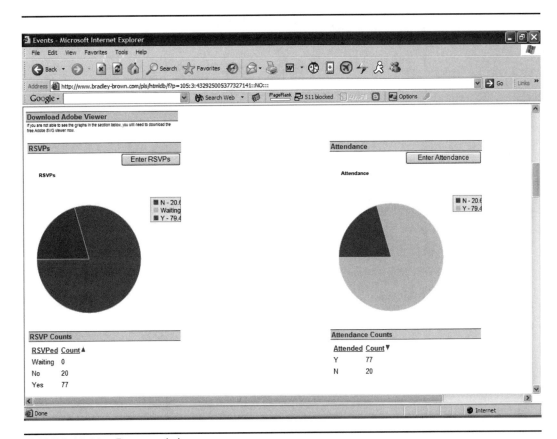

FIGURE 14-11   *Event statistics*

The summary of the event is also presented in a detailed manner. The summary page of the application reports, shown in Figure 14-12, provides information on the RSVP process, timeliness of RSVP by event type, member type, specific event, and specific member.

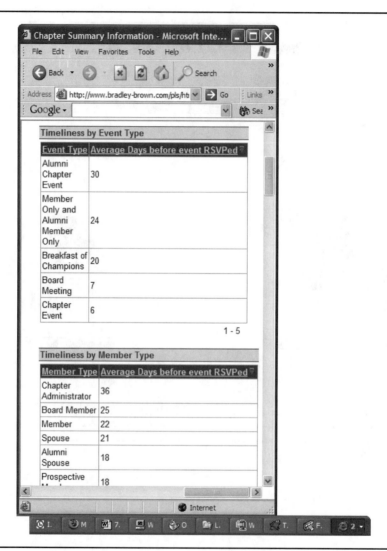

FIGURE 14-12 *Timeliness reports*

The database is also able to maintain a membership profile and provide graphs and charts related to membership, as shown in Figures 14-13 and 14-14.

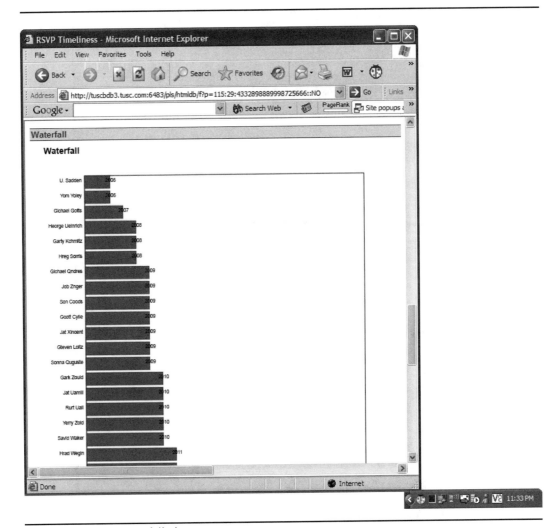

FIGURE 14-13   *Waterfall chart*

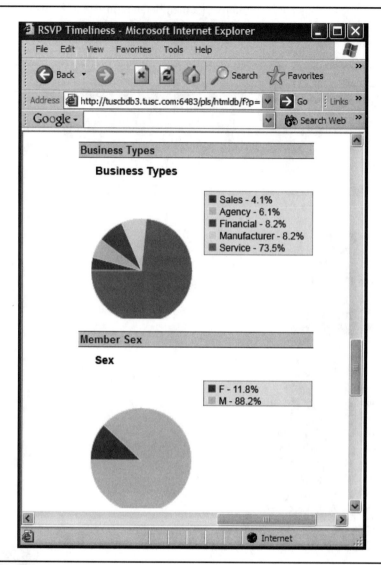

FIGURE 14-14 *Chapter statistics*

Maintenance

During configuration, any administrator is able to set rules for the chapter. For instance, in setting up the database, an administrator sets rules for how an RSVP is accepted, how member and event types are set, and how an RSVP can change during a lockdown period. Rules also call for automatic "inconsiderate" fees to be applied for a non-RSVP or for a no-show at an event. All this information is maintained through application forms. A complete maintenance menu is available only to the chapter administrator and board members of the organization.

One of the options on this menu is Send an Announcement, as shown in Figure 14-15. This functionality allows the chapter administrator to manually send an e-mail to the following:

■ Those who have not yet RSVPed for an event—to remind them to RSVP. Otherwise, they will be receiving another e-mail again shortly.

■ Those who RSVPed that they are going to attend—to remind them of the event and tell of last-minute event details.

■ Those who RSVPed that they will not attend—to beg them to attend an event.

■ Those who attended an event—to thank them for their attendance, to provide event contact follow-up, and so on.

■ Those who did not attend an event—to tell them what they missed.

■ To those who never RSVPed and those who RSVPed Yes but didn't show—to send them an invoice.

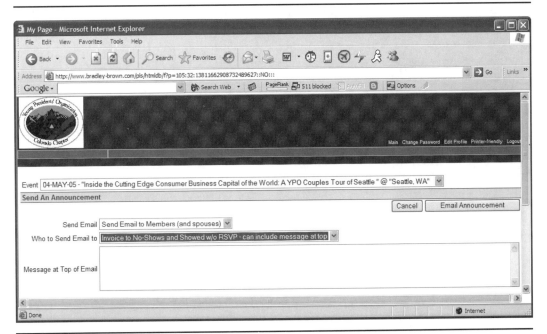

FIGURE 14-15 *Sending an announcement*

Cost Savings

HTML DB is a powerful and rapid application development tool. Not only is the application development environment user friendly, it is administratively friendly (one doesn't even need to know HTML) and secure. Using this HTML DB application, the event coordinator's role of taking RSVPs has virtually disappeared. The database provides a self-serve process that prevents human error and also provides information about recurring "problem" members. Information is tracked easily and can be presented in a variety of reports. It is also very easy to add new graphs, charts, and reports for virtually any information needed. In turn, the data stored allows the creation of other outputs, such as a directory. The grand outcome of the HTML DB is that this organization is able to manage its many events effortlessly: chapter meetings, board meetings, Breakfast of Champions Series (with limited seating), special events, joint chapter events, as well as members-only events. Due to the implementation of this HTML DB application, this organization has seen a substantial amount of savings each month—as much as $4,000. Several other chapters had considered using an ASPed event management package, which would have easily cost that much per month. When other chapters heard about our application, they came to us offering to pay to use the same HTML DB application. The international organization later came to me and asked if it could use the application. We're currently working with the international organization to integrate the application into its architecture. When users have an issue with the application, we use WebEx to connect to their machine. The ease of using the database process far outweighs the exhaustive methods used prior to its implementation.

CHAPTER
15

Building a Test
Administering Application

bike the previous chapter, this chapter will discuss the creation of a real-world application. Although this application is not an extremely complex one, it serves well as an example of putting to use the concepts we have covered so far in this book.

The Opportunity at Hand

The requirements started with the need to administer a single type of test to a group of people at many different locations. The test was a personality test, so there are no correct answers. Rather, the answers fall into categories, and the results of the test are determined based on the number of answers in each category. The requirements were later revised to include several different types of tests, including standard true/false and multiple choice.

The application needed to have two faces—an administrative face and a test-taker face. The administrative portion is where an administrator can create and edit the tests, create and edit people to take the tests, indicate the authorized people to take the tests, and view the results after the tests are completed.

The test-taker portion, on the other hand, only needed to allow authorized people access to take a test. A person could be authorized to take more than one test, so they must be able to select the test they are going to take. Because some of the tests were rather lengthy, the test taker needed to be able to stop work on the test and later return. This is not such a good idea for a test where you are attempting to measure someone's knowledge, but in this case the test had no right or wrong answers. Finally, when a test taker completes a test, they should be able to view the results of the test.

The Database

You can download the database definition and all the application files for this application at http://www.osborne.com. The database design was kept simple and was created around the implementation of the first test. Tests have questions, questions have answers. Because the personality test is not a right/wrong type of test, the answers have categories. People are authorized for (associated with) the tests they can take. When they take the test, the results of their answers are recorded. An individual's results can then be tallied and compared to the ratings criteria for the test. Particular ratings are grouped by the answer category, and the sum of an individual's results in those categories will fall into ranges for those categories. The final results for each category are brought together for an overall "rating," something like Extroverted, Sensing, with Feeling and Judging (see Figure 15-1).

Implementation

This application was one of the first HTML DB applications I created. So, as I have found with many projects, hindsight and further knowledge can provide a different perspective as to how something should be implemented. I chose this application just for that reason. Therefore, we will be able to look at one way of implementing some aspect of the application and talk of possible better solutions. Additionally, it is not so complicated that we can't dig into most of its implementation within the limitations of a single chapter.

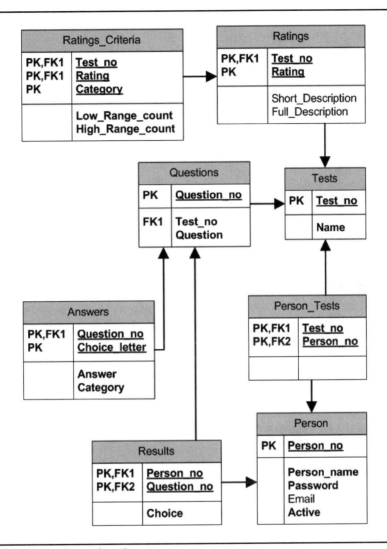

FIGURE 15-1 *Entity relationship diagram*

Security

Security requirements stated that the application should not have public access and that only authorized test takers or administrators should be able to access the application. There were also two distinct groups of users and portions of the application that needed to have access restricted based on a user's role. My initial approach was to use HTML DB's built-in users and groups with HTML DB's standard authentication scheme.

The shell application was created with the wizard, selecting to create only a single page with a single level of tabs and utilizing HTML DB's authentication. This created the standard login page and a single blank page. The idea was that all test takers would log in using a generic guest user account whose username and password were provided to all test takers.

To start with, I created two user groups—Test Taker and Test Admin—through the Manage Users section of Workspace Administration. Then I created two users—an administrative user assigned to the Test Admin group, and a guest user assigned to the Test Taker group. I then created two authorization schemes through the Security section of the application's Shared Components section. The authorization schemes are used to control access to portions of the application. Each scheme utilizes a call to a built-in function that determines if the current user belongs to a particular group Here's an example:

```
wwv_flow_user_api.current_user_in_group('Test Admin')
```

Once a test taker logs in using the guest user account, they see a page like the one shown next. They then select their name from the pop-up list of values and provide their unique password, all of which would have been e-mailed to them.

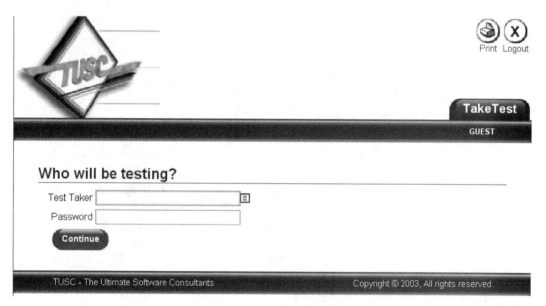

This solution works; it was easy to create and takes advantage of all the work that HTML DB has done to provide security. However, a test taker must provide two passwords (one for the guest user account and their unique password that was e-mailed to them), and they can see the names of all the other test takers. An alternate solution would be to create our own authentication scheme and utilize the person table. However, this solution requires a lot more work up front creating the authentication scheme, and we would have to create our own functions for the authorization scheme as well.

A third solution would be a combination of the two approaches. As users are created in the application, we could use the HTMLDB_UTIL.CREATE_USER procedure to add the test takers as HTML DB users in the Test Taker group. Then we could use the HTMLDB_UTIL.GET_USER_ID function to retrieve the user IDs, which we could use as the person_id in the person table. This solution allows us to take advantage of all the work HTML DB has done for us, yet still maintain our own information about each user.

When the administrator logs into the application, they have full access to the application and see a page like the one shown next. This separation of application functionality can be accomplished by simply selecting the Test Admin authorization scheme for each of the three administrative tabs in the Authorization section of their respective tab edit pages.

Build Options

Whenever I create an application, I like to specify at least one build option for testing or debugging elements. Build options are defined under the Logic section of the application's Shared Components section. For this application, I created a build option called TestFields. I use this build option on items on pages where I may want to display some information while I am developing the application, but don't want that item included in the final application. By simply changing the status of the build option to EXCLUDE, all the items are ignored.

Template and Theme

You can't see this from the black-and-white illustrations in this book, but the theme used is not one of the standard HTML DB themes. It looks similar to one, but it uses the color royal sapphire blue, which matches the blue in our company logo. I made a copy of the Opal theme (theme 5) and modified it for my own use. The bars and tabs are made up of images, so I made copies of the existing images and edited them in an image editor and changed their colors. Then I made copies of the Cascading Style Sheets and modified them to use the text colors I desired.

Test Takers' View of the World

If you have downloaded the application, you will notice that the page numbers for this application are well spread out. I like to group related pages by assigning them numerically close page numbers. I also like to try to have the page numbers be sequential as the navigation goes throughout the application. Therefore, I will have one set of pages start with 100 and another with 200 and so forth. I also skip numbers when creating pages (for example, 102, 104, 106 or 205, 210, 215) so that if I have to add a page logically between two other pages, a sequential number is available. I also take this approach when assigning sequence numbers to items on a page; it makes reordering them a lot easier.

Once a test taker logs in, selects their name, and provides their password, they will navigate to page 102, where they can select the test they want to take. Because it is possible to return to a test that has already been begun, a process on the test selection page retrieves information from the database and populates some page items used for tracking, with the total number of questions, the current question's primary key, and the current question number. This process also does this for tests the taker has yet to start. If a test taker is only authorized a single test, the page to select a test is an unnecessary step.

In order to bypass this step, yet populate the necessary items, page 102 contains a branch that is evaluated before the header of the page. If the condition of the branch is met, page 102 is never displayed. The condition in the branch is of type PL/SQL Function Body Returning a Boolean. Not only does the body of the function determine whether the page needs to be bypassed, but, in the instance where it does need to be bypassed, it retrieves the information from the database and populates the tracking page items with the required information before returning true. This causes the page to navigate on to the next page where the questions are asked.

Another bit of functionality that is performed by the logic in the process and the logic in the branch is to see whether the test the user selected, or the only test they are authorized for, has been completed. If the user has previously answered all the questions for the selected test, a flag is set in a page item on the page that asks the questions (page 103) that indicates that the user is all done with the test. This flag will be used to bypass the questions and go directly to the results.

The page that asks the questions, page 103 (shown next), is made up of two regions. The top region is a SQL Query report region that selects the current question based on the test number and question number that are saved in the tracking page items. The second region is an HTML region, which contains the answers, the question count, and the Previous, Next, and Finish buttons.

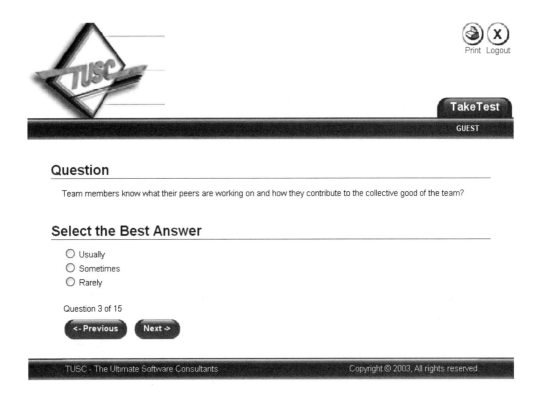

The answers are displayed as a single radio group based on the following query:

```
select answer, choice_letter
     from answers
     where question_no = NV('P102_CURRENT_QUESTION')
```

The question count is done in a display field assigned the following static value:

```
Question &P102_CUR_QUESTION_NO. of &P102_TOTAL_QUESTIONS
```

The buttons are displayed conditionally based on the values of the current question and total questions page items.

The same page is used for all the questions; it just navigates back to itself after saving the response to the current question. There are two processes on the page—one for when the Previous button is clicked and one for the Next or Finish button. The process for the Previous button resets the tracking items so that the page will query the previous question. The other process saves the response into the RESULTS table and checks to see if it was for the last question, in which case it sets a flag to indicate that the user is all done with the test. If this is not the last question, it sets the next values into the tracking page items.

Page 103 contains a before header branch that is conditional on the flag that indicates whether the test taker is all done with the test. Remember, this flag is set by the save process and was also set by page 102, where the taker selected the test to take if they had already answered all the questions. Because this is a before header branch, if the taker returns to a test they have already completed, they will branch past the questions page to the results page.

The test results page, page 104 (shown next), has several regions. The Test Results region is a simple SQL Query report. There is also a region for an HTML chart and one for an SVG chart. Finally, there is a small key region that provides information to help the user understand the graphs.

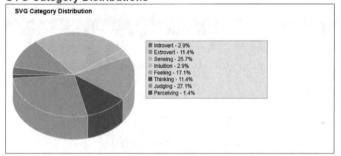

The Rating field in the test results report is a working link to an external website that provides more information on the personality rating. The link was embedded in the query for the report, as follows:

```
select '<a href="http://www.personalitypage.com/'||rating||
            '.html" target="NEW">'||rating||'</a>' rating,
         short_description, full_description
    from ratings
   where rating = v('P103_RESULTS')
     and test   = nv('P102_TEST_NO')
```

Similarly, links are embedded in the headings in the HTML chart as well as each piece of the pie in the SVG chart. The Key region is a static HTML region that contains the HTML to construct the table displayed within the region. All the regions are conditional based on which test the result page is being displayed for, because most of the tests implemented do not have the charts.

One of the tests that was added later did not fit very well into the model of a single set of answers for each question. This particular test had four responses for each question, but each of the responses had to be rated from 1 to 4, with none of the ratings being the same. In order to add this test into the application, some changes needed to be made. The path that the application took to ask the questions had to be routed to a different page. Once the questions are asked, the app will come back to the same results page.

Another before header branch was added to page 103, the questions page. This branch was conditional on the test being the new test and navigated the user through a different path for the questions to be asked.

Because the instructions for this test were not intuitive, an instruction page was put before the page that cycles through the questions. The instruction page, page 113 (shown next), provides detailed information about how the user is to take the test. The page is implemented as a series of HTML regions. The columns of radio buttons are four separate radio groups with the label defined above. The radio buttons actually function, but there is no process to support them. The Continue button navigates to the actual page that cycles through all the questions.

i Instructions

The Survey provides an opportunity for you to describe your unique strenghts and personl styles -- the actions that make you as successful as you are. The results describe your style and strengths when things are going well, and when you meet stress or conflict.

When Answering the Survey it is important to remember:

- The Survey is NOT a test--there are no right or wrong, good or bad answers.
- Think of yourself in one of the following settings: at work, with your family, as part of a specific group.
- Answer the questions to describe yourself as you are NOW--not how you would like to be, or how you used to be.

Directions

You will be given a descriptive statement, followed by four possible endings. You are to indicate the order in which you feel each ending applies to you. Each statement has a corresponding set of radio buttons. Select either 4, 3, 2 or 1 according to which ending is most like you(4) and least like you (1).

Example

Statement - Most of the time I am:

Response A - good-natured and helpful.
Response B - hard-working and full of ideas.
Response C - practical and careful.
Response D - charming and popular.

Order the responses

Select either 4, 3, 2 or 1 according to which ending is most like you(4) and least like you (1).

```
  A    B    C    D
 O 1  O 1  O 1  O 1
 O 2  O 2  O 2  O 2
 O 3  O 3  O 3  O 3
 O 4  O 4  O 4  O 4
```

DO NOT USE 4,3,2, or 1 MORE THAN ONCE.
If the statements that follow in this questionaire have two or more endings that seem equally like you, or are not like you at all, please rank them anyway, even though it may be difficult. Each ending must be ranked 4,3,2 or 1.

Continue

The new page that cycles through the questions, page 114 (shown in Figure 15-2), has four sections. The Statement section, like its counterpart on the original page, is a SQL Query report that queries from the QUESTIONS table. The template used for both this region and the next just provides a simple header.

The Responses section is also a SQL Query report with the following query:

```
select 'Response '||choice_letter||' - '||answer as answer
       from answers
       where question_no = NV('P102_CURRENT_QUESTION')
```

Notice that I am still referencing the tracking page items on page 102. Hindsight now tells me that it would have been better to define these "global variables" as application-level items.

FIGURE 15-2   *Multiresponse question page*

The Order the Responses section is just a plain HTML section containing items, but the formatting of the region holds a valuable tip. As the HTML DB engine renders an HTML region containing items, it creates a table in which it places the items. Generally the item labels are in one column of the table and the items are in another column. If you choose the No option in the Begin On New Line field of the Displayed section of an item, the HTML DB engine will add two more columns to the table.

The instructions are in the first item in this region, which is a static display text item that has no label. Therefore, the value of the item is placed in the second column of the table that will hold the region, making that column wide enough to fit all the text. The difficulty comes in trying to line up the four radio groups in nice close columns.

The second, third, and fourth radio groups are defined with the No option for the Begin On New Line field. All the radio groups are defined to display their label above the item, so each one would take up a single column. Therefore, the HTML DB engine would make the regions table four columns wide; however, the second column would be as wide as the instructions, so you end up with radio groups A, C, and D in narrow columns and radio group B centered in a wide column. Shown next is the Order the Responses section with the table cells outlined with the formatting as described. The outlining is done with a tool called Web Developer, which is discussed in Chapter 18.

Order the responses

Select either 4, 3, 2 or 1 according to which ending is most like you(4) and least like you (1).

A		B		C	D
○ 1				○ 1	○ 1
○ 2		○ 1		○ 2	○ 2
○ 3		○ 2		○ 3	○ 3
○ 4		○ 3		○ 4	○ 4
		○ 4			

In order to get around this formatting problem within regions, HTML DB provides a special item type: Stop and Start HTML Table (Displays label only). When you create an item through the wizard, this type is not one of the options. Simply create a Display Only type item and then edit the item, and in the Identification section on the edit page change the Display As field to Stop and Start HTML Table (Displays label only). This item stops the current HTML table that the engine is using to build the region and starts a new one. By placing an item of this type (with a blank label) between the instructions and the four radio groups, we get an outline of table cells as shown next.

Order the responses

Select either 4, 3, 2 or 1 according to which ending is <u>most like you(4)</u> and <u>least like you (1)</u>.

A	B	C	D
○ 1	○ 1	○ 1	○ 1
○ 2	○ 2	○ 2	○ 2
○ 3	○ 3	○ 3	○ 3
○ 4	○ 4	○ 4	○ 4

To handle the multiple radio groups, the page has validations that first check to see that every one of the radio groups has a value selected. Then it checks to see that none of the selections are the same. Like the other questions page, this one has two processes—one to save the responses and one to set the tracking page items to move back to a previous question. The page uses the same logic in setting an "all done" flag to trigger navigation to the results page.

Because the results of this test were placed in a different table, a decode statement was placed in the results queries that calls a function if the test is this special test.

Administrators' View of the World

Any user who logs in and is a member of the Test Admin group will see all the administrative tabs. If they are also a member of the Test Taker group, they will see the Take Test tab as well. The Admin Test tab provides access to the pages to create and modify tests, questions, and answers. The Applicants tab provides access to the pages to create and modify users and to assign them tests. The Reports tab provides access to the results of the test and even allows the user to drill down to see the response to the individual questions.

Administer Tests

There is nothing particularly out of the ordinary about the Administer Tests section of the application. The section is made up of a series of pages that are a hierarchical series of master detail pages:

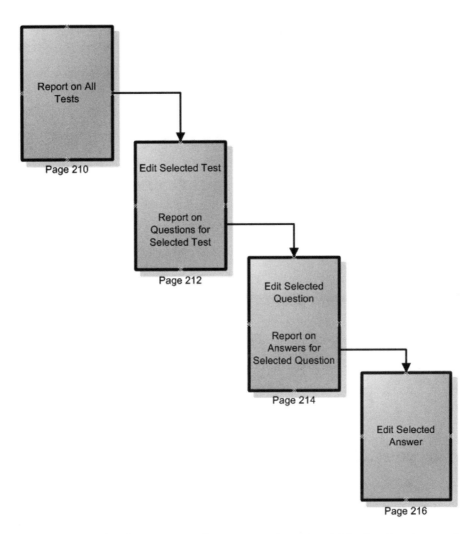

The pages were created with two trips to the page-creation wizard. The first time I created master detail pages with TESTS being the master table and QUESTIONS being the detail table. After following the wizard and selecting to create the edit page for QUESTIONS on a separate page, I ended up with all of page 210, all of page 212, and the QUESTIONS edit portion of page 214. I then returned to the page-creation wizard and created a two-page report and form on the ANSWERS table. Rather than creating two new pages, I specified to place the report on ANSWERS on page 212 and then created a new page (216) for the edit form. Within the wizard, you can specify a optional WHERE clause for the report on ANSWERS. I entered the following:

```
question_no = :P214_QUESTION_NO
```

This illustration shows part of what I ended up with.

Applicants
The Applicants section of the application is also a master detail series of pages on the PERSONS and PERSON_TESTS tables. I did something a little different with these. First, I created a two-page report and form on the PERSONS table. This gave me pages 500 and 501. For the Person Test section, shown here, I did something a little different.

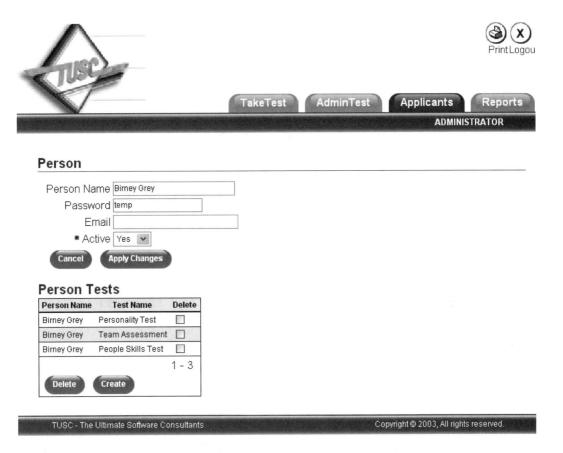

I created a SQL Query report with the following query:

```
select HTMLDB_ITEM.CHECKBOX(1,p.person_no||':'||t.test_no) " ",
          p.person_name, t.test_no, t.name test_name
       from person_tests pt, tests t, person p
      where pt.test_no    = t.test_no
        and pt.person_no = p.person_no
        and pt.person_no = :p500_person_no
```

I didn't do this to allow the user to delete more than one test at a time. Instead, it was really more of an opportunity to play with the HTMLDB_ITEM package. The check box was created with the HTMLDB_ITEM.CHECKBOX function, where I chose to include both person_no and the test_no in the value that's passed when the box is checked. To handle the deletions, I created a PL/SQL process with the following block of code:

```
begin
    for i in 1..HTMLDB_APPLICATION.G_F01.COUNT loop
        delete from person_tests
        where person_no = to_number(substr(HTMLDB_APPLICATION.G_F01(i),
                                    1,instr(HTMLDB_APPLICATION.G_F01(i),':')-1))
            and test_no = to_number(substr(HTMLDB_APPLICATION.G_F01(i),
                                    instr(HTMLDB_APPLICATION.G_F01(i),':')+1));
    end loop;
end;
```

This process uses one of the HTMLDB_APPLICATIONS.G_FXX functions to cycle through the array of values for the check boxes. Notice in the declaration of the check box that the first parameter is 1, which is the index for the item; the G_F01 function retrieves the values for the item with the index of 1.

Reports

The last piece of the administrative section of the application is the Reports section. The Reports section allows an administrative user to view a summary of test results with the ability to drill into more detail. The Reports section was also an experiment in embedding links in reports. The initial page, shown in Figure 15-3, contains a summary report of test results.

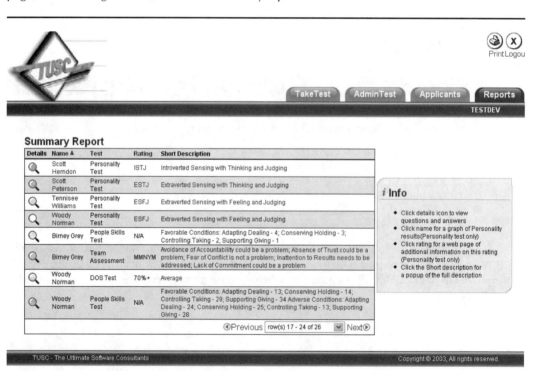

FIGURE 15-3 *Reports main page*

The icon on the left drills into a report that shows each question and all its answers, including the categories and an indicator marking the selection made by the user. The test taker's name and rating are active links only for the results of the personality test. The Name link drills into a chart that displays the distribution of answers in the different categories, whereas the Rating link opens up a new window and connects to an external website that has more information on the particular rating. Finally, the short description uses JavaScript to pop up a small window that displays the full description for the rating.

The two links that work only for the personality test are embedded in the query for the report. The following code snippet shows how this is accomplished using a decode statement:

```
select details, person_no, test_no,
            decode(name,
                   'Personality Test','<a href="f?p=&APP_ID.:303: &SES-
           SION.:::::P303_PERSON_NAME,P303_PERSON_NO,P303_TEST_NO:'||
           person_name||','||person_no||','||test_no||'">'||person_name||'</a>',
                   person_name )person_name,
               name, …
```

The Details icon and the Short Description link are implemented as links in the report's column attributes page. The short description is implemented with the following URL:

```
javascript:openPopUp('#TEST_NO#','#RATING#','#PERSON_NO#');
```

The following JavaScript function is placed in the HTML Header section of the page attributes:

```
<script language="JavaScript" type="text/javascript">
        function openPopUp(theTestNo, theRating, thePerson) {
            var targetUrl;
            targetUrl = f?p=&APP_ID.:302:::::
                        :P302_TEST_NO,P302_RATING,P302_PERSON_NO:'+
                        theTestNo+','+theRating+','+thePerson;
                        win=open(targetUrl,"ratingDet","Scrollbars=1,
                        resizable=1,width=500,height=500");
            if (win.opener == null)
               win.opener = self;
            win.focus();
        }
    </script>
```

As we walked through the testing application, hopefully you learned some valuable lessons on using some of the techniques covered in previous chapters. Looking through the implementation of applications is a great way to learn more about HTML DB. Invest the time to install and look through the sample applications that come with HTML DB. Additionally the Oracle HTML DB Studio (http://htmldb.oracle.com/pls/otn/f?p=18326) contains many applications, submitted by users, available for download and your perusal.

PART
V

Security and Administration

CHAPTER
16

Security

ecurity for any web-based application is a huge topic in and of itself. In fact, entire books have been written on the subject. This chapter will discuss some of the available security options for an HTML DB application. It does not cover security configurations such as firewall placement. It does not cover securing your application server. Some of these security topics are discussed on Oracle's marketing website in the "How To" section. The topics discussed in this chapter include the following:

- Authentication

- Authorization

- Session state protection

- Editing security attributes

- Login page

Authentication

Application authentication is where the application checks a user's identity prior to allowing access to the application. Authentication is an all-or-none situation—either users have access to the application or they don't. Which components users have access to within the application is called *authorization*. Authorization is discussed in detail later in this chapter.

Within HTML DB, several different authentication methods are available for your use. Although not required, application authentication typically asks a user to provide a username and password to access the application. Biometric authentication may only require a retinal scan or a fingerprint to identify the user.

HTML DB allows you to keep track of each user's application access by setting the value of the built-in APP_USER substitution string. As users (and developers) navigate throughout your application, HTML DB tracks each click.

No Authentication

When creating an application, you first must determine whether to include authentication. During the Create Application Wizard, shown in Figure 16-1, you can choose to not require authentication. When you choose this option, HTML DB does not check any user credentials. All pages of your application are accessible to all users. Within an HTML DB application, you can turn off all authentication requirements. This topic is discussed in detail in the "How To" section of Oracle's marketing website at http://www.oracle.com/technology/products/database/htmldb/howtos/index. html. The paper is titled "Make an HTML DB application public."

Built-in Authentication Schemes

When you create an authentication scheme, you can choose from a number of preconfigured HTML DB authentication schemes. You can also copy an existing authentication scheme, or you can create your own custom authentication scheme.

HTML DB Built-in Authentication

HTML DB's built-in authentication method uses its own tables to store authentication and authorization information. The user accounts used with the HTML DB built-in authentication scheme

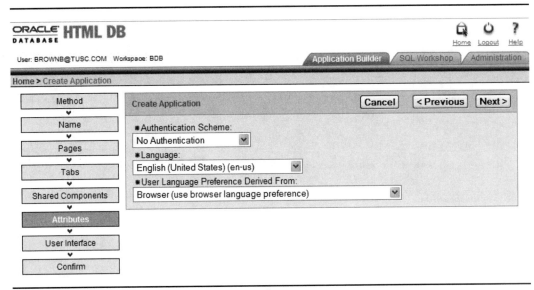

FIGURE 16-1 *Create Application with No Authentication*

are the built-in HTML DB users that are created in a workspace. See the beginning of Chapter 17 for a good discussion of the different types of workspace users. The built-in authentication method is a very effective authentication method for most applications. It is most effective for applications that have a limited number of users and companies that don't have an existing authentication scheme.

Authentication schemes (typically login IDs and passwords) and authorization schemes (what you have access to within the application) for the application are maintained in the Shared Components section of the application. The Authentication Schemes section, shown in Figure 16-2, allows you to change your authentication scheme for your application.

Workspace developers cannot add users to the application; instead, only workspace administrators can add users and groups—user administration can also be done through the INTERNAL workspace. Users can be application users, developers, or administrators, or you can place them into your own groups. For more information on managing users, refer to the "Manage HTML DB Users" section of Chapter 17. Figure 16-3 shows the HTML DB workspace home page with the Administration option and the Manage HTML DB Users option open. From this menu, you can do the following:

- Manage existing HTML DB workspace users

- Create new developers for the workspace

- Create new workspace administrators

- Create new end users

- Edit existing HTML DB user groups

- Create new HTML DB user groups

- Manage user-to-group assignments

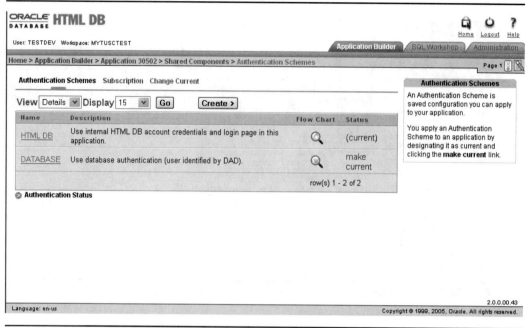

FIGURE 16-2 *Application Shared Components—Authentication Schemes*

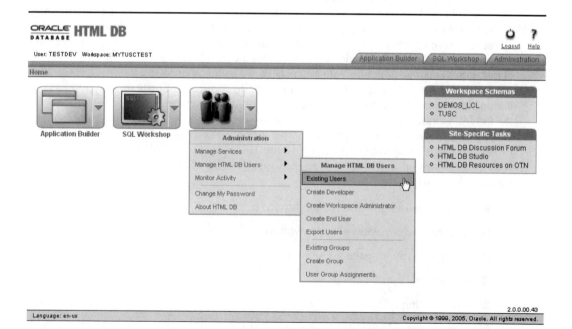

FIGURE 16-3 *Manage HTML DB Users menu*

To assign a user to one or more groups, select Existing Users under the Manage HTML DB Users menu. As shown in Figure 16-4, you can add a user to one or more groups in the User Groups section.

HTML DB built-in authentication uses these user accounts (also known as "cookie user" accounts) created and managed in the Oracle HTML DB user repository. Workspace developers can develop new applications in a workspace, and workspace administrators can create and edit user accounts using the Manage Users page. HTML DB built-in authentication is a good solution in the following situations:

- You want control of the user account repository.

- A username and password–based approach to security is sufficient.

- You do not need to integrate into a Single Sign-On or other authentication framework.

- You do not have another authentication scheme.

- You have a limited number of application user accounts.

- You need to get a group of users up and running on a new application quickly.

Database Authentication

The PL/SQL module of Oracle's Application Server, which HTML DB runs on, uses database authentication. The PL/SQL module uses database access descriptors (DAD) to define the username, password, and SQL*Net connection to log into an Oracle database and schema. The application server's URL includes the DAD. In the URL http://localhost/pls/htmldb, *http* stands for the Hypertext

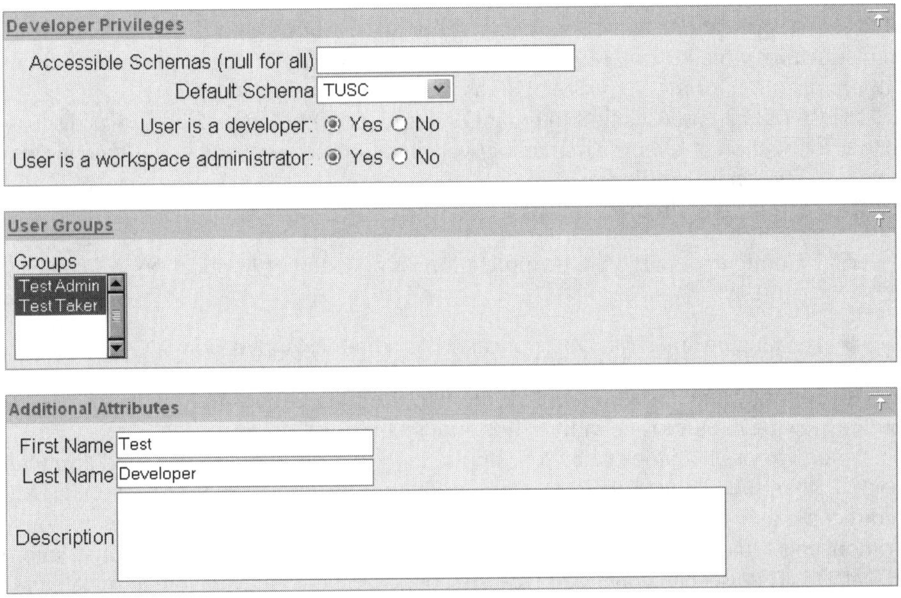

FIGURE 16-4 *Assigning a user to one or more groups*

Transfer Protocol, *localhost* is the name of the machine running the application server, *pls* stands for the PL/SQL module, and *htmldb* references the htmldb DAD.

The htmldb DAD stores a username and password to use for authenticating to (logging into) the database. To use database authentication (that is, to require that users specify a valid database username and password before entering an HTML DB application), you can create a DAD that does not store the database username and password. The application server will then prompt the user for their database username and password.

Here's what must happen to use database credentials for authentication:

- Each application user must have a user account in the Oracle database.

- You must configure a PL/SQL DAD for basic authentication (without storing the account information).

Application users will be prompted for a database username/password (that is, schema) for their browser session. The username is then made available in the APP_USER substitution variable. Database authentication is useful in the following situations:

- You wish to implement an authentication method that requires minimal setup for a manageable number of users.

- Every user already has a database username and password.

The main drawback of database authentication is the burden of database account maintenance, especially if users do not administer their own passwords, or if their database accounts exist only to facilitate authentication to your application. Your DBA may not be happy with this approach.

Oracle Internet Directory Authentication

HTML DB applications can operate as partner applications with the Single Sign-On (SSO) infrastructure, which uses Oracle Internet Directory (OID). To accomplish this, you must register your application (or register HTML DB) as the partner application.

HTML DB can use Oracle's Internet Directory (OID) or Single Sign-On as discussed in the "How To" section of Oracle's marketing website at http://www.oracle.com/technology/products/database/htmldb/howtos/index.html.

Two papers exist on this subject:

- "Configure an HTML DB Application As an External Application in Oracle AS Single Sign-On"

- "Configure an HTML DB Application As a Partner Application in Oracle AS Single Sign-On"

Additionally, there is a tip labeled "How to use OID Groups to Manage HTML DB Security" on the HTML DB Studio site in the "Tips and Techniques" section.

If you choose this approach, your application will not use an integrated application login page. Rather, when a user accesses your application in a new browser session, HTML DB will redirect the user to the Single Sign-On login page. After the user is authenticated by SSO, the SSO components redirect back to your application, passing the user identity and other information to HTML DB. The user can continue to use the application until they log off, terminate their browser session, or until some other session-terminating event occurs.

Microsoft Active Directory and Other LDAP Authentication

Any Lightweight Directory Access Protocol (LDAP) server can be used for HTML DB authentication. The authentication scheme's login page will use LDAP to verify the username and password submitted on the login page. As shown in Figure 16-5, under the Shared Components section of your application, HTML DB allows you to configure your LDAP host, port, distinguished name, and option parameters. These wizards assume that an LDAP directory accessible to your application for authentication already exists and that it can respond to a SIMPLE_BIND_S call for credentials verification. This option is discussed in detail at http://www.oracle.com/technology/products/database/htmldb/howtos/how_to_ldap_authenticate.html.

Custom Authentication

HTML DB allows you to use an existing authentication scheme or create your own custom authentication scheme. This is useful if you already have a function that can be used for authentication or if you wish to base your authentication on data (such as username and password) that already exists in your database.

Creating a custom authentication scheme provides you with complete control over your authentication interface, but may be reinventing the wheel. First consider using an existing or built-in authentication scheme. To implement a custom authentication scheme, you must provide a PL/SQL function that HTML DB will execute before processing each page request. This function's Boolean return value determines whether HTML DB processes the page normally or displays a failure (denied access) page.

HTML DB provides a wizard to assist you in creating a custom authentication scheme. To start the wizard, go to the Shared Components section for your application and click on the Authentication Schemes link under the Security section. This navigates you to the Authentication Schemes page, shown earlier in Figure 16-2. Start the wizard by clicking on the Create button.

The wizard is used to create both custom authentication schemes and the preconfigured schemes discussed earlier or to create a scheme as a copy of an existing scheme. In the first step of the wizard, you select which one of the methods you will use. For a custom authentication scheme, select the From Scratch radio button.

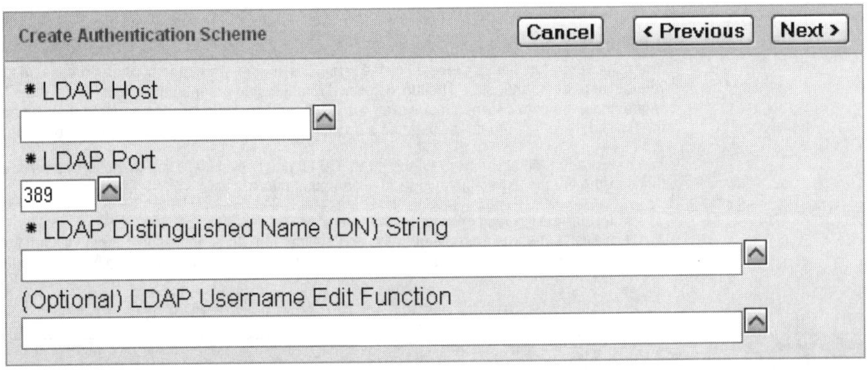

FIGURE 16-5   *LDAP configuration*

The next step in the wizard allows you to name the custom scheme and provide a description. The following step, shown in Figure 16-6, is where you will specify your sentry function. The sentry function controls access to each page; it is called prior to every page in the application. It is used to verify that the user has logged on and has a valid session. You may write your own, or you may utilize the built-in page sentry logic by leaving this field blank. The latter option is highly recommended unless you like reinventing the wheel.

Each of the next steps in the wizard is similar to the previous one. As you can see in Figure 16-6, each page provides you with fairly detailed information about each piece of the authentication scheme and how you may customize it. The following table provides insight into each piece of the authentication scheme:

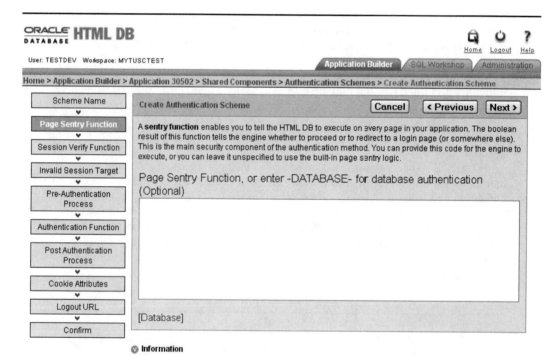

FIGURE 16-6 *Authentication Scheme Wizard's Sentry function*

Scheme Item	Comments
Sentry Function	The Sentry function returns a Boolean and is used prior to every page in the application to determine whether to proceed or redirect elsewhere. The default functionality of this function automatically calls the next item. Recommend use of built-in logic.
Session Verify Function	The purpose of this function is to verity that a valid session exists. You may write your own function here and still use the built-in sentry logic. It is recommended that you use the built in logic here as well unless you need to use multiple cookies.
Invalid Session Target	This is where you specify the target for when the Sentry function fails. Options include a built-in logon page, a page in the application, a URL, a Single Sign-On server, and none.
Pre-Authentication Process	Code that will be executed prior to validating user credentials during the processing of the submitted login page. You might set cookies or create audit records with this process.
Authentication Function	This function, which must accept a username and password as parameters and return a Boolean result, is used to validate a user's logon credentials. This is the function most typically customized. This function allows you to use your own table for users and passwords and not have to create users within HTML DB for each of your application users.
Post-Authentication Process	Code that will be executed after validating user credentials. You can set more cookies, create audit records, or redirect.
Cookie Attributes	Used to specify standard cookie attributes, including Cookie Name, Cookie Path, and Cookie Domain.
Logout URL	Specifies the URL to navigate to upon user logout.

Authentication Scheme Functions

When entering functions into the wizard, you can type the function's syntax into the page or you can call a prewritten function. The function can be standalone or in a package. For some functions you can pass parameters, such as the application username (that is, APP_USER), password, application number, and more, into the function, although some expect a specific signature.

Sample authentication schemes (that is, functions) are discussed here. These include the following:

- Simple authentication functions based on an existing member table

- Role-based authentication

- Java-based security authentication integration

- Authenticate against Oracle eBusiness Suite User Repository

Simple Authentication Functions Based on an Existing Member Table   Authentication
functions return a Boolean value. If the value returned is true, the user will be allowed to access
your application. If the value returned is false, the user will not have access to the application. In
Chapter 14, the application discussed uses a custom authentication scheme. The Sentry function
call looks like this:

```
return check_login(:p101_username, :p101_password);
```

The standalone check_login function contains the following code:

```
function check_login (p_username in varchar2, p_password in varchar2)
      return boolean
      is
      cursor member_cur (in_username varchar2, in_password varchar2) is
         select org_no
         from    member m, member_email me
         where   m.member_no               = me.member_no
         and     lower(me.EMAIL_ADDRESS) = lower(in_username)
         and     lower(m.PASSWORD)        = lower(in_password);
      begin
          if p_username is null then
               return false;
          end if;

          for member_rec in member_cur (p_username, p_password) loop
             return true;
          end loop;
       return false;
       end;
       /
```

A process is defined on the login page (page 101) that sets a number of page variables for use
in limited data throughout the application. This process contains the following code:

```
begin
          :p2_username              := :p101_username;
          :p2_password              := :p101_password;
          :p2_in_org_no             := get_default_org(:p2_username);
          :p2_in_member_no          := get_default_member(:p2_username);
          :p2_real_member_no        := get_real_member(:p2_username);
          :p2_save_member_no        := :p2_in_member_no;
          :p2_in_sub_member_no      := get_default_sub_member(:p2_username);
          :p2_save_sub_member_no := :p2_in_sub_member_no;

          wwv_flow_custom_auth_std.login(
           P_UNAME       => :P101_USERNAME,
           P_PASSWORD    => :P101_PASSWORD,
           P_SESSION_ID  => :FLOW_SESSION,
           P_FLOW_PAGE   => :FLOW_ID || ':1'
           );
       end;
```

Role-based Authentication   Another, more complex approach, discussed here, provides for an authorization function based on users and roles. You can apply it to all your applications (at the application level or lower if necessary). This will ensure that only authorized users can use a given application.

For example, your authorization function might look like this:

```
return authorize_user(:APP_ID,:APP_USER);
```

This calls the authorize_user function, which is defined as follows:

```
CREATE OR REPLACE FUNCTION authorize_user (
        app_id_in     IN   PLS_INTEGER,
        username_in   IN   VARCHAR2
    )
    RETURN BOOLEAN
IS
    CURSOR app_cur (app_id_p PLS_INTEGER, user_p VARCHAR2)
    IS
        SELECT DISTINCT wa.web_application_num
                FROM web_users wu,
                     web_user_roles wur,
                     web_roles wr,
                     web_application_roles war,
                     web_applications wa
               WHERE wu.web_user_num = wur.web_user_num
                 AND wur.web_role_num = wr.web_role_num
                 AND wr.web_role_num = war.web_role_num
                 AND war.web_application_num = wa.web_application_num
                 AND UPPER (wu.username) = user_p

                 AND wa.app_id = app_id_p;
    result_v    BOOLEAN := FALSE;
BEGIN
    FOR app_rec IN app_cur (app_id_in, username_in)
    LOOP
        result_v := TRUE;
    END LOOP;
    RETURN result_v;
END authorize_user;
/
```

Java-based Security Authentication Integration   If the integration with a technology doesn't work as you need it to, keep in mind that you can write a Java program that communicates directly with your underlying protocol. Using a Java stored procedure, you can integrate the Java-based security method with HTML DB authentication.

Authenticate Against Oracle eBusiness Suite User Repository   You can find a complete tip on how to create a custom authentication scheme for the eBusiness Suite User Repository at the

HTML DB Studio site: http://htmldb.oracle.com/pls/otn/f?p=18326:54:17407967622871653405:::
:P54_ID:621.

Viewing Authentication Reports

HTML DB allows you to view a list of users who have accessed your application. Clicking on Top
Views and By User will show you a list of users who have authenticated within the time period
specified (up to one year ago).

Authorization

Implementing an authorization scheme extends the security of your application's authentication
scheme. You can specify an authorization scheme for an entire application, a page (see the "Edit
Security Attributes" section, later in this chapter), or a specific control (such as a region), or a control
such as an item or button. For example, using an authorization scheme you could selectively
determine which tabs, regions, or navigation buttons a user sees.

Like authentication, an authorization scheme either succeeds or fails, but for a component
rather than for access to the application. You could use the same table in the database for both
functions if you wish. If your component-level authorization scheme succeeds, the user can view
the component or control. If the scheme fails, the user cannot view the component or control. If
an application- or page-level authorization scheme fails, then Oracle HTML DB displays your
authentication failure message.

Each authorization scheme is given a unique name. You can have zero to many authorization
schemes for your application. Once an authorization scheme is defined, you can attach it to any
component or control in your application. To attach an authorization scheme to a component or
control in your application, simply navigate to the appropriate attributes page and select an
authorization scheme from the Authorization Scheme list, as shown here:

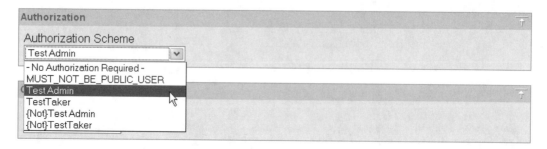

Once authenticated, users will either have access to the entire application or to specific
components within the application. If users only have access to specific components, this is
called *authorization*. HTML DB supports any number of authorization methods.

You can create a generic authorization for your application. If you do not create an application-
level authorization scheme, you can still authorize individual pages, regions, components, or
controls in your application.

Authorization schemes can be created at the application level by clicking on Authorization in
the Security section of the application's Shared Components section. This will bring up the Edit
Authorization Scheme page shown in Figure 16-7.

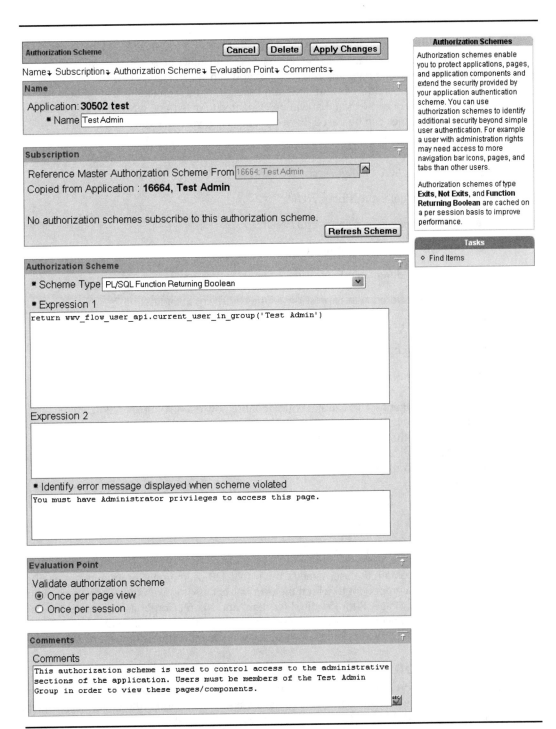

FIGURE 16-7 *Edit Authorization Scheme page*

When you create an authorization, you can create it as a copy of an authorization from another application. When you do this, you may also choose to subscribe to that authorization. This way, if there are any changes to the original, they can either be pushed down from the original or pulled from the subscribing authorization, as you can see in Figure 16-7.

The Scheme Type field in the Authorization section of the Edit Authorization Scheme page determines the type of expression that will be evaluated to determine whether a user is authorized. Authorization schemes can be based off of the following types of expressions:

- Exists SQL Query
- NOT Exists SQL Query
- Item in (page) Expression is NULL
- Item in (page) Expression is NOT NULL
- PL/SQL Function Returning Boolean
- Value of Preference in Expression 1 Equals Expression 2
- Value of Preference in Expression 1 Does NOT Equal Expression 2
- Value of Item in Expression 1 Equals Expression 2
- Value of Item in Expression 1 Does NOT Equal Expression 2

There is also a field where you can specify an error message that will be displayed when the scheme is violated.

The Evaluation Point section allows you to control how often your expression will be evaluated. The expressions can be evaluated once for a session (that is, if the expression results will not change throughout the session) or once per page view.

A sample authorization table and query follows. First, a table is created in the schema to support our authorization scheme:

```
CREATE TABLE htmldb_authorization (
    app_user        VARCHAR2(30),
    component_type  VARCHAR2(1),
    component_name  VARCHAR2(30),
    privilege       VARCHAR2(1));
```

App_user will contain the username of the HTML DB username. Component_type will contain the type of component to which the user has access (for example, A for Application/Authentication, P for Page, R for Region, I for Item, and so on). Component_name is the name of the component referenced. Privilege will contain additional information about the component access (for example, D means denied, F means full, A means Administrative, and so on).

Authorization Levels

Each page allows you to select an authorization scheme that should be used (for example, if your application supports multiple authentication schemes). Each region, button, and item on a page supports conditional display logic, which could be used for authorization of a component's display. Each component also allows you to set the authorization scheme used.

Application-level Authorization

The application-level (which is really page-level on every page) authorization schema "Exists" SQL query would look like this:

```
Select 'x'
from    htmldb_authorization
where   app_user        = :app_user
and     component_type = 'P'
and     component_name = :app_page_id
and     privilege       != 'D'
```

Page-level Authorization

Page-level authorization allows you to specify a different authorization scheme on a page-by-page basis. If your application doesn't have an application-level authorization scheme, but you want a specific page to be authorized for use, you could specify the same query as the one in the preceding section. If the page is an update page (that is, it requires special privileges of "U"), your query might look like this:

```
Select 'x'
from    htmldb_authorization
where   app_user        = :app_user
and     component_type = 'P'
and     component_name = :app_page_id
and     privilege       = 'U'
```

Component/Control-level Authorization

Component- or control-level authorization provides the same functionality as application- or page-level authorization, but at a component or control level. For example, a region could be considered a component. Your "Exists" SQL query might look like this:

```
Select 'x'
from    htmldb_authorization
where   app_user        = :app_user
and     component_type = 'R'
and     component_name = 'Bottled Water Count'
and     privilege       = 'U'
```

You might have a Delete button on a page. This control might only be available to users with the "A" (active) privilege, as shown in this query:

```
Select 'x'
from    htmldb_authorization
where   app_user        = :app_user
and     component_type = 'B'
and     component_name = 'DELETE'
and     privilege       = 'A'
```

This authorization level could be placed on all Delete buttons.

Component/Control-level Conditional Display

Component- or control-level conditional display can also be used. An item on a page, such as a column in a select region ("S") of a report, could be displayed only if the user has "S" (select) privileges for the Salary column, as shown in this query:

```
Select 'x'
from    htmldb_authorization
where   app_user       = :app_user
and     component_type = 'S'
and     component_name = 'SALARY'
and     privilege      = 'S'
```

Users without this privilege would not see the Salary column.

Adding User Authorizations

Based on your authorization scheme that you decide to use, you'll need to develop an application that allows you to maintain your authorization table. This would be an easy HTML DB application for you to build.

Session State Protection

Deep linking refers to the ability to link to an Oracle HTML DB page out of context (for example, from a hyperlink in an e-mail or workflow notification). When you link to a page out of context and the application requires user authentication, the user will be taken to the login page. After authentication, HTML DB automatically displays the page that was referenced in the original link. Deep linking is supported for applications that use authentication schemes.

As of Version 2, *Session State Protection* refers to your ability to turn off or secure the ability to link to the following:

- Page level

- Item level

- Application item level

Page Level

You can set Page Access Protection attributes for all pages in your applications. Select a specific page in order to query or set page and item session state protections attributes on that page. At the page level, you can protect the session state through the following techniques:

- Forcing the arguments to have a correct checksum value.

- Not allowing any arguments.

- Not providing any URL access to the page.

- Providing unrestricted access (that is, deep linking). This is the default mode.

Item Level

At the item level, you can protect data-entry items or display-only items by doing the following:

- Requiring a checksum at the application level.

- Requiring a checksum at the user level.

- Requiring a checksum at the session level.

- Providing unrestricted access (that is, deep linking). This is the default mode.

Application Item Level

Application-level items are used to maintain session state in your application. Application items can be set using computations or processes, or by passing values on a URL. You can use On New Instance computations to set the value of items once for a session. Application items are used to maintain session state that is not displayed and is not specific to any one page. You can protect application items by doing the following:

- Providing restricted access (the state may not be set from the browser).

- Providing unrestricted access (that is, deep linking). This is the default mode.

Edit Security Attributes

Under the Security section of the Shared Components section for your application, you will find the Edit Security Attributes link. This page, shown in Figure 16-8, allows you to set applicationwide security settings. On this page, you can establish the home link (specifies a URL or procedure that should be run when you run the application), the login URL, and the public user (that is, what APP_USER will be set to if the user is not logged into the application). Your authentication and authorization schemes and parsing schema may be set here. Note that the authorization scheme set here is applicationwide and applies to requests for all pages. Session state protection can be enabled and disabled here, and you can set the Virtual Private Database (VPD) PL/SQL call to set the security context for a VPD.

Login Page

You have full control over your application's login page. When you create a new application in HTML DB, a login page is automatically created as page 101. By default, the alias for the page is 'LOGIN'. As you can see in the previous examples, the login page is constructed with processes that call the HTML DB login API to perform credentials verification and session registration.

You can also build your own login pages using the prebuilt pages as models. From there, you have the ability to tailor all of the user interface and processing logic for your authentication and authorization requirements.

If you click on Create Page within your application, you'll see that "Login Page" is one of the predefined page types that HTML DB's wizards will create for you. The wizard will ask you for the page number, name of the login page, the template to be used, the label for the username and password fields, the page to branch to upon a successful login, whether to save the username in a

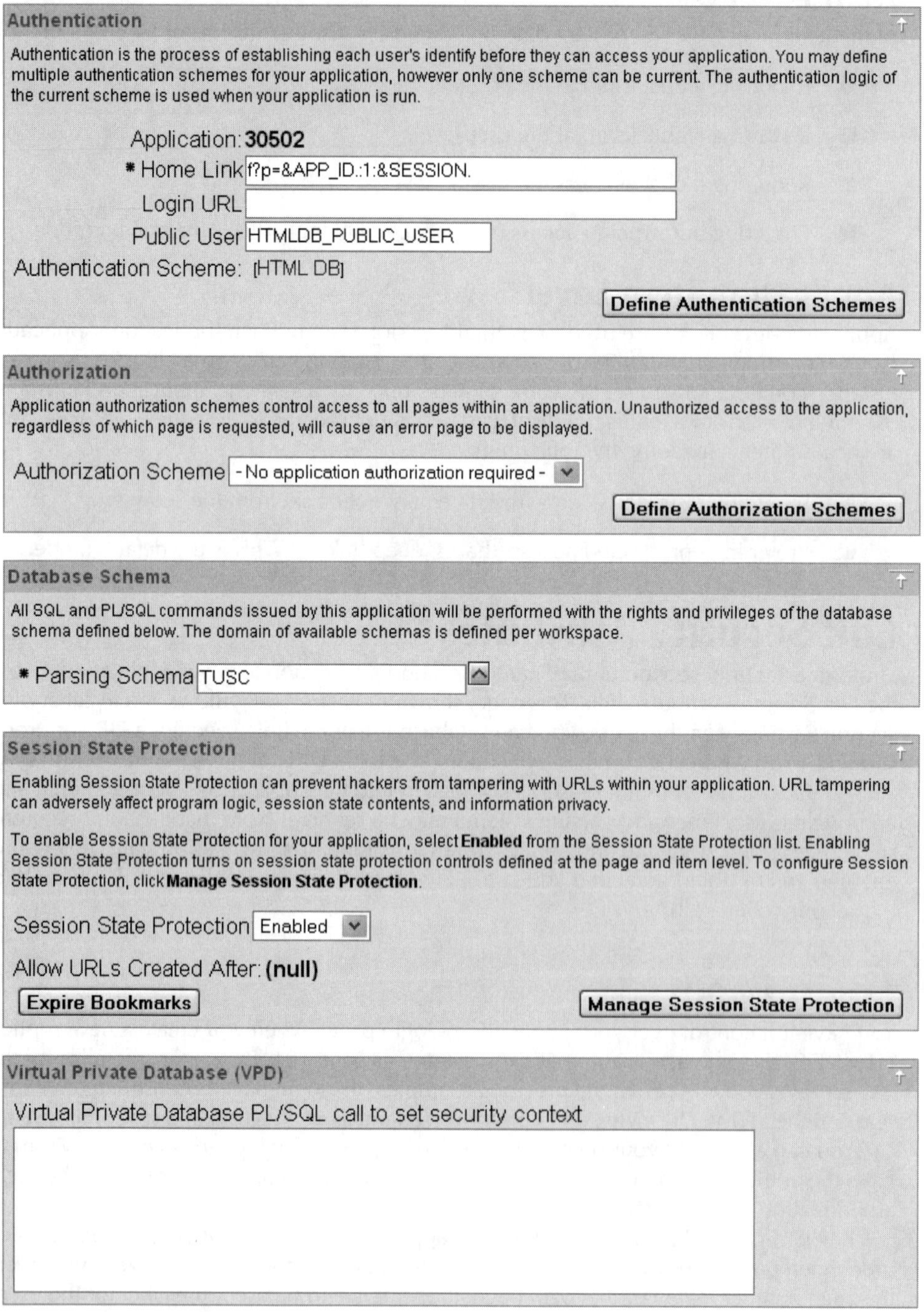

Authentication

Authentication is the process of establishing each user's identify before they can access your application. You may define multiple authentication schemes for your application, however only one scheme can be current. The authentication logic of the current scheme is used when your application is run.

Application: **30502**

* Home Link `f?p=&APP_ID.:1:&SESSION.`

Login URL

Public User `HTMLDB_PUBLIC_USER`

Authentication Scheme: [HTML DB]

Define Authentication Schemes

Authorization

Application authorization schemes control access to all pages within an application. Unauthorized access to the application, regardless of which page is requested, will cause an error page to be displayed.

Authorization Scheme | - No application authorization required - ∨ |

Define Authorization Schemes

Database Schema

All SQL and PL/SQL commands issued by this application will be performed with the rights and privileges of the database schema defined below. The domain of available schemas is defined per workspace.

* Parsing Schema `TUSC`

Session State Protection

Enabling Session State Protection can prevent hackers from tampering with URLs within your application. URL tampering can adversely affect program logic, session state contents, and information privacy.

To enable Session State Protection for your application, select **Enabled** from the Session State Protection list. Enabling Session State Protection turns on session state protection controls defined at the page and item level. To configure Session State Protection, click **Manage Session State Protection**.

Session State Protection `Enabled ∨`

Allow URLs Created After: **(null)**

Expire Bookmarks   **Manage Session State Protection**

Virtual Private Database (VPD)

Virtual Private Database PL/SQL call to set security context

FIGURE 16-8   *Edit Security Attributes page*

cookie (so that the browser remembers this next time the user logs in), and whether to set the new page as the application login page at this point in time.

As you can see from this chapter, the security options available in HTML DB are limitless. Authentication and authorization give you the power to control who has access to your applications and what they have access to. By controlling your login page, you have the ability to control exactly what users are prompted for to log in.

CHAPTER
17

Administration Functions

hen you talk about administration in HTML DB, two distinct areas must be addressed: internal administration of the entire HTML DB instance and administration within a workspace. Internal administrators manage workspaces and their resources, manage application developers, and monitor resources and activities. Workspace administrators manage workspace users and groups, monitor activity, and manage development services. In this chapter, we will address the different administrative functions throughout the HTML DB environment.

Understanding Users and Administrative Roles

To understand administrators, it is helpful to understand users and the different types of users within HTML DB. The HTML DB environment has a repository of users, which it uses to authenticate user credentials for various pieces of the HTML DB environment (SQL Workshop, Data Workshop, Application Builder, Internal Administration). Keep in mind that the HTML DB environment is itself an HTML DB application. Just as it uses the user account repository to authenticate users, so can any other HTML DB application you develop. The four distinct types of users within HTML DB are listed here in descending order of authority:

- HTML DB instance administrators

- Workspace administrators

- Application Developers

- Application users

An HTML DB instance administrator is created when an HTML DB instance is installed. To log on as the instance administrator, you can use the URL http://server:port/pls/htmldb/htmldb_admin and provide the administrator's username and password, or you can go to the normal login page and enter **INTERNAL** for the workspace and provide the administrator's username and password. Once logged on as the internal administrator, you can create workspaces and users for those workspaces. As you will see later in this chapter, when you create a workspace user, you can assign that user to be an administrator and a developer, just a developer, or neither. That is how each of the other types of users are created.

Instance administrators can only log into the INTERNAL workspace and can only do internal administration tasks, including creating any user. Recall that the instance administrator's username is ADMIN and the password was set (and should have been noted) during installation (see Chapter 2). Workspace administrators can only log into the workspace under which they were created. They can do all workspace administration tasks including creating users for their workspace as well as all developer tasks. They can also log into any workspace application that does not implement special authentication. Developers can do a few limited administration tasks and all development tasks as well as log into any workspace application that does not implement special authentication. Naturally, application users can log into any workspace application that does not implement special authentication. Additionally, they can log into the workspace under which they were created, but the only action available to them is to change their own password.

Internal Administrator Functions

Once the internal administrator has logged in by one of the methods stated previously, they will see the HTML DB Administration page, shown in Figure 17-1. The page divides tasks into four main groups: Manage Service, Manage Workspaces, Manage Applications, and Monitor Activity. Each of these navigation icons has a drop-down menu for all the options under each category. You can either select from the drop-down menu or click on the navigation icon to go to a page where all the menu options are listed. Although this looks like a whole lot of different tasks available to the administrator, the reality is that the majority of the links provide nothing more than a report. This is not to diminish the reports, because they can provide you with some very useful information about your HTML DB environment. But when it comes to actually doing something, there are only a few tasks that an internal administrator can perform.

Monitor Activity

All the links in the Monitor Activity section of the HTML DB Administration page are links to reports or charts. The link titles are fairly descriptive of their corresponding reports. These reports allow you to see details about developer and user activities on applications.

Manage Applications

The Build Status option under Manage Applications navigates to a report page that reports on and allows you to change the build status of any application to either Run and Build Application or only Run Application. The Application Attributes link navigates to a report with a few details about all instance applications. The report lists applications by workspace, detailing application name, number, language, number of pages, parse schema, and when it was last updated. The

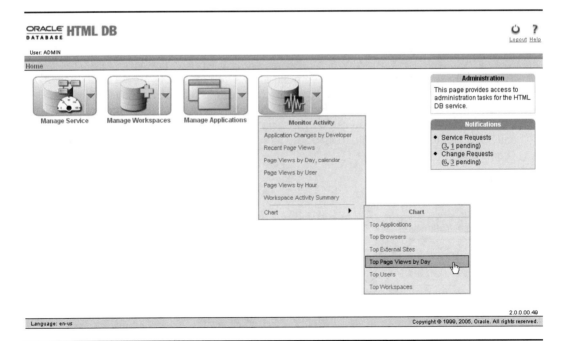

FIGURE 17-1 *HTML DB Administration page*

Parse As Schemas option is just that—a report about the schemas and the applications that are parsed with them.

Manage Workspaces

This section contains the majority of actual tasks that can be performed by an internal administrator (aside from managing users, the rest of the tasks deal with workspaces). Workspaces are the containers for applications and associated users and developers.

Create New Workspace

Before any applications can be created, you must first create a workspace. The Create Workspace link, available from the drop-down menu of the Manage Workspaces icon (shown earlier in Figure 17-1), navigates you to the first page of the Provision Workspace Wizard, shown next. Here you enter a unique name and description for the new workspace. Click on Next to navigate to the next step in the wizard.

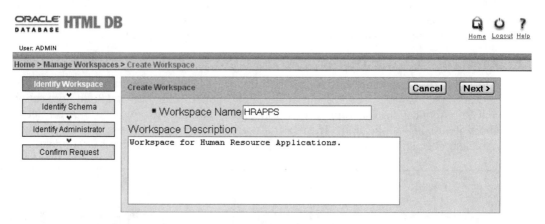

The second step in the wizard, shown next, allows you to specify the schema that will be associated with the workspace. You can utilize an existing schema and select it from the list of values, or you can specify a name for a new schema along with its password and the database space quota. At this point, you can only associate one schema with the new workspace. However, after it is created, it is possible to associate more schemas with the workspace. Click on Next to continue.

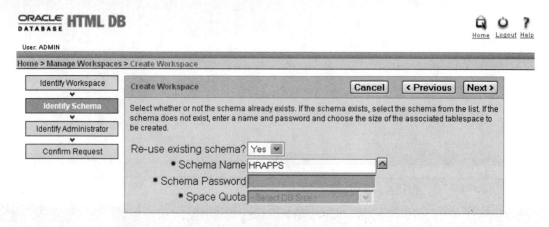

In the third step of the wizard, you specify information about the workspace administrator user, as shown next. The username for the administrator does not have to be unique to the HTML DB environment. In fact, it will be defaulted to the same administrator username and password that were entered during the creation of the HTML DB instance. It is possible to create the same user in multiple workspaces with the same password. Although it will seem like the same user, it will actually be two different users. Therefore, if the password is changed in one workspace, it will not be changed in the other. You can also specify a first and last name for the administrator. You must also enter a valid e-mail address. This address will be used for automated responses to resource requests from the workspace administrator.

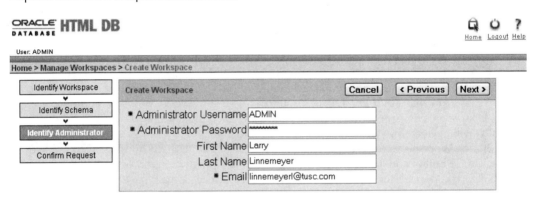

The final step in the wizard is the confirmation page, shown next. This is the final opportunity to review the information provided before proceeding with the provisioning of the workspace. After clicking on the Provision button and successful provisioning of the workspace, you will be presented with a success message.

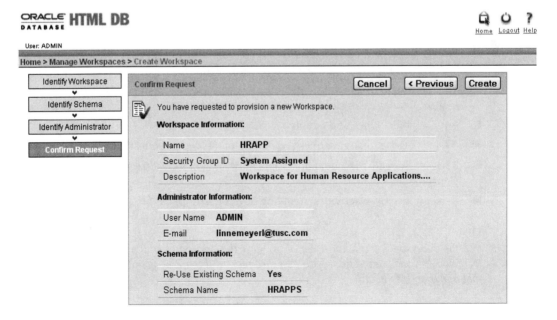

Import and Export Workspaces

The Import and Export menu options under Manage Workspaces allow you to move a workspace from one HTML DB instance to another. Exporting a workspace creates a text file that contains information about the workspace and its users and groups. Workspace exports do not include applications, images, files, or schemas. Although it is not necessary to move an application to the same workspace in a different HTML DB instance, it will make things easier if the application uses groups.

Manage Workspace and Report Workspace Attributes

The Existing Workspace and the Workspace Details menu options under the Manage Workspaces icon end up at the same final destination—the Workspace Utilization Report. The Existing Workspace link takes you there through a simple report. This report allows you to search for a workspace should your environment grow so large that this is necessary. The report lists all your workspaces with the number of users, developers, and applications, along with the provision status and date. Also, a couple navigational items take you to the other sections described; the Create Workspace button navigates you to Create New Workspace, and another for each workspace navigates you to Remove Workspace. Each listed workspace's name is an active link that will navigate you to the Workspace Detail Report.

The Workspace Detail Report menu option takes you to the Workspace Details page, which has a Go button and a single LOV for selecting the workspace upon which you want to report. Select a workspace and then click on Go for the Workspace Details page for the selected workspace. The page contains the following information for the selected workspace:

- Workspace attributes with a link to edit these attributes

- A list of the default tablespace for all schemas, with a link to Workspace to Schema Assignment page (see the section "Manage Workspace to Schema Assignments" for more detail)

- A list of the tablespaces utilized by all schemas

- A list of all applications and their owners

- A list of application developers with a link to the Manage Developers and Users page (see the section "Manage Developers and Users" for more detail)

- A list of cookie users with a link to the Manage Developers and Users page (see the section "Manage Developers and Users" for more detail)

- A list of object types and counts

- A list of service change requests, detailing name, type, request date, and status

- A list of user activities, detailing application, page, user, session ID, number of rows, and elapsed time

- A list of developer activities, detailing developer, application, page, date, and component

TIP
Use the Workspace Utilization Report to view the properties of the INTERNAL workspace. There, you can discover all the applications that make up HTML DB.

Remove Workspace

At some time it may be necessary to remove a workspace. The Remove Workspace menu option under the Manage Workspaces icon navigates you to the first page of the Remove Workspace Wizard. The first step of the four-step wizard is to select the workspace you wish to remove. The next step informs you of the number of applications and users that are contained in the workspace and requires you to verify that you want to proceed. You may also select to remove any existing requests for the selected workspace. The third step lists the schemas and their tablespaces and warns you if any other schemas are using the tablespaces. This page is informational only. Clicking on the Remove Workspace button on this page will *not* remove the database objects. If you want to remove the database objects, you must do so through some other means. The last step in the wizard is the success message.

Manage Workspace to Schema Assignments

When a workspace is created, a single schema is associated with that workspace. The Manage Workspace to Schema Assignments menu option under the Manage Workspaces icon allows you to change the schema associated with a workspace or to associate more schemas to a workspace. The Manage Schema to Workspace Assignments link navigates you to the Schemas by Workspace page, shown in Figure 17-2. From here, you can see all your workspaces and the schemas associated with each. The report is similar to many throughout the application where you can order by clicking on the column headings or limit those that are displayed by selecting a workspace or entering text to limit the schemas by.

Clicking on the workspace name takes you to a screen where you can change the schema, the workspace, or both for the selected association. To create a new association, click on the Create button. This will start a four-step wizard where you select whether you want to add an

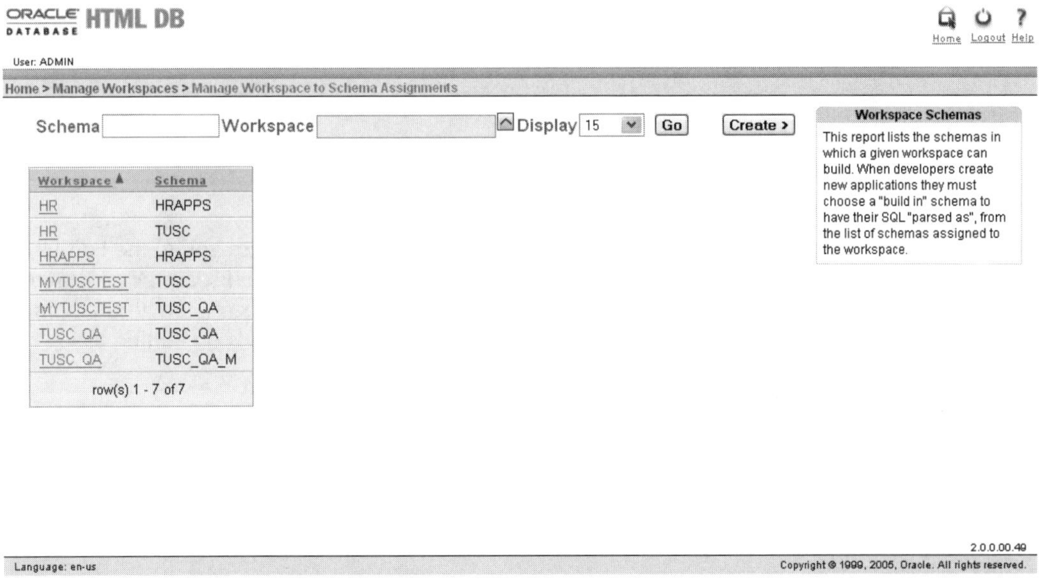

FIGURE 17-2 *Schemas by Workspace page*

existing schema or create a new schema. Then you select the workspace for which you want to create the association. Depending on whether you select to create a new schema or use an existing schema, the third step allows you to specify the schema name, password, and tablespace information to create a new schema or select from an LOV to use an existing schema. The final step in the wizard is the confirmation page.

Manage Developers and Users

The Manage Developers and Users menu item under the Manage Workspaces icon navigates you to the Manage Developers and Users page. This page is a report, like many of the pages, that allows you to search for a particular user or limit the users displayed by selecting a workspace. The report displays some basic information about the users—user ID, full name, workspace, default schema, creation date, and last update date. For each user there is also a password reset link, and the user's name is an active link to edit the user.

The password link takes you to a page where you can enter a new password, as shown next. The New Password field is populated for you with a random password. You may use the suggestion or enter your own. When you apply the change, an e-mail will be sent to the user. If you expand the User Information arrow, you can view more information about the user.

The edit icon on the Manage Developers and Users page navigates you to the Edit User page. This page is almost identical to the Edit User page available to the workspace administrator. On this page, you can edit user attributes, including their password, privileges, and group memberships. See the section "Workspace Administration Functions" for more details on editing users.

Manage Service

Once a workspace is created, a user with workspace administration privileges can request more resources for the workspace. They might request another schema or more storage space for the workspace. The Manage HTML DB Services section provides the tools to handle those requests, along with tools to manage HTML DB instance-wide resources.

Edit Environment Settings

The Manage Environment Settings page allows the administrator of the HTML DB environment to set the globally used properties. On the Manage Environment Settings page, the properties are grouped into sections listed in the following table. The properties values can be set through the Edit Environment Settings menu option under the Manage Service icon. For more detailed information on the properties, refer to the Oracle HTML DB Users Guide.

Section	Description
Application Development	Controls PL/SQL program unit editing and installation of demonstration objects
Self Service	Defines provisioning status and a service URL
Email	Defines SMTP server attributes
SQL Workshop	Sets limits for SQL Workshop
Monitoring	Enables database monitoring
Security	Disables admin and workspace login and restricts access by IP address

Manage Logs

HTML DB records information about many aspects of the environment, including developer activity and user activity. The information in these log files is viewed through the myriad of reports under the Monitor Activity icon and menu. The Manage Logs menu option under the Manage Service icon navigates to a page from which all these log files can be managed. In short, you can either truncate these log files or delete entries older than a given number of days. The log files available are the script file log, control file log, SQL command processor history log, SQL Archive log, Page view activity log, developer activity log, external click counting log, and mail log.

Manage Session State

Because HTML DB application users connect to the applications through a browser, special logic must be implemented to maintain a persistent state between each page of the application. The internal logic that maintains this stateful behavior is referred to as a *session*. Each session is tracked by a unique ID that is used by the HTML DB engine to store and retrieve information from page to page. This information is stored in the database until it is purged by an administrator. The Manage Session State menu option under the Manage Service icon navigates to a page from which you can purge sessions by age, view session state statistics, or view a report with recent sessions, with the ability to drill down to session details.

Manage Mail Queue

Many of the administration functions result in an email being generated and sent through the email server configured in the environment preferences (see the section "Edit Environment Settings" earlier in this chapter). The Manage Mail Queue menu option under the Manage Service icon navigates to a report page that displays all unsent mail messages. From there, you can delete selected messages or send all queued messages.

Manage Service and Change Request

Service requests are requests for the creation of workspaces, whereas change requests are requests for modifications to an existing workspace, such as adding a schema or increasing allocated disk space. The notification panel on the HTML DB Administration main page shows the number of service requests and change requests. The number on the left is the total number of requests, whereas the number on the right is the number of pending requests. Each of the numbers is an active link to the corresponding Manage Report page: Service Requests and Service Change Requests. The pending number link automatically sets the status parameter so the report shows only those in Requested status. The Manage Service Requests icon and the Manage Change Requests icon under the Manage Service icon also navigate to the same report pages and also limit the displayed requests to those in Requested status.

The Manage Service Requests report page will display all service requests, which can be filtered by the following statuses: Approved, Declined, In Progress, Requested, and Terminated. Each row of the report displays basic information about the request, along with an action link and the standard paper-and-pencil edit icon.

The edit icon takes you to the Provision Request page, shown in Figure 17-3. Here, you can edit the selected provisioning request. Only some of the fields actually have an impact on the provisioning of the workspace. The workspace name is already unique, but you can change it if you need to. The e-mail address is used to reply to the request. The schema can be accepted as requested or changed as needed. The database size controls the number of megabytes that will be

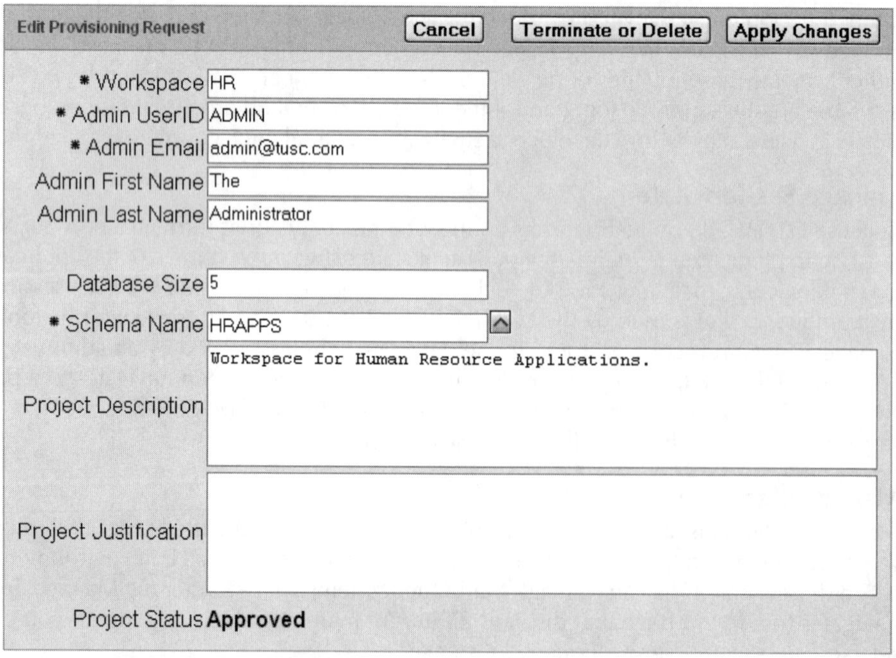

FIGURE 17-3 *Provision Request page*

allocated for the workspace. If the request has been approved, the Terminate or Delete button will appear; otherwise, there will only be a Delete button.

The action link on the Service Requests report navigates to a summary page that allows you to approve or decline a provision request still in request status. Clicking on either the Approve or Decline button will take you to a final page where you will be able to edit the e-mail that is sent to the requesting administrator. For a request that has already been approved, the action link navigates to a summary page where the status can be changed.

The Manage Change Request report page displays all change requests, which can be filtered by the following statuses: Approved, Declined, In Progress, Requested, and Terminated. Each row of the report displays basic information about the request, along with an action link. The action link navigates to the Process Change Request page, shown in Figure 17-4. The page allows the request to be processed or denied—either choice results in an e-mail being sent to the requester. As shown in Figure 17-4, below the details of the change request are sections that can be expanded for additional information about the workspace. This information can assist in making a decision about the request.

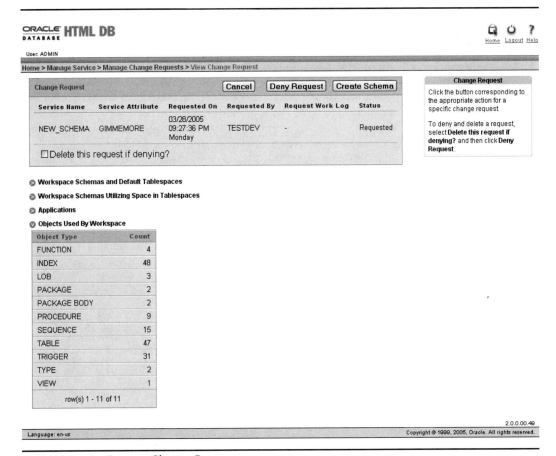

FIGURE 17-4   *Process Change Request page*

Manage Site-Specific Tasks Lists

Site-specific tasks are links displayed on either the Workspace Home page or the Workspace Login page of every workspace belonging to this HTML DB environment. They are displayed in a panel labeled Site-Specific Tasks, shown next. Links can be any valid URL. They can be used to navigate to external applications, utilities, or message pages.

The Manage Site-Specific Tasks link navigates to the Site-Specific Tasks page, which displays all defined tasks. Clicking on the edit icon or the Create button navigates to the Create/Edit Site-Specific Tasks page, shown in Figure 17-5. The display sequence determines the order in which the tasks will be displayed. The location can be either the workspace home page or the login page. The task name is displayed in the panel and navigates to the task link. Whether or not the link is displayed is determined by the Displayed pick list.

Workspace Administration Functions

In the beginning of the chapter, we discussed the different types of users. Two of these are authorized to log into the workspace development environment—developers and workspace administrators/developers. Naturally the administrator has full access to all workspace administration functions, but developers also have access to some of the administrative functions. The Administration icon on the Workspace home page navigates to the HTML DB Workspace Administration main page, shown next. This page contains three navigational icons that take you to the corresponding pages for each of the main administrative areas: Manage Services, Manage Users, and Monitor Activity. Additionally, each of these icons has an arrow on the right side that, when clicked, produces a drop-down menu to navigate directly to tasks under each of the main areas. The only navigational

ORACLE **HTML DB**
DATABASE

User: ADMIN

Home > Manage Service > Manage Site-Specific Tasks > Create/Edit Site-Specific Tasks

| Site-Specific Tasks | Cancel | Create |

* Display Sequence 10
  Display Location ○ Workspace Login ◉ Workspace Home
* Task Name `Developer Standards`
  Task Link http://ourserver.com/DevStnd.html
  Displayed Yes

Site-Specific Tasks
Specify tasks for the site-specific task lists that appear on the Workspace Login page and the Workspace Home page.

To determine whether a task displays, select **Yes** or **No** from the Displayed list.

FIGURE 17-5 *Create/Edit Site-Specific Tasks page*

icon available to developers is the Monitor Activity icon. The page also contains a link for changing the current user's password.

Change Password

The Change Password link pops up a window that allows any user to change their password. Keep in mind that if the same user is created in several different workspaces with the same password, it appears as a single user. However, there are actually two different records in the internal user account repository. Therefore, when the password is changed for one, it will not change the other accounts.

Manage HTML DB Users

The Manage Users icon navigates to the Manage Users page, shown in Figure 17-6. From here, an administrator can create new users, manage existing users, or delete existing users. They can also create and edit groups and view user-to-group assignments.

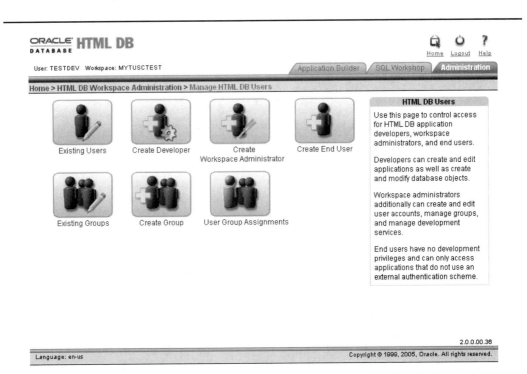

FIGURE 17-6 *Manage Users page*

Managing Users

The four icons on the top of the Manage HTML DB Users page provide the administrator access to several user-related functions. The Create User and Edit User functions use practically the same page. Each of the different Create User icons (Developer, Workspace Administrator, and End User) navigate to the Create User page, shown in Figure 17-7. The only difference is how the Developer Privileges radio buttons are defaulted.

User Name, Password, and Email Address are required fields, indicated by the asterisk. The username can be up to 100 characters long and can include periods and @, but no other special characters or spaces. Usernames are not case sensitive and must be unique within the workspace. Passwords can also be up to 100 characters long. Unlike usernames, passwords are case sensitive. The field Accessible Schemas controls a user's access to the schemas associated with the workspace. Enter a colon-delimited list for those schemas the user can access, or leave it blank to allow

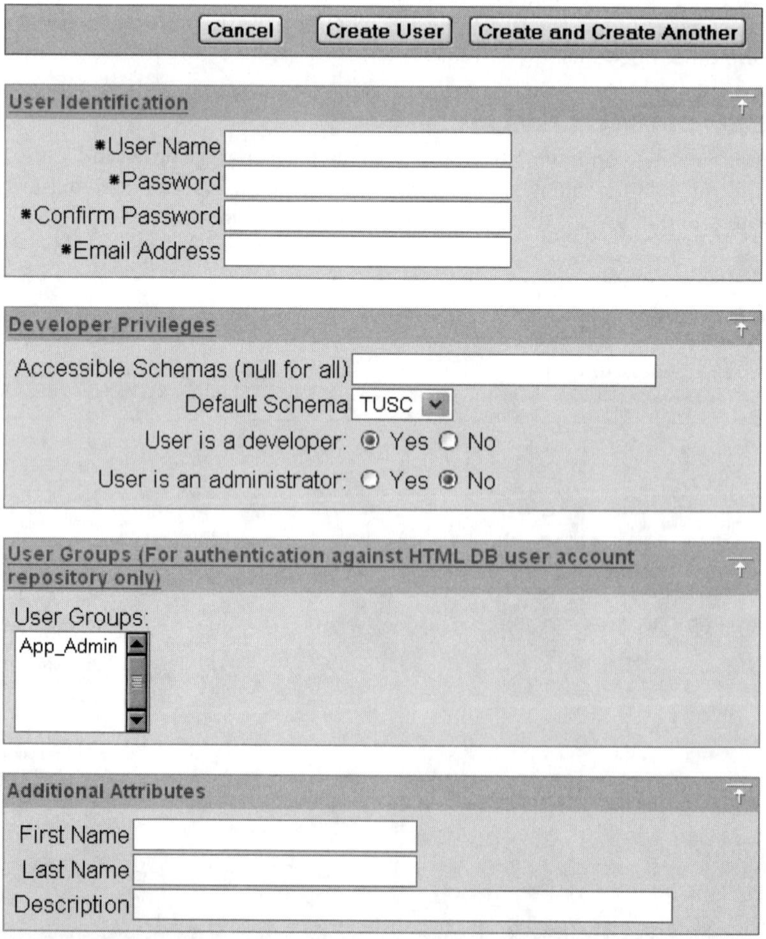

FIGURE 17-7   *Create User page*

access to all schemas. You can also specify the default schema. The radio buttons are preset based on which icon you chose, but you may change the selections. A user can be granted both developer and administrator privileges (Workspace Administrator), only developer privileges (Developer), or neither developer nor administrator privileges (End User). A user's group assignments can be made by highlighting the groups (see the section "Managing Groups" for more information on users and groups). Additionally, you may enter the user's name and a description for the user.

The Existing Users icon and link navigate to a report page that displays, by icon or by detail, all the previously created internal user accounts. Like many of the other report pages, the detail view allows you to order the report by clicking on any of the column headings: user, email, first name, last name, default schema, developer, or groups. Alternatively, the users displayed can be limited by using the find function, which will search the username and e-mail address fields. Each username is also a link that opens a User Edit page, almost identical to the Create User page shown in Figure 17-7.

Managing Groups

If an application uses HTML DB authentication, access to different parts of the application can be controlled through the use of user groups. Users are assigned to groups on the Edit User pages just covered. For more information on application security, see Chapter 16. The three icons at the bottom of the Manage HTML DB Users page, shown in Figure 17-6, provide links to pages to create groups, edit groups, and report user-to-group assignments.

The Create Group icon and link navigate to the Create User Groups page, shown next. Simply enter a unique name and an optional description and click on the Create Group button.

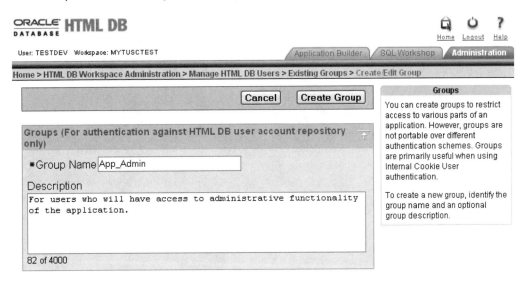

The Edit Groups icon and link navigate to a report page that displays existing groups by either icons or details. The detail report is a simple two-column report page that displays the group names and descriptions. The group name is also a link that navigates to the Create/Edit User Group page, where you can make changes.

The User Group Assignments icon and link, shown in Figure 17-6, similarly navigate to a simple three-column report page that displays group name, username, and edit links for each user group assignment. Clicking on the edit icon will navigate to the Edit User page, shown in Figure 17-7, where group assignments can be changed for that particular user.

Manage Services

The Manage Services icon and link on the HTML DB Workspace Administration page navigate to the Manage Services page, shown in Figure 17-8. This page contains a number of icons and links that navigate to individual workspace-management activities. Remember, services are the resources that the workspace utilizes—schemas and storage space.

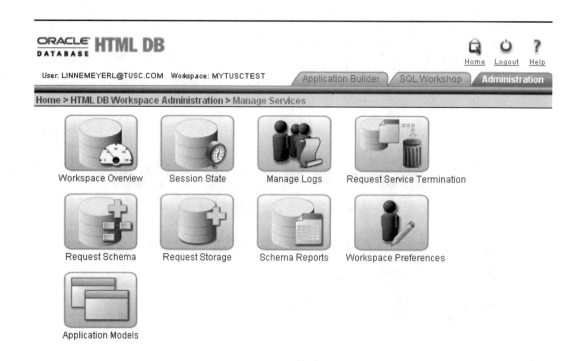

FIGURE 17-8   *Manage Workspace page*

Manage Logs

The logs available from a workspace are the Developer log and the Click through log. The data from these logs are available to both developers and administrators through the reports in the Monitor Activity section of HTML DB Workspace Administration. Developer logs track developer activity, and Click through logs track links to external applications that use the HTMLDB_UTL. COUNT_CLICK procedure. Each can be viewed though the Monitor Activity section, discussed later in this chapter. The Manage Logs icon and link on the Manage Workspace Page navigate to the Manage Logs page, shown next. From this page you can view the number of entries in each log and purge the logs if desired. Entries older than one month will automatically be purged. The Monitor Developer Activity Log link navigates to the Developer Activity by Day report page (see the upcoming "Monitor Activity" section).

Manage Logs	Cancel	Purge Developer Log	Purge Click Log

Developer activity log entries: 599
Click through log entries: 0

- Monitor Developer Activity Log

Session State

Session state was discussed in Chapter 8. The Session State icon and link, shown in Figure 17-8, navigate to the Session State Management page, shown in Figure 17-9. The first link, Current Preferences and Session State, with an option to purge, actually provides four actions. Not only can you view the values of your current session items and purge them, but you can do the same for user preferences. Session items viewed from here are for all applications, including the internal HTML DB applications. Purging your current session state allows you to run your application anew without having to log out and log back in. User preferences are those items in an application for which you have specified to maintain session state "per user" rather than "per session." These values are stored for each user. When the user exits and opens another session, the values will still be available.

The second link, Recent Sessions, with drilldown to session details, navigates to a report page that shows recent sessions. You can select a time period for which to view sessions. Each session listed has a link that navigates to a detail report about the selected session. This is a valuable debug tool for viewing session values for a normal application user. The Go button at the top allows you to refresh the view of the current session. The Remove State button allows you to clear the values stored in the session, and the Remove Session button allows you to totally remove a user's session. After you remove a user's session, they will receive an error and have to log back into the application.

TIP
Use the Recent Sessions with drilldown to session details report as a debug tool to monitor application users.

The next link, Purge Sessions by Age, provides a pick list of ages with a Report Sessions button. Select an age, click on Report Sessions, and you will see how many sessions are older

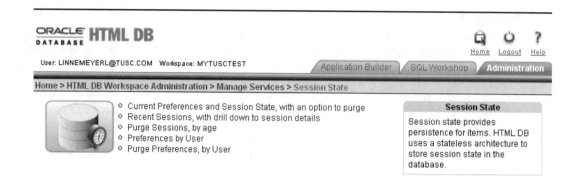

FIGURE 17-9   *Session State Management page*

than the selected age criteria. Click on the Purge Sessions button and you will purge the same sessions.

The Preferences by User link navigates to a report page that displays the user preferences for all users. The final link, Purge Preferences by User, allows you to select a user and then report on that user's preferences. Then you can purge the user's preferences if so desired.

Workspace Overview

The Workspace Overview icon and link navigate to the Workspace Overview report page. This report shows information about the workspace's schemas, tablespaces, applications, and application developers.

Request Service Termination

The Request Service Termination icon and link also navigate to the Request Service Termination report page, which is the same report for Workspace Overview, so you can see what the impact of terminating this service would be. An additional button is displayed to request termination of the workspace.

Request Schema

The Request Schema icon and link navigate to the Request Database Schema page. Here, you can choose to request a new schema or you may choose from a list of existing schemas. Simply enter a name for the new schema and click on the Next button. If the schema exists, a message will be displayed and you will be allowed to enter another schema name. If the schema name does not exist, a request will be sent to the internal HTML DB administrator. The administrator will either accept or reject the request, as described earlier in the chapter.

Request Storage

The Request Storage icon and link navigate to the Request Storage page, where you can request additional storage space: 5MB, 10MB, 50MB, 100MB, 250MB, or 500MB. Once you select the size and click on the Request Storage button, a request will be sent to the internal HTML DB administrator, who will process the request as described earlier in the chapter. The page also has a simple report that displays the tablespaces the current schemas are utilizing.

Schema Reports

The Schema Reports icon and link navigate to the Schema Reports page, which contains three links to different reports about the workspaces' schemas. One shows the utilization of workspaces by schema, another reports database privileges by schema, and the final link simply reports all schemas for the workspace and the number of privileges and applications that each has.

Workspace Preferences

Workspace Preferences is new to version 2.0. The icon and link navigate to a page where you can change whether PL/SQL program unit editing is allowed for the workspace. If it is allowed, developers will have the ability to edit and compile PL/SQL program units from the Object Browser. If it is not allowed, developers cannot change code directly from the data dictionary. However, they will still be able to make changes by running scripts or through the SQL Command Processor.

Application Models

Application Models is also new to version 2.0. The icon and link navigate to the Application Model page, where you can view current application models and delete them if you desire. As you create applications through the application-creation wizard, the option to save the definition as a design model for reuse will be offered on the final confirmation page. Once it is saved, as you create other applications through the wizard, you may select to create the application based on an existing application design model.

Monitor Activity

The Monitory Activity icon and link on the HTML DB Workspace Administration page navigate to the Monitor Activity page, shown next. From this page, developers and administrators have access to many of the same monitoring reports available to the HTML DB internal administrator, except these reports are limited to just the current workspace. As you can see by the page, the reports are grouped into three categories: reports on page views, reports on application changes, and reports on sessions.

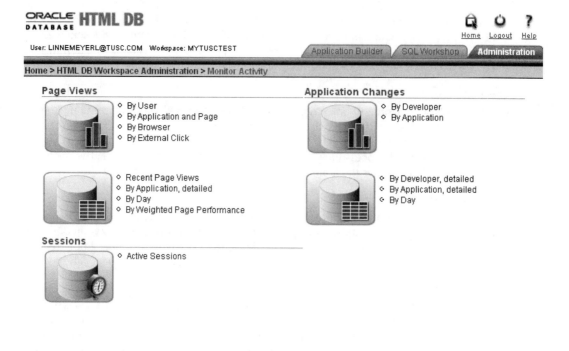

The Page View reports are a good tool to get a feel for the user activity in your applications. The Top View reports give you an overview of activity. The By User, By External Click, and By Browser reports are simple bar graph reports that allow you to select a time for how far back the report will be run. The By Application and Page report allows you to see which pages are viewed the most and what percent each page's views are of the total application. The Page View Statistics reports can give you a good feel for the utilization of the application pages. You can even see a breakdown of page views by the hour, to help manage your peak usage.

The Application Changes reports provide a view to the activity of developers within the workspace. Both administrators and developers can see statistics on activities of all developers. The By Developer and By Application reports provide total change counts in either a bar chart or a pie chart. Both reports allow you to select a time for how far back the report will be run. The Application Change Statistics reports provide different views to see changes with detail on: user, application, page, date of change, component changed, and change action.

The Active Sessions report allows developers and administrators to view a report of the current active session, which shows the session ID, the owner, when it was created, and how many items are in the session. Each session ID is an active link that drills down to a page that reports on page views and session state values.

Application Reports

Prior to version 2.0, you could access application reports from the administrative section. Access to these reports has logically been moved to the main application page. Not only were these reports moved, but many new reports have been added, for a total of some 65 reports. The View Application Reports link in the Tasks panel on the right side of any application's main page will take you to an intermediate page, shown next. From here, you can either navigate to pages that list reports for each category or navigate directly to a report using the drop-down menus from the icons.

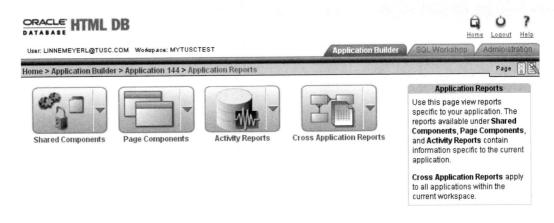

Because there are some 65 different reports available, space precludes us from describing all of the reports—besides, we want you to keep reading without falling asleep. Be sure to take the time to explore the reports available to you. If you know they are available, you will find a time when you will be able to use them.

In this chapter, we have covered the functions available to both the internal HTML DB administrator and the workspace administrator. The larger your HTML DB environment grows, the more you will utilize the functions available to these two types of administrators.

PART
VI

Advanced Topics

CHAPTER
18

Tips and Techniques

 hen it comes to developing within any application development environment, we as developers are always looking for tips and techniques to make our development lives easier. This chapter discusses a number of topics that do just that, including the following:

- Places to find new tips and techniques

- Useful supplemental tools

- Tips for the Application server and the client

- Application development

- User education

Places to Find New Tips and Techniques

It's always good to know where to go to find new tips and techniques that you can use. A number of great resources are available on the Web, including these:

- Oracle technical forum

- Oracle marketing site

- Oracle HTML DB Community blogs

- HTML DB Studio

- HTML DB hosting site

Oracle Technical Forum for HTML DB

The HTML DB forum provides answers to developers' questions. The forum can be found at http://forums.oracle.com/forums/forum.jsp?forum=137.

This site allows you to post questions and receive replies from any number of HTML DB developers. Several of the Oracle vHTML DB team members (development and product management) contribute regularly. You can search through prior threads or post new threads at any time. Take the time to post a thorough question (and especially a thorough title) so that you get appropriate responses to your question.

Oracle Marketing Site

Oracle's HTML DB marketing site is located at http://www.oracle.com/technology/products/database/htmldb/index.html. The HTML DB documentation can be found for each of the versions at this site. You'll also find good news (technical) articles and tutorials here. For example, the news story discussed later in this chapter on rendering Oracle HTML DB reports as PDFs using FOP can be found here.

In this section of the website, you'll find a technical papers section, which includes great papers on subjects such as the following:

- Integrating Oracle HTML DB with Oracle Application Server 10*g*

- Customizing user interface templates in HTML DB

- The Installation FAQ

- Oracle HTML DB best practices

- Using virtual private database and Oracle HTML DB

- Building an Oracle text application with HTML DB

- Converting a Microsoft Access application to Oracle HTML DB

- Oracle HTML DB overview

You'll also want to note the "How To's" section, which includes great information on subjects such as the following:

- Forms and JavaScript

  - How to create a form to upload spreadsheet data

  - How to create a tabular form

  - How to control form layout

  - How to build a master-detail application

  - How to build tabular forms for multirow operations

  - How to build a file upload and download application

  - How to incorporate JavaScript into an HTML DB application

  - How to build custom pop-up pages

  - How to work with check boxes

  - How to add navigation within a page

- Reports and Charts

  - How to create a stacked bar chart

  - How to create a dynamic query report

  - How to customize report columns and column headings

  - How to customize report pagination

  - How to build tree-based reports

  - How to control page sizes in result sets

  - How to extend an easy report

  - How to build a chart with drilldown to a report

- How to build drilldown reports
- How to build a report based on a dynamic query
- Security
  - How to make an HTML DB application public
  - How to change how users are authenticated
  - How to authenticate users using an LDAP server
  - How to create a login page
  - How to configure an HTML DB application as an external application in Oracle AS Single Sign-On
  - How to configure an HTML DB application as a partner application in Oracle AS Single Sign-On
- Install and Configuration
  - How to integrate Oracle Reports with Oracle HTML DB
  - How to install and configure Oracle HTML DB for use with Oracle Application Server 10*g*
  - How to install and configure Oracle HTML DB for use by a 9*i*R2 Oracle HTTP server
- Other
  - How to send e-mail from HTML DB applications
  - How to work with dates
  - How to change a logo in a page template
  - How to publish an HTML DB component as a Portlet in Oracle Application Server Portal

Oracle HTML DB Community Blogs

Links to some very useful blog pages are contained on Oracle's main HTML DB page, http://www.oracle.com/technology/products/database/htmldb/index.html. Additionally, you will want to explore http://spendolini.blogspot.com for the content of Scott Spenolini's blog page. Scott was the product manager for HTML DB at Oracle. At his blog you'll find good information about various topics, such as converting your corporate look and feel into an HTML DB theme. Scott is a regular contributor to the HTML DB Studio site and the discussion forum, as well as a regular presenter at user groups, and so much more. He's likely the world's leading authority on HTML DB, so he's a great guy to follow. Also check out the recently started HTML DB wiki at http://wiki.shellprompt.net/htmldb.

HTML DB Studio

If you're looking for useful HTML DB applications (roughly 20 out there as of today), themes (coming soon), utilities (eight as of today), or tips and tricks (roughly 50 more tips and techniques for you to check out), you'll find useful information at the HTML DB Studio site (http://htmldb. oracle.com/studio).

The utilities provide HTML DB with additional charting capabilities, mail merges, recent page view statistics, automatic session timeout, enhanced application export facilities, and more.

HTML DB Hosting Site

If you search Google for HTML DB, you'll find the HTML DB public hosting site. This site contains information on HTML DB hosting services, sample applications, and more. If you wish to have Oracle host a non-production site, you can do so for free at http://htmldb.oracle.com, but if you wish to pay for a hosted site with 99.5% availability, this is the site for you. It can be found at http://www.htmldb.com/.

Useful Supplemental Tools

Although you could use HTML DB as a standalone tool, it's recommended that you have some additional tools to help with your development. These include the following

- Development IDE

- PDF generation tool

- Browser plug-ins

Development IDE

Numerous excellent developer IDEs are available today. Oracle JDeveloper is an excellent IDE for both Java and PL/SQL (and much more). Quest's TOAD tool is my personal favorite IDE for Oracle SQL and PL/SQL-based development. An IDE can be very helpful to supplement your HTML DB development.

Use your favorite (external) SQL or PL/SQL editor (for example, Toad or Formatter) to compose and even test the code for your HTML DB report sections and complicated LOV queries. It's easier to debug, and when you are satisfied you can just copy the code into the appropriate HTML DB field.

PDF Generation Tool

There are many ways you can write PDF files. Numerous PDF toolkits are available in Java. My favorite PDF generation tool is free. It's call FOP (Formatting Objects Processor) and it's from the Apache Organization (http://xml.apache.org/fop/). You can find out more information about how to output PDFs directly from HTML DB reports at http://www.oracle.com/technology/pub/notes/technote_htmldb_fop.html.

Browser Plug-ins

One of the more useful browser plug-ins I have found is called Web Developer for Mozilla Firefox and Mozilla browsers. This tool is extremely valuable when working with templates. Among other things, it allows you to outline HTML elements such as tables and table cells. It also helps with Cascading Style Sheets. You can find out more at http://chrispederick.com/work/firefox/webdeveloper/.

Tips for the Application Server and the Client

HTML DB can run on an existing application server, or you can install a separate application server instance. Numerous papers exist on the sites listed earlier about different configuration options for your HTML DB server. Sometimes you don't have enough resources to keep HTML DB running on your portable server (that is, laptop), which the first tip discusses. Additionally, the HTML DB client can run in any browser. The second tip in this section discusses the Firefox client.

Starting and Stopping the Application Server

If you don't want your application server running all the time, you can use a bat file (on Windows) to start up and shut down your development environment as discussed here. Each of the "net start" lines starts up a Windows service. Before implementing this, you will first want to go into Windows Services and set each of the services listed next in a net start command to start manually. By default, they are installed to start automatically. The "opmnctl" lines start and stop the HTTP server. Although the HTTP server should start when the other services are started, I have found that many times it does not. Therefore, I added a command to shut down the HTTP server if it is running and then restart it.

STARTHTMLDB.BAT

- net start OracleServiceORCL

- net start OracleOraDb10g_home1TNSListener

- net start OraclehtmldbProcessManager

- net start OracleCSService

- net start OracleDBConsoleorcl

- cd \

- cd oracle\htmldb\opmn\bin

- opmnctl stopproc ias-component=HTTP_Server

- opmnctl startproc ias-component=HTTP_Server

STOPHTMLDB.BAT

- net stop OracleDBConsoleorcl

- net stop OracleCSService

- net stop OraclehtmldbProcessManager

- net stop OracleOraDb10g_home1TNSListener

- net stop OracleServiceORCL

Using the Firefox Client

Many developers are using the Mozilla Firefox browser instead of Internet Explorer or Netscape. The footprint of Internet Explorer and Netscape has become so large that it's prohibitive. In early versions of Firefox, installation of the Adobe SVG viewer was problematic. You had to copy a DLL manually for it to work. Numerous tips on this subject can be found on the HTML DB Studio site, and there are discussion threads on this topic in the HTML DB forum. Note that CTRL-ENTER normally executes a command in the SQL command window, but this does not work in earlier versions of Firefox. Some of the formatting is slightly different in Firefox, too.

Application Development

HTML DB application development is multifaceted. This section discusses various tips and techniques associated with application development in each of the following areas:

- General

- Forms

- Reports

General

A number of application tips and techniques can help make your applications more efficient and easier to maintain. These include the following:

- Page 0

- HTML DB features

- Loading and referencing images

- Debugging

- Publishing URLs

- Other tips

Global Application Regions Through Page 0

Any component that is placed on page 0 will show up on every page in the application, unless you turn it off by using conditional component/region logic. This can be a useful technique for your applications.

HTML DB Features

Into this general category I would throw all the side features in the HTML DB environment. When you get comfortable with the basics, you tend to overlook all the little features in HTML DB. Some of them are only useful in certain situations, but when you need them, they can save you a lot of time.

For instance, when you are working with a form page with a lot of fields you are trying to tweak, run the page and click on the Show Edit Links in the Developer's Toolbar. This places a small icon next to most elements on the page. Click on the icon and a pop-up window appears with that item's edit page. Make changes, apply changes, close the window, and then refresh your browser. Explore all the functionality that is offered through the side task panels. Get used to all the navigation offered; you can get from one place to another in many different ways. Take advantage of the multi-item edit pages available by clicking on section titles in the Page Definition page, such as Regions, Buttons, and Items.

Most of these have been covered elsewhere in this book, but they can quickly be forgotten. Take the time to explore the HTML DB development environment thoroughly. The better you know it, the more efficient it becomes.

Loading and Referencing Images

As part of the shared components, HTML DB allows you to load images into the database. You can include these images in your HTML DB application. For example, if you uploaded your corporate logo into the HTML DB database and you want to set the LOGO substitution variable to this image, you can set LOGO to the image location. To find the image location, go to the Shared Components images page and right-click on the image. Paste this URL into LOGO and your corporate logo will now appear on all pages of the application (that is, that include the logo in the template).

Debugging

The v2.0 User's Guide has three and a half pages on debugging. Take the time to read and understand this section of the documentation. The fifth parameter in the f?p syntax indicates whether debug mode is on or off. You can typically click the Debug link at the bottom of a page, but sometimes a broken page does not display this link. In this case, simply change the fifth parameter from NO to YES. DEBUG is also a substitution variable that your applications have access to. In other words, you can place your own debug logic into your application.

To isolate the problem on a complex page, you can turn off the display of regions and then turn them back on one at a time. Change the Conditional Display parameter to NEVER to turn regions off.

You can also enable SQL Tracing using TKPROF by adding a parameter onto the end of your URL:

&p_trace=YES

Publishing URLs

When publishing or bookmarking HTML DB URLs, omit the session ID at the end of the URL because this is assigned for each session. For example, instead of saving or publishing the URL

http://xyz.com/pls/test/f?p=152:1:875877720339413092

use this instead:

http://xyz.com/pls/test/f?p=152:1.

Other General Tips

Additional general tips exist on other sites. Rather than repeating these tips, I've listed them here along with their location. There are many more tips than mentioned here; these are simply some of the top ones:

- HTML DB Studio

  - Installing HTML DB into multiple Oracle instances using a single Oracle HTTP server

- Favorites icon

- Searching across an application through all region source

- Dynamic select list

- Dynamic drop-down menu

- Setting regions with a scroll bar

- Text parsing of file upload

- Adding a "Top of Page" bookmark in a Region header

- Building page-level help in a pop-up window

- Application versioning

- Using the Z-link to track external clicks

- Adding a border to Forms or Reports region

- Quick tip for displaying properly formatted XML data

- HTML DB Forum

  - Using external tables with HTML DB

  - How to handle multiple conditional display

  - Source code / version control

  - Highlighting a row (on a page)

  - Plotting multiple series on an SVG chart

  - Referencing uploaded files

  - Integrating HTML DB in Portal

Forms

HTML DB forms are powerful for querying, inserting, updating, or deleting data from your database. Topics discussed for HTML DB forms include the following:

- Tabular form validation

- Barcode scanner integration

- PDA compatibility

- Other tips

Tabular Form Validation

Tabular forms can be useful for editing multiple records on the same page. Tabular forms can be effective, but when it comes to forms that require extensive validation, it's best not to use them. If you search the forum for information on "tabular form validation," you will find a number of tips that might be helpful in this regard. However, because validation in tabular forms is limited, it's recommended that you not use tabular forms if you need to perform operations such as the following:

- Setting the value of specific fields in the form (for example, setting fields such as last_update_date)

- Making sure a series of values aren't null

- Turning off/disabling a field if another field value is set to a specific value

Barcode Scanner Integration

Placing a GO button immediately after the last field in a form improves the usability of HTML DB applications with barcode scanners. Set the scanner to output a tab character after each barcode's data and you can advance from field to field, ending on the GO button. Pressing the ENTER/RETURN key will then submit the completed form.

PDA Compatibility

HTML DB applications run fine on most handheld computers and PDAs that have a browser application. You may, however, need to add your own JavaScript to initially position the cursor on a given field. To do this, add a region (and don't use a template) with a display point before the footer and put your script in the region header. Here's an example:

```
<script language=javascript>
function first_field()
{
  window.document.wwv_flow.P2_ITEM_ID.focus();
  return true;
}
</script>
```

Other Forms Tips

Additional general tips exist on other sites. Rather than repeating them, I've listed them here along with their location. There are many more tips than mentioned here; these are simply some of the top tips:

- HTML DB Studio

  - Processing multiselect lists and check boxes for insert

  - Setting the value of a select list using a link

  - Using ORA_ROWSCN in your HTML DB application (optimistic locking)

  - Adjusting radio group layout

  - Formatting radio buttons

- Controlling runaway fields
- Adding blank rows to a tabular form with the click of a button
- Using fixed-width select lists
- Creating "check all" functionality for dynamically created check boxes
- Adding form control with tags
- Rejecting a field containing blanks only or a null string
- Refreshing the calling page of a pop-up
- HTML DB Forum
  - Using multirecord forms threads
  - Using a select list to branch
  - Creating a bold value from a pop-up LOV
  - Using a master/detail form with modal edit
  - Disabling an item

Reports

HTML DB reports are powerful for displaying data that exists in your database. Reports can also provide links to other components and pages in your application. Topics covered in this section include the following:

- Favorite reporting feature
- Instant drilldown
- Tuning your pagination style
- Long pages with multiple sections
- Other tips

Favorite Reporting Feature

The Report with Links to Form on a Table (2 Pages) Wizard is one of the most used reporting features. Use this wizard to get a basic functional application started, and you can begin customizing to get the functionality needed for your application.

Instant Drilldown

The ability to make the data in a report column automatically link to another page is a powerful feature. This can easily provide drilldown capabilities for detailed information. Many developers don't notice this feature because it is "hidden" behind the Column Attributes icon on the Report Attributes tab. Clicking on the magnifying glass icon to edit a specific column attribute takes you to the detailed attribute editing form. Using this form makes it easy to generate the proper link format the first time. Optionally, you can write SQL to output the necessary links, but this is much more difficult to get right the first time.

Tuning Your Pagination Style

Reports allow you to set a pagination (or paging logic) style. Some of the styles must count the number of rows in the entire set so that they can display a message (for example, Rows 1-25 of more than 500). Don't choose these styles when a large number of rows exist in the query set.

Long Pages with Multiple Sections

The nice little jump to tags that HTML DB commonly has at the top of long pages with multiple sections (like in the templates) can be created with a simple HTML region at the top of the page referencing HTML anchors, which you define in the Region Header area. Examples of this can be seen by going to the edit page for a page template. Just below the title bar that includes the Cancel, Delete, and Apply Changes buttons is a series of links with little down-arrow images (for example, Subscriptions, Template, Display Points, Sub Templates). These would be defined as

    <a href=#Subscriptions>Subscriptions</a>

They reference anchors defined at the top of sections. They would look like this:

    <a name="Subscriptions">

Other Reports Tips

Additional general tips can be found on other sites. Rather than repeating these tips, I've listed them here along with their location. There are many more tips than mentioned here; these are simply some of the top tips:

- HTML DB Studio

    - Building trees using multiple tables

    - Building a hierarchical report

    - Highlighting calendar date range

    - Highlighting report rows based on a column value

    - Ordering states logically in reports

    - Using the new 10g string syntax to simplify HTML DB reports

    - Embedding uploaded images in a report

    - Creating a page view summary report

    - Simulating a correlated subquery in report LOVs

    - Creating reports with links to pop-up page

    - Downloading report data to a spreadsheet

    - Using ALT text on an image to save report space

- ■ Highlighting report rows on MouseOver

- ■ Using rowselector in report regions other than "SQL Query(updatable report)"

■ HTML DB Forum

- ■ Dynamically calculating values and validating in reports

- ■ Creating a report of a report

- ■ Using report breaks, formatting, attributes, totals, sorts, and sums

- ■ Customizing reports

- ■ Using check boxes in a report

User Education

With any application development environment, it's important to tell your users the best practices for using the tool and minimizing error generation. Browser-based applications are more "breakable" because of the nature of browsers. A browser provides functionality to the user that can "break" the application. For example, to avoid error messages, it's important that users use the HTML DB navigation buttons rather than the browser's Forward and Back buttons to navigate whenever possible. Take the time to educate your users on how best to use your HTML DB applications.

Tips and techniques compilation is a living document. As you find new avenues to speed up your development, take a minute to forward them to the authors so that we may include them in our next version of this book.

CHAPTER
19

Best Practices

 hen installing, configuring, developing, testing, and deploying applications, best practices are always an important consideration. This chapter will discuss some of the best practices for HTML DB environments, which include the following topics:

- Installation

- Development

- Security

- Testing

Installation

The HTML DB environment can be configured any number of ways. HTML DB can be installed as a standalone environment or within a 10AS environment. The application server can reside outside the firewall or behind the firewall. Numerous white papers on these topics can be found on Oracle's HTML DB marketing site. Follow the Technical Papers link from the Oracle HTML DB main page at http://www.oracle.com/technology/products/database/htmldb/index.html.

Development

When it comes to HTML DB development, the best-practice topics of discussion include:

- Workspaces

- Schemas

- Application templates

- Database administration

- HTML DB application configuration

Workspaces

Think of workspaces as development environments for HTML DB. Many applications can be grouped into a workspace. Workspaces will typically contain related applications because they will deal with the same (or related) schemas.

Development, Test, and Production Workspaces

Ideally the development, test, and production instances of your HTML DB applications will be on three separate boxes, but you could also segregate them as three separate workspaces on the same box if you need to. Regardless of the physical location of your workspaces, it is recommended that you have a development, test, and production workspace for your applications.

Power User Workspace

You may wish to create a workspace for individual power users or you might want to create a workspace for all your power users. You may even wish to create a "starting" or base application for your power users. The application could contain all the necessary lists of values, images, and other shared components for your business. Keep in mind that in HTML DB, you're either a developer or you're not. In other words, there is no way to restrict what functionality individual developers have access to within a workspace in HTML DB.

Schemas

An HTML DB workspace can access multiple schemas, but an HTML DB application can only access one schema at a time. This schema is called the "parsing schema" for the application. For an application, it's as if it is logged into one and only one schema—like any application would be. Therefore, when it comes to organizing your schemas, if you have your application data split across multiple schemas, you'll likely want to set up an application schema that has the necessary access to each of the other schemas' objects. Ideally, everything for an application will be in one schema, but that's not always possible. If you create a schema called APPS, for example, and you grant access to the tables and views contained in other schemas, HTML DB does not "see" those tables/views/sequences unless they are owned by the APPS schema. Therefore, you may wish to create views in the APPS schema for all the tables/views that you wish to "see" (that is, in the pop-up list of tables and views) from the HTML DB development environment. Synonyms (or granted access) will provide objects to the HTML DB schema—it uses a view similar to the USER_ views to obtain its list of valid objects to display.

Application Templates

HTML DB doesn't officially support application templates. However, if you would like for your "developers" or power users to be able to create a new application using your official corporate application template, you can achieve this by creating an application, exporting it, and requiring (or requesting that) developers create new applications by importing your "corporate application template."

Database Administration

Like any development environment, an HTML DB development environment should be designed (or at least reviewed) by your DBA group. It's ideal to have database integrity, which is typically obtained by enforcing integrity (that is, primary and foreign key constraints). Other considerations, such as using sequence numbers to populate primary keys, are also important to good database design. To simplified application development, design your database to the third normal form (that is, no duplication of data).

HTML DB Application Configuration

A number of components in HTML DB should be configured for any application. These include the following:

- List of values
- Themes and templates
- UI defaults
- Substitution strings

- No hardcoding

- SQL tuning

- Code modularization and reuse

- Use of built-in functionality

- Error handling

- PL/SQL error handling

List of Values
It's important to establish your application's list of values early on.

Themes and Templates
You may have already established a corporate look and feel for your web applications. If so, you'll want to check out Scott S's blog (mentioned in Chapter 18), which discusses converting your corporate look and feel to an HTML DB theme.

Otherwise, you may choose to use one (or many) of the pre-established HTML DB themes. The HTML DB developers have simplified getting your logo onto all the pages using the LOGO section of the application attributes. Set this to the location of your logo image.

UI Defaults
UI defaults (under the SQL Workshop) are important to set up for all your developers within the environment. These defaults simplify application development by automating column headings, defaulting whether to display items in reports, presetting display sequences for items, and providing types, format masks, groupings, and so on, for forms and reports.

Substitution Strings
One of the nice features with HTML DB is the concept of a global substitution string, much like the LOGO substitution mentioned in the "Themes and Templates" section. If you have items that will be used in your templates that are ideal for global substitution, use substitution strings. Maybe you know your corporate name is about to change or perhaps your department name changes every week. Maybe it's the name of a product or service that you offer. For instance, if the department name changes often, a substitution string could be used as follows:

The Official &Department_Name Website

No Hardcoding
For portability of your applications, it's important not to hardcode items such as URLs in your application. For example, you could hardcode the application number in the URLs. However, instead it's ideal to use the built-in &APP_ID variable in your URLs. Make use of these variables, such as SESSION_ID, IMAGE_PATH, LOGO, and so on.

It's also important to use bind variables in your queries. This way, your queries are dynamic and are shared in the database across application users.

SQL Tuning
Most application performance problems in the database world are the result of poorly tuned database queries. Inefficient queries can quickly bring an entire system to its knees. Take the

time to tune your SQL queries. For more information on this topic, read Rich Niemiec's book, "Oracle 9*i* Performance Tuning Tips & Techniques", by Oracle Press.

Code Modularization and Reuse
As with any programming tool, it's good practice to modularize your code. This is easiest to accomplish in HTML DB by calling procedures rather than embedded anonymous PL/SQL blocks. This technique also allows for the reuse of your PL/SQL code.

Use of Built-in Functionality
HTML DB has a considerable amount of functionality that is built in (that is, preprogrammed). Don't reinvent the wheel, but rather use the functions that exist. For example, to check to see if a field is numeric, use the built-in function rather than writing your own function for this purpose.

Error Handling
One way to handle errors in HTML DB is to create a generic error page in all your applications and then use your procedures to set text fields on the generic error page and branch errors to that page. For example, if you were to create a generic error page with an error message, error number, and so on, and the error page was on page 1000, your PL/SQL code might look something like this:

```
Begin
    Procedure_call_1(:p1_field1, :p1_field2);
Exception when no_data_found then
    :p1000_error_message := 'There was no data in the XYZ table...';
    :p1000_error_number := '101';
End;
```

Page 1000 could simply be an HTML region containing the following text:

```
Generic Error Page for HTML DB<hr>
Error Message: &p1000_error_message;<br>
Error Number: &p1000_error_number;<br>
```

PL/SQL Error Handling
At TUSC, we have developed our Server Core Toolkit, which we use for all our development projects. The "default" installation of the toolkit uses database pipes to provide transaction-independent writing of error and debugging messages. A generic procedure provides all the behind-the-scenes error logic. An alternate "message writer" package can be installed that will switch to autonomous transactions instead of database pipes. The autonomous transactions version is slightly easier to maintain because it does not require the running (via dbms_job) of messaging daemons. However, Oracle still throws errors when you attempt to use an autonomous transaction across a database link. So, if the application uses distributed transactions, you are best sticking with the "default" install. We throw this toolkit in with every project we do. So if you're interested in our toolkit, which includes the error logic, hire us for a project. Otherwise, it's recommend that you develop your own error logic library.

Security
Develop a single authorization function that you use throughout all your HTML DB applications. This will ensure that only authorized users can use a given application, even if they are

authenticated and jump into an app from something else or by manually entering the URL. See Chapter 16 for more information on security options available to your application.

Testing

Testing of an HTML DB application should follow your standard testing processes and procedures. You can use automated testing tools or perform manual testing of your application.

When it comes to unit testing, go back to the basics of Programming 101. Do you remember in your first programming class when they told you to only change one section of your code and then compile it? This is true for HTML DB application development as well—do only *one* thing then *test* it. Because the additions and changes you make are instantly available, you should test functionality in small "chunks" rather than doing a number of things prior to testing. This way, if testing uncovers problems or unexpected behavior, you can be reasonably certain that these problems are related to the small section of code you just added or changed.

Like tips and techniques, HTML DB best practices are a living document. As you come upon new best practices, feel free to forward them to the authors for inclusion in our next book.

PART
VII

Appendixes

APPENDIX
A

The HTML DB Packages, Procedures, Functions, and Views

he HTML DB development environment contains several hundred stored procedures that are used by the HTML DB engine. Many of these are also available for use by developers. This appendix covers some of the packages, procedures, functions, and views of HTML DB.

Packages

The HTML DB packages can contain global variables, procedures, and functions. The HTML DB packages include:

- HTMLDB_APPLICATION
- HTMLDB_APPLICATION_GLOBAL
- HTMLDB_CUSTOM_AUTH
- HTMLDB_ITEM
- HTMLDB_LANG
- HTMLDB_LDAP
- HTMLDB_MAIL
- HTMLDB_PLSQL_JOB
- HTMLDB_UTIL
- WWV_CALCULATOR
- WWV_CRYPT
- WWV_EXECUTE_IMMEDIATE

HTMLDB_APPLICATION

The HTMLDB_APPLICATION API package is useful for accessing the following global HTML DB variables:

- **G_USER**   The user currently logged into HTML DB
- **G_FLOW_ID**   The ID of the application currently running
- **G_FLOW_STEP_ID**   The ID of the page currently running
- **G_FLOW_OWNER**   The schema to parse for the currently running application
- **G_REQUEST**   The request variable that was most recently used

HTMLDB_APPLICATION_GLOBAL

HTMLDB_APPLICATION_GLOBAL references the wwv_flow_global package. This package allows you to share data within a session that does not belong to any given package.

HTMLDB_CUSTOM_AUTH

The HTMLDB_CUSTOM_AUTH API package contains a variety of procedures and functions related to authentication and session management. These program units allow you to check to see if an object exists, if a session is valid, or if pages are public. You can set the current user and session with the program units. You can also retrieve the session ID, cookie values, LDAP properties, current username, or security group. You can generate session IDs as well as log users in or out using these program units, too.

This API is covered in depth in the online help/documentation.

HTMLDB_ITEM

The HTMLDB_ITEM API package allows you to dynamically (that is, on the fly) create HTML DB form elements and items such as check boxes, dates with pop-ups, hidden fields, select lists, text area fields, text fields, radio groups, and the like.

This API is covered in depth in the online help/documentation.

HTMLDB_LANG

The HTMLDB_LANG API package facilitates the translation of text strings from one national language to another. This package contains a message function, a message procedure, and a lang function.

The message function returns a message from the HTML DB message repository. The parameters include the name of the message to be printed (p_name), the substitution parameters that replace the text strings %0 through %9 (p0–p9), and an optional parameter to override the language (p_lang). The syntax for each procedure and function is shown here:

```
function message (
    p_name                   in varchar2 default null,
    p0                       in varchar2 default null,
    p1                       in varchar2 default null,
    p2                       in varchar2 default null,
    p3                       in varchar2 default null,
    p4                       in varchar2 default null,
    p5                       in varchar2 default null,
    p6                       in varchar2 default null,
    p7                       in varchar2 default null,
    p8                       in varchar2 default null,
    p9                       in varchar2 default null,
    p_lang                   in varchar2 default null)
    return varchar2;
```

The message procedure contains the same inputs, but has no output.

The lang function retrieves a translated text string from the translatable messages repository within HTML DB. The input parameters for this function include the text string to be translated (p_primary_text_string), the substitution parameters that replace the text strings %0 through %9 (p0–p9), and the primary language (p_primary_language). The syntax for the lang function is shown here:

```
function lang (
    p_primary_text_string    in varchar2 default null,
```

```
p0                          in varchar2 default null,
p1                          in varchar2 default null,
p2                          in varchar2 default null,
p3                          in varchar2 default null,
p4                          in varchar2 default null,
p5                          in varchar2 default null,
p6                          in varchar2 default null,
p7                          in varchar2 default null,
p8                          in varchar2 default null,
p9                          in varchar2 default null,
p_primary_language          in varchar2 default null)
return varchar2;
```

HTMLDB_LDAP

The HTMLDB_LDAP package references the wwv_flow_ldap package. This package contains functions and procedures used to extract data from an LDAP server, such as Oracle Internet Directory (OID).

The authenticate function returns a Boolean indicating whether a username (p_username) authenticates for a specific password (p_password) and search base (p_search_base). The host (p_host) and optionally the port (p_port) of the LDAP server are provided to the function. Here is the syntax:

```
function authenticate(
        p_username      in varchar2 default null,
        p_password      in varchar2 default null,
        p_search_base   in varchar2,
        p_host          in varchar2,
        p_port          in varchar2 default 389)
        return boolean;
```

The is_member function returns a Boolean indicating whether a username (p_username) is a member of a specific group (p_group) and group base (p_group_base) for a specific password (p_pass) and authorization base (p_auth_base). The host (p_host) and optionally the port (p_port) of the LDAP server are provided to the function. Here is the syntax:

```
function is_member(
        p_username      in varchar2,
        p_pass          in varchar2 default null,
        p_auth_base     in varchar2,
        p_host          in varchar2,
        p_port          in varchar2 default 389,
        p_group         in varchar2,
        p_group_base    in varchar2)
        return boolean;
```

The member_of function returns an array of groups that a specific username (p_username), password (p_pass), and search base (p_auth_base) have access to. The host (p_host) and optionally the port (p_port) of the LDAP server are provided to the function. Here is the syntax:

```
function member_of(
      p_username      in varchar2 default null,
      p_pass          in varchar2 default null,
      p_auth_base     in varchar2,
      p_host          in varchar2,
      p_port          in varchar2 default 389)
      return wwv_flow_global.vc_arr2;
```

The member_of2 function returns a string containing the groups that a specific username (p_username), password (p_pass), and authorization base (p_auth_base) have access to. The host (p_host) and optionally the port (p_port) of the LDAP server are provided to the function. Here is the syntax:

```
function member_of2(
      p_username      in varchar2 default null,
      p_pass          in varchar2 default null,
      p_auth_base     in varchar2,
      p_host          in varchar2,
      p_port          in varchar2 default 389)
      return varchar2;
```

The get_user_authenticate procedure returns an array of user attribute values (p_attribute_values) for a specific username (p_username), password (p_pass), authorization base (p_auth_base), and specified attributes (p_attributes). The host (p_host) and optionally the port (p_port) of the LDAP server are provided to the function. Here is the syntax:

```
procedure get_user_attributes(
      p_username            in  varchar2 default null,
      p_pass                in  varchar2 default null,
      p_auth_base           in  varchar2,
      p_host                in  varchar2,
      p_port                in  varchar2 default 389,
      p_attributes          in  wwv_flow_global.vc_arr2,
      p_attribute_values    out wwv_flow_global.vc_arr2);
```

The get_all_user_authenticate procedure returns an array of user attribute names (p_attributes) and a corresponding array of attribute values (p_attribute_values) for a specific username (p_username), password (p_pass), and authorization base (p_auth_base). The host (p_host) and optionally the port (p_port) of the LDAP server are provided to the function. Here is the syntax:

```
procedure get_all_user_attributes(
      p_username            in  varchar2 default null,
      p_pass                in  varchar2 default null,
      p_auth_base           in  varchar2 default null,
      p_host                in  varchar2,
      p_port                in  varchar2 default 389,
      p_attributes          out wwv_flow_global.vc_arr2,
      p_attribute_values    out wwv_flow_global.vc_arr2);
```

HTMLDB_MAIL

The HTMLDB_MAIL API points to the wwv_flow_mail package, which contains the HTML DB generic e-mail routines. The columns you pass to the send module include the e-mail address to which to send the message (p_to), the e-mail address the message is from (p_from), the text body of the message (p_body), the HTML body of the message (p_body_html), the subject of the message (p_subj), the e-mail addresses to include as carbon copies (p_cc), and the blind carbon copy e-mail addresses (p_bcc). This package is overloaded, so the text body and HTML body of the message can be passed as a varchar2 or CLOB value. The syntax for the send procedure is shown here:

```
procedure send( p_to           in varchar2,
                p_from         in varchar2,
                p_body         in varchar2,
                p_body_html    in varchar2 default NULL,
                p_subj         in varchar2 default NULL,
                p_cc           in varchar2 default NULL,
                p_bcc          in varchar2 default NULL);
procedure send( p_to           in varchar2,
                p_from         in varchar2,
                p_body         in clob,
                p_body_html    in clob     default NULL,
                p_subj         in varchar2 default NULL,
                p_cc           in varchar2 default NULL,
                p_bcc          in varchar2 default NULL);
```

A mail queue background process can be kicked off for a specific SMTP host and port using the background procedure. The parameters of this procedure include the ID of the background process (p_id), the hostname of the SMTP server (p_smtp_hostname), and the port number for the SMTP server (p_smtp_portno). The syntax for this procedure is shown here:

```
procedure background( p_id in number,
                      p_smtp_hostname in varchar2,
                      p_smtp_portno in varchar2 );
```

If a background e-mail process has not been established, you can manually push the queued messages using the push_queue procedure. This procedure accepts the hostname and the port number of the SMTP server. Here is the syntax:

```
procedure push_queue( p_smtp_hostname in varchar2,
                      p_smtp_portno in varchar2 );
```

HTMLDB_PLSQL_JOB

The HTMLDB_PLSQL_JOB package references the wwv_flow_plsql_job package, which updates the wwv_flow_jobs table with values passed in. This package allows your application to see all its own outstanding jobs running and their status or error text.

To update a job's status, call the update_job_status procedure. The parameters include the job number (p_job), which can be passed with the reserved word JOB, the current status (p_status) you want associated with this job, and an additional text field (p_desc) for explaining the status field or the job description. Here is the syntax:

```
procedure update_job_status(
    p_job                   in number,
    p_status                in varchar2,
    p_desc                  in varchar2 default null)
```

If you wish to submit a job process to be placed in the "background" of your session, call the submit_process procedure. This procedure accepts the SQL or PL/SQL code you wish to run in your job (p_sql), when you want to run it (p_when), for which the default is immediately, the total number of units of work to be accomplished (p_totalwork), which is useful when you are checking status, the plain text status information for this job (p_status), which will eventually be updateable through this API as discussed previously, and the plain-text value of what "units" p_totalwork refers to (p_units). Here is the syntax:

```
function submit_process(
    p_sql                   in varchar2,
    p_when                  in varchar2     default sysdate,
    p_status                in varchar2     default 'PENDING')
    return number
```

To purge a specific job number (p_job), you can call the purge_process procedure. A process may only be removed if it is not currently running. The syntax for this procedure is shown here:

```
procedure purge_process(
    p_job                   in number)
```

If you wish to verify that the HTML DB database instance is configured to run jobs, you can call the jobs_are_enabled function. This function returns a Boolean indicating whether jobs are enabled for the server. Here is the syntax:

```
function jobs_are_enabled
    return boolean
```

To determine the amount of time that has elapsed since a specific job (p_job) was submitted, you can call the time_elapsed function, which shows elapsed time as a number. Here is the syntax:

```
function time_elapsed(
    p_job                   in number)
    return number
```

HTMLDB_UTIL

The HTMLDB_UTIL API package contains a number of programming utilities for HTML DB. These utilities clear user and page caches as well as allow you to set or change account attributes such as passwords, e-mail addresses, first name, last name, username, preferences, and session state. This API allows you to create new users and new groups for users. You can check to see if a user is in a group, if a password is valid, or if a username is unique. Users can be exported through a procedure in this package. The utilities in this package allow you to remove preferences as well as sort preferences or users. You can retrieve app items, user information, security groups, workspace information, attributes, current user ID, e-mail addresses, files, file IDs, first name, last name, group ID, group name, username, preferences, session state, and user roles. Other utilities in this package allow you to perform string-to-table or table-to-string conversions. URLs can be encoded using a procedure in this package.

This API is well defined in the online help/documentation.

WWV_CALCULATOR

The WWV_CALCULATOR package can be called to display a JavaScript-based calculator, passing a value back to a form field (p_field). To generate the JavaScript code for the calculator, but not display it, you can embed the call to this package in your page process. This will create two JavaScript functions: calculatorFill_{p_field} passes the value back to p_field, and calculatorPopUp_{p_field} pops up the calculator for the field p_field. Calling the show procedure displays the calculator in the browser window you designate. Clicking on the DONE button on this page passes the value back to p_field. The syntax for each procedure is shown here:

```
procedure draw(p_field varchar2);
procedure show(p_field varchar2);
```

WWV_CRYPT

The WWV_CRYPT package provides functions you can use to encrypt and decrypt strings, RAWs, BLOBs, and CLOBs. The algorithm used (single DES or triple DES with two keys or three keys) for encryption will be decided based on the key length. If you pass an 8-byte key, single DES (56-bit key) will be used. When you use a 16-byte key, triple DES with two keys (112-bit key) is used, and when you pass a 24-byte key, triple DES with three keys (168-bit key) is used. The key may be passed in with each call, or it may be set for the package (for setting a global variable) by calling the setKey function one time. The setKey function takes either RAW or varchar2 input. The syntax is shown here:

```
procedure setKey( p_key in varchar2 );
```

If you are encrypting/decrypting RAW or BLOB data, you must use a RAW key. If you are decrypting string or CLOB data, you must use a VARCHAR2 key. In addition to providing a layer on top of encryption, this package provides access to the MD5 routines if installed.

You use the encryptString and decryptString to encrypt/decrypt any string, date, or number data (p_data) up to 32K in size. If you do not pass a key (p_key), because it's optional, you must call setKey first. To save space, we're only showing the varchar2 syntax. The syntax is the same for all the data types. If you look at the package definition, you will see that this package is overloaded for each data type. Here is the syntax:

```
function encryptString( p_data in varchar2,
                        p_key  in varchar2 default NULL )
return varchar2;
function decryptString( p_data in varchar2,
                        p_key  in varchar2 default NULL )
return varchar2;
```

WWV_EXECUTE_IMMEDIATE

The WWV_EXECUTE_IMMEDIATE package allows you to immediately execute a block of SQL code (not a select, but DML or DDL) or PL/SQL code.

The get_userid function returns the user ID for a specific username (p_username). Here is the syntax:

```
function get_userid( p_username in varchar2 ) return int
```

The run_block procedure simply executes a block of code with no inputs or outputs. It automatically binds the necessary variables using the GET_BINDS and V() functions. The parameters include the SQL code (p_sql) and the user to run this code as (p_user). Here is the syntax:

```
procedure run_block
        ( p_sql     in    varchar2,
          p_user    in varchar2 );
```

If you wish to execute a block of SQL code (with no outputs), while passing in and binding variables in the process, use the following run_block syntax:

```
procedure run_block
        ( p_sql     in    varchar2,
          p_names   in dbms_sql.desc_tab,
          p_values  in wwv_flow_global.vc_arr2,
          p_user    in varchar2 );
```

If you wish to run a block of PL/SQL and pass the bind names and values as a varchar array (instead of a dbms_sql.varchar2s data type for the names), use the run_block2 procedure. If p_preserve_state is true, the output values will be saved in the respective session variables. Here is the syntax:

```
procedure run_block2
        ( p_sql     in    varchar2,
          p_names   in wwv_flow_global.vc_arr2,
          p_values  in wwv_flow_global.vc_arr2,
          p_user    in varchar2,
          p_preserve_state in boolean default TRUE );
```

If you wish to run a block of SQL and additionally pass the data types and masks for the input variables, use run_block3:

```
procedure run_block3 (
          p_sql     in varchar2,
          p_names   in wwv_flow_global.vc_arr2,
          p_values  in wwv_flow_global.vc_arr2,
          p_types   in wwv_flow_global.vc_arr2,
          p_masks   in wwv_flow_global.vc_arr2,
          p_user    in varchar2,
          p_preserve_state in boolean default TRUE );
```

To run a block of code without any binding variables, use the run_block4 procedure. The state will not be preserved with this version. run_block4 is used by wwv_flow_dml.insert_row and wwv_flow_dml.update_row. Here is the syntax:

```
procedure run_block4
        ( p_sql     in    varchar2,
          p_names   in wwv_flow_global.vc_arr2,
          p_values  in wwv_flow_global.vc_arr2,
          p_user    in varchar2 );
```

To run a set of DDL statements (each statement in a dbms_sql.varchar2s array record), use the run_ddl procedure with the following syntax:

```
procedure run_ddl
        ( p_sql     in dbms_sql.varchar2s,
          p_user    in varchar2 );
```

To check the syntax of your PL/SQL code, you can execute the check_plsql function, passing the SQL or PL/SQL code (p_sql), the application ID (p_flow_id), and security group ID (p_security_group_id). Here is the syntax:

```
function check_plsql (
        p_sql                 in varchar2,
          p_flow_id             in number,
          p_security_group_id in number
) return varchar2;
```

If you wish to count the number or rows that match a query or execute a result set that returns a single column, you can use the countem function. It returns the single value as a string. The valueof_vc function performs the same purpose. The valueof_num function returns the single column value as a number. The valueof_date function returns the single column as a date. Here is the syntax:

```
function countem( p_sql in varchar2,
                      p_user in varchar2 ) return varchar2;
function valueof_vc( p_sql in varchar2,
                        p_user in varchar2 ) return varchar2;
function valueof_num( p_sql in varchar2,
                          p_user in varchar2 ) return number;
function valueof_date( p_sql in varchar2,
                          p_user in varchar2 ) return date;
```

The select_vc, select_num, and select_date functions are the same as the valueof functions. Their syntax is shown next:

```
function select_vc( p_sql in varchar2,
                        p_user in varchar2 ) return varchar2;
function select_num( p_sql in varchar2,
                          p_user in varchar2 ) return number;
function select_date( p_sql in varchar2,
                          p_user in varchar2 ) return date;
```

To return a cursor value for a SQL statement, use the func_returning_cursor function. Here is the syntax:

```
function func_returning_cursor( p_sql in varchar2,
                                p_user in varchar2 ) return number;
```

HTML DB Procedures

The HTML DB procedures are useful to understand. They include the following:

- DEVELOPMENT_SERVICE_HOME
- DEVELOPMENT_SERVICE_HOME_LOGIN
- HTMLDB
- HTMLDB_ADMIN
- HTMLDB_DATA_WORKSHOP
- HTMLDB_LOGIN
- HTMLDB_SQL_WORKSHOP

DEVELOPMENT_SERVICE_HOME

The DEVELOPMENT_SERVICE_HOME procedure takes you directly to the HTML DB development service home. This is the same as the following HTML DB procedure. Here's an example:

http://machine/pls/HTMLDB/ DEVELOPMENT_SERVICE_HOME

DEVELOPMENT_SERVICE_HOME_LOGIN

The DEVELOPMENT_SERVICE_HOME_LOGIN procedure takes you directly to the HTML DB login page. Here's an example:

http://machine/pls/HTMLDB/ DEVELOPMENT_SERVICE_HOME_LOGIN

HTMLDB

The HTMLDB procedure is the default procedure that is executed for the HTMLDB DAD. This procedure takes you directly to the HTML DB development service home. Here's an example:

http://machine/pls/HTMLDB/ htmldb

HTMLDB_ADMIN

The HTMLDB_ADMIN procedure contains the application and starting page for the administration pages of HTML DB. The defaults for these values are 4050 and 3, respectively. You can change these values by editing this procedure if you wish. When you log into the INTERNAL workspace, this procedure is called.

You can also use this procedure as a template to create another quick starting point for an HTML DB application. For example, to start the RSVP application, you could copy this procedure to a new procedure called RSVP and change the application and page numbers accordingly. You could then direct users to the following URL:

http://machine/pls/HTMLDB/rsvp

This would start the RSVP application directly.

HTMLDB_DATA_WORKSHOP

The HTMLDB_DATA_WORKSHOP procedure takes you directly to the HTML DB data workshop file repository page. Here's an example:

http://machine/pls/HTMLDB/htmldb_data_workshop

HTMLDB_LOGIN

The HTMLDB_LOGIN procedure takes you directly to the HTML DB application login page. Here's an example:

http://machine/pls/HTMLDB/htmldb_login

HTMLDB_SQL_WORKSHOP

The HTMLDB_SQL_WORKSHOP procedure takes you directly to the HTML DB SQL Workshop. Here's an example:

http://machine/pls/HTMLDB/htmldb_sql_workshop

HTML DB Functions

The HTML DB functions include the following:

- WWV_FLOWS_RELEASE
- WWV_FLOWS_VERSION

WWV_FLOWS_RELEASE

The WWV_FLOWS_RELEASE function returns the HTML DB version as a string.

WWV_FLOWS_VERSION

The WWV_FLOWS_VERSION function returns the date this version of HTML DB was released as a string in the format yyyy.mm.dd.

HTML DB Views

The HTML DB views reference queries against HTML DB base tables. These include the following:

- HTMLDB_ACTIVITY_LOG
- HTMLDB_APPLICATION_FILES

- HTMLDB_COLLECTIONS

- HTMLDB_MAIL_LOG

- HTMLDB_MAIL_QUEUE

- HTMLDB_PLSQL_JOBS

HTMLDB_ACTIVITY_LOG
The HTMLDB_ACTIVITY_LOG view provides a detailed activity log for HTML DB workspaces.

HTMLDB_APPLICATION_FILES
The HTMLDB_APPLICATION_FILES view points to the WWV_FLOW_FILES view, which references all records from WWV_FLOW_FILE_OBJECTS$ for the current workspace.

HTMLDB_COLLECTIONS
The HTMLDB_COLLECTIONS view points to the WWV_FLOW_COLLECTIONS view, which is accessible to the users for collections.

HTMLDB_MAIL_LOG
The HTMLDB_MAIL_LOG view points to the WWV_FLOW_USER_MAIL_LOG table, which contains a lot of the e-mail messages that have been sent.

HTMLDB_MAIL_QUEUE
The HTMLDB_MAIL_QUEUE view references the WWV_FLOW_USER_MAIL_QUEUE table, which contains all the messages currently in the outbound e-mail queue.

HTMLDB_PLSQL_JOBS
The HTMLDB_PLSQL_JOBS view references the WWV_FLOW_PLSQL_JOBS table, which contains information about the previously queued PL/SQL jobs.

APPENDIX
B

PL/SQL Web Toolkit and
Packages

he PL/SQL Web Toolkit is a set of PL/SQL packages that can be used in HTML DB dynamic regions. These packages can obtain information about an HTTP request, specify HTTP response headers, such as cookies, content-type, and mime-type, and for HTTP headers they can set cookies and generate standard HTML tags.

Typically when you use the PL/SQL Web Toolkit with HTML DB you are also going to use some of the HTML DB packages covered in Appendix A.

The following piece of code was taken from a PL/SQL Procedure region. The region creates a multirow edit form where the rows are displayed vertically.

```
-- populate table of detail measurement records
htp.p('<table >');
--
--create a delete checkbox row
--
htp.p('<tr><th class="'||v_th_class||'">Delete This Record</th>');
for x in 1..v_loop_count loop
   htp.p('<td  class="'||v_td_class||'">');
   htp.p(htmldb_item.checkbox(24,x,null, null));
   htp.p('</td>');
end loop;
htp.p('<th class="'||v_th_class||'">Delete This Record</th>');
htp.p('</tr>');
--
-- create and populate time_id row
--
htp.p('<tr><th width="10%" class="'||v_th_class||'">Time</th>');
for x in 1..v_loop_count loop
  if x <= v_count then
    v_value := v_table(x).time_id;
  else
    v_value := null;
  end if;
   htp.p('<td  class="'||v_td_class||'">');
   htp.p(htmldb_item.select_list_from_lov(2,v_value,'TIME',
                         'onChange="javascript:check4DupTimes(this);"',
                         NO',null,null,'F02_'||x));
 --
 -- create data field measurement_id and populate with a value (if exists)
 -- and do not display
 --
   if x <= v_count then
     v_value := v_table(x).measurement_id;
    else
      v_value := null;
    end if;
   htp.p(htmldb_item.hidden(1,v_value));
   htp.p('</td>');
end loop;
htp.p('<th width="10%" class="'||v_th_class||'">Time</th>');
```

```
htp.p('</tr>');
......
......
htp.p('</table>');
```

Structure Tags

Syntax	Generates
`htp.htmlOpen;`	`<HTML>`
`htp.htmlClose;`	`</HTML>`
`htp.headOpen;`	`<HEAD>`
`htp.headClose;`	`</HEAD>`
`htp.bodyOpen (cbackground, cattributes);`	`<BODY background="cbackground" cattribute>`
`htp.bodyClose;`	`</BODY>`
`htp.Comment (ctext);`	`<!-- ctext -->`

Head-related Tags

Syntax	Generates
`htp.base (ctarget, cattributes);`	`<BASE HREF={current URL} TARGET=ctarget cattributes>`
`htp.isindex (cprompt, curl);`	`<ISINDEX PROMPT="cprompt" HREF="curl">`
`htp.linkRel (crel, curl, ctitle)`	`<LINK REL="crel" HREF="curl" TITLE="ctitle">`
`htp.linkRev (crev, curl, ctitle);`	`<LINK REV="crev" HREF="curl" TITLE="ctitle">`
`htp.meta (chttp_equiv, cname, ccontent);`	`<META HTTP-EQUIV="chttp_equiv" NAME="cname" CONTENT="ccontent">`
`htp.title (ctitle);`	`<TITLE>ctitle</TITLE>`

Functional Object Tags

Syntax	Generates
`htp.anchor (curl, ctext, cname, cattributes);`	`<A HREF="curl" NAME="cname" cattributes>ctext</A>`
`htp.anchor2 (curl, ctext, cname, ctarget, cattributes);`	`<A HREF="curl" NAME="cname" TARGET = "ctarget" cattributes>ctext</A>`

Syntax	Generates
htp.area(ccoords, cshape, chref, cnohref, ctarget, cattributes);	`<AREA COORDS="ccoords" SHAPE="cshape" HREF="chref" NOHREF TARGET="ctarget" cattributes>`
htp.bgsound(csrc, cloop, cattributes);	`<BGSOUND SRC="csrc" LOOP="cloop" cattributes>`
htp.img (curl, calign, calt, cismap, cattributes);	`<IMG SRC="curl" ALIGN="calign" ALT="calt" ISMAP cattributes>`
htp.img2 (curl, calign, calt, cismap, cusemap, cattributes);	`<IMG SRC="curl" ALIGN="calign" ALT="calt" ISMAP USEMAP="cusemap" cattributes>`
htp.mailto (caddress, ctext, cname, cattributes);	`<A NAME=cname HREF="mailto:caddress" cattributes>ctext</A>`
htp.mapOpen(cname, cattributes);	`<MAP NAME="cname" cattributes>`
htp.mapClose;	`</MAP>`

List Tags

Syntax	Generates
htp.dirlistOpen;	`<DIR>`
htp.dirlistClose;	`</DIR>`
htp.dlistDef (ctext, cclear, cattributes);	`<DD CLEAR="cclear" cattributes>ctext`
htp.dlistOpen (cclear, cattributes);	`<DL CLEAR="cclear" cattributes>`
htp.dlistClose	`</DL>`
htp.dlistTerm (ctext, cclear, cattributes);	`<DT CLEAR="cclear" cattributes>ctext`
htp.listHeader (ctext, cattributes);	`<LH cattributes>ctext</LH>`
htp.listItem (ctext, cclear, cdingbat, csrc, cattributes);	`<LI CLEAR="cclear" DINGBAT="cdingbat" SRC="csrc" cattributes>ctext`
htp.menulistOpen;	`<MENU>`
htp.menulistClose;	`</MENU>`
htp.olistOpen (cclear, cwrap, cattributes);	`<OL CLEAR="cclear" WRAP="cwrap" cattributes>`
htp.olistClose;	`</OL>`

Syntax

```
htp.ulistOpen (cclear, cwrap,
cdingbat, csrc, cattributes);

htp.ulistClose;
```

Generates

```
<UL CLEAR="cclear" WRAP="cwrap"
DINGBAT="cdingbat" SRC="csrc"
cattributes>

</UL>
```

Table Tags

Syntax

```
htp.tableOpen (cborder,
calign, cnowrap, cclear,
cattributes);

htp.tableClose;

htp.tableCaption
(ccaption, calign,
cattributes);

htp.tableData (cvalue,
calign, cdp, crowspan,
ccolspan, cnowrap,
cattributes)

htp.tableHeader (cvalue,
calign, cdp, cnowrap,
crowspan, ccolspan,
cattributes);

htp.tableRowOpen (calign,
cvalign,cdp, cnowrap,
cattributes);

htp.tableRowClose;
```

Generates

```
<TABLE "cborder" NOWRAP ALIGN="calign"
CLEAR="cclear" cattributes>


</TABLE>

<CAPTION ALIGN="calign"
cattributes>ccaption</CAPTION>


<TD ALIGN="calign" DP="cdp"
ROWSPAN="crowspan" COLSPAN="ccolspan"
NOWRAP cattributes>cvalue</TD>


<TH ALIGN="calign" DP="cdp"
ROWSPAN="crowspan" COLSPAN="ccolspan"
NOWRAP cattributes>cvalue</TH>


<TR ALIGN="calign" VALIGN="cvalign"
DP="cdp" NOWRAP cattributes>


</TR>
```

Form Tags

Syntax

```
htp.formOpen (curl,
cmethod, ctarget,
cenctype, cattributes);

htp.formClose;

htp.formCheckbox (cname,
cvalue, cchecked,
cattributes);

htp.formHidden (cname,
cvalue, cattributes);
```

Generates

```
<FORM ACTION="curl" METHOD="cmethod"
TARGET="ctarget" ENCTYPE="cenctype"
cattributes>

</FORM>

<INPUT TYPE="checkbox" NAME="cname"
VALUE="cvalue" CHECKED cattributes>
<Command>

<INPUT TYPE="hidden" NAME="cname"
VALUE="cvalue" cattributes>
```

Syntax	Generates
`htp.formImage (cname, csrc, calign, cattributes);`	`<INPUT TYPE="image" NAME="cname" SRC="csrc" ALIGN="calign" cattributes>`
`htp.formPassword (cname, csize, cmaxlength, cvalue, cattributes);`	`<INPUT TYPE="password" NAME="cname" SIZE="csize" MAXLENGTH="cmaxlength" VALUE="cvalue" cattributes>`
`htp.formRadio (cname, cvalue, cchecked, cattributes);`	`<INPUT TYPE="radio" NAME="cname" VALUE="cvalue" CHECKED cattributes>`
`htp.formReset (cvalue, cattributes);`	`<INPUT TYPE="reset" VALUE="cvalue" cattributes>`
`htp.formSubmit (cname, cvalue, cattributes);`	`<INPUT TYPE="submit" NAME="cname" VALUE="cvalue" cattributes>`
`htp.formText (cname, csize, cmaxlength, cvalue, cattributes);`	`<INPUT TYPE="text" NAME="cname" SIZE="csize" MAXLENGTH="cmaxlength" VALUE="cvalue" cattributes>`

Select

Syntax	Generates
`htp.formSelectOpen (cname, cprompt, nsize, cattributes);`	`cprompt <SELECT NAME="cname" PROMPT="cprompt" SIZE="nsize" cattributes>`
`htp.formSelectOption (cvalue, cselected, cattributes);`	`<OPTION SELECTED cattributes>cvalue`
`htp.formSelectClose;`	`</SELECT>`
`htp.formTextarea (cname, nrows, ncolumns, calign, cattributes);`	`<TEXTAREA NAME="cname" ROWS="nrows" COLS="ncolumns" ALIGN="calign" cattributes></TEXTAREA>`
`htp.formTextarea2 (cname, nrows, ncolumns, calign, cwrap, cattributes);`	`<TEXTAREA NAME="cname" ROWS="nrows" COLS="ncolumns" ALIGN="calign" WRAP="cwrap" cattributes></TEXTAREA>`
`htp.formTextareaOpen (cname, nrows, ncolumns, calign, cattributes);`	`<TEXTAREA NAME="cname" ROWS="nrows" COLS="ncolumns" ALIGN="calign" cattributes>`

Syntax	Generates

`htp.formTextareaOpen`
`(cname, nrows,`
`ncolumns, calign,`
`cwrap, cattributes);`
	`<TEXTAREA NAME="cname" ROWS="nrows"`
	`COLS="ncolumns" ALIGN="calign" WRAP =`
	`"cwrap" cattributes>`

`htp.` `formTextareaClose;`	`</TEXTAREA>`

Frame Tags

Syntax	Generates
`htp.framesetOpen`	`<FRAMESET>`
`htp.framesetClose;`	`</FRAMESET>`

`htp.frame(csrc, cname,`
`cmarginwidth, cmarginheight,`
`cscrolling, cnoresize,`
`cattributes);`
	`<FRAME SRC="csrc" NAME="cname" MARGIN`
	`WIDTH="cmarginwidth" MARGINHEIGHT="c`
	`marginheight" SCROLLING="cscrolling"`
	`NORESIZE cattributes>`

`htp.noframesOpen;`	`<NOFRAMES>`
`htp.noframesClose;`	`</NOFRAMES>`

General Format Tags

Syntax	Generates
`htp.div(calign, cattributes);`	`<DIV ALIGN="calign" cattributes>`

`htp.header (nsize, cheader,`
`calign, cnowrap, cclear,`
`cattributes);`
	`<Hnsize ALIGN="calign"`
	`NOWRAP CLEAR="cclear"`
	`cattributes>cheader</Hnsize>`

Lines

Syntax	Generates
`htp.line (cclear, csrc,` `cattributes);`	`<HR CLEAR="cclear" SRC="csrc" cattributes>`

Breaks and No Breaks

Syntax	Generates
`htp.br (cclear, cattributes);`	`<BR CLEAR="cclear" cattributes>`

Syntax	Generates
`htp.nl (cclear, cattributes);`	`<BR CLEAR="cclear" cattributes>`
`htp.nobr(ctext);`	`<NOBR>ctext</NOBR>`
`htp.wbr;`	`<WBR>`

Paragraphs

Syntax	Generates
`htp.para`	`<P>`
`htp.paragraph (calign, cnowrap, cclear, cattributes);`	`<P ALIGN="calign" NOWRAP CLEAR="cclear" cattributes>`

Formatting Text and Images

Syntax	Generates
`htp.address (cvalue, cnowrap, cclear, cattributes);`	`<ADDRESS CLEAR="cclear" NOWRAP cattributes>cvalue</ADDRESS>`
`htp.blockquoteOpen (cnowrap, cclear, cattributes);`	`<BLOCKQUOTE CLEAR="cclear" NOWRAP cattributes>`
`htp.blockquoteClose;`	`</BLOCKQUOTE>`
`htp.center(ctext);`	`<CENTER>ctext</CENTER>`
`htp.centerOpen;`	`<CENTER>`
`htp.centerClose;`	`</CENTER>`
`htp.listingOpen;`	`<LISTING>`
`htp.listingClose;`	`</LISTING>`
`htp.preOpen (cclear, cwidth, cattributes);`	`<PRE CLEAR="cclear" WIDTH="cwidth" cattributes>`
`htp.preClose;`	`</PRE>`

Character Format for Fonts

Syntax	Generates
`htp.basefont(nsize);`	`<BASEFONT SIZE="nsize">`
`htp.fontOpen(ccolor, cface, csize, cattributes);`	`<FONT COLOR="ccolor" FACE="cface" SIZE="csize" cattributes>`
`htp.fontClose;`	`</FONT>`

Special Character Format

Syntax	Generates
`htp.big(ctext, cattributes);`	`<BIG cattributes>ctext</BIG>`
`htp.dfn(ctext);`	`<DFN>ctext</DFN>`
`htp.plaintext(ctext, cattributes);`	`<PLAINTEXT cattributes>ctext</PLAINTEXT>`
`htp.s(ctext, cattributes);`	`<S cattributes>ctext</S>`
`htp.small(ctext, cattributes);`	`<SMALL cattributes>ctext</SMALL>`
`htp.strike(ctext, cattributes);`	`<STRIKE cattributes>ctext</STRIKE>`
`htp.sub(ctext, calign, cattributes);`	`<SUB ALIGN="calign" cattributes>ctext</SUB>`
`htp.sup(ctext, calign, cattributes);`	`<SUP ALIGN="calign" cattributes>ctext</SUP>`

Character Format Tags

Syntax	Generates
`htp.cite (ctext, cattributes);`	`<CITE cattributes>ctext</CITE>`
`htp.code (ctext, cattributes);`	`<CODE cattributes>ctext</CODE>`
`htp.em (ctext, cattributes);`	`<EM cattributes>ctext</EM>`
`htp.emphasis (ctext, cattributes);`	`<EM cattributes>ctext</EM>`
`htp.kbd (ctext, cattributes);`	`<KBD cattributes>ctext</KBD>`
`htp.keyboard (ctext, cattributes);`	`<KBD cattributes>ctext</KBD>`
`htp.sample (ctext, cattributes);`	`<SAMP cattributes>ctext</SAMP>`
`htp.strong (ctext, cattributes);`	`<STRONG cattributes>ctext</STRONG>`
`htp.variable (ctext, cattributes);`	`<VAR cattributes>ctext</VAR>`

Physical Format Tags

Syntax	Generates
`htp.bold (ctext, cattributes);`	`<B cattributes>ctext</B>`

Syntax	Generates
`htp.italic (ctext, cattributes);`	`<I cattributes>ctext</I>`
`htp.teletype (ctext, cattributes);`	`<TT cattributes>ctext</TT>`

OWA Packages

The PL/SQL Web Toolkit contains utility packages that are commonly referred to as the OWA packages because they all start with the prefix OWA, which stands for Oracle Web Agent.

OWA_COOKIE Package

Syntax	Generates
`owa_cookie.send(name, value, expires, path, domain, secure)`	`Set-Cookie: <name>=<value> expires=<expires> path=<path> domain=<domain> secure`
`owa_cookie.get(name)`	`Get-cookie: <name>`
`owa_cookie.get_all(names, vals, num_vals)`	Output contains an array of cookie names, an array of cookie values, and the number of cookie-value pairs.
`owa_cookie.remove(name, value, path)`	`Set-Cookie: <name>=<value> expires=01-JAN-1990 path=<path>`

OWA_IMAGE Package

Syntax	Generates
`owa_image.get_x(p)`	x-coordinate as integer
`owa_image.get_Y(p)`	y-coordinate as integer

OWA_OPT_LOCK Package

Syntax	Generates
`owa_opt_lock.checksum(p_buff in varchar2) return number;`	A checksum value
`owa_opt_lock.checksum(p_owner in varchar2, p_tname in varchar2, p_rowid in rowid) return number;`	A checksum value
`owa_opt_lock.get_rowid(p_old_values in vcArray) return rowid;`	A row ID
`owa_opt_lock.store_values(p_owner in varchar2, p_tname in varchar2, p_rowid in rowid);`	A series of hidden form elements

Syntax	Generates
`owa_opt_lock.verify_values(p_old_values in vcArray) return boolean;`	TRUE if no other update has been performed; FALSE otherwise

OWA_PATTERN Package

Syntax	Generates
`owa_pattern.match(line, pat, flags)`	Boolean indicating whether match was found.
`owa_pattern.match(line, pat, backrefs, flags)`	Boolean indicating whether match was found.
`owa_pattern.match(mline, pat, rlist, flags)`	Boolean indicating whether match was found.
`owa_pattern.amatch(line, from_loc, pat, flags)`	Location (in number of characters from the beginning) to the end of the match. 0 if there are none.
`owa_pattern.amatch(line, from_loc, pat, backrefs, flags)`	Location (in number of characters from the beginning) to the end of the match. 0 if there are none.
`owa_pattern.change(line, from_str, to_str, flags)`	Revises the line parameter. Function outputs the number of substitutions made.
`owa_pattern.change(mline, from_str, to_str, backrefs, flags)`	Revises the mline parameter. Function outputs the number of substitutions made.
`owa_pattern.change(mline, from_str, to_str, flags)`	Revises the mline parameter.
`owa_pattern.getpat(arg, pat)`	Pattern.

OWA_SEC Package

Syntax	Generates
`owa_sec.get_client_hostname return varchar2;`	The hostname
`owa_sec.get_client_ip return owa_util.ip_address;`	IP address of the client
`owa_sec.get_password return varchar2;`	The password
`owa_sec.get_user_id return varchar2;`	The username
`owa_sec.set_authorization(scheme in integer);`	Sets authorization scheme for PL/SQL gateway

Syntax	Generates
`owa_sec.set_protection_realm(realm in varchar2);`	Sets the realm of the page that is returned to the user

OWA_TEXT Package

Syntax	Generates
`owa_text.stream2multi(stream, mline)`	`multi_line`
`owa_text.add2multi(stream, mline, continue)`	`multi_line`
`owa_text.new_row_list(rlist)`	Actual output generated by `htp.print`
`owa_text.print_multi(mline)`	Actual output generated by `htp.print`
`owa_text.print_row_list(rlist)`	Actual output generated by `htp.print`

OWA_UTIL Package

Syntax	Generates
`owa_util.bind_variables(theQuery in varchar2 DEFAULT NULL, bv1Name in varchar2 DEFAULT NULL, bv1Value in varchar2 DEFAULT NULL, bv2Name in varchar2 DEFAULT NULL, bv2Value in varchar2 DEFAULT NULL, bv3Name in varchar2 DEFAULT NULL, bv3Value in varchar2 DEFAULT NULL, ...`	Prepares a SQL query by binding variables to it, and stores the output in an opened cursor.
`bv25Name in varchar2 DEFAULT NULL, bv25Value in varchar2 DEFAULT NULL) return integer;`	An integer identifying the opened cursor.
`owa_util.calendarprint (inDate in date default sysdate)`	Creates a calendar in HTML.
`owa_util.choose_date(p_name in varchar2, p_date in date DEFAULT SYSDATE);`	Select an option for dates.
`owa_util.dateType Datatype (Date Datatype)`	The type is defined as table of `varchar2(10)` index by `binary_integer`.

Syntax	Generates
`owa_util.get_cgi_env(param_name in varchar2) return varchar2;`	
`owa_util.get_owa_service_path return varchar2;`	A virtual path of the PL/SQL cartridge that is handling the request.
`owa_util.get_procedure return varchar2;`	The name of a procedure, including the package name if the procedure is defined in a package.
`owa_util.http_header_close;`	A newline character, which closes the HTTP header.
`owa_util.ident_arr Datatype` (Miscellaneous)	The type is definded as table of `varchar2(30)` index by `binary_integer`.
`owa_util.ip_address Datatype` (Miscellaneous)	The type is defined as table of `integer` index by `binary_integer`.
`owa_util.listprint(p_theQuery in varchar2, p_cname in varchar2, p_nsize in number, p_multiple in boolean DEFAULT FALSE);`	
`owa_util.listprint(p_theCursor in integer, p_cname in varchar2, p_nsize in number, p_multiple in boolean DEFAULT FALSE);` `<SELECT NAME="p_cname" SIZE="p_nsize">` `<OPTION SELECTED value='value_from_the_first_column'>value_from_the_second_column` `<OPTION SELECTED value='value_from_the_first_column'>value_from_the_second_column` `...` `</SELECT>`	
`owa_util.mime_header(ccontent_type in varchar2 DEFAULT \`text/html', bclose_header in boolean DEFAULT TRUE);`	`Content-type: <ccontent_type>\n\n`
`owa_util.print_cgi_env;`	`cgi_env_var_name = value\n`

Syntax	**Generates**
`owa_util.redirect_url( curl in varchar2, bclose_header in boolean DEFAULT TRUE);`	`Location: <curl>\n\n`
`owa_util.showpage;`	The output of the `htp` procedure is displayed in SQL*Plus.
`owa_util.showsource (cname in varchar2);`	The source code of the specified function, procedure, or package.
`owa_util.signature;`	

`owa_util.signature (cname in varchar2);`	Without a parameter, the procedure generates a line that looks like the following:
	`This page was produced by the PL/ SQL Agent on August 9, 2005 09:30`
	With a parameter, the procedure generates a signature line in the HTML document that might look like the following:
	`This page was produced by the PL/ SQL Agent on 6/14/05 09:30`

View PL/SQL Source

`owa_util.status_line( nstatus in integer, creason in varchar2 DEFAULT NULL, bclose_header in boolean DEFAULT TRUE);`	`Status: <nstatus> <creason>\n\n`
`owa_util.tablePrint( ctable in varchar2, cattributes in varchar2 DEFAULT NULL, table_ type in integer DEFAULT HTML_ TABLE, ccolumns in varchar2 DEFAULT `*`, cclauses in varchar2 DEFAULT NULL, ccol_ aliases in varchar2 DEFAULT NULL, nrow_min in number DEFAULT 0, nrow_max in number DEFAULT NULL )`	
`return boolean;`	A preformatted or HTML table.
`owa_util.todate(p_dateArray in dateType) return date;`	A standard date.
`owa_util.who_called_me( owner out varchar2, name out varchar2, lineno out number, caller_t out varchar2);`	Calling procedure name.

Index

B

N

O

P

Q

R

T

GET YOUR FREE SUBSCRIPTION
TO ORACLE MAGAZINE

Oracle Magazine is essential gear for today's information technology professionals. Stay informed and increase your productivity with every issue of *Oracle Magazine*. Inside each free bimonthly issue you'll get:

- Up-to-date information on Oracle Database, Oracle Application Server, Web development, enterprise grid computing, database technology, and business trends
- Third-party vendor news and announcements
- Technical articles on Oracle and partner products, technologies, and operating environments
- Development and administration tips
- Real-world customer stories

IF THERE ARE OTHER ORACLE USERS AT YOUR LOCATION WHO WOULD LIKE TO RECEIVE THEIR OWN SUB-SCRIPTION TO ORACLE MAGAZINE, PLEASE PHOTOCOPY THIS FORM AND PASS IT ALONG.

Three easy ways to subscribe:

① Web
Visit our Web site at otn.oracle.com/oraclemagazine. You'll find a subscription form there, plus much more!

② Fax
Complete the questionnaire on the back of this card and fax the questionnaire side only to +1.847.763.9638.

③ Mail
Complete the questionnaire on the back of this card and mail it to P.O. Box 1263, Skokie, IL 60076-8263

FREE SUBSCRIPTION

O **Yes, please send me a FREE subscription to *Oracle Magazine*.**
To receive a free subscription to *Oracle Magazine*, you must fill out the entire card, sign it, and date it (incomplete cards cannot be processed or acknowledged). You can also fax your application to +1.847.763.9638.
Or subscribe at our Web site at otn.oracle.com/oraclemagazine

O **NO**

O From time to time, Oracle Publishing allows our partners exclusive access to our e-mail addresses for special promotions and announcements. To be included in this program, please check this circle.

signature (required)   date

X

O Oracle Publishing allows sharing of our mailing list with selected third parties. If you prefer your mailing address not to be included in this program, please check here. If at any time you would like to be removed from this mailing list, please contact Customer Service at +1.847.647.9630 or send an e-mail to oracle@halldata.com.

name   title

company   e-mail address

street/p.o. box

city/state/zip or postal code   telephone

country   fax

YOU MUST ANSWER ALL TEN QUESTIONS BELOW.

(1) WHAT IS THE PRIMARY BUSINESS ACTIVITY OF YOUR FIRM AT THIS LOCATION? (check one only)
- ☐ 01 Aerospace and Defense Manufacturing
- ☐ 02 Application Service Provider
- ☐ 03 Automotive Manufacturing
- ☐ 04 Chemicals, Oil and Gas
- ☐ 05 Communications and Media
- ☐ 06 Construction/Engineering
- ☐ 07 Consumer Sector/Consumer Packaged Goods
- ☐ 08 Education
- ☐ 09 Financial Services/Insurance
- ☐ 10 Government (civil)
- ☐ 11 Government (military)
- ☐ 12 Healthcare
- ☐ 13 High Technology Manufacturing, OEM
- ☐ 14 Integrated Software Vendor
- ☐ 15 Life Sciences (Biotech, Pharmaceuticals)
- ☐ 16 Mining
- ☐ 17 Retail/Wholesale/Distribution
- ☐ 18 Systems Integrator, VAR/VAD
- ☐ 19 Telecommunications
- ☐ 20 Travel and Transportation
- ☐ 21 Utilities (electric, gas, sanitation, water)
- ☐ 98 Other Business and Services

(2) WHICH OF THE FOLLOWING BEST DESCRIBES YOUR PRIMARY JOB FUNCTION? (check one only)
Corporate Management/Staff
- ☐ 01 Executive Management (President, Chair, CEO, CFO, Owner, Partner, Principal)
- ☐ 02 Finance/Administrative Management (VP/Director/ Manager/Controller, Purchasing, Administration)
- ☐ 03 Sales/Marketing Management (VP/Director/Manager)
- ☐ 04 Computer Systems/Operations Management (CIO/VP/Director/ Manager MIS, Operations)
IS/IT Staff
- ☐ 05 Systems Development/ Programming Management
- ☐ 06 Systems Development/ Programming Staff
- ☐ 07 Consulting
- ☐ 08 DBA/Systems Administrator
- ☐ 09 Education/Training
- ☐ 10 Technical Support Director/Manager
- ☐ 11 Other Technical Management/Staff
- ☐ 98 Other

(3) WHAT IS YOUR CURRENT PRIMARY OPERATING PLATFORM? (select all that apply)
- ☐ 01 Digital Equipment UNIX
- ☐ 02 Digital Equipment VAX VMS
- ☐ 03 HP UNIX

- ☐ 04 IBM AIX
- ☐ 05 IBM UNIX
- ☐ 06 Java
- ☐ 07 Linux
- ☐ 08 Macintosh
- ☐ 09 MS-DOS
- ☐ 10 MVS
- ☐ 11 NetWare
- ☐ 12 Network Computing
- ☐ 13 OpenVMS
- ☐ 14 SCO UNIX
- ☐ 15 Sequent DYNIX/ptx
- ☐ 16 Sun Solaris/SunOS
- ☐ 17 SVR4
- ☐ 18 UnixWare
- ☐ 19 Windows
- ☐ 20 Windows NT
- ☐ 21 Other UNIX
- ☐ 98 Other
- ☐ 99 None of the above

(4) DO YOU EVALUATE, SPECIFY, RECOMMEND, OR AUTHORIZE THE PURCHASE OF ANY OF THE FOLLOWING? (check all that apply)
- ☐ 01 Hardware
- ☐ 02 Software
- ☐ 03 Application Development Tools
- ☐ 04 Database Products
- ☐ 05 Internet or Intranet Products
- ☐ 99 None of the above

(5) IN YOUR JOB, DO YOU USE OR PLAN TO PURCHASE ANY OF THE FOLLOWING PRODUCTS? (check all that apply)
Software
- ☐ 01 Business Graphics
- ☐ 02 CAD/CAE/CAM
- ☐ 03 CASE
- ☐ 04 Communications
- ☐ 05 Database Management
- ☐ 06 File Management
- ☐ 07 Finance
- ☐ 08 Java
- ☐ 09 Materials Resource Planning
- ☐ 10 Multimedia Authoring
- ☐ 11 Networking
- ☐ 12 Office Automation
- ☐ 13 Order Entry/Inventory Control
- ☐ 14 Programming
- ☐ 15 Project Management
- ☐ 16 Scientific and Engineering
- ☐ 17 Spreadsheets
- ☐ 18 Systems Management
- ☐ 19 Workflow

Hardware
- ☐ 20 Macintosh
- ☐ 21 Mainframe
- ☐ 22 Massively Parallel Processing
- ☐ 23 Minicomputer
- ☐ 24 PC
- ☐ 25 Network Computer
- ☐ 26 Symmetric Multiprocessing
- ☐ 27 Workstation
Peripherals
- ☐ 28 Bridges/Routers/Hubs/Gateways
- ☐ 29 CD-ROM Drives
- ☐ 30 Disk Drives/Subsystems
- ☐ 31 Modems
- ☐ 32 Tape Drives/Subsystems
- ☐ 33 Video Boards/Multimedia
Services
- ☐ 34 Application Service Provider
- ☐ 35 Consulting
- ☐ 36 Education/Training
- ☐ 37 Maintenance
- ☐ 38 Online Database Services
- ☐ 39 Support
- ☐ 40 Technology-Based Training
- ☐ 98 Other
- ☐ 99 None of the above

(6) WHAT ORACLE PRODUCTS ARE IN USE AT YOUR SITE? (check all that apply)
Oracle E-Business Suite
- ☐ 01 Oracle Marketing
- ☐ 02 Oracle Sales
- ☐ 03 Oracle Order Fulfillment
- ☐ 04 Oracle Supply Chain Management
- ☐ 05 Oracle Procurement
- ☐ 06 Oracle Manufacturing
- ☐ 07 Oracle Maintenance Management
- ☐ 08 Oracle Service
- ☐ 09 Oracle Contracts
- ☐ 10 Oracle Projects
- ☐ 11 Oracle Financials
- ☐ 12 Oracle Human Resources
- ☐ 13 Oracle Interaction Center
- ☐ 14 Oracle Communications/Utilities (modules)
- ☐ 15 Oracle Public Sector/University (modules)
- ☐ 16 Oracle Financial Services (modules)
Server/Software
- ☐ 17 Oracle9*i*
- ☐ 18 Oracle9*i* Lite
- ☐ 19 Oracle8*i*
- ☐ 20 Other Oracle database
- ☐ 21 Oracle9*i* Application Server
- ☐ 22 Oracle9*i* Application Server Wireless
- ☐ 23 Oracle Small Business Suite

Tools
- ☐ 24 Oracle Developer Suite
- ☐ 25 Oracle Discoverer
- ☐ 26 Oracle JDeveloper
- ☐ 27 Oracle Migration Workbench
- ☐ 28 Oracle9*i*/AS Portal
- ☐ 29 Oracle Warehouse Builder
Oracle Services
- ☐ 30 Oracle Outsourcing
- ☐ 31 Oracle Consulting
- ☐ 32 Oracle Education
- ☐ 33 Oracle Support
- ☐ 98 Other
- ☐ 99 None of the above

(7) WHAT OTHER DATABASE PRODUCTS ARE IN USE AT YOUR SITE? (check all that apply)
- ☐ 01 Access
- ☐ 02 Baan
- ☐ 03 dbase
- ☐ 04 Gupta
- ☐ 05 IBM DB2
- ☐ 06 Informix
- ☐ 07 Ingres
- ☐ 08 Microsoft Access
- ☐ 09 Microsoft SQL Server
- ☐ 10 PeopleSoft
- ☐ 11 Progress
- ☐ 12 SAP
- ☐ 13 Sybase
- ☐ 14 VSAM
- ☐ 98 Other
- ☐ 99 None of the above

(8) WHAT OTHER APPLICATION SERVER PRODUCTS ARE IN USE AT YOUR SITE? (check all that apply)
- ☐ 01 BEA
- ☐ 02 IBM
- ☐ 03 Sybase
- ☐ 04 Sun
- ☐ 05 Other

(9) DURING THE NEXT 12 MONTHS, HOW MUCH DO YOU ANTICIPATE YOUR ORGANIZATION WILL SPEND ON COMPUTER HARDWARE, SOFTWARE, PERIPHERALS, AND SERVICES FOR YOUR LOCATION? (check only one)
- ☐ 01 Less than $10,000
- ☐ 02 $10,000 to $49,999
- ☐ 03 $50,000 to $99,999
- ☐ 04 $100,000 to $499,999
- ☐ 05 $500,000 to $999,999
- ☐ 06 $1,000,000 and over

(10) WHAT IS YOUR COMPANY'S YEARLY SALES REVENUE? (please choose one)
- ☐ 01 $500, 000, 000 and above
- ☐ 02 $100, 000, 000 to $500, 000, 000
- ☐ 03 $50, 000, 000 to $100, 000, 000
- ☐ 04 $5, 000, 000 to $50, 000, 000
- ☐ 05 $1, 000, 000 to $5, 000, 000

100103